T0215794

Healthy SQL

A Comprehensive Guide to Healthy SQL
Server Performance

Robert Pearl

Apress®

Healthy SQL

ISBN-13 (pbk): 978-1-4302-6773-7

ISBN-13 (electronic): 978-1-4302-6772-0

Managing Director: Welmoed Spahr
Lead Editor: Jonathan Gennick
Development Editor: Douglas Pundick
Technical Reviewer: Steve Jones
Editorial Board: Steve Anglin, Mark Beckner, Gary Cornell, Louise Corrigan, Jim DeWolf, Jonathan Gennick, Robert Hutchinson, Michelle Lowman, James Markham, Susan McDermott, Matthew Moodie, Jeffrey Pepper, Douglas Pundick, Ben Renow-Clarke, Gwenan Spearing, Matt Wade, Steve Weiss
Coordinating Editor: Jill Balzano
Copy Editor: Kim Wimpsett
Compositor: SPi Global
Indexer: SPi Global
Artist: SPi Global
Cover Designer: Anna Ishchenko

Distributed to the book trade worldwide by Springer Science+Business Media New York, 233 Spring Street, 6th Floor, New York, NY 10013. Phone 1-800-SPRINGER, fax (201) 348-4505, e-mail orders-ny@springer-sbm.com, or visit www.springeronline.com. Apress Media, LLC is a California LLC and the sole member (owner) is Springer Science + Business Media Finance Inc (SSBM Finance Inc). SSBM Finance Inc is a Delaware corporation.

For information on translations, please e-mail rights@apress.com, or visit www.apress.com.

Apress and friends of ED books may be purchased in bulk for academic, corporate, or promotional use. eBook versions and licenses are also available for most titles. For more information, reference our Special Bulk Sales–eBook Licensing web page at www.apress.com/bulk-sales.

Any source code or other supplementary material referenced by the author in this text is available to readers at www.apress.com. For detailed information about how to locate your book's source code, go to www.apress.com/source-code/.

Without hesitation and with all my heart and soul, I dedicate this book to my beautiful wife, Milana, and my three beautiful children, Ilan, Gabriella, and Nicole, without whom my life would have no purpose. They are my everything, the blessings and light in my life, as well as the inspiration and impetus to drive toward success. They are immensely talented and bright, each in their own unique ways. Everything that I do and strive for is to enrich their lives first and foremost, even as I make modest achievements and reach toward my own personal success. Success for me is nothing, only bittersweet, without the pillar of my family to stand on and provide each other with mutual support. I strive to be and hope that I was, am, and will be the best dad and husband I can be. With love, loyalty, and dedication, I strive to balance work/life and even to sacrifice some opportunity to be part of my family's everyday world. No matter what twists and turns or what curveballs life throws at us, I hope they realize and know that I love each and every one of them, and my heart is always filled with the best intentions. To spend time with them and see them grow every day before my eyes is unmatched by any other life experience. I also hold up this book as an example to them that you can accomplish anything and everything you desire and put your mind to if you are determined, steadfast, and maintain an unyielding positive outlook on life. May they have health, happiness, prosperity, and all the best life has to offer.

"If you can dream it,

you can become it!"

Testimonials

"A few years back the company I worked for contracted Robert to help us establish a process to baseline and monitor our servers. During this time Robert became our go-to person to escalate issues that the team simply didn't have the experience or knowledge to handle. Having a resource like Robert helped the DBA team grow, and having access to historical trending data of the environment aided the team in noticing trends and patterns of how the systems were being used as well as gave them the ability to see what was going on with the server hours or days past when a user noticed a decrease in performance.

"Having these continual health checks being performed allowed a very small team to be much more proactive, enabled us to quickly find servers with configuration settings outside of the normal baseline, and, more importantly, provided us with solid data to help us prove or disprove that there was a problem with the database server."

—Tim Radney, SQL Server MVP, author, SQLSkills

"Every DBA wants a checklist on what to look for when trying to determine the state of affairs on their servers. Not only is a checklist one of those sought-after things, but how to use that checklist and how to check the "health" of the server. With this book by Robert Pearl, we now have ready-made access to these essential tools. Robert guides you through how to perform a health check, how to baseline your server health, how to routinely compare current health to that baseline, and how to report on the server health. This book is a great resource to have on the bookshelf and in your tool belt."

—Jason Brimhall, SQL Server MVP/MCM, author, speaker

"I have worked with Robert Pearl on several projects and envied his ability to perform health checks and assessments. He is well known in the industry for his performance monitoring, assessment, and health check tools for SQL Server. In this book he dives into SQL Server internals and monitoring and provides readers with a solid foundation to perform health checks on the SQL Servers they manage. This resource is sure to be a valuable companion to both novice and seasoned DBAs."

—Hilary Cotter, SQL MVP, speaker, author, SQL replication industry expert

"I've known of Robert Pearl, his great experience as a DBA, his scripts, and his work within the SQL community for quite some time. From his work on different forums and advice, I've always thought very highly of him and his technical abilities. Recently, I've also had the pleasure of working with Robert in a DBA capacity. Let me assure you that my impressions were not only well founded but have been expanded. I have watched Robert troubleshoot critical outages, researched issues with him, and reached out for help and found a talented ally in the fight against SQL misuses and misconfigurations, in troubleshooting, and in performance tuning. As a new MVP, I've also been able to see Robert in action, in the way only a few lucky others ever have. Robert is a top-notch DBA and a SQL Server expert, and we are all better for having read the words he has written!"

—Bradley Ball, SQL Server MVP, trainer, speaker, data platform management lead
and PM at Pragmatic Works

"Robert Pearl is a Microsoft MVP and a first-class DBA. His new book, *Healthy SQL*, provides a holistic approach to maintaining a well-functioning, stable, and healthy SQL environment for enterprises of any size."

—Michael Coles, aka Sergeant SQL, former SQL Server MVP,
speaker, author, XML guru, BI expert

"Robert Pearl is an excellent technologist and expert in Microsoft SQL Server. Having worked with him on improving the performance of an existing SQL Server installation, I know he brings experience and insight to every project. The analyses and procedures he outlines in this book are indispensable to those tasked with the day-to-day management of SQL Server or managers who wish to understand more about the daily duties and maintenance tasks required of a Microsoft SQL Server administrator. If you want to learn how to reduce downtime of your SQL Server by implementing an ongoing management and monitoring program, buy this book."

—Brad Irby, .NET architect, speaker, and author of *Reengineering.NET*

"In the world of the DBA, system DBAs come and go. The longevity of the priceless DBA stems from knowing and liking to work nights, weekends, and holidays as well as the normal daily grind. Robert is a system DBA who has outstanding knowledge of SQL Server. This book is the result of Robert's dedication to that knowledge from the early days of SQL Server to the present. Robert has the ability to break down seemingly complex issues into interesting tidbits of solid information. This helps the readers apply that information to their own situations. Robert has dedicated his career to learning the ins and outs of SQL Server and its interaction with the Windows operating system."

—Chuck Kelley, enterprise data architect and data warehousing pioneer

"As an experienced database administrator and architect (and a reader and author of SQL Server books), I have learned that a good approach for a book is to more focused on the book's subject matter. This is where I commend my fellow professional and SQL Server MVP Robert Pearl, industry expert, and his new book, *Healthy SQL: A Comprehensive Guide to Healthy SQL Server Performance*. Instead of delving into every aspect of performance tuning and monitoring, the book emphasizes a rigorous routine of data platform health check procedures.

"You are in good hands because Rob is an accomplished SQL Server professional with practical experience to share. I have known him personally for the last ten years, and his work in the SQL Server community is commendable as someone who spends great deal of time helping users and fellow professionals. I congratulate Robert Pearl for this big venture in the world of authoring."

—Satya Shyam K. Jayanty, aka SQL Master, SME, SQL MVP, author, speaker

Contents at a Glance

Contents

About the Author

Robert Pearl, president and founder of Pearl Knowledge Solutions, Inc., has been a Microsoft SQL Server MVP since 2009, having received his fifth MVP recognition award. Professionally, he is a solutions-oriented senior DBA with 15+ years of experience and is considered a subject-matter expert on SQL Server technology.

He also coined the terms Healthy SQL™ and SQL Fitness™ to kick off the worldwide healthy SQL campaign to highlight the need for regular health checks to ensure that everyone's SQL Server environment has achieved healthy SQL.

He is a SQL Community/SQL Saturday evangelist, promoter, and speaker and maintains his regular blog at SQLServerCentral.com, called Pearl Knows. He was voted Top Blogger in the 2011 SQL Mag Community Choice Awards. He is also the creator/developer of the award-winning SQL Centric—a web-based database monitoring and alert system for DBAs.

Robert is a SQL Saturday organizer and co-chair of the successful New York Metro PASS SQL Saturdays.

About the Technical Reviewer

Steve Jones has been working with SQL Server since 1991, from version 4.2 through SQL Server 2014. He has been a DBA in a variety of large and small companies and industries. In 2001 Steve founded SQL Server Central with two partners and has been publishing technical articles and facilitating discussions among SQL Server professionals ever since. He currently is the full-time editor of SQL Server Central, owned by Red Gate Software. Steve is a Microsoft SQL Server MVP and a D&B MVP.

Acknowledgments

There is a short list of professional folks who I would like to thank for their contributions big and small, whether direct or indirect. I consider myself lucky to have them as my friends. I am thanking them here for allowing me to complete this book, which indeed was a monumental task and a difficult balance between my challenging family obligations on the home front; my professional career and day job; my entrepreneurial endeavors; my blogging, speaking, and presenting at local user groups and SQL Saturday events; and my MVP status and volunteerism for my second family, affectionately the SQL Community. I'd like to thank those who either helped materially with the book or provided me with inspiration to continue on my writing journey and bring this enlightening and awesome experience to conclusion and the final published book to fruition! I know this isn't the Academy Awards, but nonetheless I feel I must give the thanks that is well-deserved and express my gratitude for the folks who helped me along the way.

Specifically, not necessarily in any order, thanks to Steve Jones, SQL Server MVP and editor-at-large for the largest SQL Server community site, which published my many articles and hosts my blog, Pearl Knows. I am most grateful and appreciative for all he has done for me through the years. Steve almost instantly agreed to be technical editor and reviewer for my book and did an awesome job of tearing many of my initial chapters to pieces so I could modify, rewrite, and produce the high-quality technical work and professional development book that you are reading today. Steve and I go way back, and like many others, he has provided a platform to advance my own career as a DBA but also to contribute and share my knowledge on SQLServerCentral.com and eventually become a Microsoft SQL Server MVP, for which I am most honored and humbled to have received my fifth MVP award as of this writing. Steve generously gave his valuable time not only to review the book but to author the foreword as well.

I'd also like to thank Jonathan Gennick (and the Apress team of Jill Balzano, Douglas Pundick, and others) for his consummate professionalism and editorship of this book, as well as the extraordinary opportunity to publish *Healthy SQL* under the Apress name. Without Jonathan, you would not be reading this book today! Thank you for believing in the idea and all the phone calls, e-mails, logistics, and guidance on how to write, format, and produce a published technical book, for which this has been a joyous journey and excellent experience.

Thanks to Jason Brimhall, SQL Server MCM/MVP and author, who collaborated with me on many of the technical aspects of the book and who provided me with hours of conversation and Skyping to bounce a billion ideas off him, which helped me move the book forward when I was stuck. He also helped sell the idea of my book to Apress and Jonathan.

Edwin Sarmiento, SQL Server MCM/MVP and inspirational speaker and motivator, has helped me on a few occasions when I was stuck on a topic and not sure how to present some of the book's technical information, often dry and regurgitated in white papers, blogs, and other sources. He inspired me to introspection on how to tell a story that would be understood by readers and connect to them through real-world experiences and everyday examples.

Timothy Radney, SQL MVP and rising SQL star, now at one of the most well-known and top SQL consulting firms in the world, SQL Skills, gave me the unique opportunity to work remotely for his then workplace, a top bank in Columbus, Georgia. This project came exactly at the right time in my life, when I was between gigs, during extraordinarily personal and challenging circumstances that required me to be close to home. Moreover, this project gave me the groundwork to build a comprehensive automated health check system, for which I based my ideas, professional service offering, and inspiration for this book! I will always be grateful for what he has done to help me.

Thanks also to Chuck Kelley, data warehouse guru. I have had the pleasure to meet, know, work with, and maintain a continuous friendship with one of the world's renowned and industry-known data warehouse architects. To say that he is one of the "founding fathers" of data warehousing is not an understatement. He worked with William Inmon and Kimball in its infancy during the advent of modern data warehousing theory. He has taught me a lot about databases, datamarts, and data warehousing, as well as provided professional interaction with C-level folks. But, the irony here is that Mr. Kelley was more than just a technical mentor. In fact, he was a source of personal inspiration, advice, and fortitude, being there for me through some of my darkest and challenging moments in my life, including the passing of my dear dad. Even though our professional paths parted ways, we kept in touch, and he was always a phone call away, even though across a few times zones. He provided me with words of wisdom and professional advice, including about authoring a book. You are a kind humanitarian, sir!

Thanks to Michael Coles, author, speaker, BI architect, developer, XML guru, strong business leader, and former SQL MVP. He is one of the smartest guys I know, not only about code and SQL Server but is a well-rounded guy full of real-world experiences. He's been there, done that. He's a take-charge kind of person who knows how to negotiate and get what he wants! He's not afraid to call a spade a spade; if you are a cushy consultant stacking the hours and Mike comes in to clean up, get ready to shape up or ship out! He has offered up invaluable advice on SQL, business, and personal interrelationships. He also made the initial connection to Jonathan Gennick at Apress for me and sold my book idea to them. No wonder they call him Sergeant SQL!

Finally, thank you, dear reader, for deciding to buy *Healthy SQL* for your guide to achieving a healthy SQL Server environment.

Now for some personal thanks and appreciation.

Wife: Milana, if you read this, now you finally know why I spent so much time in the corner at the dining room table, pounding at my keyboard into the wee hours of the night. My two words "thank you" are not nearly enough to express my gratitude for having you in my life. Any time during "family time" when I was working on the book was time that my wife was being Supermom with three needy kids and time when I skipped a chore or two. I really, really needed to finish those chapters. I guess after this, I'll be spending a lot of time doing household chores and watching the kids. It is truly an amazing display of strength and fortitude to raise three beautiful children so close together in age. That they are very opinionated and often disagree is an enormous understatement. No matter how impossible and crazy things seem, we're in it together. I know that each one of them will make us proud. Only now I know it takes a village—or at least one of you.

Dad: He may not be here physically anymore, but he is in spirit. He provided me with many life lessons that are apparent today. He was my moral compass growing up and was the dad who seemed to know everything and provided me with a solid foundation. He was a well-rounded, learned, and highly educated man. I often hear his voice in my head, especially in my own interactions with my son and daughters. Like all human beings, he was not infallible but tried his best to let me experience the world as a child and teenager. I know he was proud of me and probably his "great-white hope." I'm also sure I disappointed him on many fronts, but he was confident in my abilities to succeed at whatever I did and excel where others couldn't. I hope this accomplishment would make him proud.

Baba Riva: An amazing, unique, and remarkable individual, my wife's grandmother was the matriarch of our family. She was the rock-solid foundation and an endless fountain of wisdom, full of grand experiences and guidance. Yet she was a simple, family-oriented woman, who was always selfless, loyal, and giving, and she showed my wife, my children, and me unconditional love and dedication. She had a heart of gold and was an inspiration and example of inner beauty, grace, will power, and strength. No matter how challenging and uncertain things in life would get, you always knew everything would be OK when she was around. To speak and spend time with Riva was always enlightening, interesting, and intriguing. She was a true friend and family member. We were all one family, and that was all that mattered. I was lucky to have known her and have her in my life. Her soft-spoken words, uplifting optimism, soothing spirit, and comforting presence are sorely missed.

Nana Helen: Known throughout my whole life as Nana, my maternal grandmother and only grandparent growing up was always there at all our holidays, our family get-togethers, graduations, my wedding, and my son's first birthday party. Helen always maintained a sunny and optimistic attitude, even through some of life's most challenging times. She practically raised two children on her own, as a widow, and was a testament to strength and longevity. She was going back and forth to Atlantic City well into her 80s. She departed us at 96, which is a blessing that we had her in our lives so long.

God: I'm actually not a religious person, but I've learned to seek a higher authority, sometimes the only one left to turn to in times of trouble and times of need. In fact, my own belief is that religion is the technology to reach and attain the same results. So, you don't have to be religious, nor does it matter what faith you follow. Call it what you want, but if you channel your inner strength and seek divine help, whatever you put out into the "universe" will come back to you.

I believe there is an overarching connection to the universe that interconnects physicality and spirituality. In quantum physics we have the string theory of everything, which talks about vibrations that bring things into existence. This model is a version of string theory, which posits that at the tiniest levels all particles are fundamentally little loops of string that vibrate at different frequencies. And, if true, all matter and energy would follow rules derived from the nature of these strings. So, in my own layman's, nonseminal theory, positive energy vibrations attract positive energies, and negative vibrations attract negativity. Stay away from negative influences!

May he give you the desire of your heart and make all your plans succeed. —Psalm 20:4

Foreword

Maintaining a healthy SQL Server database system can seem deceptively simple at times. Once the software is installed, it seems as though the server might just manage itself for a significant period of time. However, many times problems lie just out of sight of the users, waiting for another row of data or one additional user to tip the response time from acceptable to problematic.

Indeed, this is the situation with many SQL Server instances, where an organization sets up the platform and seemingly out of the blue finds itself in need of expensive consulting help. Even when there are administrative staff members available, they are caught off-guard when some part of their database server fails and their entire application becomes unusable.

Many of these problems could be prevented, or mitigated, if the people in charge of SQL Server had gathered more information and performed preventative maintenance to ensure a healthy SQL Server. That has been the aim of Robert Pearl for most of his career, and he has compiled his extensive knowledge into this book.

Many of the tools and techniques that a savvy system administrator can use to maintain their system are introduced and demonstrated in this book. You will learn how to use the information captured and recorded inside SQL Server DMVs to assess the health of a server. A variety of free utilities and scripts are given to allow professionals on a limited budget to learn about the state of their server. Even those readers who can purchase third-party tools will benefit from understanding the information captured by the software they use.

There are also chapters on indexing for better performance, as well as the performance-tuning method called waits and queues. The process of examining waits and queues has become the de facto standard for determining the bottlenecks on a system and focusing your efforts to improve the performance of your system.

You will learn how to gather and keep historical information in a repository that can be used to determine in an objective fashion what the expected performance of the system should be. Chapter 8 covers reporting on the health of your server, which is often important for management, even when the system is running smoothly.

Security, auditing, high availability, disaster recovery, and more are sometimes not considered when monitoring and maintaining your server on a daily basis, but they can be just as important to the health of your system as any other tasks. There are quite a few thoughts and considerations brought to your attention, some based on Robert's extensive time with large financial institutions and his experience from the 9/11 disaster in New York City.

I hope you will study the information presented in this book and work to implement the processes and tools on your own servers. Move carefully and deliberately, ensuring you understand each section of code you run or change you make. This book contains much of what you need to learn to maintain a well-running SQL Server, but you will need to use the references and links provided to expand your knowledge of the incredibly complex and powerful platform known as SQL Server.

Whether you are a dedicated database professional or an accidental DBA, you can benefit from the wealth of information contained in this book. I hope you will treat the concepts discussed here and the scripts provided as the valuable tools they are for your SQL Servers.

—Steve Jones
Editor, SQL Server Central

CHAPTER 1

■ ■ ■

Introduction to Healthy SQL

Microsoft SQL Server has become an eminent relational database management system (RDBMS) in the marketplace. The SQL Server engine has come a long way from being just another RDBMS; it's an end-to-end business intelligence platform with built-in options for reporting; extract, transform, load (ETL); data mining; and high availability/disaster recovery (HA/DR). Its rich feature set provides a comprehensive solution for deploying, managing, monitoring, maintaining, auditing, reporting, and backing up and restoring databases; building data warehouses; and more! You will learn all about this as you journey through this book toward achieving healthy SQL.

Whether it's small, medium, or large enterprise infrastructures, it is common for organizations to have deployed multiple SQL Server instances in their environments, and as companies deploy various applications, many have had to deal with what's known as *SQL sprawl*. This is the 1:1 ratio explosion of deploying every new application to its own SQL Server. The implementation of multiple SQL Server instances has made it difficult for database administrators to manage and maintain them. It is not uncommon to eventually embark on a SQL Server database consolidation project with the assistance of a qualified SQL Server database professional.

Another common scenario is that third-party vendors will deploy their applications on back-end SQL Server instances and leave their clientele to their own devices. They will install SQL Server even though it's doubtful that they know what the proper installation and configuration settings are. The goal of a vendor is to install and set up its application without regard for the ongoing health or performance of SQL Server. This is known as "Set it and forget it."

In a situation of "Set it and forget it," as the application usage increases, as new records are continuously inserted, updated, and deleted, and as users place demand on the application, response times will eventually slow down, as will the overall performance of the SQL Server database back end. Indexes become fragmented, excessive page splitting occurs, and backups are not properly configured.

All these issues that occur on the back-end SQL Server instance frustrate users, and organizations don't usually have the database administrator (DBA) skill set in-house to fix these performance problems. Often the application vendor will not even have the right know-how or database expertise required to resolve these issues. In these situations, there are a myriad of questions that companies and database professionals need to ask themselves. For example, can SQL Server perform better? Can the application scale if it is necessary? Do we have a recent backup? Is there a disaster recovery plan? Can the database be restored?

Enter the DBA

In addition to the previous questions, businesspeople, chief executive officers (CEOs), analysts, customer service personnel, and the like, might even ask, "What is a DBA?" To a nontechnical CEO, the acronym DBA traditionally stands for "doing business as." According to Wikipedia, this means that the trade name, or fictitious business name, under which the business or operation is conducted and presented to the world is not the legal name of the legal person (or people) who actually owns the business and is responsible for it. Obviously that's not what we mean by DBA in this book.

1

Most businesspeople today recognize the importance that technology plays in their business and the need for people to manage that technology, but often the distinction blurs among the individual information technology (IT) roles. People assume the appointed IT director, chief information officer (CIO), or chief technical officer (CTO) will take care of all the IT needs, without ever coming in contact with the DBA.

Even at the department level, there is a balance between the business department and the IT department. In reality, they depend on each other—the business to fund IT and IT to support the business. The perception often is that the business needs are more important than the IT needs. The chicken-vs.-egg question becomes, does the business drive IT, or does IT drive the business? It is my opinion that IT is the most critical need because trying to run the business without IT, let alone the databases, is untenable.

Often in traditional corporate firms, IT serves as a "cost center" and supports the business. Every time the IT department assesses that it needs more resources such as hardware, software, and human capital in order to adequately support the business, the business in some cases perceives it as "whining again" for a bigger budget and sucking capital out of the bottom-line profit.

However, the value of the IT department can be enhanced by making all of the IT functions "billable," or part of the charge-back system. Once IT becomes billable, the business is motivated to assign more work and create new, often unnecessary projects because of individual budgets, and suddenly the value of everyone in IT goes up.

The division of labor balances out, in that you will not blindly throw more work at your IT employees, hire more employees, or raise the salary of those already employed. This also depends upon the size of the organization. In smaller firms, newer, more modern CEOs are a bit savvier and willing to invest in IT infrastructure and human resources to expand their business.

In my personal experience, once I took the helm of the database infrastructure as the organization's first official DBA. (Perhaps there should be a plaque somewhere with my name on it!) It was a well-known financial services firm, with more than $75 billion in assets, and the CEO did not know what a DBA was. The company chugged along with SQL sprawl in the form of exponential growth in its SQL Server infrastructure, with a combination of overworked system administrators, developers, and even somewhat semi-technical business application owners all managing the SQL Server instances. Obviously, this didn't scale, and the need for a DBA became abundantly clear.

So in sum, the DBA is the IT professional who performs all activities related to ensuring and maintaining a healthy and secure database environment. The DBA has several responsibilities related to the well-being of the database environment including, but not limited to, designing, implementing, maintaining, and monitoring the database system. When a database system begins to perform sluggishly, the DBA must be able to identify and resolve performance bottlenecks, as well as be able to do performance tuning and optimization.

Moreover, the DBA must ensure the continuation of database functions, the integrity of the database, and that databases are backed up regularly and are easily restorable. The DBA is instrumental in establishing policies, procedures, and best practices, and in enforcing their use across the enterprise. As database platforms have become more sophisticated over the years, DBAs have inherited more and more tasks and responsibilities than ever before. Nowadays for example, you can be a hybrid DBA performing overlapping database functions for your company. You'll learn throughout this book about the roles and responsibilities of the traditional DBA as defined here in this section.

Who Cares?

Why should you care about health checks? The answer is short and simple. If you are a database administrator or anyone who is in charge of managing one or more SQL Server instances, then you should care because you are the guardian of the company's data. You are vested with the huge responsibility to make sure that data is maintained, always available, easily retrievable, and quickly attainable.

If that data is lost, corrupted, compromised, or not available when needed, your neck is on the line and the company's business could be jeopardized. It is not an overstatement to suggest that billions of dollars are at risk, as well as the very business that employs you, if that data is not properly guarded and secured.

This book contains a lot of useful information that will help organize your DBA day and give you a clear road map to ensuring that your SQL Server environment is healthy. I will discuss a number of tools, methodologies, and SQL Server features that will help you achieve healthy SQL. You will be a better database professional by using this book as a guideline in your everyday job and when challenged to manage multiple SQL Server instances.

There are key elements to be aware of as a database administrator, and like any serious diet, if you follow the plan, your SQL Server instances and your career prospects will benefit. I will provide you with the methods, processes, knowledge, and the wherewithal to accomplish this. I suggest that you the entire the book, at least once, and then feel free to use it in your daily arsenal as a cross-reference to improved SQL Server health.

SQL Fitness

If you want to excel in your career as a data professional or DBA, then you need to be concerned about your companies' SQL fitness. *SQL fitness* simply means that the SQL Server instances are healthy, that they are regularly maintained, and that performance is optimal. It also means you can ostensibly prove this and back it up with documentation. Such documentation will include graphs, charts, measures, and statistics. It must be demonstrable to anyone who asks. You should easily be able to run reports or pull up data on the status and health of your SQL Server instances.

Documentation is particularly important to be in legal compliance with Sarbanes-Oxley (SOX) and Health Insurance Portability and Accountability Act (HIPPA) laws. There is much confusion as to what information is needed to collect to pass an actual audit. Such an audit is not as esoteric as it sounds. Despite the pages and pages of laws written on this topic, it boils down to "document what you do and do what you document." I will discuss this and explain it in more depth later in the book.

Moreover, if you perform regular health checks, run scheduled maintenance on the servers, keep the servers on the latest service packs, and apply cumulative updates as required, you are ensuring the servers' SQL fitness.

You can ask a series of questions and use carefully compiled checklists to make sure your organization's SQL fitness is high. The higher your SQL Server's SQL fitness is, the better performance, security, and stability of the system. Once you go through the process of a SQL Server health check, ranking the SQL fitness, you can give your SQL Server instances a clean bill of health. Even if your company does not have to comply with SOX/HIPPA laws, enabling your SQL Server to pass an audit with flying colors will make it certifiably healthy!

What You Will Learn?

In this book, you will learn what every DBA needs to know about maintaining a healthy SQL Server. You will be educated on the what, why, when, which, where, and how of a SQL Server health check. The goal of this book is to provide you with an easy way to determine whether your servers are healthy and to be able to prove it to your peers and managers during an IT audit. At the end of this book, you will be able to answer affirmatively to all the aforementioned questions. Specifically, you will learn the following:

- What a SQL Server health check is about

- Why you want to perform a SQL Server health check

- When you should perform a SQL Server health check

- Which tools you should use to perform a SQL Server health check

- Where to store the information collected from a SQL Server health check

- How to review and analyze data collected in a SQL Server health check

What Is Healthy SQL?

I've coined the term *healthy SQL* as part of my campaign to spread the word to anyone managing a SQL Server database infrastructure that you should perform health checks on each server and repeat them often. The purpose is to get database professionals, or those managing the SQL databases, to ensure that all their SQL Server instances are healthy and can pass a health check. For the rest of the book, I will simply refer to the person managing the SQL Server instances as the database professional or the DBA. The book aims to build awareness that your SQL Server instances need regular checkups and need to maintain a fit and healthy lifestyle to increase your longevity.

In today's age, health and fitness is a billion-dollar industry. It is on the mind of every human being at some point in their life. We are in a society obsessed with maintaining our health, youth, and longevity. People spend a significant portion of their money on trying to stay healthy and in shape. Healthy foods, vitamins, supplements, books, magazines, fitness and training videos, spas and gyms, weight loss centers, trendy fad diets, exercise equipment—the list goes on and on.

The healthcare debate, and making individual healthcare affordable, has dominated the national headlines in recent years. In some extreme circumstances, the government regulates what is healthy for people and what is not. While human health and life are unmatched in importance, the economic well-being and prosperity of companies are inextricably linked to human capital, and the ability to provide business continuity is uninterrupted. Likewise, if the health and well-being of our SQL Server database environment is not properly monitored, managed, and maintained, then companies will incur huge business losses and place the business and its ability to operate unhindered at enormous risk, including ultimately your job and career.

Another analogy could be that of a car, as shown in Figure 1-1. To maintain its proper function and not break down unexpectedly, you need to bring the car to the shop for regular maintenance and of course pass inspection. Every car needs its engine tuned; your database is no different! The message here is, "Don't forget to change the oil."

Figure 1-1. *A database is like a car: both need tuning from time to time*

Moreover, we also have car insurance to guarantee we can recover our losses quickly (in case of an accident or vandalism) by getting the car repaired and running optimally again. Likewise, having a dedicated DBA or specialized managed service provider to look after your SQL Server instances is insurance against your SQL Server instances going down, your databases going offline or becoming corrupt, and your data being stolen or lost. While I'm on the topic of engines, it is essential for business owners, executives, managers, users, and so on, to understand and realize that data is the engine that drives the business. Where else does data live, if not the database?

This begets the question, what happens to the business if you lose data because of a number of seen and unforeseen circumstances? What happens to the people who are responsible for managing these systems? I think the answer is quite obvious; the bottom line is that if the business loses its data and cannot recover fairly quickly, the business loses money and credibility, damages their reputation, and in the extreme case shuts its doors. As for the manager of databases, that person will find themselves quickly on the unemployment line.

Simple routine preventative maintenance can avert disaster, minimize losses, and avoid costly technical support down the road. This applies to health, cars, and, in our case here, databases. As a database administrator or anyone who has inherited the awesome responsibility of managing their company's SQL Server infrastructure, you want to ensure that every SQL Server instance is performing optimally; is stable, secure, and highly available; and can pass an audit. I will discuss all these concepts throughout the book.

So, how healthy are your SQL Server instances? How do you know? Can you prove this in an IT audit? Are all the SQL Server instances you manage performing optimally? Are you providing the high availability your organization expects? Do you have a DR plan, and can you ensure business continuity in the event of a disaster? If the answer to any of these questions is no, then you need to ask how long you intend to keep your job.

The goal of this book is to help you, the database professional, answer all these questions in the affirmative. You can use this book as a guide to understanding the business end-user perspective, as well as the technical knowledge and tools in accomplishing this stated objective.

What Is a Health Check?

The concept of a health check is an important one and also the foundation around which this book was written. A SQL Server *health check* is simply a routine SQL Server performance assessment and review. You can also refer to this process as a *performance audit* or *analysis.*

This assessment can be an initial snapshot of a SQL Server instance at any point in time or an ongoing regular routine to continuously collect, sample, analyze, and report on a collection of metadata statistics. The statistics comprise metrics derived from performance counters and dynamic management objects and views.

Counters are part of Windows Performance Monitor and are used to provide information about how well an operating system, application, service, or driver is performing. You can use the counter data to determine system bottlenecks and modify the system's or application's performance. There are hundreds of performance counters available. In this book, I will focus on a specific set of performance counters and how they affect your SQL Server's performance, both in real time and by collecting log data for later analysis. How the server's resources are being used will help you identify why your SQL Server is running slow or suboptimally.

Dynamic management objects (DMOs), collectively called dynamic management views and functions, were introduced with the release of SQL Server 2005 and are useful in monitoring SQL Server instance health because of the server state information they return. By exposing to the user internal metadata about the state of your SQL Server, you can more easily diagnose problems and tune performance. DMOs are aggregated metadata statistics at the database and server levels. The two types of dynamic management views and functions are server-scoped and database-scoped. They both require a specific set of permissions.

- Server-scoped dynamic management views and functions require VIEW SERVER STATE permission on the server.

- Database-scoped dynamic views and functions require VIEW DATABASE STATE permission on the database.

The information from the health check will be used to highlight areas of concern and how you can improve the performance and configuration of SQL Server. The collected data will also allow you to compare and to implement industry-recommended best practices and, in fact, create your own best practices. In addition, you will be able to document and create standardization across the enterprise.

Recent Infamy

Two critical junctures, I believe, are historically significant to the way government and businesses think about the health and security of their computer systems. These recent events underscored the need to ensure that their infrastructure and servers are performing optimally and securely and that, in the event of unforeseens circumstance (man-made or natural disasters), business continuity will be guaranteed.

Both events were intentional and malicious acts intended to inflict maximum damage and destruction. The first obvious tragic day was September 11, 2001. The financial markets on Wall Street were down for a week, as were hundreds of businesses. Some never recovered. This was a physical event in the sense of physical infrastructure—and lives—being lost. The other event was a computer worm, known as the SQL Slammer, that infected networks worldwide, specifically targeting and exploiting a weakness in the SQL Server stack. I can say that I was a witness to both historical events and involved in both recovery efforts.

As some seasoned IT and DBA professionals may recall, back on January 25, 2003, precisely at 12:30 a.m., the exploitation of a security flaw with Microsoft SQL Server 2000 affected networks worldwide. Known as the SQL Slammer, it took advantage of buffer overflow vulnerability in SQL 2000 servers. SQL Slammer could best be described as a worm that exploited these vulnerabilities specifically in version 2000, before Service Pack 3a.

SQL Slammer was spread by scanning the Internet for vulnerable systems and open ports, using SQL Server UDP port 1434 as an entry into the network. An infected instance could then scan for other instances on random Transmission Control Protocol/Internet Protocol (TCP/IP) ports. This scanning activity degraded service across the entire Internet, and the worm itself was file-less.

Rather than actually do anything to the SQL Server instances, such as maliciously creating or deleting files, it remained resident in-memory, scanning for vulnerable Microsoft SQL Server instances. It was the infinite scanning that slowed Internet traffic to a crawl by overloading many networks, tantamount to a denial-of-service (DOS) attack. SQL Slammer was only one infamous example of infiltration into networks and SQL Server instances, as related to UDP port 1434.

Because of this highly publicized exploit and security threat, it is recommended that you assign a fixed port to your SQL Server instance and use an alias to access the named instance through a firewall without exposing UDP port 1434. You can use the Client Network Utility to create a client-side alias for a named instance that includes the IP address and port that the instance uses. Therefore, the client connecting to the server must know the TCP/IP port number in advance.

Despite the insidious nature of this attack and that it took many companies and organizations by surprise, the important lesson to note here is it was completely avoidable, if DBAs took preventative measures and followed best practice to continuously patch their systems. In fact, Microsoft identified this threat months earlier and released a patch to remove the buffer flow vulnerability. In other words, the ability to fix to this was already publicly available.

SQL Server 2000 Service Pack 3a is one that stands out as an historical example of what can happen if you don't keep up with regular service pack upgrades, hotfixes, and cumulative updates. The underlying Server Resolution service buffer overrun flaw exploited by SQL Slammer was first reported in June 2002 and patched in MS02-039. When the dust settled, it was realized that it was not the fault of Microsoft but directly because of the large number of unpatched systems that accounted for the worm's rapid spread across the Internet that fateful day on January 25, 2003. Remember, there is no patch for laziness.

In the final analysis, the advent of what's known as Microsoft Patch Tuesday was introduced in 2003, shortly after the fallout of SQL Slammer. Patch Tuesday is the second Tuesday of each month, when Microsoft releases the newest fixes for its Windows operating system and related software applications such as SQL Server.

By streamlining the process, patches are downloaded and installed automatically and delivered via Windows Update. Of course, administrators can schedule this and select only critical updates they feel are relevant to their infrastructure. Systems are kept up-to-date, and patching is made easier to ensure the latest security and to reduce maintenance costs.

For good or for bad, Microsoft's attempt to come up with a way to deliver important updates and security fixes in a standardized way was a worthwhile intention to get companies in the habit of regular patch maintenance. There are varying opinions on the execution, but several companies still use Patch Tuesdays to update their Windows infrastructures, which is still highly recommended.

However, the SQL Server and .NET cumulative updates and service packs should not be included in an automatic monthly patching cycle. Infrastructure operations should make the DBA team aware of available updates on a monthly basis. The DBA teams are then responsible for liaising with appropriate project teams and stakeholders to ensure that application testing is done on development and test environments first and that the updates are applied through the stack in a timely fashion.

In multi-instance environments, cumulative updates and service packs should be applied to all instances and shared components on the host or cluster at the same time, so the DBA team should ensure that testing has been carried out across all tenants before the patches are applied. For all of the security exploits that occurred with version SQL Server 2000, Microsoft sought to reduce the surface area of attack in its next big release of SQL Server 2005. This was truly a change in the overall architecture and security enhancements because the need for database professionals to have more tools to fight security threats was recognized.

Database administrators must properly secure their databases from both internal and external threats as databases are increasingly exposed through web servers. In addition, administrators must establish a strong security and password policy to lock down SQL Server.

When the long-anticipated SQL Server 2005 was released to manufacturing, it was marketed as "the security-enhanced database platform" and was secure by default, out of the box. This was a concentrated effort to keep customers already invested in Microsoft SQL Server technology, as well as win new business. The desire was for companies to upgrade and for easing the concerns of new and existing customers alike about prior historical software vulnerabilities. Automated Software Updates was presented as one of SQL Server 2005's security features.

Why Perform a Health Check?

Of course, you can ask the inverse as well: why *not* perform a health check? There is no good reason for not doing one, so what I aim to do here is show you the importance of this process and how to do it. The worst excuse for not doing a health check is that the DBA is just too busy. If servers go down or data is lost, you soon won't be too busy. Obviously, from a professional career standpoint, job security is a good reason to perform a health check, as mentioned earlier. However, from the standpoint of a healthy SQL Server, there are several reasons that I will discuss.

To review the "whys" of doing a health check, I will cover the essential elements that you must focus on to completely ensure that your SQL Server instances are healthy and running optimally and that your entire SQL environment is well maintained and has a clean bill of health.

- These are the eight areas why you should be performing regular health checks:
- Performance
- Security
- Stability
- Audits
- Migration
- Upgrade
- Backup and restore
- Business continuity

To expound upon these, you perform health checks to ensure optimal server and database performance to make sure your SQL Server instances are secure and stable. You do health checks to guarantee that your SQL Server instances are audit-proof and can pass audits on demand on any single day. You regularly health check your servers before and after migration and upgrades. You must safeguard your databases by making sure you have good, corruption-free backups and the ability to restore them at a moment's notice. And finally, you perform health checks to ensure business continuity and rapid recovery by implementing high availability and having a solid DR plan. Let's examine each one of these in greater detail.

Performance

Performance is the number-one reason to perform a health check. You want to ensure that response times are efficient and applications are not running slow. Performance is most noticeable by end users when their web pages don't render, their reports run indefinitely, or their application screens don't load. Often this will escalate into a crisis for the business, even when this could be easily avoided. By performing regular health checks, you will be able to spot potential issues before they arise. If you do it right, by creating and maintaining your baselines, you will immediately be aware of any deviations from normal operating server and database behavior. Baselines are defined extensively in Chapter 2.

Ideally, if you can automate this, you can be alerted to such deviation via e-mail, text, or pager. Based on the underlying issue, you can get in front of this and prevent it from becoming a larger issue and one that eventually impacts the business. There is usually a window of opportunity here before escalation.

It is essential to be proactive rather than reactive. Sure, you may be a skilled troubleshooter and even heartily praised for resolving the issue in record time, but how much downtime was incurred, and how much money was lost while you recovered the databases?

From another, perhaps cynical perspective, if you tune your databases so well and everything is humming along without any issues, you might be worried that the perception will be that a DBA is not needed because everything is working just fine. In this case, creating small fires to put out is worthy of a Dilbert comic, but I highly advise against it.

There are other ways, from the point of view of the business, to present statistics, data, and reports to prove your worth as a database administrator. Part of what I do in this book is to show how to build some simple yet effective automation and reporting that will please and impress your managers.

The way to avoid being reactive and move away from the traditional break/fix approach is one of the goals of the health check, by implementing preventive maintenance and ongoing performance monitoring, with a great degree of automation. Automating routine maintenance and continuously capturing performance data to compare to your initial baselines will ensure that the SQL Server daily operations are smooth and efficient.

This will relieve some of the pressure off the DBA to have to go through manual checklists, especially when managing multiple SQL Server instances; it will actually strengthen the position of the DBA and reduce monotonous and repetitive tasks.

If you can accomplish this as part of the healthy SQL goal, you will see more SQL Server instances performing optimally, fewer server crashes, fewer memory dumps, fewer corrupt databases, less downtime, and fewer on-call and after-hours put in. Fewer wake-up calls in the middle of the night will make for happier database professionals, who will more likely to succeed in their chosen field. Businesses can focus on the business and maintain customer credibility as well as profitability, and customers will be satisfied. Moreover, it will help free up DBA time to focus on more creative, constructive, and necessary database projects.

The proactive model endorsed by this book will allow the database professional to excel in the workplace and differentiate themselves from someone who puts out fires by being someone who prevents fires. By presenting the healthy SQL road map, I will lay out exactly what you need to know as a database professional and provide the methodology, the tools, and the resources that you will need in your job. In fact, in Chapter 2, I describe exactly what data you need to collect, describe how to do a SQL Server inventory, and introduce you to the key concepts of measuring and analyzing SQL performance metrics, as well as best practices. In Chapters 5 and 6, you will learn about specific tools, features, and scripts that will help collect all the necessary data. Chapter 3 discusses the one of the most effective yet underutilized techniques: performance tuning.

Security

Security is a critical function to ensuring that your servers are locked down and secure. There are several measures necessary to ensure that your SQL Server instances are secure, not only from within the organization but from external threats as well.

Some security threats are targeted and aim to breach systems for the sole purpose of stealing proprietary data, corporate secrets, and individual identities. Others are simply malicious attempts to bring networks and systems to their knees. Either way, such security breaches are dangerous and threaten to cripple the flow of business and their very existence. Downed systems mean loss of dollars; stolen data means loss of credibility and ultimately can put a company out of business.

With data centers communicating over open networks and connecting to the Internet, network engineers, administrators, and database professionals must be aware of the potential threats out there and lock down access to these vulnerable ports.

The TCP/IP port numbers that Microsoft SQL Server requires to communicate over a firewall are assigned a random value between 1024 and 5000. The default port that SQL Server listens on is 1433. With respect to named instances, UDP port 1434 needs to be open if you have to determine the TCP/IP port that a named instance is using or if you connect to the server by using only the name of the instance. However, since it is well-known that many attacks have exploited vulnerabilities to UDP port 1434, it is generally a good idea to keep it closed. An example of this exploitation was evident with SQL Slammer, as discussed earlier in this chapter.

By limiting the surface area exposure to potential exploitation and attack, maximum security of the database can be achieved, and vulnerabilities can be greatly reduced. With SQL Server 2005, Microsoft introduced the Surface Area Configuration (SAG) tool, which allows administrators to manage services and connections, thus limiting the exposure of these services and components. This includes analysis services, remote connections, full-text search service, SQL Server browser service, anonymous connection, linked objects, user-defined functions, CLR integration, SQL Mail, and native XML web services.

Another example of "secure by default" is turning off features that were previously on by default, such as xp_cmdshell and OLE automation procedures. xp_cmdshell is an extended stored procedure that can execute a given command string as an operating system command shell and returns any output as rows of text. It is a prime example of a security vulnerability that can potentially wreak havoc on a Windows server, where the person executing this command has full control of the operating system as though they were running in DOS. This powerful stored procedure can bring down the server. For example, imagine running the command xp_cmdshell 'shutdown' in the middle of a production day.

One common usage of xp_cmdshell is to be able to execute a .bat file from within a SQL Server stored procedure. It is a fairly simple construct.

```
CREATE Procedure [dbo].[sp_callbatfile]
AS
BEGIN
execute master.sys.xp_cmdshell 'C:\Test.bat '
END
```

Nowadays, the administrator can control, via sp_configure, whether the xp_cmdshell extended stored procedure can be executed on a system at all.

If you attempted to execute xp_cmdshell, you would get an error message as follows:

> "SQL Server blocked access to procedure 'sys.xp_cmdshell' of component 'xp_cmdshell' because this component is turned off as part of the security configuration for this server. A system administrator can enable the use of 'xp_cmdshell' by using sp_configure. For more information about enabling 'xp_cmdshell,' see "Surface Area Configuration" in SQL Server Books Online."

With some sophistication and distribution among newer component features, the Surface Area Configuration tool was discontinued in SQL Server 2008. Much of the SAG functionality was relegated to the SQL Server Configuration Manager (or programmatically sp_configure) and replaced by individual component property settings, as well as the arrival of policy-based management in SQL Server 2008.

SQL Server 2008 introduced policy-based management (PBM) as a means to define rules for one or more SQL Server instances and enforce them. PBM can be used in a variety of ways, most of which augment a documented policy manual, which was the only previous way to ensure compliance. PBM can now streamline this manual task and allow policy violations to be discovered, along with who is responsible via the SQL Server Management Studio.

The policy-based management framework can be extremely helpful in standardizing and enforcing SQL Server configuration and other policies across the enterprise. Database professionals can configure different conditions that prevent servers from being out of compliance with internal database policies that allow you to discover when one of those servers goes out of compliance. Indeed, PBM can prove instrumental with complying with SOX/HIPPA laws and proving to auditors that your servers are actively enforcing such compliance.

The introduction of policy-based management in SQL Server 2008 solves the problem of policy enforcement and can be a significant time-saver. It is now possible to define how servers are to be configured and have SQL Server create these policies to enforce the rules. Relevant to security, you can set up a policy to prohibit xp_cmdshell usage, for example. While the xp_cmdshell configuration option is disabled by default, there is no enforcement or preventative measure to preclude someone from enabling it.

Another important aspect of security is password policy enforcement. SQL Server allows you during installation to select the preferred authentication mode. Available choices are Windows Authentication mode and Mixed mode. Windows Authentication mode only enables Windows Authentication and therefore disables SQL Server Authentication. Mixed mode enables both Windows Authentication and SQL Server Authentication. Windows Authentication is always available and cannot be disabled.

For a time, I recall the purist recommendation to enable Windows Authentication only, as a means to preventing weak SQL Server passwords. Many unenlightened folks managing SQL Server instances and application development will simply create passwords or common simple password schemes so that they can easily remember them. You will see a lot more about SQL Server password enforcement, techniques, scripts, and details later in the book.

In fact, part of the healthy SQL security checks is to look for and flag weak SQL Server passwords, such as blank, one-character, reverse, and reused passwords. This occurrence, however, is not because of any insecure system or flawed technology but because of human nature. If you don't adhere to best practices, there will always be a weak link in the chain.

Windows Authentication mode only means that password enforcement will be managed by Active Directory and managed by the Windows administrators. It was previously known as *integrated security*; SQL Server does not need to validate the user identity but rather trusts the credentials given by Windows. This is the reason why I often refer to this as a *trusted* connection. This makes Windows security much stronger because it uses the security protocol Kerberos. Kerberos provides password policy enforcement with regard to complexity validation for strong passwords, provides support for account lockout, and supports password expiration.

From a logistical point of view, every time a request comes in to create a new account for SQL Server, you would always have to enlist the help of your Windows administrators' friends. Their time spent on other things would create more red tape and limit the control that qualified database administrators have over their own SQL Server database environment.

In many legacy applications that are still around today, SQL Server passwords are often stored in configuration files in clear text, thus exposing SQL Server to potential hacking. In reality, disabling SQL Server Authentication would cause unnecessary complexities for application developers and database administrators. There are better ways than to store passwords in clear text. Enforcing password policies is part in parcel of what is suggested, and you will learn how to do this in Chapter 10.

Strong password policies require and check for minimum password length, proper character combinations, and passwords that are regularly changed. Many companies require Windows user accounts to change their password every 90 days. This practice leads to more secure passwords and makes security breaches of database servers much more avoidable.

Microsoft SQL Server now allows Mixed mode where a SQL Server–authenticated account and password is enforced by the same API and protocol that enforces Windows login policies.

SQL Server now supports password complexity and password expiration, which allows for more secure password policies. Therefore, database security is now enhanced by the same Windows password policies that can also be applied to SQL Server password policies. Figure 1-2 shows the creation of a new user login and the password enforcement options available in SQL Server Authentication.

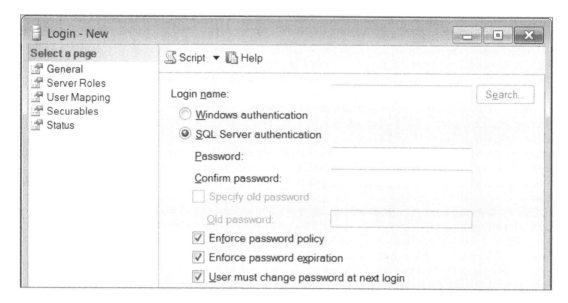

Figure 1-2. *The Login – New dialog in SQL Server 2012 password enforcement options*

There are even further encryption options to map a user to a certificate. These advanced features are available depending on the complexity of the company's security needs.

Furthermore, while on the topic of security, in the most pristine environments, especially those that must adhere to SOX and HIPPA compliance laws, you must have a separation of duties and separate environments each for production, development, quality assurance (QA), and user acceptance testing (UAT).

A hierarchy for code releases and access to production machines must be implemented to ensure the stability and compliance of these systems. There is a bit of cultural and organizational change that must take place as well. It is the database administrator's job to periodically create a security report and review developer access to production (DAP).

For a myriad of reasons, it is ideal *not* to grant developers access to production in coordination with tight change control processes. Organizations need to make sure that all changes are documented and scheduled, and the database administrator must enforce these rules, as well as perform a new health check, once code changes are implemented. I will discuss these concepts later in-depth and provide information on how to pass an audit (with flying colors) and certify that your SQL Server is healthy and in compliance.

The good news is that with all the security feature enhancements, Microsoft has recognized that security is a top priority in locking down your SQL Server environment and has positioned itself in the marketplace as a serious enterprise-class database platform.

Stability

Along with security, stability is another critical aspect to maintaining healthy SQL Server instances. You certainly want to make sure that your SQL Server databases and applications are stable. For example, you must make sure that your servers are up-to-date with the proper service packs and cumulative updates. I discussed this in context of security patches, but such important updates also include fixes to a whole host of potential bugs and flaws that can wreak havoc on your SQL Server.

Failure to be aware of the new code releases, hotfixes, cumulative updates, and service packs, as well as failure to apply these in a timely manner, can certainly make your SQL Server systems less stable. In the extreme, there can be fixes that prevent database corruption, fix critical mathematical calculations and formulas, plug memory leaks and fatal errors, and so on.

It is of utmost importance, as the database professional in an organization, to stay abreast of all these developments and releases. The database administrator must present this information to their management and infrastructure teams, make best-practice recommendations, and schedule deployment accordingly. You must also make the proper determination as to whether new fixes, features, and enhancements apply to your current database systems.

Another important consideration is the life cycle of Microsoft SQL Server, which is critical to your company's ability to keep up with and deploy the latest technology and SQL versions, as well as take advantage of new features. The Microsoft SQL Server product life cycle will greatly impact your upgrade and migration timelines and implementation.

According to the Microsoft product life-cycle support page, "Microsoft Support Lifecycle policy provides consistent and predictable guidelines for product support availability when a product releases and throughout that product's life. By understanding the product support available, customers are better able to maximize the management of their IT investments and strategically plan for a successful IT future."

Technology continues to transform and often outpaces an organization's own internal timelines for upgrading. You as the database professional must present your organization with the facts, as well as product life-cycle dates specifically when mainstream and extended support options officially end for a particular SQL Server version and service pack level.

Because there is a lot of confusion about mainstream support vs. extended support and what it exactly entails, Microsoft has provided the table shown in Figure 1-3 to describe the support for each scenario.

Available Support	Mainstream Support	Extended Support
Paid support (per-incident, per hour, etc.	✓	✓
Security update support	✓	✓
Non-security hotfix support	✓	Extended hotfix agreement required – must purchase w/in 90 days of mainstream support end.
No-charge incident support	✓	
Warranty claims	✓	
Design changes/feature requests	✓	
Microsoft Knowledge Base available online about specific product information.	✓	✓
Support site usage at Microsoft Help/Find answers to technical questions about the product	✓	✓

Figure 1-3. The main differences between Microsoft mainstream and extended support phases

Information and end dates about mainstream and extended support, as well as service pack and security updates, are available to the public at http://support.microsoft.com/lifecycle. You can learn all about the timelines, support phases, and answers to frequently asked questions at http://support.microsoft.com/gp/lifePolicy.

Another important area that the database professional must keep informed about is not only what's new in the latest version of SQL Server but also what's old. When I say what's old, I mean the features that are being deprecated. Deprecation basically means the gradual phasing out and eventual removal of a feature in some later version.

Often when folks hear about features that are being deprecated, they go into panic mode worrying about what's going to break or what will no longer be functional if they upgrade to the newer version of SQL Server. In reality, this is not the case.

Deprecated features are generally announced with the release of the Community Technology Previews (CTP) of the next upcoming version. With respect to the life cycle of features, it indicates that a particular feature or set of features is flagged for removal, usually within three version releases.

This too can change, and I've seen such legacy deprecated features still available more than three versions later. However, note that use of such features will no longer be supported, and users should stop using deprecated features in their continued development. Users should also understand that these features may be removed without further notice. Failure to discontinue use of these features can result in broken code and application instability.

The whole point of deprecating features is to get users to focus on changing and regression testing their code in order to be compatible with new versions and features. Microsoft does provide good references for deprecated features, such as Books Online (BOL) on TechNet (www.technet.microsoft.com)..

For the latest version, as of this book's publication, you can visit http://technet.microsoft.com/en-us/library/ms143729(v=sql.120).aspx to see the Deprecated Database Engine Features list for SQL Server 2014. (You can also Google this phrase.) You will find information on each deprecated feature and its replacement, if any.

Finally, if you're looking for a technical way to monitor and keep track of deprecated features, SQL Server provides the SQL Server: Deprecated Features object performance counter for version 2008 and newer. Therefore, you can run the following Transact-SQL (T-SQL) script, which queries the sys.dm_os_performance_counters view, to find out which features are affected:

```
SELECT instance_name
FROM sys.dm_os_performance_counters
WHERE OBJECT_NAME like '%Deprecated Features%'
and cntr_value > 0
```

Audits

Because of a number of reasons, IT environments may come under an audit. This could be an internal audit, a self-audit, or an actual federal audit by various legal and government entities. Because of the serious impact activities whether criminal, malicious, accidental, or even by omission could have on the welfare of a business or organization, many laws have been passed. These laws are intended to ensure certain compliance policies are enforced and adhered to. A breach or loss of data, for example, can have broad legal implications. You hear a lot about SOX-404 and HIPPA compliance, where the former usually affects financial firms and the latter affects health organizations.

Auditing can take several forms, but in the context of healthy SQL, I am referring to IT audits, drilling down to the SQL Server database systems. Many questions arise around who is doing what to the server and when. The purpose of an IT audit is to review and evaluate the internal controls, policies, and procedures and ensure that they are being adhered to. There was much confusion as to what an organization needs to do to be in compliance with SOX 404, for example, at its inception. The regulations do not specifically state what to do. One requirement includes the "segregation of duties." Another is to record who has access to systems, as well as keep track of changes made to the system. Change control processes should be in place. However, it boils down to "do what you say and say what you do" In other words, if you document your company's policy where you must do A-B-C in order to implement a new code change, stored procedure, and so on, you must in fact be able to demonstrate you are doing A-B-C.

SQL Server has evolved as such that it has made several features available and given you the technical capacity to help audit your SQL Server and enforce policies: password policy enforcement, complex password requirements, default trace, extended events, change data capture, SQL Server audit, and policy-based management, to name a few.

The point of healthy SQL is to make sure that your servers can pass an audit and that your servers are audit-proof with the ability to produce proof anytime required. This is one of the goals you will be working toward in this book. Database compliance, change control, auditing, and the like, are all discussed in great detail in Chapter 10.

Migration

From a healthy SQL standpoint, migrating from one server to another, from one platform to another such as physical to virtual, and from one data center to another all introduce new variables into your SQL Server environment. Therefore, any established baselines are no longer valid, and new baselines must be created. Migration definitely warrants another health check to see how the SQL Server will perform in the new environment and how it handles its load.

Upgrade

Upgrades also necessitate a new performance review and health check since all the data previously collected is not valid. Upgrading can include any of the following tasks. It could be as simple as applying a new service pack or cumulative update or upgrading to a new SQL Server version, OS, or hardware. It can also mean upgrading from a 32-bit platform to a 64-bit platform. With all things being equal, an upgrade is often an opportunity to refresh and provision new hardware, storage, and software, which all often occur together.

My experience is that if you are coming from an older or no longer supported version of SQL, the OS is likely to be older as well. I have seen SQL Server 32-bit versions now upgraded to 64-bit versions, which is now very much the standard. The software and OS upgrades also usually happen all at once with a hardware refresh. Because of all these significant changes, once the server is built and up and running, the database professional must once again perform a health check of the server environment and establish new baselines.

As far as best-practice recommendations go, I strongly caution against any upgrade in-place. An in-place upgrade is basically a one-way trip to the next version. However, it is potentially a high-risk upgrade that leaves little room for failure and a painful fallback plan. There is usually no easy way to roll back.

The only possible way back from a failed in-place upgrade is to rebuild it from scratch, with all previous versions and service packs, cumulative updates, and so on, and then to restore all the databases. This of course is not an ideal situation, and therefore I highly recommend an upgrade that consists of moving to a new server (whether physical or virtual) and that is consistent with a hardware refresh because of hardware no longer supported by the vendor.

Backups

If I have one word to ensure DBA job security, it would be *backups*. If I had a few words to emphasize, they would be *good database backups*. Databases must be backed up consistently. Backups are a big deal, not only because of their importance to recovery but because they are a moving target and they themselves utilize server resources. Backups use storage and disk space, they are I/O-intensive operations, and they use even more CPU resources if using compression.

In other words, you have to do something more than just back up the database. You must devise a comprehensive backup strategy to meet the needs and expectations of the business. You need to consider recovery point objective (RPO) and recovery time objective (RTO). (These are concepts I will discuss later in the book.) You need to schedule them to occur accordingly, and you need to manage them and ensure they complete in a timely fashion.

In addition, you must set the file retention period of backups so you don't run out of space. Retention period is also determined by the business needs. You must also make sure they are corruption free and check database integrity. To help make sure of all this, there must be extensive monitoring of your backup process.

When all goes wrong and you need to recover, backups are your first line of DBA defense. Your job security as well as your database is only as good as your last backup. Good backups are part of your healthy SQL strategy. One important thing to remember as a DBA is that it is simply not good enough to say you have backed up the databases. A DBA must be able to verify backups. The time-tested way to verify a backup is to periodically restore the database and ensure that it comes online. Often, it is recommended that a database consistency check (DBCC CheckDB) be run against the restored database to check integrity and ensure that it is free of any corruption. Another occasion to restore your databases is to test your DR plan. Chapter 9 discusses planning, features, and methodologies for backups and for ensuring HA/DR.

Business Continuity

Although the concepts of high availability and disaster recovery are not new, September 11 was a pivotal date in elevating the awareness among government and private industry of the necessity to have a comprehensive disaster recovery plan in place that will assure business continuity in the event of a disaster, natural or man-made.

Besides the enormous and tragic loss of life and property on that fateful day, hundreds of small and big businesses, including Wall Street and the entire stock exchange, were brought to their knees. The financial markets were shut down for a week, and many computer systems, applications, and databases were offline without any type of redundancy.

To share my own personal experience, I witnessed the destruction of the World Trade Center, having arrived in downtown Manhattan on my way to work in 1 World Financial Center—across the street from the South Tower. I won't recount all the firsthand and secondhand stories here in this book, but I will note that in terms of disaster recovery and business continuity, the investment bank that I worked for was caught totally unprepared.

They had two offices in New York, one downtown and one in midtown. Both locations had local data centers that hosted their own servers, yet they served completely different lines of business, and neither of them was redundant. Of course, each data center, even though only across town, should have been each other's colocation site (*colo*) for disaster recovery.

We all eventually moved and merged into the midtown facility. The recovery efforts were of enormous magnitude. It took some months to get back to 100 percent capacity. "Rack, stack, and build" went on 24/7. For the servers and databases, we totally relied on tape backup retrieved from offsite. At that time, there were even SQL Server 6.5 databases that needed to be recovered, and anyone who has worked with pre-7.0 versions knows how much of a pain 6.5 was to install and rebuild.

Once we were back to normal operating levels, we embarked on an elaborate disaster recovery planning project and colo site preparation. The infrastructure was eventually migrated out of New York, but all this was of course done after the fact.

Had we even had some minimal form of redundancy between the two locations across town, we would have been back online in a matter of days. Hindsight is 20-20, and far too many companies found themselves in this predicament, totally unprepared. Business continuity became the new corporate mantra and a boon to the economy as new IT workers and businesses specializing in this area were sought after. Even more consequential, the government and insurance companies required businesses to have a business continuity and DR plan as a federal and state compliance necessity, as well as to acquire insurance coverage.

From a healthy SQL perspective, having a comprehensive DR plan in place is definitely part of an overall healthy SQL Server strategy. The primary objective of SQL health checks is to help prevent unnecessary downtime by ensuring that your SQL Server instances are performing optimally and that they are well maintained. However, in the event of unforeseen circumstances, you need to prepare for every possible contingency.

In Chapter 9, I will discuss strategies, documentation, best practices, and the need for every company to have a "run book" with respect to bringing SQL Server instances back online and ensure they are up and running with minimal effort. To do this, I will point out how to leverage the existing features and technologies available out of the box.

When to Perform a Health Check

When should you perform a SQL Server health check? There is no better time like the present. More specifically, it's a process you want to do regularly, but as a starting point, you should initiate a review if your servers (including servers you may have inherited from other departments or acquired companies) were never documented. I will discuss more in the next chapter about when and how often to collect performance information for the health check.

A great time to learn about the SQL Server environment is when you start a new job as a DBA or you need to get up to speed on your client's SQL Server instances, if you are coming in as a consultant. Once an initial health check is performed, it should be repeated regularly to ensure the continued health of your SQL Server instances. Follow-up health checks will be much faster because you already have collected the basics.

Before getting into the doomsday scenarios, I'll first lay out a road map for you for a healthy SQL Server infrastructure. The next chapter will discuss where to start, how to identify your SQL Server instances, and how to collect pertinent information. You will learn the building blocks of how to conduct a thorough performance review, as well as about important concepts in collecting and analyzing performance metadata. After the next chapter, you will be able to get handle on your SQL Server environment and subsequently ensure better centralized management of your SQL Server instances.

■ ■ ■

CHAPTER 2

Creating a Road Map

You will begin your journey on the road to a healthy SQL Server infrastructure with a checklist. A checklist is a simple way to organize the things you'll need to do, both long and short term. It provides an agenda to keep you on track and is a tangible item that you can refer to and affirmatively say, "I am done with these items; only three more to go." It is also something you can present to management and colleagues to show that you have documented your servers. Moreover, the checklist gives you clarity and purpose, allows you to focus on what needs to be done, keeps you on schedule, and acts as a motivator when you're not sure what to do next. Follow the checklist and follow the road map that I am laying out for you here to achieve a certifiably healthy SQL Server environment.

The checklist serves three major purposes, which will be expanded upon in this chapter. It helps you know what to collect, it helps you know what to compare, and it helps you know what to document. By starting out with a checklist, you can be methodical about thoroughly evaluating your SQL Server instances.

Before you proceed to build your checklist, I will talk about the terms you will need to know. This terminology will help you sound intelligent when talking about how you know your servers are healthy and what you are doing to make them so. Then I will discuss the need for an inventory and show you how to take one. Afterward, you will return to building the healthy SQL checklist.

Statistics and Performance

Enter the world of statistics 101. No, you don't need to be a statistician (statistics are boring!); you should just be familiar with basic terms so you can discuss certain topics with your peers, project managers, and higher-ups in relation to how your SQL Server instances are performing and so you can build reports based on performance trends.

Understanding the Terms

One nonstatistical term you will be hearing a lot throughout this book and your database administrator (DBA) travels with respect to performance is *bottleneck*. Literally, a bottleneck means the narrowest part of a bottle. In SQL Server usage, a bottleneck is something that slows down the performance of a server, usually to a point noticeable by the end user. A bottleneck implies an impasse and is an occurrence that affects the entire SQL Server system or component that is limited by resources. You might say there is a "resource bottleneck" on your server.

I'll be using the following terms extensively throughout the book:

- *Baseline*: The baseline is the norm. It is the measure of performance of your SQL Server instances when they are operating normally without any issues and is your typical state of performance. It is a starting point to use for future data comparisons; you can use this calculation to measure average performance over time.

- *Delta*: Delta's most common meaning is that of a difference or change in something. To calculate the delta as the difference, you must have two points to work with. You need a starting point and an ending point (or two points in between if you are looking for a specific difference). To figure out the change, you subtract your beginning point from your ending point.

- *Deviation*: This just means how far from the normal baseline the performance statistics are or how varied they are from the average baseline numbers.

- *Trending*: This means beginning to deviate from normal operation. Over time you will see your baselines move in a particular direction, which will indicate the prevailing tendency of the performance of your SQL Server.

- *Measures*: This is an instrument or a means to measure or capture data on how a SQL Server is performing. One example of a measure is a performance counter or object. You use counters and objects to measure your performance.

- *Metric*: A metric is the measurement of a particular characteristic of a SQL Server's performance or efficiency.

- *Metadata*: Basically this is informational data about, or properties of, your data. The information that you will collect about the performance of your SQL Server is referred to as metadata.

- *Historical data*: Historical data is data saved, stored, and persisted beyond the restart of services of the SQL Server instance, in-bound memory processes, or statistics cleared manually. It exists in tables on the disk storage in the database and enables you to view and compare performance (statistics) over time, reaching into historical points in time.

- *Peak*: Peak is the time during your busiest server activity, usually during production/business hours or during batch processing.

- *Nonpeak*: Conversely, nonpeak time is the most inactive period, usually off-peak or during nonbusiness hours. Activity is at its quietest during nonpeak hours.

Applying Real-World Principles of Statistics to Performance

Let's look at establishing a baseline as an example of applying a principle of statiscs to performance management of your database. To increase the performance of your database applications, you monitor your database for a few days on your server during regular business hours. You'll also find yourself monitoring daily after you install and deploy your SQL Server, when you start to add load to it. If your peak load continues to operate at the same level, without any ostensible performance issues, then you are operating at a normal baseline. This will be your average norm. As long as you are not experiencing any serious bottlenecks or downtime, your SQL Server is in a good, average range. This is your *mean* (or average) performance range. Take performance measurements at regular intervals over time, even when no problems occur, to establish a server performance baseline. In addition, you can use your baseline to discern frequent patterns and understand how the server is utilizing resources. To determine whether your SQL Server system is performing optimally, you can then compare each new set of measurements with those taken earlier.

The following areas affect the performance of SQL Server:

- System resources (hardware)
- Network architecture
- The operating system
- Database applications
- Client applications

At a minimum, use baseline measurements to determine the following:

- Peak and off-peak hours of operation
- Production query or batch command response times
- Database backup and restore completion times

Once you've established a server performance baseline, you then can compare the baseline statistics to the current server performance. Numbers far above or far below your baseline may indicate areas in need of tuning or reconfiguration and are candidates for further investigation. For example, if the amount of time to execute a set of queries increases, examine the queries to determine whether they can be rewritten, whether column statistics can be updated, or new indexes must be added. Real-time performance and trend analysis of resource utilization is also possible.

You may even need to create multiple baselines on a single SQL Server, depending on the situation. Even though you can expect your performance to be steady without any changes, you can expect your SQL Server to perform differently under different circumstances. Your servers may be humming along from your starting baseline, and then at night your backup operations kick in, or you run DBCC integrity checks. Both of these are I/O-intensive operations and will surely send the I/O stats higher than the usual baseline.

Therefore, you may want to create another baseline for different periods, when you expect performance behavior to change. The maintenance window where you take backups, rebuild indexes, run database integrity checks, and so on, is grounds for another baseline. So, you'll have your typical performance during normal business hours but have alternate performance, which in fact would be typical and consistent with overnight maintenance or batch processing. Another period where you can expect performance to be taxed is in companies that have monthly, quarterly, and year-end processing, when users are running reports at these times. You can expect an increase in load and therefore can have another baseline.

Once you establish a baseline for each server, you continuously collect and sample data and observe whether there are any changes since the baseline was first created. If all the server measurements are performing well within the mean and operating at the expected baselines, you can consider SQL Server to be healthy. If there are any differences, you will have to determine what in the environment may have changed and why these changes are occurring and then adjust your baselines accordingly.

Any change going forward in time from the original baseline is a deviation from the norm. The incremental changes are what are known as the *deltas*. Deltas could indicate a number of changes in the environment and could be as simple as a service pack upgrade, code change, new database created, and so forth. It could be related to performance changes over time, say because of index fragmentation; a depletion of resources; or something deployed to the server.

The changes that occur may skew your baseline. The changes that you make can resolve the performance issue, and then you need to reset the baseline. When you observe these deviations, you can identify any health issues and seek to remediate them in accordance with best practices. You can further compare collected data to established best practices and identify these potential changes to your SQL Server instances.

Once you've had a chance to analyze the data and examine the differences, you can determine what changes, if any, should be implemented. Sometimes, established or industry best practices may not be a best practice in your environment. What is best practice for some may not necessarily be best practice for others. That is why to truly establish your own best practices, you set a baseline, trend the data over time, measure the deltas, and determine which best practices should be implemented.

Creating and maintaining a baseline is similar to the life-cycle development process, which consists of the analysis and requirements phase, the design and development phase, then testing and QA, and finally deployment.

Inventories

Of course, before you can build and use your checklist, you will want to create another list, called the *inventory list*. If you are a new database administrator (DBA) on the job, an accidental DBA inheriting new SQL Server instances, or a database consultant at a new client site, you want to first answer the question, "Where are all the SQL Server instances?" You need to find out basic information about the currently existing SQL Server instances in the environment. You can call this elementary and important exercise *discovery*. In other words, before you can do anything else, you need to do a discovery of the SQL Server landscape and answer these questions to create an inventory:

- Where are the servers? Are they in the same domain?

- What are the server names/instance names/ports/IP addresses?

- Can you connect? Do you connect via SQL Server Management Studio (SSMS) or Remote Desktop Protocol (RDP) using the command mstsc?

- What version, build, service pack, and edition are the servers?

- Are they set up with Windows Authentication or SQL Authentication (sysadmin/sa passwords)?

- Are they clustered? Are they virtual or physical?

■ **Note** Before you do anything else, you need to do a discovery of the SQL Server landscape by taking inventory.

Ideally, you also can get this inventory from existing documentation, spreadsheets, and asset management repositories. If none of this exists, then you will have to discover them on your own, with the help of some scripts. You can use a handy little command-line utility called sqlcmd, available and updated since SQL Server.

In SQL Server 2005 as part of the Microsoft SQL Server bundle, you can use sqlcmd to execute Transact-SQL (T-SQL) queries and procedures directly from the command line. For the full syntax of the commands, refer to the following TechNet page:

http://technet.microsoft.com/en-us/library/ms162773%28v=sql.100%29.aspx

You can get a list of all the SQL Server instances broadcasting in a Windows network by opening a DOS window command prompt and running sqlcmd -L. Figure 2-1 shows a DOS window with sqlcmd -L running.

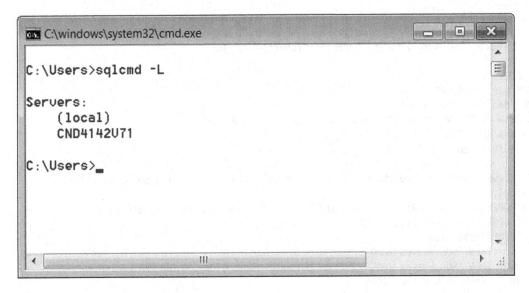

Figure 2-1. *Sample output of sqlcmd –L*

There are a number of ways to collect basic information about SQL Server, such as its version, edition, and other top-level properties. What is the build and current service pack level? What is the instance name vs. the actual server name? Is it clustered or stand-alone? Is it virtual or physical? What is the security mode of the server? Another thing I'm often asked is what version of .NET is currently installed on SQL Server? In the following text, I will provide a simple and quick way to get all this information from one script.

Although you can get some of this information from the older, time-tested T-SQL command select @@version, which returns system and build information for the current installation of SQL Server, its output is one long nvarchar string. You can find @@version information on the following MSDN page:

http://msdn.microsoft.com/en-us/library/ms177512.aspx

You would in fact need to parse the string to derive some of its useful information in a readable format that could be output to a column and thus stored in a table. You can also use, as is suggested, the SERVERPROPERTY (T-SQL) function to retrieve the individual property values. You can find a complete reference to this on MSDN here:

http://msdn.microsoft.com/en-us/library/ms174396.aspx

The SERVERPROPERTY function has been around for several versions now and has added some useful parameters for SQL Server 2012 to 2014. One obvious example, with the release of 2012, is the AlwaysOn parameter IsHadrEnabled. This parameter when tells you whether AlwaysOn availability groups are enabled on a server instance. Again, this is available only in versions SQL Server 2012 and newer.

So, when I need a quick way to retrieve this basic data, I run a script that I put together that uses both SERVERPROPERTYand @@version. You can use a batch script to run it against multiple SQL Server instances in the environment. Here is the GetSQLServerEngineProperties script:

```
SET NOCOUNT ON
DECLARE @ver NVARCHAR(128)
DECLARE @majorVersion NVARCHAR(4)
SET @ver = CAST(SERVERPROPERTY('productversion') AS NVARCHAR)
SET @ver = SUBSTRING(@ver,1,CHARINDEX('.',@ver)+1)
SET @majorVersion  = CAST(@ver AS nvarchar)

SELECT SERVERPROPERTY('ServerName') AS [ServerName],SERVERPROPERTY('InstanceName') AS
[Instance],
SERVERPROPERTY('ComputerNamePhysicalNetBIOS') AS [ComputerNamePhysicalNetBIOS],
SERVERPROPERTY('ProductVersion') AS [ProductVersion],
    CASE @MajorVersion
WHEN '8.0' THEN 'SQL Server 2000'
WHEN '9.0' THEN 'SQL Server 2005'
WHEN '10.0' THEN 'SQL Server 2008'
WHEN '10.5' THEN 'SQL Server 2008 R2'
WHEN '11.0' THEN 'SQL Server 2012'
WHEN '12.0' THEN 'SQL Server 2014'
END AS 'SQL',
SERVERPROPERTY('ProductLevel') AS [ProductLevel],
SERVERPROPERTY('Edition') AS [Edition],
SERVERPROPERTY ('BuildClrVersion') AS NET,
    CASE SERVERPROPERTY('IsClustered')
        WHEN 0 THEN 'NO'
        WHEN 1 THEN 'YES'
    END
    AS [IsClustered],
CASE WHEN CHARINDEX('Hypervisor',@@VERSION)>0
    OR CHARINDEX('VM',@@VERSION)>0 THEN 'VM'
    ELSE 'PHYSICAL'
    END
    AS [VM_PHYSICAL],
    CASE SERVERPROPERTY('IsIntegratedSecurityOnly')
    WHEN 1 THEN 'WINDOWS AUTHENTICATION ONLY'
    WHEN 0 THEN 'SQL & WINDOWS AUTHENTICATION'
  END AS 'SECURITY MODE'
```

You can also use a central management server (CMS), on versions SQL Server 2008 and newer, to run T-SQL scripts and queries against multiple instances of SQL Server simultaneously by creating server groups that contain the connection information for one or more instances of SQL Server. You designate one instance to manage all the others and serve as the CMS. You can create a CMS in SSMS by selecting View ➤ Registered Servers ➤ Central Management Servers. Right-click and select Register Central Management Server to register an instance of the CMS, as shown in Figure 2-2. To learn more on how to create a CMS, visit MSDN here:

```
http://msdn.microsoft.com/en-us/library/bb934126.aspx
```

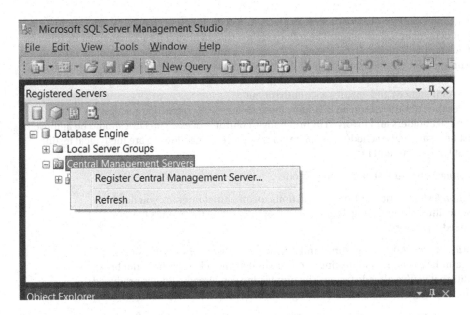

***Figure 2-2.** Registering the CMS*

The script uses what I see as the most significant properties for the purposes I mentioned. It comes in handy when doing inventory and Microsoft licensing true-ups, which are similar to audits, to reconcile the number of purchased SQL Server licenses vs. the number of running and deployed SQL Server engines. After you collect the data, you can store it, parse it, query it, and run reports on it. You also can add some of the other properties and modify the script to your own desires.

You can take a look at the SQL Server properties via T-SQL. The script I use runs on versions SQL Server 2005 through SQL Server 2014. Figure 2-3 shows the output for one SQL Server instance.

sults	Messages					
ServerName	Instance	ComputerNamePhysicalNetBl...	ProductVers...	SQL		ProductLe...
SQLServerName	SQLInstanceName	SERVERNAME	11.0.3128.0	SQL Server 2012		SP1

Edition	NET	IsCluster...	VM_PHYSICAL	SECURITY MODE
Enterprise Edition (64-bit)	v4.0.30319	NO	PHYSICAL	WINDOWS AUTHENTICATION ONLY

***Figure 2-3.** Server properties for one server*

For the SQL Server DBA and from a healthy SQL perspective, when it comes to implementing changes in production, you must take a measured approach. Any changes, whether it is new code, a new service pack or update, or a modification in configuration settings, must be tested on a separate SQL Server that is dedicated to thorough and scripted testing.

Once you determine which changes should be made and go through the testing cycle, the changes should be documented and approved by some change-control process. Change control can be as simple as multiple signatures on a piece of paper from all the stakeholders, agreeing that these are the changes that will be made. More sophisticated systems include enterprise change control systems that serve as a ticketing, documenting, and approval mechanism to track, streamline, and automate the process as much as possible.

In addition to having a change-control process in place, especially for code changes, there should be a rigorously tested deployment or rollout script. The rollout scripts should always be accompanied by rollback scripts. These rollback scripts, which will roll back any changes should the deployment fail for any reason, will quickly and seamlessly let you fall back to where the server was, before the changes. This is almost on par with a Windows OS systems restore to a recovery point. Such a script contains all the changes that will be made to the SQL Server instances and ensures a smooth rollout.

The sign-off gives the DBA the go-ahead to deploy these changes. Of course, I argue that the DBA should be one of the stakeholders and involved in the change-control process. The DBA should be at those meetings, or at least be aware of the scheduled changes to take place. The following are the typical testing life-cycle phases that lead to implementation:

- *Unit testing*: You unit test each piece of code.

- *Integration testing*: When putting several units together that interact, you need to conduct integration testing to make sure that integrating these units has not introduced any errors.

- *Regression testing*: After integrating (and maybe fixing), you should run your unit tests again. This is regression testing to ensure that further changes have not broken any units that you've already tested. The unit testing you already did has produced the unit tests that can be run again and again for regression testing.

- *Acceptance tests*: When a user/customer/business receives the functionality, they (or your test department) will conduct acceptance tests to ensure that the functionality meets their requirements.

Once you approve the changes, go through the normal testing cycles, and send the changes to production deployment, your baseline will be out-of-date. Since SQL Server instances are never static, you need to repeat the data collection process by updating your baselines.

Essentially, the process of creating and modifying baselines, comparing them to evolving data trends, and implementing changes is what makes up the SQL Server health check flow and part of the performance tuning life cycle (PTL). The PTL essentially organizes database performance tuning in a way that allows you to methodically capture and compare metrics and identify performance issues.

The PTL is similar to the SQL Server health check and follows a similar pattern as shown in Figure 2-4. Each step is part of the integral Healthy SQL methodology by which you determine what to collect, establish a baseline of the collected data, calculate the changes or delta of changes over time, and identify any potential health issues. Then you establish in-house best practices that keep data close to the baseline or norm. Then you determine and document the changes to be implemented in production. Once any changes are made, you repeat the cycle from the beginning. In other words, any time there is a change, you need to start collecting new performance data and establish a new baseline or norm.

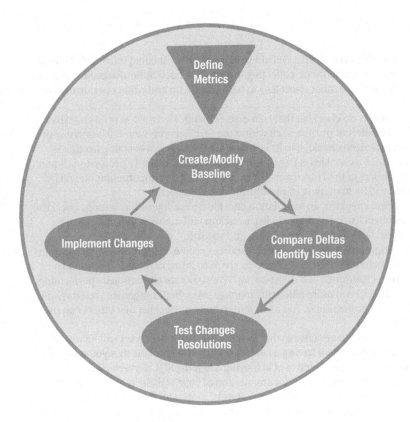

Figure 2-4. *The PTL*

To summarize, the following are the steps taken in a SQL Server health check:

1. Collect (via the checklist)

2. Baseline

3. Compare/delta

4. Identify any health issues

5. Establish best practices

6. Determine changes/implement in production

7. Rinse/repeat

You can also see the similarities of the healthy SQL health check compared to the PTL cycle in Figure 2-4.

The PTL consists of defining metrics to collect, creating your baseline, comparing deltas and identifying bottlenecks or any health issues, testing changes/resolutions, implementing, and modifying your baseline. You regularly repeat this exercise because SQL Server performance is never static! It constantly changes over time.

The Checklist

Let's get back to the business of checklists. A checklist will aid you in gathering detailed information about your SQL Server instances and help document them, collecting information such as hardware, instance, and operating system configuration. You can use other checklists to help you set up and collect performance metadata and statistics.

You must also be aware that there is no checklist that is one-size-fits-all. There are several checklists that collect different information for different purposes, all within the SQL Server realm. Each organization or company might have its own customized checklist to fit its internal needs. It is an evolving list that is constantly updated and changed. Once a checklist is in place, it can be used by other IT professionals and is a great place to start for new members of the DBA team. To wit, the checklist as documentation will be extremely valuable to anyone who will be managing or monitoring the databases.

You might have a pre-installation checklist, an installation checklist, a configuration settings checklist, a cluster checklist, a SQL services checklist, an audit checklist, a backup and maintenance checklist, a currently installed features checklist, DBA daily task checklists, and so forth.

So, where does the checklist originate? There are several resources online and checklists put together by various database professionals, including myself, available on the Web. Most of the information in a solid checklist comes primarily from experience and observation. When you are continuously performing repetitive tasks, a DBA checklist will help you more efficiently manage tasks, better organize your day, and ultimately make you a better database professional. You also want to build a checklist that others can use and ultimately follow.

So, while I will include a template for you to create your own healthy SQL checklist, I will focus on key areas about health checks and the importance of having a DBA checklist. The checklist that you are going to use and create is one that helps you with your objective of achieving a healthy SQL Server environment.

The key to a checklist is that it creates your initial documentation of your SQL Server instances. Now there are several ways to document your SQL Server, and many scripts, tools, and third-party software programs can effectively automate this process. You will learn about these tools later in the book.

In addition, a checklist serves as a foundation for creating a baseline of data that you can use for future comparison. A baseline is a major component of healthy SQL and one that will be covered extensively in this book. To accurately measure performance, a baseline of data is essential for future comparison. You create and use a checklist to keep track of the items you want to capture for the health check. The checklist helps you know what information to collect.

Before you collect this information, you should first know exactly what this collection of information is. So, what is metadata? *Metadata* is simply data about your data. Traditionally, there is *structural metadata*, in which you can get information about the structure of a database schema, such as tables, columns, data types, and so on, rather than the data itself. There is also *system metadata*, in which the functions SERVERPROPERTY and @@version (covered earlier in the chapter), which return data about your various SQL Server properties, are prime examples.

When I begin to talk about dynamic management views (DMVs) and functions in more depth, you will be heavily relying on what I call *performance metadata*. When you query these system views and functions, you are accessing a goldmine of performance data. The workload on the server impacts the system resources when doing such operations as updating, inserting, deleting, and retrieving data. Throughout the next chapters, you will be collecting, storing, and analyzing all of this performance metadata and using it to determine whether there are any performance issues that should be addressed. You will then create reports to visualize this data and present it to management. The report will help you identify areas for improvement and help you determine what steps to take.

It is important to understand metadata as an essential term, because every piece of information about the state of health of your SQL Server instances and the performance and configuration data that you will collect and use as the main artery of healthy SQL is metadata.

What to Collect

To do a comprehensive performance analysis and review of the company's SQL Server infrastructure, its existing SQL Server instances, and the databases residing there, you will want to collect several metrics in specific categories.

You want to collect a pool of data that will give you an overview of the server and database configurations, the key performance indicator (KPI) performance counters and measures, the SQL Server metadata, and other various information that will be included in a health check. This information will be used to highlight where the SQL Server instance can be improved.

Because there are so many things that can affect performance, security, and the overall health of your SQL Server instances, a good place to start is getting an existing snapshot of the SQL Server environment. What I am going to share with you in this book is my somewhat-famous, 15-point health check, which is what I offer my clients (see Figure 2-5). When I first come into a client's network, it is what I use to find out the current state of affairs of their SQL Server instances. I can come into an environment and pretty much know the versions, configuration, and resources without asking any questions. This is based on the scripts I use to capture the information set out by the checklists I use.

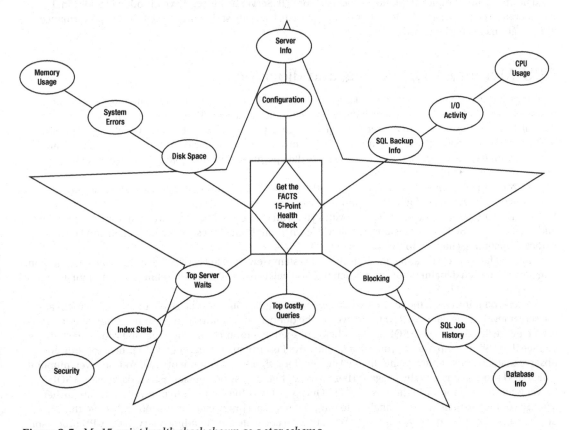

Figure 2-5. *My 15-point health check shown as a star schema*

It is this precise list that I have used successfully with all my clients. This initial metadata capture is an important start in identifying any issues that will potentially degrade performance and compromise security. I run some various scripts I have compiled and created over the years to take a snapshot of the SQL Server.

This snapshot reflects a point-in-time overview on the state of the health of the SQL Server. A report is generated that you can use to identify areas for improvement, present to the client, and make best-practice recommendations.

Here are the top-level categories:

- Health or state of the SQL Server information

- Configuration

- Performance

- Security

Optimal performance means sufficient resources are allocated for SQL Server instances. You must consider these resources in your performance review and overall system health. Prime factors, relating to adequate resources, are the central processing unit (CPU), memory, and disk I/O. Other configuration factors, such as proper tempdb configuration, also help with improved performance. Drilling down into query performance, locking, blocking, and deadlocks are common causes of slow performance. Virtualization and its rapid adaptation, especially for SQL Server instances, have introduced additional considerations and caveats. While CPU, memory, and disk I/O are still critical to SQL Server performance, virtualization can mask the issue.

CPU, Memory, I/O, Locking, and Blocking

There are key areas to focus on when seeking to identify bottlenecks. If you can capture this data, create a baseline, and trend it over time, you can discern when things go awry with performance. In many cases, you will leverage the available dynamic management objects (DMOs) in SQL Server, which do not persist this data; they only aggregate it since the SQL Server instance was last started or the statistics were cleared. Therefore, for each category of measure, you create data points in time and collect historical data by persisting this information in archive tables.

So, categorically from a high-level view, the things you should capture for your performance health check review are system configuration options, performance counters (Windows OS and SQL Server), DMOs, and wait statistics. Each of these provides you with a piece of the puzzle and window into the state and health of your SQL Server instances. You will learn about each of these in further detail, and I even dedicate upcoming chapters to them.

You will heavily rely on a specific collection of system views, mostly DMOs that are available to you from more than 200 such dynamic views and functions. You will use the DMOs to baseline CPU, random access memory (RAM), and I/O usage.

When you think about the resources that SQL Server uses, you can analyze the utilization of them at the server level, at the database level, and even at the query level. Capturing the resource bottleneck at the server level will tell you where SQL Server is being pegged. For example, say by analyzing your wait statistics, you see that CPU is a top wait, so you subsequently run Performance Monitor on CPU processor time and observe that it is consistently greater than 90 percent for a significant amount of time. You can even pinpoint which CPU processor is actually pegged. Then, you can find out, by percentage, which database on SQL Server is accounting for the highest use of CPU. Once you know the database in question, you can further arrange your top expensive query analysis to pinpoint the exact query causing the most CPU and then begin to fine-tune your query accordingly. You can even correlate the offending query to the CPU processor or scheduler reporting high CPU time. I will provide several methods and scripts to correlate this data throughout the book.

Collecting Information from the System Catalog

The system catalog is a set of views showing metadata that describes the objects in an instance of SQL Server. This metadata is fairly static; it changes occasionally but not often. Nonetheless, it is something that should be monitored; that is, you want to capture it if there are any changes to the SQL Server configuration values and even set up an alert. The catalog views replaced many of the system stored procedures and system tables. The catalog views in SQL Server are organized into more than two dozen categories. For a complete list of these categories, you can visit the following page on MSDN:

```
http://msdn.microsoft.com/en-us/library/ms174365(v=sql.110).aspx
```

With respect to the SQL Server system catalog information, you will capture only some basic metadata pertinent to your health checks. `sys.configurations`, part of the serverwide configuration catalog views, will provide serverwide configuration options set at the server level. This information is commonly displayed via the legacy `sp_configure` system stored procedure. You can also view configuration settings via `sys.sysconfigures`. Among the most relevant of settings you will find here are maximum memory and minimum memory configuration options. These are often the ones that are not properly configured and should be changed accordingly from the default values.

`Select * from sys.dm_os_performance_counters` will get the total existing SQL Server performance counters, including the `object_name`, `counter_name`, `instance_name`, the counter value, and the type. How this data can be calculated will be explained in the next chapter.

You can find more information about your databases, such as names, IDs, status, database options, recovery models, sizes, physical locations, and more in the Database and Files Catalog Views category. You can inspect the data from `sys.database_files`, `sys.databases`, and `sys.master_files` to find the database settings and parameters that are of interest. You can find the complete MSDN reference to these catalog views here:

```
http://msdn.microsoft.com/en-us/library/ms180163(v=sql.110).aspx
```

Information in the final report will contain the detailed drill-down data along with recommendations and best practices, as assessed by the DBA on the project. The main areas studied, some of which will require further drill-down and analysis, in this initial "collection and analysis" period can be categorized as follows:

- State of Health
- Configuration and Server Information
- Performance, CPU, and Memory
- Security

State of Health can be broken down as follows:

- Disk space full/used/percentage free
- Database log file usage
- Database status check (online, in-recovery, suspect, read-only, and so on)
- Check all service statuses (such as clustering, replication, service broker, log shipping, database mirroring) to verify that they are running correctly
- Uptime status (how long the server has been online and running)
- Error log checking for severity 17 and greater

- Error log check for 701 insufficient memory errors and I/O requests taking longer than 15 seconds

- Error log check for disk/subsystem errors 823, 824, and 825

- Last time database backups/`dbcc checkdb`

- List of scheduled jobs (backups, maintenance, and so on)

Configuration and Server Information includes:

- OS build, settings, IsClustered

- Database sizes, parameters, settings

- SQL Server settings, configurations

- Memory settings/AYOU/target versus total memory/VAS/MemtoLeave

- CPU processor/parallelism settings

- Virtual page size

- Active traces/default

The Performance, CPU, and Memory category encompasses a great many items:

- Memory usage/stats

- Buffer cache hit ratio

- Page life expectancy

- IO activity/databases using the most I/O

- CPU usage/processors

- Causes of the server waits

- Index information

- Count of missing indexes, by database

- Most important missing indexes

- Unused indexes

- Most costly indexes (high maintenance)

- Most used indexes

- Most fragmented indexes

- Duplicate indexes

- Most costly queries, by average IO

- Most costly queries, by average CPU

- Most executed queries

- Queries suffering most from blocking

- Queries with the lowest plan reuse

- Top stored procedure usage by execution count

- Top stored procedure usage by I/O pressure

- Top stored procedure usage by CPU pressure

- Top stored procedure usage by memory pressure

And finally Security is broken down as follows:

- Security mode

- Super admin (sa) access check

- Weak password/blank/reverse passwords

- Database/DBO/user rights (SOX/HIPPA compliance)

- List of logins

- Information about remote servers (linked servers)

Table 2-1 details the overall general categories and subcategories of the 15-point health check that I employ at various clients.

Table 2-1. *15-Point Health Check and Subcategories*

Cat	Subcat	Description
1		General Server Info
	1.11	Server Instance Properties
2		SQL Server Configuration Parameters
3		SQL Memory Usage Stats
	3.1	Cache Statistics
4		Error Captures (in last 24 hours)
5		Logical Disc Volumes
6		Historical CPU Usage
7		Database Parameters
	7.1	Database Size Summary and Distribution Statistics
	7.2	Database Recovery Model
	7.3	Database Log Utilization
8		Database Backup Information
9		SQL Job Information
	9.1	Long-running Jobs and Average Runtime
	9.2	Maintenance Plan Jobs
10		I/O Activitity
	10.1	I/O Activity Ranked by Database
	10.2	I/O Activity Ranked by I/O Stalls

(*continued*)

Table 2-1. (*continued*)

Cat	Subcat	Description
11		Top Server Waits
12		Historical Blocking Information
13		Index Usage and Statistics
	13.1	Unused Indexes
	13.2	Most-Used Indexes
	13.3	Logical Index Fragmentation
	13.4	Most-Costly Indexes
14		Top Query Performance
	14.1	Most-Executed Queries
	14.2	Most-Costly Queries by Memory Usage
	14.3	Most-Costly Queries by I/O Volumes
	14.4	Most-Costly Queries by CPU
15		Security Checks
	15.1	Passwords
	15.2	Windows Accounts with Admin Privileges
	15.3	Database and User rights, including DBO
	15.4	Remote Servers

Virtually Speaking...

Many companies have made virtualization a major part of their deployment and disaster recovery strategy. Virtualization technologies have come to the point where production SQL Server instances are commonly being provisioned as virtual machines. There is still some debate about whether virtualization can support SQL Server efficiently, although recent developments have narrowed this gap. There are many benefits to virtualization, including administrative management, resource management, high availability, recovery, streamlined provisioning of SQL Server instances, rack space, and cost savings on hardware power, and cooling.

However, it doesn't make the DBA's job any easier. When there is a SQL Server performance issue, the DBA is the first person who is approached. Unfortunately, virtualization doesn't make some performance issues transparent. This is a case where you need to work with your virtual machine (VM) administrator because in most instances the VM host is not visible or accessible to the DBA. Therefore, the DBA must be aware of how virtualization works, as well as the specific performance metrics to pay attention to. Many of the SQL Server best-practice recommendations for physical servers don't necessarily work well for virtual servers.

When I first encountered virtualization, it wasn't quite up to par yet and so was used to rapidly provision and deploy test and development servers. You could test new features, service packs, hot fixes, code, and so on. As part of my disaster recovery strategy, the limits of virtualization were then stretched by using a process to move servers from a physical box to a virtual machine, otherwise known as physical to virtual (P2V). My company's physical production servers resided in the NYC data center, and the virtual infrastructure was across the river in New Jersey at the colo site. The hardware was backed by blades with the latest, at that time, VMware platform. At the time, in the event of a DR scenario, the company would temporarily operate at a slightly degraded performance level. This made virtualization a perfect component for my DR plan.

A significant problem early on with SQL Server performance and virtualization was that the additional layer (the hypervisor) between the OS/SQL Server and the hardware (memory, CPU, and disk) in and of itself was the cause of some latency unacceptable to high-transaction online transaction processing (OLTP) systems. Recent developments have significantly improved the ability for SQL Server to scale and perform optimally on a virtual platform and reduce the overhead associated with the translation layer. Second Level Address Translation (SLAT) is one technology that supports virtual to physical memory address translation, which can significantly reduce CPU time and conserves memory resources for the VM.

Each processor type, Intel or AMD, has its own name known as Extended Page Tables (EPT) or Rapid Virtualization Indexing (RVI), respectively. The performance penalty is reduced by allowing the host to directly handle the mapping between the virtual memory used in the VMs and the physical memory in the virtualization host.

Although virtualization technologies have improved by leaps and bounds, it does not mean that every SQL Server machine should be virtualized. In some cases, such as a SQL Server cluster, physical servers may be a better option, even though it is possible to cluster across virtualized environments. Again, there is some debate about virtualizing your SQL clusters among SQL Server pros, but as the technology advances, use cases do become more attractive. Microsoft SQL Server 2008 R2 and newer supports advanced capabilities for high availability, such as guest and host clustering.

The reasons against such an implementation have more to do with who will manage the cluster failover, and not to minimize the DBA's role here. The advances in virtualization will overcome the existing technical complexities.

■ **Note** Do not cluster your virtual SQL Server nodes on one VM host because this is a single point of failure (SPOF).

If you do decide to set up SQL Failover Clustering on a virtual environment, remember that it is clustered across different physical VM hosts. If you're a DBA, it may seem that I am stating the obvious; nonetheless, I recently came across a client with multiple SQL Server instances that were clustered on the same VM host. This is an obvious single point of failure and defeats the purpose of a high-availability cluster, so be aware in your DBA travels.

The virtualization debate, however, is beyond the scope of this book. What is relevant here is that the DBA managing a SQL Server environment where several instances, if not all, are virtualized needs to adhere to certain best practices and performance measures.

Let's come back to what you need to know as a DBA to get healthy SQL performance. If you have a SQL Server instance that is virtual, you have an additional layer of abstraction (in other words, the hypervisor) between you and your data. The host's allocations of resources are often the cause of unseen performance issues that are not apparent by observing the VM guest. The trouble is that you need to know which layer is causing you performance issues. Is it the host? Or is it the guest? As such, you need to rely on the VM performance counters to get a complete picture of what is happening.

Memory Ballooning

Memory ballooning is a memory management technique that allows a physical host to take advantage of unused memory on its guest virtual machines. This is bad for SQL Server!

If the VM host attempts to retake the memory, there is an option available to reserve the guest memory assigned to individual virtual machines, called "Reserve all guest memory (All locked)." By enabling this feature—located under the Virtual Hardware settings for the virtual machine (vSphere 5.5), as shown in Figure 2-6—the selected virtual machine is not impacted, as shown in Figure 2-6. In the event that this option is not enabled, there may be a case for enabling the Lock Pages In Memory option in SQL Server, which is under DBA control.

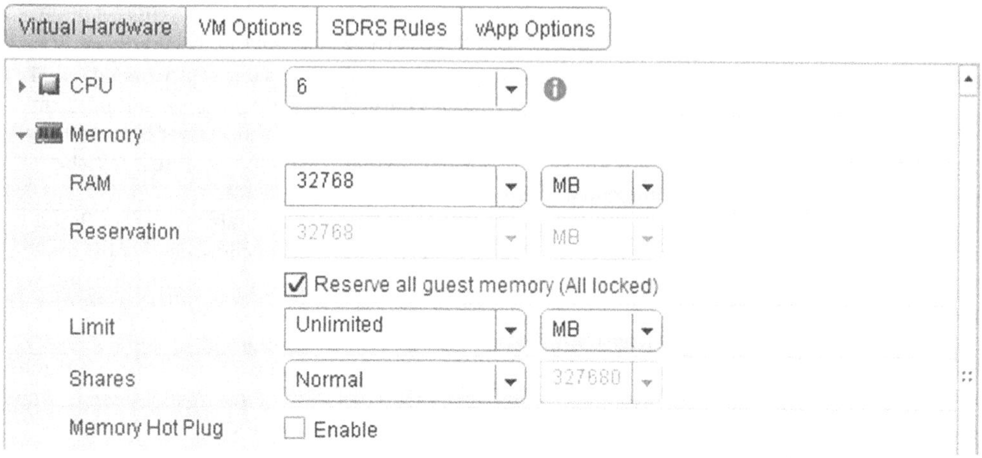

Figure 2-6. *VM configuration for guests: "Reserve all guest memory (All locked)"*

If your production virtual SQL Server instances are located on shared hosts, it is recommended that this feature is enabled on your virtual machines. Since the DBA is unaware how the host is configured, the DBA must consult with the VM administrator and ensure it is enabled. The last thing you want is for any process to take away memory from one of your SQL Server instances. Although this is the intended function of the memory balloon driver, you don't want this to happen because it will have a negative impact on SQL Server performance.

Over-allocation of Memory/CPU

It's OK to want to over-allocate your memory and CPU resources. What you don't want is to have them over-committed because that's where performance issues manifest themselves.

CPU Ready is a metric that measures the amount of time a VM is waiting ready to run against the pCPU (the physical CPU). In other words, CPU Ready indicates how long a vCPU (virtual CPU) has to wait for an available core when it has work to perform. So, while it's possible that CPU utilization may not be reported as high, if the CPU Ready metric is high, then your performance problem is most likely related to the CPU. CPU Ready Time, for example, is one of the VM-specific counters to look at and is the amount of time the virtual machine (guest) is ready to use a pCPU (host) but has to wait to get time on it.

The Balloon KB values reported for the balloon indicate that the host cannot meet its memory requirements and is an early warning sign of memory pressure on the host. The Balloon driver is installed via VMware Tools onto Windows and Linux guests, and its job is to force the operating systems of lightly used guests to page out unused memory back to ESX so that ESX can satisfy the demand from hungrier guests.

In the next chapter, I will discuss and call attention to some key performance counters to monitor, as they relate to virtualized SQL Server instances.

Best Practices: Says Who?

Most often, when a new DBA comes on the job or is interested in performance tuning a slow-running SQL Server, they seek out information on best practices. So, what exactly is a best practice, who is the authority, and who's to say that their best practices are your best practices? Where do these "best practices" come from?

This is especially true when you're looking for specific thresholds with performance counters. When setting these up, you often misconstrue what numbers are good and bad for SQL Server. The truth of the matter is that these numbers don't always tell the whole story. They need context, and they need correlation. I'm not going to list commonly accepted, and in many cases folklore, best-practice numbers. Instead, I am going to talk about how to establish your own best practices based on the performance of your SQL Server instances.

There are many common misconceptions when it comes to setting a number in stone. Often the benchmark numbers are based on specific tests, in specific environments, on specific hardware. Instead, this book is going to talk about best practices in general and how they are all related to your healthy SQL environment. Obviously, you want to adhere to best practices in order to achieve this and create best practices of your own for your company's needs. Therefore, the best thing to remember about best practices is that they are not always best.

■ **Tip**   The best thing to remember about best practices is that they are not always best.

Some Not-So Best Practices

Beware of bad practices often disguised as best practices. The superinformation highway, as the Internet used to be referred to, contains a lot of misinformation, roadblocks, and confusing signs. I want to dispel these notions here to emphasize that not all best practices should be blindly followed. As I discussed earlier in the chapter, only when you monitor your own SQL Server instances and see the numbers stray from the baseline should you consider a potential performance issue developing.

A couple of typical examples that many folks incorrectly accept as best practices are regarding the Page Life Expectancy (PLE) performance counter, the CXPACKET wait type, and tempdb configuration. PLE deals with how long you expect a data page to remain in the buffer cache in memory, on average. The number is represented in seconds, so the special number everyone talks about is 300, which is 5 minutes.

Therefore, when new pages are being read into memory, in essence the entire SQL Server memory buffer, the pages being replaced are flushed from cache every five minutes. If you think about this, especially nowadays with servers with large amounts of RAM, that's a lot of pages being flushed, and it's pretty risky to wait until your PLE is anywhere near that number.

■ **Note**   Some commonly accepted best practices are myths.

Another misunderstanding is with one of the commonly occurring wait types, CXPACKET. This particular wait type often comes to the top of the wait list when querying the sys.dm_os_wait_stats DMV. (Wait types and this DMV will be talked about more in-depth in Chapter 3.) This wait type is related to parallelism and parallel query processing. Many uninformed folks who see this show up as a top wait on their SQL Server automatically think that this is a problem. What follows from that line of thought are two wrong assumptions. The first one is that this in fact indicates there is a parallelism performance problem. The second one is the oft-accepted recommendation to turn parallelism off.

In reality, the nature of the OLTP system is to manage the query processes in which each process is always waiting on some resource at some point in time to run. The key question is, how long is it waiting? The facts that you see CXPACKET appear as your top wait is not necessarily a problem, unless there are excessive wait times.

Whether this wait is a problem or not depends on the type of system. In an OLTP environment, excessive CXPACKET waits can affect the throughput of other OLTP traffic. In a data warehouse environment, CXPACKET waits are expected for multiple-processor environments.

Figure 2-7 shows sample output of the sys.dm_os_wait_stats view where CXPacket is among the top waits.

Wait Type	Wait Time %	% Waiting
CXPACKET	4162790	25.90
CLR_AUTO_EVENT	2556444	15.91
OLEDB	2550596	15.87
PAGEIOLATCH_SH	1693645	10.54

Figure 2-7. *The top five waits from the* sys.dm_os_wait_stats *DMV*

The longer the query is waiting for a particular resource, the slower performance is perceived by the end user. While a query, thread, or process is waiting (the differences in these terms will be defined in Chapter 3), it sometimes holds up other queries, threads, and processes waiting to execute. This holdup creates the performance bottleneck. What to do next is the foundation for Chapter 3, which covers the methodology of waits and queues. In that chapter, you will learn one of the most effective performance troubleshooting techniques.

One final example of misconstrued best practice is the configuration of the system database tempdb. The name itself is a misnomer because without this database, SQL Server will not start up. The purpose of this system database is basically a work-and-sort space for database operations. Temporary tables, variables, stored procedures, cursors created by the user, and internal objects created by SQL Server get used here. tempdb is used also for row versioning and snapshot isolation and other such snapshot operations such as when executing certain DBCC commands. All of these objects are dropped once the session is disconnected.

The function of tempdb is critical to the overall performance of SQL Server, and the size, placement, and number of tempdb files directly affect performance. That is where urban legend kicks in as database professionals seek some guidelines on sizing, disk placement, and number of tempdb data files to create. An outdated recommendation was to create one additional database file for tempdb for each number of processor CPUs on the system.

With an ever-increasing number of physical processors, multicores, and hyperthreading, this recommendation will not give you any significant performance gains and becomes a point of diminishing returns. It may even degrade performance.

It Depends

With all the confusion out there as to what are best practices, the best answer to this is "it depends." It all depends on your environment and your server's specific workload. There are several factors that come into play. The purest form of best practices comes from your own testing, trending, baselining, and benchmarking. The numbers themselves matter little if they are near or trending at your typical baseline.

As technical as performance tuning will get, it is truly more art than science and experience over training. You don't need to completely throw out what are commonly accepted as industry best practices. You can use these as a guideline for your own testing. Some of them may be more applicable than others. What this section aims to do is arm you with knowledge on how to establish your own best practices, rather than spoonfeed you theoretical numbers that may not apply. Once you get through this book, you ideally will have created your own best practices to follow.

So, one way to establish your best practices is to compare the data you have collected during your health check data collection. This is the starting point to determine your ideal numbers. Using your baseline data, you will use this as a point of reference to determine whether your server is "healthy." All the measures and statistics that are captured at or near your baseline in essence become your best-practice standards. These standards should in turn be documented as a guide of best practices for your company to follow and assist with future SQL Server builds and deployments.

Perhaps if you are not yet comfortable or ready to create your own best-practice documentation, you can start looking at authoritative and reliable resources. (See some of my common best-practice recommendations at the end of this chapter.) Industry best practices and recommendations from Microsoft are a good place to start. Its white papers, knowledge base articles, TechNet, and MSDN are solid references, and I'll tell you why. Though some of their information may not always be 100 percent accurate, the documentation goes through a fairly rigorous technical-editing process before being released to the public.

Because of the high industry reputation of Microsoft and obligation to the customer, its information and documentation are vetted and validated. Even further, you can expect your group of Microsoft SQL Server MVPs, whose expertise is often unmatched with the product line, to always be reviewing, validating, and correcting any technical errors or omissions. Indeed, the MVP community plays a symbiotic relationship between Microsoft and the customers.

As a final point, with respect to establishing your best practices, you will soon see how it all gels together. Your inventory and baseline performance data becomes your documentation, which allows you to establish internal best practices, which in turn become your standards guide. Finally, you will be able to publish an operations manual that will become your *run book*. This term is discussed in the next section.

Your documentation and run book will be the key to a certifiably happy and healthy SQL server infrastructure and something you can immediately produce in the event of an audit. You managers will be happy, your colleagues will be happy, your auditors will be satisfied (but always grumpy), and you will be a happy database professional and exceptional DBA, worthy of praise, accolades, and, most important, a raise!

Run Book

The road map now brings me to what will become one of the most essential pieces of documentation the organization will ever have, collated into one book, with respect to your IT SQL Server infrastructure: the *run book*. When I refer to the run book here, it can, but not necessarily mean, an actual printed book. It is the collection of your documents, whether it's hard copy sitting on your desk, in the data center, or in the safe or an electronic repository located on a network share, in a document management system, on SharePoint, or even in the cloud. The run book can be any format and contain Word documents, Excel spreadsheets, Visio diagrams, PowerPoint slides, and so on.

Far too few companies have a run book, and yours will be fortunate enough to have one on hand once you complete this book. The run book in essence will be the organization's SQL Server instruction and operations manual, and such a book will provide the keys to the kingdom.

Now that I have built up the significance of the run book, let me define its purpose. The run book can have multiple uses. Wikipedia defines an IT run book as "a routine compilation of procedures and operations that the system administrator or operator carries out." Indeed, the run book is used as a reference by the interrelated IT teams, DBAs, help-desk staff, and network operations centers (NOCs), internally or externally. It stands alone as something that can be used as a training tool and to get junior staff and DBAs up to speed. The run book can also be used by project and database consultants that come in for a short-term assignment and need to quickly get up to speed on the logistics and technical specifications of the SQL Server environment.

So, what if you're a new DBA on the job? Wouldn't it be great to be able to refer to an all-encompassing run book that contains inventory, checklists, diagrams, performance data, and procedural and operational guides? The first thing I ask for at a new job or project is existing documentation. More often than not, there is no existing documentation, which is unfortunate. When some forms of documentation are available, usually they are not very good or useful. If you are lucky enough that a previous DBA or IT professional was mindful to put together some useful and valid documentation, consider yourself ahead of the game.

Nonetheless, this awesome responsibility will more than likely fall on your shoulders, and this book aims to make you aware of the significance that detailed documentation can make. It can make or break an organization's ability to troubleshoot issues, ensure business continuity, and recover quickly from a disaster, as well as pass an audit.

In addition, the run book will aid in performance tuning, as well as allow you or help-desk staff to triage issues through step-by-step instructions, decision trees, and contingencies. A good example is the DBA who is on-call, especially where there is escalation procedures in place. If a technically capable help-desk admin is manning the operations center and is the first call, a run book can allow the person to actually troubleshoot and resolve simple issues.

For example, if a simple script can be run to restart a failed job, truncate a transaction log, or rerun a backup, why escalate the issue up the chain? A run book can empower the junior technicians to grow their experience, technical know-how, and careers. It makes the difference between a call center where tickets are logged and delegated and a first-class, quality technical support center. This has positive benefits for all involved, including the organization as a whole.

Having thorough documentation is essential to building an efficient SQL Server infrastructure and is key to healthy SQL. You don't have to be the best writer (you're not writing a best-selling novel here); you just need to write things down in an organized way. And while it may be a daunting task, it is an undertaking that is well worth the effort. From a career perspective, it will mean the difference between an ordinary DBA and an exceptional DBA.

■ **Tip**   Career-wise, having a run book in your organization will mean the difference between an ordinary DBA and an exceptional DBA.

Keep in mind that the data is out there for the taking, and you must make sure you collect the right data and the right amount of data to allow you to make the proper analysis. Having too much data or not enough data will lead you to bad decisions. Analyzing the data will lead you to make decisions that will affect your SQL Server instances and impact performance. Therefore, you must be careful not to misinterpret the data and its meaning. Moreover, if you have all this data at your disposal and choose to ignore it, that in and of itself is a bad decision.

Now that you know about the run book, the information you need to collect, and the need to create a baseline, I will give you the knowledge, the tools, and the methods to collect this data throughout the rest of this book.

To sum up, having a run book will assist you with the following:

- Training

- Procedural operations and contingencies

- Performance tuning

- Troubleshooting

- Standardization

- Disaster recovery

- Audit

Road Map Essentials

I've talked about all the essential components involved in creating a healthy SQL Server environment road map. Here's a review of the items necessary for conducting a healthy SQL health check:

- Checklist

- Inventory

- Statistical terms: baseline, delta, deviation, and so on

- Metadata

- Collection data

- Compare data

- Performance life cycle

- Testing life cycle

- Best practices

- Documentation

- Run book

The road map for healthy SQL is now complete. Here I have given you the foundation of what you need to know to move toward a healthy SQL Server Infrastructure. You're ready to move forward to understanding and using the methodologies you will employ.

Rob's Bonus Best Practice Considerations

Here are ten quick best practice considerations (there are tons of them throughout this book, so this is just a preview) of things to consider when provisioning and deploying a new SQL Server. I don't make any specific recommendation because, as always, "it depends," but these areas should be considered for optimal performance at the server level when first deploying and configuring a new SQL Server instance.

- The Disk Layout for SQL Server should ideally separate Data, Log, tempdb, Binaries, and SQL Backups to separate physical disks.

- You should consider enabling LockPagesInMemory for both physical and clustered SQL Servers.

- Enable Instant File Initialization by assigning the Perform Volume Maintenance Tasks Windows policy to the SQL Server service account.

- Always set the SQL Server configuration options Maximum Server Memory andMinimum Server Memory.

- Exclude all data, log, backup, and SQL Server files from antivirus scans.

- The rule of thumb for the number of Tempdb Files to create for a SQL Server is the number of Logical Cores/4.

- Use the Startup Trace Flag T-1118 to reduce allocation contention in the SQL Server tempdb database.

- Enable the SQL Server configuration setting Optimize For AdHoc Workloads for better query performance.

- Increase the SQL Server configuration setting Cost Threshold for Parallelism to specify the threshold at which SQL Server creates and runs parallel plans for queries.

- Consider using native backup compression for your SQL Server backups.

CHAPTER 3

■ ■ ■

Waits and Queues

Now that the road map has been built, you are on your way to a healthy SQL Server infrastructure. In this chapter, you will learn about one of the most effective methodologies for performance tuning and troubleshooting. The key methodology is *waits and queues*, which is an accurate way to determine why your SQL Server is performing slowly and to pinpoint where the bottleneck is. By analyzing the wait statistics, you can discover where SQL Server is spending most of the time waiting and focus on the most relevant performance counters. In other words, by using this process, you will quickly discover what SQL Server is waiting on.

Anyone who is involved in the development or performance of SQL Server can benefit from this methodology. The purpose of this chapter is to help DBAs, developers, and other database professionals by spreading the word about waits and queues. The objective here is to lay a foundation for your own independent investigation into the more advanced aspects of this in-depth topic. Consider this chapter your performance-tuning primer to identifying and understanding SQL Server performance issues.

Introducing Waits and Queues

The methodology known as waits and queues is a performance-tuning and analysis goldmine that came with the release of SQL Server 2005. However, there was not a lot of fanfare around it, nor was there significant adoption of it by those who would benefit from it the most: database administrators. There was not a lot of early promotion of the concept or a complete understanding of how to use it, especially the correlation between waits and queues. I began writing and speaking about the topic some time ago and was amazed at how many DBAs had not heard about it or used it. Today, this is not the case, and many SQL Server MVPs, speakers, and presenters have effectively created an awareness of the methodology. Moreover, many vendors have built third-party monitoring software built upon this methodology.

Before drilling down into how to use this methodology, I'll define what a wait state is and how it works internally. Because a resource may not be immediately available for a query request, the SQL Server engine puts it into a wait state. Therefore, waits and queues is also known as *wait state analysis*. The official definition according to Microsoft is as follows:

> *"Whenever a request is made within SQL Server that—for one of many reasons—can't be immediately satisfied, the system puts the request into a wait state. The SQL Server engine internally tracks the time spent waiting, aggregates it at the instance level, and retains it in memory."*

SQL Server now collects and aggregates in-memory metadata about the resources that a query or thread is waiting on. It exposes this information through the primary DMVs with respect to wait statistics: sys.dm_os_wait_stats and sys.dm_os_waiting_tasks. When one or more queries start to wait for excessive periods of time, the response time for a query is said to be slow, and performance is poor. Slow query response times and poor performance are the results that are apparent to end users. Once you know where the contention is, you can work toward resolving the performance issue.

The "queue" side of the waits and queues equation comes in the form of Windows OS and SQL Server performance counters, which are discussed later in this chapter. All of the SQL Server performance counters that are available can also be viewed by using the sys.dm_os_performance_counters DMV. This DMV replaced the sys.sysperfinfo view, which was deprecated in SQL Server 2005 and therefore shouldn't be used. There will be broader discussion of how to calculate and derive useful numbers from the counter values exposed by sys.dm_os_performance_counters in this chapter briefly and in the upcoming chapters. Moreover, when I show you which counters to use for monitoring performance, relative to the various wait types, I will not necessarily define each one. You can see the counter detail from within Performance Monitor by clicking the Show Description checkbox for each counter, as shown in Figure 3-1. Or, you can look up more information about each counter by searching on MSDN.com.

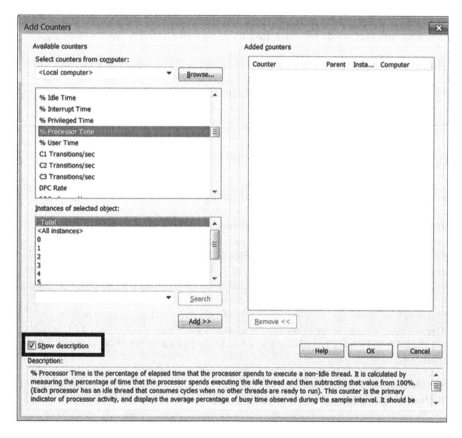

Figure 3-1. Performance Monitor displays a detailed description for each counter

You can run this quick SELECT statement to view the columns and inspect the raw data:

```
SELECT object_name,
            counter_name,
            case when instance_name =''
then @@SERVICENAME end as instance_name,
            cntr_type,
            cntr_value
FROM  sys.dm_os_performance_counters
```

Figure 3-2 shows the results from this query and shows a sample of the myriad of performance counters and objects available in the system view.

	object_name	counter_name	instance_name	cntr_type	cntr_value
1	SQLServer:Buffer Manager	Buffer cache hit ratio	MSSQLSERVER	537003264	14
2	SQLServer:Buffer Manager	Buffer cache hit ratio base	MSSQLSERVER	1073939712	14
3	SQLServer:Buffer Manager	Page lookups/sec	MSSQLSERVER	272696576	7022262
4	SQLServer:Buffer Manager	Free list stalls/sec	MSSQLSERVER	272696576	0
5	SQLServer:Buffer Manager	Database pages	MSSQLSERVER	65792	6909
6	SQLServer:Buffer Manager	Target pages	MSSQLSERVER	65792	64012288
7	SQLServer:Buffer Manager	Integral Controller Slope	MSSQLSERVER	65792	10
8	SQLServer:Buffer Manager	Lazy writes/sec	MSSQLSERVER	272696576	0
9	SQLServer:Buffer Manager	Readahead pages/sec	MSSQLSERVER	272696576	13547
10	SQLServer:Buffer Manager	Page reads/sec	MSSQLSERVER	272696576	29363
11	SQLServer:Buffer Manager	Page writes/sec	MSSQLSERVER	272696576	28693
12	SQLServer:Buffer Manager	Checkpoint pages/sec	MSSQLSERVER	272696576	28115
13	SQLServer:Buffer Manager	Background writer pages/sec	MSSQLSERVER	272696576	0
14	SQLServer:Buffer Manager	Page life expectancy	MSSQLSERVER	65792	1369218

Figure 3-2. *A sample of the myriad of performance counters and objects via the sys.dm_os_performance_counters DMV*

S-l-o-w Performance

The term *slow performance* is broad, often used by end users when they can't get their reports to run, their data to display, or their front-end application screens to render in a timely manner. Usually, the cause of this slowness is happening on the backend. As database professionals, you know there is a much deeper technical explanation.

Poor performance is often because of a resource limitation. Either a SQL query is waiting on a resource to become available or the resources themselves are insufficient to complete the queries in a timely manner. Insufficient resources cause a performance bottleneck, and it is precisely the point of resource contention that the waits and queues methodology aims to identify and resolve. Once the bottleneck is identified, whether it is CPU, memory, or I/O, you can tune the query. Query optimization may make the query use the existing resources more efficiently, or you may need to add resources, such as more RAM or faster CPU processors and disks.

The delay experienced between a request and an answer is called the *total response time* (TRT). In essence, the request is called a *query*, which is a request to retrieve data, while the answer is the output or data that is returned. TRT, also called the *total query response time*, is the time it takes from when the user executes the query to the time it receives the output, after a query is run against SQL Server. The TRT can be measured as the overall performance of an individual transaction or query.

You can also measure the average cumulative TRT of all the server queries running. Many developers often ask whether there is a way to calculate the total query response time. In this chapter, I will discuss CPU time, wait time, and signal waits; what they represent; and how you can calculate each of these individually. However, for now, know that if you add these wait times together (as in CPU time + wait time + signal wait time), you can derive the overall total query response time, as shown in Figure 3-3.

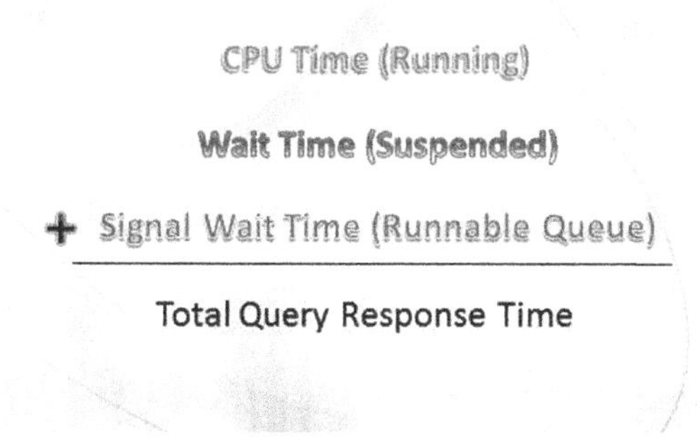

CPU Time (Running)

Wait Time (Suspended)

+ Signal Wait Time (Runnable Queue)

Total Query Response Time

Figure 3-3. *Computing the total query response time*

One way you can get the average total query response time is to use the sys.dm_exec_query_stats DMV, which gives you the cumulative performance statistics for cached query plans in SQL Server. Within the cached plan, the view contains one row per query statement. The information here is persisted only until a plan is removed from the cache and the corresponding rows are deleted. You will have more use for this _query_stats view later in the book. In the meantime, you can focus on the total_elapsed_time column in this view, which will give you the time for all the executions of the cached queries. So, for completed executions of the query plan, you take the total_elapsed_time value and divide it by the number of times that the plan has been executed since it was last compiled, which is from the execution_count column. Here's an example:

```
SELECT avg(total_elapsed_time / execution_count)/1000 As avg_query_response_time
--total_avg_elapsed_time (div by 1000 for ms, div by 1000000 for sec)
FROM sys.dm_exec_query_stats
```

The output in my case is as follows:

```
avg_query_response_time
153
```

Likewise, you can use the same formula to approximate the total query response time for the individual cached queries, along with the average CPU time and statement text. This can help you identify which queries are taking a long time to return results. Here is the script:

```
SELECT TOP 20
    AVG(total_elapsed_time/execution_count)/1000000 as "Total Query Response Time",
SUM(query_stats.total_worker_time) / SUM(query_stats.execution_count)/1000 AS "Avg CPU Time",
    MIN(query_stats.statement_text) AS "Statement Text"
```

```
FROM
    (SELECT QS.*,
    SUBSTRING(ST.text, (QS.statement_start_offset/2) + 1,
    ((CASE statement_end_offset
        WHEN -1 THEN DATALENGTH(ST.text)
        ELSE QS.statement_end_offset END
            - QS.statement_start_offset)/2) + 1) AS statement_text
    FROM sys.dm_exec_query_stats AS QS
    CROSS APPLY sys.dm_exec_sql_text(QS.sql_handle) as ST) as query_stats
WHERE statement_text IS NOT NULL
GROUP BY query_stats.query_hash
ORDER BY 2 DESC; -- ORDER BY 1 DESC - uncomment to sort by TRT
```

The following is the output. (I've elided text from some of the longer statements in order to fit within the limitations of the page.)

Total Query Response Time	Avg CPU Time	Statement Text
10	59256	SELECT DISTINCT Status FROM dbo.rpt_...
45	41982	SELECT DISTINCT dep.DeploymentName AS ...
0	9430	SELECT [ReportComponent_ID], ...

Blame Game: Blame SQL Server

When something goes wrong and performance is slow, there is often a visceral instinct to attribute immediate blame to SQL Server. The database is often the usual suspect, so SQL Server must be the cause. Directly translated, this puts you, the DBA, in the line of fire. Thus, the quicker you can identify and resolve the performance issue, the more confident the users will be in your technical, troubleshooting, database administration, and tuning skills. You must also gather evidence and document your findings, explaining and identifying the true cause.

You might ask why it is that everyone blames SQL Server and points their finger at the DBA. One common reason is the database is always at the scene of the crime; another reason is that people target SQL Server because they don't understand much about it. It is easier to blame that which you don't know. SQL Server used to be, and still is in some respects, a black box to nondatabase professionals. Oftentimes, SQL Server will record an error message that is intended to lead you in the right direction as to where the bottleneck is located. The nondatabase professional will use this as "evidence" of database culpability, and end users will pile on. I will highlight some of these "blame game" antics throughout the chapter.

■ **Caution**   Remember, the database is the usual suspect, so the DBA will be to blame.

Back to Waiting

If I haven't convinced you yet why you want to use waits and queues in your performance troubleshooting, tuning, and monitoring, let's consider the following scenarios. An end user has a 4 p.m. dead line to generate some important reports from SQL Server, and the server has crawled to a halt. He calls to complain about the slowness in performance. Not very detailed, is he? Take another example: it's Friday afternoon, and suddenly the developers find that the application is running slow and it's time to deploy code into production.

The application is poorly designed; there are no indexes, no primary keys, and no standards, so there are many performance problems. The project managers get wind of this and, fearing missing their project milestones, escalate it to your higher-ups. Your managers then tell you to immediately drop everything and resolve these performance problems as a top priority. These folks likely don't understand the time it might take to identify the cause of the problem, let alone to resolve it, and most times they don't care. They know only one thing: they want it fixed now, and they know the DBA is the person to do it.

Traditionally, to analyze and discover the root cause of the performance bottleneck, you needed to employ various methods and tools such as Performance Monitor, profiler traces, and network sniffers. Since there were some limitations in versions of SQL Server 2000 and earlier, many companies turned to expensive third-party software solutions. Another challenge with identifying and isolating a performance issue is knowing the right counters to set up. If at the outset you are uncertain whether the bottleneck is a memory, CPU, or I/O issue, it makes troubleshooting more difficult. Once you collect all the performance data, you still need to parse it. When setting up performance counters, you need to cast a wide net, and such methods are time-consuming and often frustrating.

Moreover, what do tell your users, colleagues, clients, and managers when they call complaining about slow performance? Do you let them know that you need to set up about 20 or so Perfmon counters, collect the data over a period of a few days, trend it against peak and nonpeak hours, and get back to them "real soon"? The next time you have half your company and irate users approaching your desk like zombies from the *Night of the Living Dead* complaining about some vague or urgent performance issue, remember that wait stats can quickly identify the cause of the bottleneck and what SQL Server is waiting on.

Therefore, the quickest way to get to the root cause is to look at the wait stats first. By employing the use of waits and queues, you can avoid troubleshooting the wrong bottleneck and sidestep a wild-goose chase. Once you identify what a query or session is waiting on, you have successfully uncovered the likely bottleneck. To dig deeper, the next step you will want to take is to set up the relevant performance counters related to the resource wait. Using the waits and queues methodology can offer the best opportunities to improve performance and provide the biggest return on time invested in performance tuning. Microsoft has proclaimed that this methodology is "the biggest bang for the buck." And that is why you should use it and why it is a major component to healthy SQL.

■ **Note** The waits and queues methodology offers the biggest bang for the buck and has a significant return on the performance-tuning time investment, according to the Microsoft engineering team.

So, let's continue and correlate a query request with the wait queue. When a query is run and SQL Server cannot complete the request right away because either the CPU or some other resource is being used, your query must *wait* for the resource to become available. In the meantime, your query gets placed in the *suspended* or *resource* queue or on the *waiter list* and assigned a wait type that is reflective of the resource the query is waiting for. By examining the wait stat DMVs, you can answer this question and track how such waits are affecting overall performance.

Wait Type Categories

SQL Server tracks more than 400 wait types; I will discuss only a handful of them in this chapter, focusing on potential resource contention and bottlenecks, such as CPU pressure, I/O pressure, memory pressure, parallelism, and blocking. These cover the most typical and commonly occurring waits. Before digging into the different wait types, I'll discuss the four major categories of wait types.

To help you understand what you will be looking at before running any wait stats queries, you should be familiar with the categories of waits types. Since there are so many, two great resources you should refer to are "SQL Server 2005 Waits and Queues," by Microsoft, and "The SQL Server Wait Type Repository," by the CSS SQL Server engineers. "SQL Server 2005 Waits and Queues" was published originally for SQL Server 2005 but is an invaluable resource that I have based my waits and queues presentations on, as well as information in this chapter. It is very much valid for all subsequent versions and can be downloaded from http://technet.microsoft.com/en-us/library/cc966413.aspx.

The Microsoft CSS SQL Server engineers maintain a wait type repository on their official blog. Not only can you find a description for every wait type, but it describes the type of wait; the area it affects, such as IO, memory, network, and so on; and possible actions to take. You can access the wait repository here:

http://blogs.msdn.com/b/psssql/archive/2009/11/03/the-sql-server-wait-type-repository.aspx

The various waits can be broadly categorized as follows:

- *Resource waits* occur when a worker thread requests access to a resource that is not available because it is being used by another worker and is not yet available. These are the most common types of waits. These wait types typically surface as locks, latches, network, and I/O wait states.

- *Signal waits* are the time that worker threads spend waiting for the CPU to become available to run. The worker threads are said to be in the runnable queue, where they wait until it's their turn. Since there is no specific wait type that indicates CPU pressure, you must measure the signal wait time. Signal wait time is the difference between the time the waiting thread was signaled and when it started running.

- *Queue waits* occur when a worker is idle, waiting for work to be assigned. This wait type is most typically seen with system background tasks, such as the deadlock monitor and ghost record cleanup tasks.

- *External waits* occur when a SQL Server worker is waiting for an external event, such as an extended stored procedure call or a linked server query, to finish.

Table 3-1 sums up each of these categories.

Table 3-1. Details for Each Wait Category

Category	Details
Resource waits	Locks, latches, memory, network, I/O
Signal waits	Time spent waiting for CPU
Queue waits	Idle workers, background tasks
External waits	Extended procs (XPs), linked server queries

Is Waiting a Problem?

The key misconception by database professionals, and other folks looking at top wait stats, is that the wait type at the top of the list of results is the problem. So, let's compare waits to our everyday lives to make this easier to understand. When you go to the supermarket and complete your shopping, you must get in line and wait your turn until the cashier calls you. Waiting in line is certainly expected, and you wouldn't consider a fast-moving line a problem. Only when the little old lady, who I will call Granny, begins to argue with the cashier about the soap being 10 cents cheaper in last week's circular does the waiting become longer, as does the line. Now you have a performance problem. SQL Server has a line too, and its queries (the customers) must get inline and wait to be called.

Although the length of a queue may indicate a busy OLTP system, the line itself (the runnable queue) is not necessarily a problem. Therefore, the queue length will not cause a performance issue if the queue is getting processed in a speedy manner. If this is the case, there should be no high wait times, which is the nature of a healthy SQL Server. However, when the line becomes too long and the time it takes to get the customers to the cashier is excessive, this indicates a different type of problem. In other words, if the queue is long and the thread cannot get to the CPU to be processed, it indicates there is CPU pressure. CPU pressure is measured a little differently than all other resource waits.

With the SQL Server scheduling system, keep in mind that a queue of queries waiting on resources to become available will always be present. If wait times are high and one query then blocks the other queries from executing, you must discover the cause of the bottleneck, whether it is I/O, memory, disk, network, or CPU.

I will focus on the central concepts of query queues and provide an overview of the engine internals and how they apply to an OLTP system. You will learn how the process or query queue works so that you understand that processes waiting for available resources are normal when managing threads and query execution. All threads basically must wait in line to get executed, and only when these wait times become high does it become a concern.

For example, just because you see that the PAGEIOLATCH_X wait type accounts for 85 percent of your waits does not immediately imply a performance issue. What users need to be concerned with are recurring waits where the total wait time is greater than some number, let's say greater than 30 seconds. People will run scripts and see that a particular resource wait is their top wait on the system, but all in all they have a very low wait time, as in the previous example. They automatically assume it is a problem and attempt to troubleshoot the issue. However, the top waits are only part of the story. What matters are top waits having excessive wait times.

Observing Wait Statistics

One of the most significant system views discussed in this chapter is sys.dm_os_wait_stats. As the primary DMV for collecting wait statistics, you will use this view that shows the time for waits that have already completed. Within this DMV, you will see the wait type, the number of waits for each type, the total wait time, the maximum wait time, and the signal wait time.

The columns and description of the sys.dm_os_wait_stats DMV are as follows:

- wait_type: The name of the wait type

- waiting_tasks_count: The number of waits on this wait type

- wait_time_ms: The total wait time for this wait type in milliseconds (includes signal_wait_time)

- max_wait_time_ms: The maximum wait time on this wait type for a worker

- signal_wait_time_ms: The difference between the time the waiting thread was signaled and when it started running (time in runnable queue!)

These metrics are shown at the instance level and are aggregated across all sessions since SQL Server was last restarted or since the last time that the wait statistics were cleared. This means that the metrics collected are not persisted and are reset each time SQL Server is restarted. You also need to know that the waits and related measures in the table are cumulative and won't tell you what the top waits are at this moment.

If you want to store this data beyond a restart, you must create a historical user-tracking table. You can easily dump this information into your tracking table for later use and historical trend analysis. Therefore, to derive any useful information for any point-in-time analysis, you need to take at least two snapshots of the data. The first snapshot is your baseline, and the second snapshot is your comparative delta.

When querying or building historical data from the `sys.dm_os_wait_stats` view, there are a number of system and background process wait types that are safe to ignore. This list changes and grows all the time, but you definitely want to filter out as much of these harmless waits that can be excluded from your analysis. You may want to even store these in a table so you can dynamically keep your wait stats analysis queries up-to-date. Here is a quick list of these typical wait types that can be excluded. These are the system and background process wait types to ignore.

- LAZYWRITER_SLEEP
- BROKER_TO_FLUSH
- RESOURCE_QUEUE
- BROKER_TASK_STOP
- SLEEP_TASK
- CLR_MANUAL_EVENT
- SLEEP_SYSTEMTASK
- CLR_AUTO_EVENT
- SQLTRACE_BUFFER_FLUSH
- DISPATCHER_QUEUE_SEMAPHORE
- WAITFOR
- FT_IFTS_SCHEDULER_IDLE_WAIT
- LOGMGR_QUEUE
- XE_DISPATCHER_WAIT
- CHECKPOINT_QUEUE
- XE_DISPATCHER_JOIN
- REQUEST_FOR_DEADLOCK_SEARCH
- BROKER_EVENTHANDLER
- XE_TIMER_EVENT
- TRACEWRITE
- FT_IFTSHC_MUTEX
- BROKER_TRANSMITTER
- SQLTRACE_INCREMENTAL_FLUSH_SLEEP
- SQLTRACE_WAIT_ENTRIES
- BROKER_RECEIVE_WAITFOR
- SLEEP_BPOOL_FLUSH
- ONDEMAND_TASK_QUEUE
- SQLTRACE_LOCK

- DBMIRROR_EVENTS_QUEUE

- DIRTY_PAGE_POLL

- HADR_FILESTREAM_IOMGR_IOCOMPLETION

Using sys.dm_os_wait_stats, you can isolate top waits for server instance by percentage; you use a popular DMV query written by SQL MVP Glenn Berry that gets the top waits on the server by percentage and converts the wait time to seconds. You will see that you can set the percentage threshold and eliminate nonimportant wait types.

```
WITH Waits AS
(SELECT wait_type, wait_time_ms / 1000. AS wait_time_s,
100. * wait_time_ms / SUM(wait_time_ms) OVER() AS pct,
ROW_NUMBER() OVER(ORDER BY wait_time_ms DESC) AS rn
FROM sys.dm_os_wait_stats
WHERE wait_type NOT IN
('CLR_SEMAPHORE','LAZYWRITER_SLEEP','RESOURCE_QUEUE','SLEEP_TASK'
,'SLEEP_SYSTEMTASK','SQLTRACE_BUFFER_FLUSH','WAITFOR', 'LOGMGR_QUEUE','CHECKPOINT_QUEUE'
,'REQUEST_FOR_DEADLOCK_SEARCH','XE_TIMER_EVENT','BROKER_TO_FLUSH','BROKER_TASK_STOP',
'CLR_MANUAL_EVENT'
,'CLR_AUTO_EVENT','DISPATCHER_QUEUE_SEMAPHORE', 'FT_IFTS_SCHEDULER_IDLE_WAIT'
,'XE_DISPATCHER_WAIT', 'XE_DISPATCHER_JOIN', 'SQLTRACE_INCREMENTAL_FLUSH_SLEEP'))
SELECT W1.wait_type,
CAST(W1.wait_time_s AS DECIMAL(12, 2)) AS wait_time_s,
CAST(W1.pct AS DECIMAL(12, 2)) AS pct,
CAST(SUM(W2.pct) AS DECIMAL(12, 2)) AS running_pct
FROM Waits AS W1 INNER JOIN Waits AS W2 ON W2.rn <= W1.rn
GROUP BY W1.rn, W1.wait_type, W1.wait_time_s, W1.pct
HAVING SUM(W2.pct) - W1.pct < 99 OPTION (RECOMPILE) -- percentage threshold
```

```
wait_typewait_time_spctrunning_pct
CXPACKET1207834.0451.0351.03
ASYNC_NETWORK_IO572210.6424.1875.21
LCK_M_IS138015.655.8381.04
LCK_M_SCH_M136508.055.7786.80
LCK_M_IX134139.235.6792.47
LATCH_EX47457.312.0194.48
OLEDB22417.760.9595.42
BACKUPIO14730.440.6296.05
LCK_M_SCH_S13530.930.5796.62
SOS_SCHEDULER_YIELD12422.100.5297.14
LCK_M_S9392.840.4097.54
WRITELOG8574.280.3697.90
BACKUPBUFFER6454.240.2798.17
PAGELATCH_UP6006.460.2598.43
ASYNC_IO_COMPLETION5947.370.2598.68
THREADPOOL5101.040.2298.89
CXROWSET_SYNC5091.040.2299.11
```

When establishing a baseline of wait stat data for performance monitoring, you may want to first manually clear the wait stat data by running the following command:

```
DBCC SQLPerf('sys.dm_os_wait_stats',CLEAR)
```

You should run this only in your test and development environments. Before you do this, you may want to save the current data in an archive table first. You can do this by running the following SELECT INTO statement. You can add a column called ArchivedDate that will append the current datetime to the data rows, indicating the time each row was captured. Here I will call the new table Waits_Stats_History:

```
SELECT *, getdate() as ArchiveDate
INTO Wait_Stats_History
FROM Sys.dm_os_wait_stats
WHERE wait_type NOT IN
 ('CLR_SEMAPHORE','LAZYWRITER_SLEEP','RESOURCE_QUEUE','SLEEP_TASK'
,'SLEEP_SYSTEMTASK','SQLTRACE_BUFFER_FLUSH','WAITFOR', 'LOGMGR_QUEUE','CHECKPOINT_QUEUE'
,'REQUEST_FOR_DEADLOCK_SEARCH','XE_TIMER_EVENT','BROKER_TO_FLUSH','BROKER_TASK_STOP',
'CLR_MANUAL_EVENT'
,'CLR_AUTO_EVENT','DISPATCHER_QUEUE_SEMAPHORE', 'FT_IFTS_SCHEDULER_IDLE_WAIT'
,'XE_DISPATCHER_WAIT', 'XE_DISPATCHER_JOIN', 'SQLTRACE_INCREMENTAL_FLUSH_SLEEP')
```

You can check the results of this table by querying the newly created Wait_States_History table using the following query:

```
select * from Wait_Stats_History
```

The following are the results, with the ArchiveDate column data appended to the sys.dm_os_wait_stats view. This shows a simple example of creating an archive table to persist historical data for wait stats. Here the data from the sys.dm_os_wait_stats view is appended with the current datetime stamp.

```
wait_typewaiting_tasks_countwait_time_msmax_wait_time_mssignal_wait_time_msArchiveDate
MISCELLANEOUS00002014-11-01 19:49:34.423
LCK_M_SCH_S266135309281799933322014-11-01 19:49:34.423
LCK_M_SCH_M7913650805443338629222014-11-01 19:49:34.423
LCK_M_S907939283629996559242014-11-01 19:49:34.423
LCK_M_U202519367165983971752014-11-01 19:49:34.423
LCK_M_X1990184713200153256202014-11-01 19:49:34.423
LCK_M_IS4869138015645179999261602014-11-01 19:49:34.423
LCK_M_IU145645602014-11-01 19:49:34.423
LCK_M_IX8895134139231179999915822014-11-01 19:49:34.423
LCK_M_SIU00002014-11-01 19:49:34.423
LCK_M_SIX00002014-11-01 19:49:34.423
LCK_M_UIX00002014-11-01 19:49:34.423
LCK_M_BU00002014-11-01 19:49:34.423
LCK_M_RS_S00002014-11-01 19:49:34.423
LCK_M_RS_U00002014-11-01 19:49:34.423
LCK_M_RIn_NL00002014-11-01 19:49:34.423
LCK_M_RIn_S00002014-11-01 19:49:34.423
LCK_M_RIn_U00002014-11-01 19:49:34.423
LCK_M_RIn_X00002014-11-01 19:49:34.423
LCK_M_RX_S00002014-11-01 19:49:34.423
LCK_M_RX_U00002014-11-01 19:49:34.423
LCK_M_RX_X00002014-11-01 19:49:34.423
LATCH_NL00002014-11-01 19:49:34.423
```

The overall wait time reflects the time that elapses when a thread leaves the RUNNING state, goes to the SUSPENDED state, and returns to the RUNNING state again. Therefore, you can capture and derive the resource wait time by subtracting the signal wait time from the overall wait time. You can use the simple query to get the resource, signal, and total wait time, as shown next. You would also want to order by total wait time descending to force the highest wait times to the top of the results.

You can calculate all the wait times by querying the sys.dm _wait_stats DMV as follows:

```
Select wait_type, waiting_tasks_count, wait_time_ms as total_wait_time_ms,
signal_wait_time_ms,
(wait_time_ms-signal_wait_time_ms) as resource_wait_time_ms
FROM sys.dm_os_wait_stats
ORDER BY total_wait_time_ms DESC
```

The following output shows the raw output from the sys.dm_os_wait_stats DMV top wait stats data, ordered by the total wait time in milliseconds, with the highest total wait times at the top, along with the waiting task count and signal and resource wait times.

```
wait_type waiting_tasks_count total_wait_time_ms signal_wait_time_ms resource_wait_time_ms
BROKER_TASK_STOP 8545 105170818 1098 105169720
SQLTRACE_INCREMENTAL_FLUSH_SLEEP 10617 104810645 49 104810596
HADR_FILESTREAM_IOMGR_IOCOMPLETION 84757 104810120 625 104809495
LOGMGR_QUEUE 329469 104809280 1449 104807831
```

A Multithreaded World

Multithreading is the ability of a process to manage its use by more than one user at a time. The smallest unit that can be managed independently by a scheduler is a *thread*. All threads follow a first-in-first-out (FIFO) model. Multiple threads can exist within the same process and share resources such as memory, while different processes do not share these resources. More than one thread can be simultaneously executed across multiple processors. This is an example of multithreading. SQL Server also uses what's called *cooperative scheduling* (or *nonpreemptive scheduling*), where a thread voluntarily yields the processor to another thread when it is waiting for a system resource or non-CPU event. These voluntary yields often show up as SOS_SCHEDULER_YIELD waits, which require further investigation to determine whether there is CPU pressure. When the current thread does not yield the processor within a certain amount of time, the thread expires. When a thread expires, it is said to have reached its execution quantum. *Quantum* is the amount of time a thread is scheduled to run.

The SQLOS layer implements what is called *thread scheduling*. An individual scheduler maps to a single CPU, equivalent to the number of logical CPUs on the system. So, if there are 8 OS schedulers, there are 8 logical CPUs. Sixteen OS schedulers equals 16 logical CPUs, and so forth.

For each logical CPU, there is one scheduler. It should be noted that scheduler mapping is not to physical CPU cores or sockets but to logical CPU. If you want to get a count of the existing number of SQLOS schedulers on the system, you can query the sys.dm_os_schedulers view as follows:

```
SELECT COUNT(*) AS NO_OF_OS_SCHEDULERS FROM sys.dm_os_schedulers
WHERE status='VISIBLE ONLINE'

NO_OF_OS_SCHEDULERS
32
```

You can take a look at the sys.dm_os_schedulers DMV, which shows all the activity associated with each scheduler, such as active tasks, number of workers, scheduler status, context switching, and runaway tasks. This DMV is useful in troubleshooting issues specifically related to CPU pressure.

A scheduler is mapped to an individual physical or logical CPU, which manages the work done by worker threads. Once the SQLOS creates the schedulers, the total number of workers is divided among the schedulers.

Context switching occurs when the OS or the application is forced to change the executing thread on one processor to be switched out of the CPU so another process can run. Since the scheduler is doing the work, this keeps context switching to a minimum. Context switching is a natural occurrence in any CPU system, but when this happens excessively, you have a potential performance problem.

A scenario where excessive context switching can cause high CPU and I/O contention is a potentially expensive operation and can have a serious impact on performance. Only one scheduler is created for each logical processor to minimize context switching.

The Execution Model

How does SQL Server manage the execution of user requests? To answer this question, you can examine what's known as the SQL Server SQLOS execution model. This model will help you understand how SQL Server uses schedulers to manage these requests.

Let's go back to the example of the old lady in the supermarket holding up the line to see how the SQL Server execution model works (Figure 3-4). I will focus here on what happens on one OS scheduler for simplicity and easy visualization. First, let's set up the scenario. Compare the SQL execution model to the supermarket checkout line. You have the supermarket, the customers, the line, and the cashier. During the course of the transaction, the customer will be in three states (not U.S. states). The customers are running, runnable, or suspended. The customer is equivalent to a thread. The line is the runnable queue, the cashier is the CPU, and the price is the resource. The person or thread that is at the front of the line about to be checked out is said to be *running*, or currently using the CPU. A thread using the CPU is running until it has to wait for a resource that is not available. Each thread is assigned a SPID or session_id so SQL Server can keep track of them.

Figure 3-4. A graphic depiction of the execution model running process

So, Granny, despite her age, is in a running state, and the rest of the customers in line are waiting to be "checked out" (waiting for the cashier to become available), like the threads in SQL Server are waiting for the CPU to become available. However, because Granny is arguing that the soap should be on sale, the cashier must ask for a price-check. Fortunately for the other customers, Granny must step aside and wait for the price check or, in essence, for the price to become available.

She is now in a suspended state, and the next customer moves to the front of the line to checkout. The Granny thread gets assigned a wait type and is in the suspended (or resource) queue, waiting for the resource (the price) to become available. All the threads (or customers) like Granny that stay in the suspended queue go on the waiter list. You can measure the time that Granny spends in this queue by measuring the resource wait time. Meanwhile, the next customer, now in the running state getting checked out, continues with the transaction until it is complete. Like the thread running on the CPU, if the resource is available to proceed, it continues until the execution of the query is completed. Figure 3-5 shows what the suspended state would look like in the execution model.

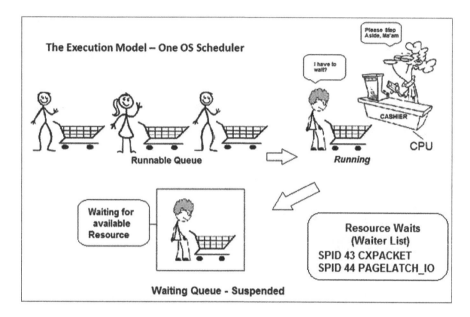

Figure 3-5. *The execution model: the suspended queue*

If for any reason the thread needs to wait again, it goes back on the waiter list into the SUSPENDED queue, and the process continues in a circular and repeatable manner. Let's not forget about Granny, who's still in the SUSPENDED state, waiting for the price check. Once she gets her price check confirmed, she can proceed again toward getting checked out. Granny is signaled that the price or the resource is now available. However, the cashier "CPU" is busy now checking out other customers, so she must go to the back of the line. The line getting longer at the supermarket while Granny is arguing over 10 cents savings is stressing out the cashier, like the CPU. The thread, now back in the RUNNABLE queue, is waiting on the CPU, like Granny is waiting again on the cashier. Again, as discussed, the waiting time spent in the runnable queue is called *signal wait time*. In terms of resource versus signal waits, the price check Granny was waiting for is a *resource wait*, and waiting in line for the cashier is the *signal wait*.

Figure 3-6 shows an example of the RUNNABLE queue. It shows the time spent waiting in the RUNNABLE queue(the transition from the suspended to runnable queue) or waiting for the CPU to become available; this time spent waiting is known as the *signal wait time*. You will learn more about signal wait time in the "CPU Pressure" section.

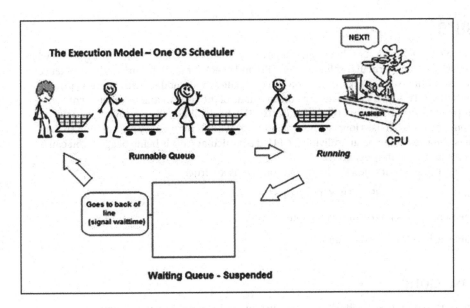

Figure 3-6. *A visual example of signal wait time or transition from the suspended queue to the runnable queue*

As expected, Granny is pretty mad she has to wait in line again, and since she was already waiting, the sympathetic customers might, like the other threads, yield to Granny as a higher-priority customer. Higher-priority tasks will run before lower-priority tasks when there are yields or preemption. As mentioned earlier, these yields will show up in the wait stat view as SOS_SCHEDULER_YIELD. The threads alternating between the three states, RUNNABLE, RUNNING, and SUSPENDED, until the query is completed is known as the *query lifecycle*. By querying the DMV sys.dm_exec_requests, you can see the current status of a thread. Figure 3-7 gives a visual demonstration of the query life cycle.

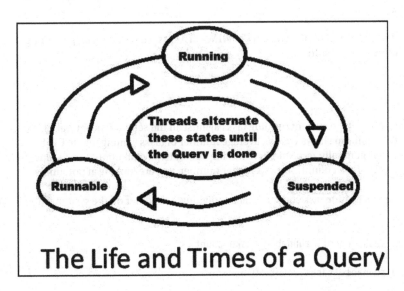

Figure 3-7. *Query life cycle and what happens to a query that starts out executing on the CPU*

CPU Pressure

On a multiprocessor system, you can see what queries are running on a particular CPU. One way to see what activity is currently assigned to a particular scheduler or CPU and check for any CPU pressure is to exeucet the query I present next in "Runnable Task Count". You can correlate scheduler data with queries currently running against the system. This query captures the current status of the session and number of context switches, as well as pending disk I/O count, the scheduler (CPU), the database, the command, and the actual statement being executed. It uses joins with some other DMVs and returns key information such as the SQL query that is being executed on an individual CPU. If a particular CPU is being pegged, you can see which queries are currently executing against it.

CPU pressure may be apparent when the following conditions are true:

- High number of SOS_SCHEDULER_YIELDS waits

- High percentage of signal waits over resource waits

- Runnable task counts greater than zero

Runnable Task Count

You can also get an overall count of the RUNNING (that is, current) and RUNNABLE tasks by querying sys.dm_os_schedulers. If the SQL Server tasks are waiting on the CPU (in other words, if the runnable_task_counts value is greater than 0), this can be another indicator of an increase in CPU pressure. The higher the runnable task count, the busier the CPU is processing. Here is a query that can get you the average task counts against the SQL Server schedulers:

```
SELECT AVG(current_tasks_count) AS [Avg Current Task],
AVG(runnable_tasks_count) AS [Avg Wait Task]
FROM sys.dm_os_schedulers
WHERE scheduler_id < 255
AND status = 'VISIBLE ONLINE'
```

The query results show the average count for the current (RUNNING) tasks, as well as the average waiting (RUNNABLE) tasks. Here is an example of the result:

```
Avg Current Task
2
```

The value here is an average count of the current running tasks against all the schedulers or total CPU processors. The Average wait task column shows you the average number of tasks waiting on the CPU that are in the RUNNABLE state. The result is generally zero, and here it is important to pay attention to any value greater than zero. If the Average Wait Task column shows a higher number, you are looking at potential CPU pressure on SQL Server.

You can view a raw current versus waiting task count for each individual scheduler on the system with the following query:

```
SELECT scheduler_id, current_tasks_count, runnable_tasks_count
FROM sys.dm_os_schedulers
WHERE scheduler_id < 255 AND runnable_tasks_count >0
```

In this query, you are asking only that it return counts where runnable_tasks_count is greater than zero. You can use a query similar to this for monitoring and tracking CPU pressure.

Signal Waits

Although excessive thread yields on the system can indicate potential CPU contention, there is no specific wait type to indicate CPU pressure. Therefore, by looking at the signal wait time, stored in the `signal_wait_time_ms` column of the wait stat DMV `sys.dm_os_wait_stats`, you can compare the two major categories of waits. Taking an overall snapshot of whether SQL Server is waiting mostly on resources to become available (resource waits) or waiting for the CPU (signal waits) to become available can reveal whether you have any serious CPU pressure. You will measure the resource waits (all the threads that are put into a suspended or resource queue) and signal waits (the time waiting for the threads to run on the CPU). So, let's use the following query to compare resource waits to signal waits:

```
Select
    ResourceWaitTimeMs=sum(wait_time_ms - signal_wait_time_ms)
    ,'%resource waits'= cast(100.0 * sum(wait_time_ms - signal_wait_time_ms) / sum
    (wait_time_ms) as numeric(20,2))
    ,SignalWaitTimeMs=sum(signal_wait_time_ms)
    ,'%signal waits' = cast(100.0 * sum(signal_wait_time_ms) / sum (wait_time_ms) as
    numeric(20,2))
from sys.dm_os_wait_stats
```

The query output shown next gives percentages for signal waits, as compared to resource waits. What you also see are cumulative wait times since SQL Server was last restarted or the statistics were cleared. The output shows you the percentage of overall wait time versus signal waits.

```
ResourceWaitTimeMs%resource waitsSignalWaitTimeMs%signal waits
1610223683281.57363752045018.43
```

Remember that I said SQL Server waiting on resources is the healthy nature of a busy OLTP system? The query results are the resource waits versus signal waits as a percentage of the overall wait time. So, what this tells you is that the percent of resource waits is significantly higher than the percent of signal waits and is exactly what you want to see (more resource waits than signal waits). Higher resource waits should not be misinterpreted as a performance issue. However, if the CPU itself is the bottleneck, the percentage with respect to signal waits will show up much higher. Relative to the overall wait time on the server, you want to see that signal waits are as low as possible. A conceivable percentage of greater than 30 percent of signal waits may be actionable data to lead you considering CPU pressure, depending on the workload. For example, you may need faster or more CPUs to keep up with the workload requests, since too slow or too few cores can be one reason for a stressed CPU to cause a performance bottleneck.

Anatomy of a CPU Metadata Query

Here is a query that will identify lots of interesting information you can use to pinpoint the offending query that is causing CPU pressure:

```
Select
t.task_state,
r.session_id,
s.context_switches_count,
s.pending_disk_io_count,
s.scheduler_id AS CPU_ID,
s.status AS Scheduler_Status,
db_name(r.database_id) AS Database_Name,
```

```
r.command,
px.text
 from sys.dm_os_schedulers as s
INNER JOIN sys.dm_os_tasks t on s.active_worker_address = t.worker_address
INNER JOIN sys.dm_exec_requests r on t.task_address = r.task_address
CROSS APPLY sys.dm_exec_sql_text(r.plan_handle) as px
WHERE @@SPID<>r.session_id -- filters out this session
-- AND t.task_state='RUNNABLE' --To filter out sessions that are waiting on CPU uncomment.
```

Let's breakdown this query and discuss the pieces of information available. You can see it is possible to identify the point of contention down to the exact CPU or scheduler and what query is causing the query or process to be bound. If you query the sys.dm_os_tasks DMV, all sorts of interesting information is displayed about what tasks are currently running. This DMV returns one row for each task that is active in the instance of SQL Server. Here is sample output of the query:

```
task_state session_id context_switches_count pending_disk_io_count CPU_ID Scheduler_Status
Database_Name command text
RUNNING    83          6757589                0                     12     VISIBLE ONLINE
master          [Actual Query Statement Text here]
```

In addition, you have the scheduler_id value, which is associated with a particular session_id (or spid). The scheduler_id value is displayed as the CPUID, which was discussed earlier as each scheduler mapped to an individual CPU. For all intents and purposes, the scheduler and CPU are equivalent terms and used interchangeably. One piece of information is pending_IO_Count, which is the count of physical I/O that is being performed by a particular task. Another is the actual number of context_Switches that occur while performing an individual task. You learned about context switching earlier in the chapter.

Another column that is relevant here is task_address. The task address is the memory address allocated to the task that is associated with this request. Because each DMV has some information you need and the others don't have, you will need to join them together, as well as use the APPLY operator to get everything you want in the results.

To get the actual query that is executing on the CPU, you need to get the plan_handle value, which is *not* available in sys.dm_os_tasks. Therefore, you will need to join the sys.dm_os_tasks view to the sys.dm_exec_requests view. Both of these have the actual task_address information and can be joined on this column. sys.dm_exec_requests is another handy DMV, even by itself, that returns information about each request that is executing within SQL Server. You will find a lot of useful statistics and information here, such as wait_time, total_elapsed_time, cpu_time, wait_type, status, and so on. With the sys.dm_exec_requests, you can also find out whether there is any blocking or open transactions; you can also do this by querying the blocking_session_id and open_transaction_count columns in this view. Please note, for the purpose of this discussion, that these columns are filtered out but worth mentioning in general. One piece of information that is also not in sys.dm_os_tasks, but available in sys.dm_exec_requests, is database_id. Thus, you can find out what database the request is executing against. There is a lot more useful data in this view; visit TechNet for more information about thesys.dm_exec_requests DMV:

http://msdn.microsoft.com/en-us/library/ms177648.aspx

You also use the task_state column from the sys.dm_os_tasks view, which shows you whether the task is PENDING, RUNNABLE, RUNNING, or SUSPENDED. Assuming the task has a worker thread assigned (no longer PENDING), when the worker thread is waiting to run on the CPU, you say that it is RUNNABLE. The thread is therefore in the RUNNABLE queue. The longer it must wait to run on the CPU, the more pressure is on the CPU. As discussed earlier in the chapter, the signal wait time consists of the threads spending a lot of time waiting in the runnable queue.

Finally, to complete the query, you need to use the `APPLY` operator to derive the text of the SQL batch that is identified by the specified SQL handle using the `sys.dm_exec_sql_text` function. This invaluable DMF replaces the system function `fn_get_sql` and pretty much makes the old `DBCC INPUTBUFFER` command obsolete. If you want to see only the sessions that are waiting for CPU, you can filter the query by using `where task_state='RUNNABLE'`.

A number of factors can affect CPU utilization adversely such as compilation and recompilation of SQL statements, missing indexes, excessive joins, unneeded sorts, order by, and group by options in your queries, multithreaded operations, disk bottlenecks, and memory bottlenecks, among others. Any of these can force the query to utilize more CPU. As you can see now, other bottlenecks can lead to CPU bottlenecks. You can either tweak your code or upgrade your hardware. This goes for any of the resource bottlenecks.

More often than not, rewriting the code more efficiently and employing proper indexing strategies can do great wonders and is in the immediate control of the DBA. Throwing more hardware at a performance problem can help only so much. Therefore, the key to healthy CPU utilization, as well as healthy SQL, is ensuring that the CPU is spending its time processing queries efficiently and not wasting its processing power on poorly optimized code or inefficient hardware.

Ideally, the aforementioned query will be useful in your performance-tuning efforts, especially when you need to pinpoint which CPU is causing the most contention and what query is causing it.

■ **Note** Throwing more hardware at a performance problem can help only so much.

So, you have observed various CPU-related queries and conditions that can help you identify CPU pressure. To further investigate and gather conclusive data, you will now want to set up some specific Performance Monitor counters to support your findings. Some of the traditional Performance Monitor counters specific to CPU performance that you would want to set up are as follows:

- Processor: % Processor Time

- System: Processor Queue Length

- System: Context Switches/sec

You may also want to take a look at the SQL Compilations, Re-compilations, and Batch Requests per second counters. The reason to consider these has to do with plan reuse and how it affects CPU performance. When executing a stored procedure or a query, if the plan does not yet exist in memory, SQL Server must perform a compilation before executing it. The compilation step creates the execution plan, which is then placed in the procedure cache for use and potential reuse. Once a plan is compiled and stored in memory, or *cache*, SQL Server will try to use the existing plan, which will reduce the CPU overhead in compiling new plans.

Excessive compilations and recompilations (essentially the same process) cause performance degradation. The fewer the compilations per second, the better, but only through your own performance baselines can you determine what an acceptable number is. When a new plan is compiled, you can observe that the SQLCompilations/sec counter increases, and when an existing plan gets recompiled (for a number of reasons), you can see that the Re-compilations/sec counter is higher. Based on these respective counters, you look to see whether a large number of queries need to be compiled or recompiled. When you are performance tuning a query or stored procedure, the goal is to reduce the number of compilations.

Batch Requests per second shows the number of SQL statements that are being executed per second. A batch is a group of SQL statements. Again, I can't say what an ideal number is here, but what you want to see is a high ratio of batches to compiles. Therefore, you can compare the Batch Requests/sec counter to the SQLCompilations/sec and Re-compilations/sec counters. In other words, you want to achieve the most batch requests per second while utilizing the least amount of resources. While these performance counters don't tell you much by themselves, the ratio of the number of compilations to the number of batch requests gives you a better story on plan reuse and, in this case, CPU load.

Therefore, to get an overall understanding of how your server is performing, you need to correlate with other metrics. So, you usually look at these three together and can calculate them to get the percentage of plan reuse. The higher the plan use, the less CPU is needed to execute a query or stored procedure. Here are the counters referred to:

- SQL Statistics\Batch Requests/sec

- SQL Statistics\SQL Compilations/sec

- SQL Statistics\SQL Re-Compilations/sec

You can also see an example of the Performance Monitor counters in Figure 3-8.

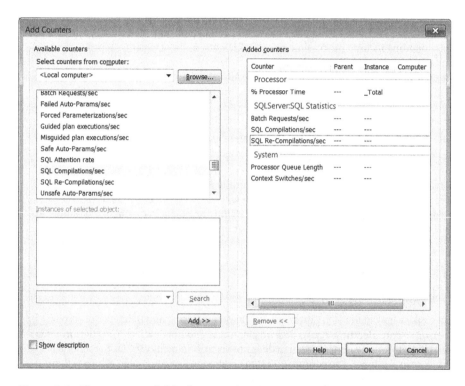

Figure 3-8. *The recommended Performance Monitor counters for CPU utilization*

You can calculate the overall percentage for plan reuse as follows:

```
plan_reuse = (BatchRequestsperSecond – SQLCompilationsperSecond) / BatchRequestsperSecond
```

Here is the script I wrote to derive this data using the sys.dm_os_performance_counters DMV:

```
select t1.cntr_value As [Batch Requests/sec],
t2.cntr_value As [SQL Compilations/sec],
    plan_reuse_percentage =
convert(decimal(15,2),
    (t1.cntr_value*1.0-t2.cntr_value*1.0)/t1.cntr_value*100)
```

```
from
    master.sys.dm_os_performance_counters t1,
    master.sys.dm_os_performance_counters t2
where
    t1.counter_name='Batch Requests/sec' and
    t2.counter_name='SQL Compilations/sec'
```

Based on the results, as shown next, a high percentage number would indicate the plan reuse is high and thus reduces the amount of server resources required to run the same queries over and over again. Therefore, a high percentage for plan_reuse is ideal. This type of calculation is somewhat discounted as an accurate indicator of actual plan reuse, though. Later in the book, you will see more accurate ways to measure and analyze plan cache usage, using DMVs.

```
Batch Requests/secSQL Compilations/secplan_reuse
190154542681777.55
```

While sys.dm_os_wait_stats provides you with the aggregated historical data, it does not show current sessions that are waiting. To know what's happening right now on your server, you can use the following DMVs and join them together to get a holistic view:

- sys.dm_os_waiting_tasks

- sys.dm_exec_requests

By using the sys.dm_os_waiting_tasks DMV, you can know what SQL Server is waiting on "right now," as well as the current suspended sessions that are waiting in the SUSPENDED queue. In fact, the actual waiter list of all waiting sessions, with the reasons for the waits, are revealed, as well as any blocking and all the sessions involved. The waiting_tasks DMV is helpful in that it filters out all other nonwaiting sessions. For a full reference on this DMV, please visit the MSDN library here:

http://msdn.microsoft.com/en-us/library/ms188743(v=sql.110).aspx

The sys.dm_exec_requests DMV shows you can see the current status of a thread and all its associated metadata. All the current activity (for example, active sessions) on the server can be viewed by using sys.dm_exec_requests. Each SQL Server session has a unique session_id value, and you can filter out the system queries from the user queries by specifying session_id > 50 or, more accurately, where user_process = 1. This DMV returns a lot of information, and you can see the entire list of column data available on the MSDN library here:

http://msdn.microsoft.com/en-us/library/ms177648(v=sql.110).aspx

The following query joins sys.dm_os_waiting_tasks and sys.dm_exec_requests to return the most important columns of interest:

```
SELECT dm_ws.session_ID,
dm_ws.wait_type,
UPPER(dm_es.status) As status,
dm_ws.wait_duration_ms,
dm_t.TEXT,
dm_es.cpu_time,
dm_es.memory_usage,
dm_es.logical_reads,
dm_es.total_elapsed_time,
```

```
dm_ws.blocking_session_id,
dm_es.program_name,
DB_NAME(dm_r.database_id) DatabaseName
FROM sys.dm_os_waiting_tasks dm_ws
INNER JOIN sys.dm_exec_requests dm_r ON dm_ws.session_id = dm_r.session_id
INNER JOIN sys.dm_exec_sessions dm_es ON dm_es.session_id = dm_r.session_id
CROSS APPLY sys.dm_exec_sql_text (dm_r.sql_handle) dm_t
WHERE dm_es.is_user_process = 1
```

The following is a sample of the output from the previous query:

```
session_IDwait_typestatuswait_duration_ms(No column name)cpu_timememory_usagelogical_
readstotal_elapsed_timeblocking_session_idprogram_nameDatabaseName
70WAITFORRUNNING3235DECLARE @time1 DATETIME;
DECLARE @time2 DATETIME;
0000NULL.Net SqlClient Data ProviderMyTroubledDB
72OLEDBRUNNING0SELECT dm_ws.session_ID,
dm_ws.wait_type,
UPPER(782132698NULLMicrosoft SQL Server Management Studio - QueryMyTroubledDB
122WAITFORRUNNING3110DECLARE @time1 DATETIME;
DECLARE @time2 DATETIME;
0000NULL.Net SqlClient Data ProviderMyTroubledDB
```

CPU Blame Game

Now that I've discussed the internals of waits and queues, the categories, and the DMVs to report on wait statistics and I've shown some basic queries, let's focus on the key bottleneck areas. I also detailed performance issues with respect to signal waits and CPU pressure. In this section, I will highlight some of the resource wait types you will typically see associated with I/O, memory, locking and blocking, and parallelism issues. Once you identify and translate the wait types, you can provide further troubleshooting and analysis by setting up the proper Performance Monitor objects and counters.

Let's play another quick round of the blame game, CPU edition. Suddenly, there are CPU spikes on your SQL Server, and CPU utilization is trending over 90 percent. The system administrator takes screenshots of the CPU usage on the Performance tab of Windows Task Manager. He also shows some Performance Monitor information that the Processor time is consistently greater than 90 percent. Then, he identifies the box as a SQL Server instance. Blame time. He tells all the managers that SQL Server must be the problem, and you, the DBA, are contacted to look into the issue. What do you do? Fortunately for you, you're reading this book, and you will run a handy little CPU script that shows historical CPU utilization derived from the sys.dm_os_ring_buffers view. The advantage of this script over looking at Task Manager is that it will break down CPU time into three key columns by the percentage used bySQLProcessUtilization, SystemIdle, and OtherProcessUtilzation, along with the event time.

```
set nocount on
declare @ts_now bigint
select @ts_now = cpu_ticks /( cpu_ticks / ms_ticks )
from sys.dm_os_sys_info
select /*top 1*/ record_id,dateadd(ms, -1 * (@ts_now - [timestamp]), GetDate()) as
EventTime,
SQLProcessUtilization,SystemIdle,100 - SystemIdle - SQLProcessUtilization as
OtherProcessUtilization
```

```
from (select record.value('(./Record/@id)[1]', 'int') as record_id,
    record.value('(./Record/SchedulerMonitorEvent/SystemHealth/SystemIdle)[1]', 'int') as
    SystemIdle,
record.value('(./Record/SchedulerMonitorEvent/SystemHealth/ProcessUtilization)[1]', 'int')
as SQLProcessUtilization,
timestamp from (select timestamp, convert(xml, record) as record
from sys.dm_os_ring_buffers
where ring_buffer_type = N'RING_BUFFER_SCHEDULER_MONITOR' and record like
'%<SystemHealth>%') as x
) as y order by record_id desc
```

Since the instance was last started (or statistics cleared), you will clearly see whether SQL Server is in fact the cause for high CPU. If the SQLProcessUtilization column shows zero or a low value and there is a high value in either the OtherProcessUtilization or SystemIdle column, SQL Server has been cleared as the suspect. Specifically, if the values in the OtherProcessUtilization column are consistently high, this means that there are other applications or processes causing high CPU utilization. The question now is shifted to the system administrators as to why there are CPU-bound applications sharing with SQL Server. The following are some results from the previous CPU query. They show the historical total CPU process utilization of SQL versus other processes since the instance was last restarted.

```
record_idEventTimeSQLProcessUtilizationSystemIdleOtherProcessUtilization
61522014-11-03 15:53:51.0276913
61512014-11-03 15:52:51.0271963
61502014-11-03 15:51:51.0270973
61492014-11-03 15:50:51.0270973
61482014-11-03 15:49:51.0270973
```

I/O May Be Why Your Server Is So Slow

SQL Server under normal processing will read and write from disk where the data is stored. However, when the path to the data on the I/O subsystem is stressed, performance can take a hit, for a number of reasons. Performance will suffer if the I/O subsystem cannot keep up with the demand being placed on it by SQL Server. Through various performance-tuning strategies, you can minimize IO bottlenecks in order to retrieve and write data from disk. When I speak of performance related to disk or storage, it's called I/O. You can measure I/O per second (IOPS) as well as latency with respect to I/O. You will take a look at I/O usage, which can be useful in many scenarios.

Tasks that are waiting for I/O to finish can surface as IO_COMPLETION and ASYNC_IO_COMPLETION waits, representing nondata page I/Os. When an SPID is waiting for asynchronous I/O requests to complete, this shows up as ASYNC_IO_COMPLETION. If you observe these common I/O wait types consistently, the I/O subsystem is probably the bottleneck, and for further analysis you should set up I/O-related physical disk counters in Performance Monitor (counters such as Disk sec/read and Disk sec/write).

I/O Blame Game

An example of such an occurrence, one that I experienced first-hand in my DBA travels, is an error message relating to I/O requests taking a long time to complete. There are various reasons this can occur. Specifically, as in my case, the latency between SQL Server and communication with the SAN storage can cause poor I/O performance. If you are experiencing suboptimal throughput with respect to I/O, you may examine the wait statistics and see PageIOLatch_ wait types appear. Values that are consistently high for this wait type indicate I/O subsystem issues. I will discuss these waits more in-depth later in the chapter. This of course affects database integrity and performance but is clearly not the fault of SQL Server. In SQL Server 2005 SP2, an error message was added to help diagnose data read and write delays occurring with the I/O subsystem. When there are such issues, you may see this in the SQL Server error log:

> *"SQL Server has encountered n occurrence(s) of I/O requests taking longer than 15 seconds to complete on file <filename> in database <dbname>."*

The intention of this error message was in fact to help pinpoint where the delay is and what SQL Server is waiting on, not indict SQL Server itself as the cause. In a situation where SQL Server was cluster attached to a SAN, it was consistently crashing. After examining the error logs and encountering the previous "I/O requests taking longer than 15 seconds…"error, the IT folks and management incorrectly determined that SQL Server was corrupt. It took several conference calls and production downtime to convince everyone to check the SAN drivers and firmware versions.

For various reasons, sometimes the server may fail to access the SAN altogether. Poor I/O throughput commonly occurs when a SAN's firmware is out-of-date. If the hardware bus adapter(HBA) drivers are not updated, an insufficient HBA queue length will cause poor I/O as well. This I/O problem can occur when one or both have not been upgraded. Be aware that if you upgrade SAN firmware, you need to upgrade the HBA drivers at the same time. In the scenario I am describing, the SAN firmware had been upgraded but not the HBA drivers, which caused poor I/O throughput, and the subsystem couldn't keep up with the I/O requests generated from SQL Server. The SAN firmware and the HBA drivers should have been upgraded simultaneously. This in fact was the cause of SQL Server crashing, as indicated by the error message, and another instance of blaming SQL Server as the culprit.

Other reasons why I/O performance is not good is the I/O load. Did you ever have a situation where there are I/O issues at night but SQL Server performs well during the day with no warnings in the logs? This is usually because of more intensive I/O operations that are running, such as batch jobs, backups, and DBCC checks. Moreover, several such jobs may be running at the same time because of poor scheduling or because one or more jobs are overlapping each other. Provided there is sufficient free time, you can reschedule one or more jobs and monitor for a couple of days to see whether the changes have made a difference in I/O.

Another cause of poor I/O performance, which also can have a significant negative impact on SQL Server, is if you have antivirus software installed on your SQL Server. You need to ensure that .mdf, .ndf, .ldf, .bak, and .trn files are added to the exclusion list. In addition, you will also want to exclude filestream/filetable/OLTP files and folders. If possible, exclude the entire directory tree for SQL Server. In addition, real-time virus checking should be disabled completely, and any virus scans should be scheduled at off-peak times instead.

■ **Note**   If you have antivirus (AV) software installed on your SQL Server, this can negatively impact I/O performance, and you need to exclude SQL Server from AV scans.

Fragmentation Affects I/O

Fragmentation is another issue that can occur with respect to I/O and may be internal (within tables/indexes) or external (file fragmentation on the disk). Physical file fragmentation can contribute to an additional load on your I/O subsystem and reduce performance because the disks have to work harder to read and write data. To find all of the required data, the disk needs to hop around to different physical locations as a result of files not being on the disk contiguously. A physically fragmented file is when it is stored noncontiguously on disk. When file data is spread all over various locations on a disk that is fragmented, this will often result in slower I/O performance.

Things to do to reduce fragmentation is to pre-allocate data and log file size (instead of using default auto-grow), never use the AutoShrink option on databases, and never manually shrink data files. Shrinking databases will rapidly cause major fragmentation and incur a significant performance penalty. In some cases, you can and will need to shrink data files but will need to rebuild your indexes to ensure you have removed any fragmentation in the database. In addition, the disk should be dedicated for SQL Server and not shared with any other applications. Log files can be shrunk without issue if need be. Sometimes they grow out of control because of certain factors and you can reclaim space from the log, after active transactions are committed to disk. I mention this because this distinction is often the cause of confusion when shrinking database files in general. For shrinking out-of-control log files, you would run a DBCC Shrinkfile(2), with 2 representing the log.

■ **Caution** Never, ever use the AutoShrink database option; avoidDBCC ShrinkDatabase!

I/O Latch Buffer Issues

Another category of I/O wait types relate to buffer I/O requests that are waiting on a latch. These types of waits show up as PAGEIOLATCH wait types, as described next. Pending the completion of a physical disk I/O, PAGEIOLATCH wait types can occur when there are buffer requests that are currently blocked. The technical definition of a latch is that they are "lightweight internal structures" used to synchronize access to buffer pages and are used for disk-to-memory transfers. As you should be aware, data modifications occur in an area of the memory reserved for data, called the *buffer* or *data cache*. Once the data is modified there, it then is written to disk. Therefore, to prevent further modifications of a data page that is modified in memory, a latch is created by SQL Server before the data page is written to disk. Once the page is successfully written to disk, the latch is released. It is similar in function to a lock (discussed further in the "Blocking and Locking" section in this chapter) to ensure transactional consistency and integrity and prevent changes while a transaction is in progress. Many papers cover the subjects of locks and latches together.

Books Online describes some of the PAGIOLATCH wait types as follows:

> PAGEIOLATCH_DT: Occurs when a task is waiting on a latch for a buffer that is in an I/O request. The latch request is in Destroy mode. Long waits may indicate problems with the disk subsystem.

> PAGEIOLATCH_EX: Occurs when a task is waiting on a latch for a buffer that is in an I/O request. The latch request is in Exclusive mode. Long waits may indicate problems with the disk subsystem.

> PAGEIOLATCH_KP: Occurs when a task is waiting on a latch for a buffer that is in an I/O request. The latch request is in Keep mode. Long waits may indicate problems with the disk subsystem.

> PAGEIOLATCH_SH: Occurs when a task is waiting on a latch for a buffer that is in an I/O request. The latch request is in Shared mode. Long waits may indicate problems with the disk subsystem.

> PAGEIOLATCH_UP: Occurs when a task is waiting on a latch for a buffer that is in an I/O request. The latch request is in Update mode. Long waits may indicate problems with the disk subsystem

When the percentage of the total waits on the system is high, it can indicate disk subsystem issues but possibly memory pressure issues as well. High values for both PageIOLatch_ex and PageIOLatch_sh wait types indicate I/O subsystem issues. PageIOLatch_ex indicates an exclusive I/O page latch, while PageIOLatch_sh is a shared I/O page latch. I will talk about steps to take to minimize these waits, but first let's talk about which DMVs can help you with analyzing I/O statistics.

A particularly useful DMV for observing I/O usage is sys.dm_io_virtual_file_stats, which returns I/O statistics for database files, both data and log. This DMV's num_of_bytes_read and num_of_bytes_written columns let you easily calculate total I/O. In addition to calculating total I/O, you can use common table expressions (CTEs) to determine the percentage of I/O usage, which tells you where most of the I/O is occurring.

You can view the default column data output with the following query:

```
SELECT * FROM sys.dm_io_virtual_file_stats (NULL, NULL)
```

With sys.dm_io_virtual_file_stats, you can look for I/O stalls, as well as view the I/O usage by database, file, or drive. An I/O stall is a situation because of disk latency, for example, where I/O requests are taking a long time to complete its operation. You can also refer to an I/O stall as stuck or stalled I/O. I/O stall is the total time, in milliseconds, that users waited for I/O to be completed on the file. By looking at the I/O stall information, you can see how much time was waiting for I/O to complete and how long the users were waiting.

Aside from the actual latency of I/O, you may want to know which database accounts for the highest I/O usage, which is a different metric than I/O stalls. Regardless of the disk layout of the particular database, the following query will return the I/O usage for each database across all drives. This will give you the opportunity to consider moving files from one physical disk to another physical disk by determining which files have the highest I/O. As a result of high I/O usage, moving data, log, and/or tempdb files to other physical drives can reduce the I/O contention, as well as spread the I/O over multiple disks. A percentage of I/O usage by database will be shown with this query:

```
WITH Cu_IO_Stats
AS
(
  SELECT
    DB_NAME(database_id) AS database_name,
    CAST(SUM(num_of_bytes_read + num_of_bytes_written) / 1048576.
        AS DECIMAL(12, 2)) AS io_in_mb
  FROM sys.dm_io_virtual_file_stats(NULL, NULL) AS DM_IO_Stats
  GROUP BY database_id
)
SELECT
  ROW_NUMBER() OVER(ORDER BY io_in_mb DESC) AS row_num,
database_name,
  io_in_mb,
  CAST(io_in_mb / SUM(io_in_mb) OVER() * 100
AS DECIMAL(5, 2)) AS pct
FROM Cu_IO_Stats
ORDER BY row_num;
```

The results that you will see from this query highlight the database with the highest I/O usage out of the total database I/O in descending order, with the highest percentage at the top. Here's an example:

```
row_numdatabase_nameio_in_mbpct
1MDW_HealthySQL3171.1487.64
2msdb218.626.04
3tempdb206.955.72
4model4.840.13
5ReportServer3.940.11
```

6master3.850.11
7ReportServerTempDB2.750.08
8XEvents_ImportSystemHealth2.350.06
9TEST2.020.06
10Canon1.970.05

With respect to these I/O results, keep in mind that although you can identify which database is using the most I/O bandwidth, it doesn't necessarily indicate that there is a problem with the I/O subsystem. Suppose you determine the I/O usage of the files or databases on a server and that a database's I/O usage is 90 percent. However, if an individual file or database is using 90 percent of the total I/O but there's no waiting for reads or writes, there are no performance issues. The percentage that you see is out of the total I/O usage of all the databases on the instance. Please note that all the percentages here add to 100percent, so this represents only SQL Server I/O. It is possible that other processes can be using I/O and impacting SQL Server. Again, it comes down to how long the system is waiting. The more users wait, the more performance is potentially affected. So, in this case, you also need to look at statistics that tell you how long users have to wait for reads and writes to occur.

In the next I/O query, you can calculate the percentage of I/O by drive (letter):

```
With IOdrv as
(select db_name(mf.database_id) as database_name, mf.physical_name,
left(mf.physical_name, 1) as drive_letter,
vfs.num_of_writes,
vfs.num_of_bytes_written as bytes_written,
vfs.io_stall_write_ms,
mf.type_desc, vfs.num_of_reads, vfs.num_of_bytes_read, vfs.io_stall_read_ms,
vfs.io_stall, vfs.size_on_disk_bytes
from sys.master_files mf
join sys.dm_io_virtual_file_stats(NULL, NULL) vfs
on mf.database_id=vfs.database_id and mf.file_id=vfs.file_id
--order by vfs.num_of_bytes_written desc)
)
select database_name,drive_letter, bytes_written,
Percentage = RTRIM(CONVERT(DECIMAL(5,2),
bytes_written*100.0/(SELECT SUM(bytes_written) FROM IOdrv)))
--where drive_letter='D' <-- You can put specify drive )))
+ '%'
from IOdrv --where drive_letter='D'
order by bytes_written desc
```

Results will resemble the output shown here, showing the top five results by percentages of I/O usages by drive letter:

```
database_namedrive_letterbytes_writtenPercentage
tempdbD160263987262.75%
tempdbD53869772821.09%
DBABCD1786675207.00%
DBABCD1096734724.29%
DB123D996510723.90%
```

Another way to look at I/O waiting is to use the io_stall column in sys.dm_io_virtual_file_stats. This column can tell you the total time that users waited for I/O on a given file. You can also look at the latency of I/O, which is measured in I/O stalls as defined earlier in this section. I/O stalls is a more accurate way to measure I/O since you are concerned with the time it takes to complete I/O operations, such as read and write, on a file. Here's an example query:

```
WITH DBIO AS
    (
      SELECT
          DB_NAME(IVFS.database_id) AS db,
          CASE WHEN MF.type = 1 THEN 'log' ELSE 'data' END AS file_type,
          SUM(IVFS.num_of_bytes_read + IVFS.num_of_bytes_written) AS io,
          SUM(IVFS.io_stall) AS io_stall
      FROM sys.dm_io_virtual_file_stats(NULL, NULL) AS IVFS
          JOIN sys.master_files AS MF
            ON IVFS.database_id = MF.database_id
            AND IVFS.file_id = MF.file_id
      GROUP BY DB_NAME(IVFS.database_id), MF.type
    )
    SELECT db, file_type,
      CAST(1. * io / (1024 * 1024) AS DECIMAL(12, 2)) AS io_mb,
      CAST(io_stall / 1000. AS DECIMAL(12, 2)) AS io_stall_s,
      CAST(100. * io_stall / SUM(io_stall) OVER()
            AS DECIMAL(10, 2)) AS io_stall_pct
    FROM DBIO
    ORDER BY io_stall DESC;
```

The query results show the top ten results of databases by number of I/O stalls:

```
dbfile_typeio_mbio_stall_sio_stall_pct
DBA123data8083.681128.4891.89
tempdblog1641.3327.912.27
DBABCdata265.6725.382.07
tempdbdata905.2915.551.27
msdbdata247.6514.331.17
DBABClog119.624.020.33
SQLDB1data24.943.080.25
DBCUPlog99.282.770.23
DBA_statsdata63.151.520.12
ReportServerdata10.021.420.12
```

You can use the io_stall_read_ms and io_stall_write_ms columns in sys.dm_io_virtual_file_stats. These columns tell you the total time that users waited for reads and writes to occur for a given file.

As mentioned in the previous paragraphs, if the I/O subsystem cannot keep up with the requests from SQL Server, you say that there is latency in the communication between SQL Server and the disk that affects the rate of reads and writes to and from. With one comprehensive script, provided by Paul Randal, industry-known SQL Microsoft MVP, you can examine the latencies of the I/O subsystem. This next script is the query that filters the stats to show ratios when there are reads and writes taking place and shows you where the latencies on reads and writes are occurring. Also, you can see the database names and file paths by joining the sys.master_files view.

```
SELECT
    --virtual file latency
    [ReadLatency] =
        CASE WHEN [num_of_reads] = 0
            THEN 0 ELSE ([io_stall_read_ms] / [num_of_reads]) END,
    [WriteLatency] =
        CASE WHEN [num_of_writes] = 0
            THEN 0 ELSE ([io_stall_write_ms] / [num_of_writes]) END,
    [Latency] =
        CASE WHEN ([num_of_reads] = 0 AND [num_of_writes] = 0)
            THEN 0 ELSE ([io_stall] / ([num_of_reads] + [num_of_writes])) END,
    --avg bytes per IOP
    [AvgBPerRead] =
        CASE WHEN [num_of_reads] = 0
            THEN 0 ELSE ([num_of_bytes_read] / [num_of_reads]) END,
    [AvgBPerWrite] =
        CASE WHEN [num_of_writes] = 0
            THEN 0 ELSE ([num_of_bytes_written] / [num_of_writes]) END,
    [AvgBPerTransfer] =
        CASE WHEN ([num_of_reads] = 0 AND [num_of_writes] = 0)
            THEN 0 ELSE
                (([num_of_bytes_read] + [num_of_bytes_written]) /
                ([num_of_reads] + [num_of_writes])) END,
    LEFT ([mf].[physical_name], 2) AS [Drive],
    DB_NAME ([vfs].[database_id]) AS [DB],
    --[vfs].*,
    [mf].[physical_name]
FROM
    sys.dm_io_virtual_file_stats (NULL,NULL) AS [vfs]
JOIN sys.master_files AS [mf]
    ON [vfs].[database_id] = [mf].[database_id]
    AND [vfs].[file_id] = [mf].[file_id]
-- WHERE [vfs].[file_id] = 2 -- log files
-- ORDER BY [Latency] DESC
-- ORDER BY [ReadLatency] DESC
ORDER BY [WriteLatency] DESC;
GO
```

You can observe where the read and write latencies are happening by examining the output results showing read-write I/O latency, as well as other stats, including drive, db_name, and file path, as shown here:

ReadLatency	WriteLatency	Latency	AvgBPerRead	AvgBPerWrite	AvgBPerTransfer	Drive	DB
19	11	13	15559	3803	6161	D:	msdb
13	10	12	113430	8291	85619	D:	eip_sp_prod
21	10	17	115512	8192	83033	D:	model

```
physical_name
D:\Program Files\Microsoft SQL Server\MSSQL11.MSSQLSERVER\MSSQL\DATA\MSDBLog.ldf
D:\Program Files\Microsoft SQL Server\MSSQL11.MSSQLSERVER\MSSQL\DATA\eip_sp_prod.mdf
D:\Program Files\Microsoft SQL Server\MSSQL11.MSSQLSERVER\MSSQL\DATA\model.mdf
```

Pending I/O requests can be found by querying both the sys.dm_io_virtual_file_stats and sys.dm_io_pending_io_requests DMVs and can be used to identify which disk is responsible for the bottleneck. Remember, pending I/O requests are themselves not necessarily a performance problem, but if there are several consistent such I/O requests that are waiting to complete for long periods of time, whether they are slow or blocked, then you can certainly assume you have an I/O bottleneck and consider options discussed toward the end of this section. The processing of I/O requests takes usually subseconds, and you will likely not see anything appear in these results, unless they are waiting long to complete. Here is a pending I/O requests query:

```
select database_id,
       file_id,
       io_stall,
       io_pending_ms_ticks,
       scheduler_address
from sys.dm_io_virtual_file_stats(NULL, NULL) iovfs,
     sys.dm_io_pending_io_requests as iopior
where iovfs.file_handle = iopior.io_handle
```

As you can see from the number of queries that can be run against the sys.dm_io_virtual_file_stats DMV alone, there are several ways to analyze and view I/O statistics. Looking at I/O stalls, as well as at read-write latencies, is most useful in finding out the I/O contention hotspots for databases and their file locations. Let's now set up the related Performance Monitor counters you can use for further I/O analysis.

Related Performance Monitor Counters

If any buffer I/O latch issues occur and the PAGEIOLATCH waits value shows high wait times, you may want to take a look at Perfmon counters that relate to memory under Buffer Manager Object. The counters here can monitor physical I/O as database pages are read and written to and from disk, as well as how memory is used to store data pages.

- Page Lookups/sec
- Page Life Expectancy
- Page Reads/sec
- Full Scans/sec

In Figure 3-9, you can see a Perfmon screen that includes several of the relevant counters that show both physical and logical I/O.

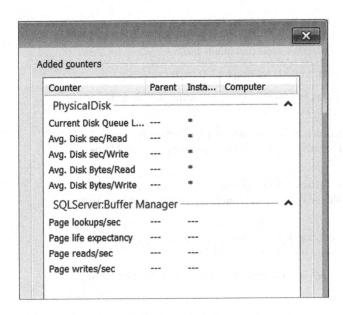

Figure 3-9. Physical and logical I/O disk counters

Another type of I/O wait types are categorized as nondata page I/O, which occurs while waiting for I/O operations to complete. As such with nondata page I/O operations, they usually appear as IO_Completion waits. Therefore, you will want to set up physical disk counters that measure the following:

- Current Disk Queue Length

- Avg Disk sec/Read

- Avg Disk sec/Write

- Avg Disk Bytes/Read

- Avg Disk Bytes/Write

- Avg Disk sec/Transfer

The numbers that you get will determine whether you have an I/O bottleneck. What you're looking for are numbers that fall outside your normal baselines.

I'll now list some action steps to reduce and minimize I/O bottlenecks. There are a number of things you can do from the SQL Server performance-tuning DBA perspective to reduce I/O bandwidth with proper indexing and fixing bad queries that are I/O intensive. You can also work to reduce the number of joins and eliminate table scans by replacing them with seeks. When there are missing indexes, this means there will be more time that SQL Server spends waiting on the disk to dot able scan operations to find records. Unused indexes waste space and should be dropped because this can cause more I/O activity. Another thing to look at is that if you see high I/O usage percentages on databases and their files, for example, you should be concerned with proper file placement. By checking the file system for where the files reside, you can identify where the I/O contention lies and move the database files to separate, dedicated, and faster storage.

As mentioned in the previous chapter, ideally LDF, MDF, and TempDB should all be on their own separate drives. If you identify the top hotspot tables by I/O, you can place them on their own separate filegroup on a separate disk. Here are some other specific I/O-related waits that might surface:

- ASYNC_IO_COMPLETION: Occurs when a task is waiting for I/Os to finish.

- IO_COMPLETION: Occurs while waiting for I/O operations to complete. This wait type generally represents nondata page I/Os.

- PAGEIOLATCH_EX: Occurs when a task is waiting on a latch for a buffer that is in an I/O request. The latch request is in Exclusive mode. Long waits may indicate problems with the disk.

- PAGEIOLATCH_SH: Occurs when a task is waiting on a latch for a buffer that is in an I/O request. The latch request is in Shared mode. Long waits may indicate problems with the disk subsystem.

- WRITELOG: Occurs while waiting for a log flush to complete. Common operations that cause log flushes are checkpoints and transaction commits.

- BACKUPIO: Occurs when a backup task is waiting for data or is waiting for a buffer in which to store data.

Memory Pressure

In the prior section on I/O, I discussed how such I/O buffer issues are related to memory pressure since the lack of available memory will force a query to use disk resources. Because it is desirable for a query to run in memory, if there is not enough memory resources to complete the query request, you say the system is under memory pressure, which will of course affect query performance. There are a number of things to look at to ensure that SQL Server has sufficient memory to perform optimally and prevent paging to disk. You will look at memory usage and the waits that can show up if under memory pressure.

Before a query actually uses memory, it goes through several stages, prior to execution. Parsing and compiling a query execution plan was already discussed, but in addition, SQL Server requires the query to reserve memory. To reserve memory, it must be granted to the query. Referred to as a *memory grant*, it is memory used to store temporary rows for sort and hash join operations. A query will be allowed to reserve memory only if there is enough free memory available. The Resource Semaphore, which is responsible for satisfying memory grant requests, keeps track of how much memory is granted.

The Resource Semaphore also keeps overall memory grant usages within the server limit, and rather than letting a query fail with out-of-memory errors, it will make it wait for the memory. The life of a memory grant is equal to that of the query. So, much of the memory pressure SQL Server will experience is related to the number of memory grants pending and memory grants outstanding. *Memory grants pending* is the total number of processes waiting for a workspace memory grant, while *memory grants outstanding* is the total number of processes that have already acquired a workspace memory grant. If query memory cannot be granted immediately, the requesting query is forced to wait in a queue and is assigned the Resource Semaphore wait type.

When you look the number of memory grants, as you will with some diagnostic queries in this section, you typically want to see this queue empty. If Memory Grants Pending is averaging greater than 0 for extended periods of time, queries cannot run because they can't get enough memory.

To find out all the queries waiting in the memory queue or which queries are using the most memory grants, you can run the following queries, using the very specific system view sys.dm_exec_query_memory_ grants.

If there are any queries waiting in the memory queue for memory grants, they will show up in response to the following SELECT statement:

```
SELECT * FROM sys.dm_exec_query_memory_grants where grant_time is null
```

To find queries that are using the most memory grants, run this query:

```
SELECT mg.granted_memory_kb, mg.session_id, t.text, qp.query_plan
FROM sys.dm_exec_query_memory_grants AS mg
CROSS APPLY sys.dm_exec_sql_text(mg.sql_handle) AS t
CROSS APPLY sys.dm_exec_query_plan(mg.plan_handle) AS qp
ORDER BY 1 DESC OPTION (MAXDOP 1)
```

When there is a user query waiting for memory, as you can see from the output, it will display how much memory is being granted in kilobytes, the session ID, the statement text, and the query plan shown as XML.

```
granted_memory_kbsession_idTextquery_plan
74504229CREATE PROCEDURE [dbo].[sp_syscollector_purge_collection_logs]<ShowPlanXML
xmlns="http://schemas.microsoft.com/sqlserver/2004/07/showplan">
```

SQL Server is a memory hog. The more memory available, the better for SQL Server performance, and rest assured that it will take and use most of the memory from the buffer pool if there is no upper limit defined. SQL Server is a memory-intensive application that may drain the system dry of buffer pool memory, and under certain conditions, this can cause Windows to swap to disk. You of course don't want this to occur, and you also need to take into account the memory needed for the OS. Competition for memory resources between SQL Server and the OS will not make for a well-tuned database engine. Plus, if you add other applications to the mix that may reside on the same server, including the OS, which all require memory, resources can starve. These other resources will compete with SQL Server, which will attempt to use most of the available memory. The ideal scenario is to have a well-balanced and properly configured system. It is usually a good idea to set the maximum server memory and minimum server memory for each instance to control memory usage. Setting the maximum server memory will ensure that an instance will not take up *all* the memory on the box. It is also recommended that a box is dedicated to SQL Server, leaving some room for the OS. The minimum server memory option guarantees that the specified amount of memory will be available for the SQL instance. Once this minimum memory usage is allocated, it cannot be freed up until the minimum server memory setting is reduced. Determining the right number will depend on collecting and reviewing memory counter data under load.

Once you know what thresholds you will set for your minimum and maximum memory usage, you can set them through SSMS or by using sp_configure. Since you configure the memory here in megabytes, you must multiply it by 1024 KB. So, for example, if you want the maximum memory SQL Server to use to be 8GB (assuming this much or even greater physical memory on the box is available), you would get this number by multiplying 8 by 1,024, which equals 8,192. Changing memory settings is an advanced user option, so you will need to show these as well. Since the memory settings are dynamic, they will start taking effect right away without the need to restart the instance.

Here is how you would set the maximum memory setting to 8GB:

```
sp_configure 'show advanced options',1
go
reconfigure
go
```

```
sp_configure 'max server memory (MB)', 8192
go
reconfigure
go
```

Once configuration changes are executed, you will receive the following message:

```
Configuration option 'show advanced options'changed from 1 to 1. Runthe RECONFIGURE
statement to install.
Configuration option 'max server memory (MB)'changed from 2147483647 to 8192. Runthe
RECONFIGURE statement to install.
```

You can use the DBCC MEMORYSTATUS command to get a snapshot of the current memory status of Microsoft SQL Server and help monitor memory usage, as well as troubleshoot memory consumption and out-of-memory errors. You can find a reference to this command on Microsoft's website:

```
http://support.microsoft.com/kb/907877/en-us
```

Additionally, you can investigate some of the other available memory-related DMVs to monitor memory usage. Some to look at include the following:

- sys.dm_os_sys_info
- sys.dm_os_memory_clerks
- sys.dm_os_memory_cache_counters
- sys.dm_os_sys_memory (SQL 2008 and greater)

Using Performance Monitor, you can setup the memory-related object counters, which monitor overall server memory usage.

- Memory: Available MBytes
- Paging File: % Usage
- Buffer Manager: Buffer Cache Hit Ratio
- Buffer Manager: Page Life Expectancy
- Memory Manager: Memory Grants Pending
- Memory Manager: Memory Grants Outstanding
- Memory Manager: Target Server Memory (KB)
- Memory Manager: Total Server Memory (KB)

Figure 3-10 shows the memory-related Performance Monitor counters you would select to monitor memory usage.

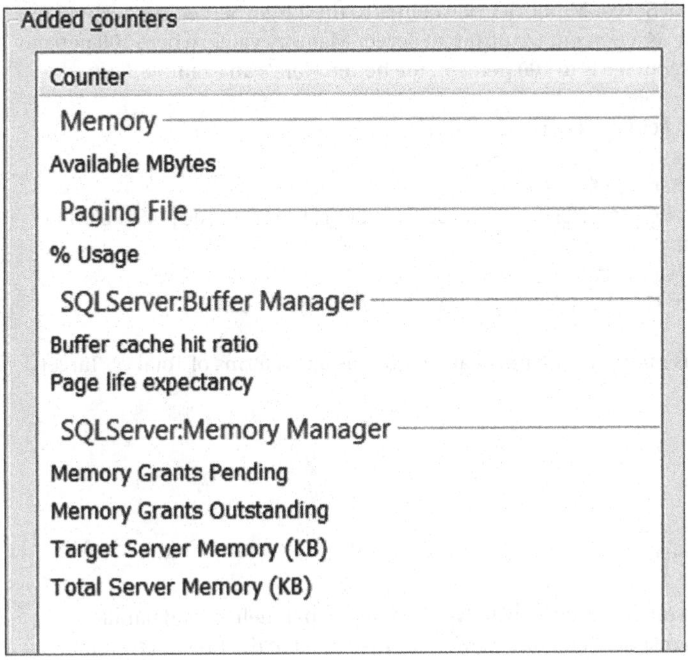

Figure 3-10. *Memory-related performance counters*

Particularly of interest is the Target Server Memory value versus Total Server Memory. The Target Server Memory value is the ideal memory amount for SQL Server, while the Total Server Memory value is the actual amount of committed memory to SQL Server. The Target Server Memory value is equal to the Max Memory setting under sys.configurations. These numbers will ramp up during SQL Server instance startup and stabilize to a point where the total should ideally approach the target number. Once this is the case, the Total Server Memory value should not decrease and not drop far below the Target Server memory because this could indicate memory pressure from the OS because SQL Server is being forced to deallocate its memory. You can measure these using sys.dm_os_performance_counters.

```
SELECT [counter_name], [cntr_value]
FROM sys.dm_os_performance_counters
WHERE [object_name]
LIKE '%Memory Manager%'
AND [counter_name] IN ('Total Server Memory (KB)', 'Target Server Memory (KB)')
```

The raw counter data output would look like this:

```
counter_namecntr_value
Target Server Memory (KB)
23017744
Total Server Memory (KB)
1420592
```

A good way to see how close the Total Server Memory value comes to the Target Server Memory value is to calculate Total Server Memory value as a percentage of Target Server Memory value, where 100 percent means they are equal. The closer the percentage is to 100 percent, the better. Here's an example:

```
SELECT ROUND(100.0 * ( SELECT CAST([cntr_value] AS FLOAT)
FROM sys.dm_os_performance_counters
WHERE [object_name] LIKE '%Memory Manager%'
AND [counter_name] = 'Total Server Memory (KB)' ) / ( SELECT CAST([cntr_value] AS FLOAT)
FROM sys.dm_os_performance_counters
WHERE [object_name] LIKE '%Memory Manager%'
AND [counter_name] = 'Target Server Memory (KB)') , 2)AS [IDEAL MEMORY USAGE]
```

The following output of the previous query shows the ideal memory usage in terms of Total vs. Target Server Memory.

```
IDEAL MEMORY USAGE
99.8
```

Parallelism and CXPACKET

In the previous chapter I mentioned one of the common wait types related to parallelism and parallel query processing, called CXPACKET. With respect to memory grants, as discussed in the previous section, parallelism can affect the query memory requirement. As multiple threads are created for a single query, not all threads are given the same amount of work to do; this causes one or more to lag behind, producing CXPACKET waits affecting the overall throughput. However, just because you see a majority of these wait types doesn't mean it's necessarily actionable.

The biggest misconception among DBAs is that in order to reduce the occurrence of CXPACKETS, you need to turn parallelism off by changing the instance-level MAXDOP setting to 1. You need to understand and factor in other considerations before you do that. I would avoid turning it off altogether, instead setting it to some number equal to the number of physical processors, not exceeding 8, after which it becomes a point of diminishing returns. Testing your MAXDOP settings is essential, measuring query performance for each, before you settle on an optimal value.

The idea is that SQL Server's internal optimizer determines opportunities to execute a query or index operation across multiple processors in parallel via multiple threads so that the operation can be completed faster. This concept of parallelism is intended to increase performance rather than degrade it.

Moreover, the execution plan for a parallel query can use more than one thread, unlike a serial execution plan. Parallelism is usually best left to SQL Server to determine the most optimal execution plan. However, sometimes performance is not always optimum. You can manually control it at the server and at the individual query level by setting Maximum Degrees of Parallelism, which is the maximum number of CPUs used for query execution. You can modify this using sp_confgure max degree of parallelism. By default, SQL Server uses all available processors or 0 as the value.

You can also set this option at the database level by using the query hint MAXDOP=x, where x is the number of processors used for the specific query. Oftentimes, this is a better option than to change the setting server-wide. This way you can control the behavior and parallelism of a particular offending query without affecting the parallelism of the entire instance.

If you see that parallelism is becoming a performance issue, before you change your MAXDOP configuration, consider changing the cost threshold for parallelism configuration option, via sp_configure, to a higher value than the default, which will reduce the number of queries running under parallelism but still allow more expensive queries to utilize parallelism. Another thing you want to do at the table level is to correct any index issues you might have so as to prevent large table scans, often caused by missing indexes. Missing indexes can cause the query optimizer to use a parallel plan to compensate for the missing index and therefore should all be identified. I will provide some missing index scripts later in the book. Such behavior will unnecessarily increase parallelism and create disk and CPU-bound performance penalties. In addition, ensure statistics are up-to-date on your tables to prevent a bad query plan. Please refer to Books Online or MSDN to run `sp_updatestats`.

Blocking and Locking, Oh My!

What is blocking, and how does this show up as a wait? When one SQL Server session puts a lock on one or more records while the second session requires a conflicting lock type on the records locked by the first session, this is *blocking*. Blocking will occur when the second session waits indefinitely until the first releases, significantly impacting performance. If the second session continues to wait on the first session and another session ends up waiting on the second session, and so on, this creates a blocking chain. Blocking and locking for short periods of time are part of the normal SQL Server processes and ensure a database's integrity and that all transactions have certain characteristics.

Let's discuss SQL Server ACID properties. Going back to database theory 101, SQL Server must ensure through its locking mechanisms that transactions are atomic, consistent, isolated, and durable. These properties are known as ACID. Atomicity ensures that a transaction is all or none, meaning that it is completed in its entirety (with no errors), has not yet begun, or is rolled back. Once the transaction is completed, it must be in a valid or consistent state; consistency ensures that the system is valid with all the changes made, before and after the transaction takes place. Isolation of a transaction (or transaction isolation) is the key to making sure that an individual transaction believes it has exclusive access to the resources needed to complete. It also prevents a transaction from accessing data that is not in a consistent state. So, each and every transaction needs to run in isolation until it finishes, or is rolled back, where once the changes are successfully completed, it is made permanent or durable. Durability prevents the loss of information essentially saved and written to disk.

Therefore, a normal amount of locking and blocking is expected, but when it begins to degrade SQL Server performance, then you have an issue that requires troubleshooting and resolution. Two blocking scenarios can occur that slow performance; one is where it holds a lock on resources for a long period of time but eventually releases them, and the other is where blocking puts a lock on resources indefinitely, preventing other processes from getting access to them. This latter example does not resolve itself and requires DBA intervention.

With respect to this topic, you would typically see various `LCK_M_x` wait types that indicate blocking issues or sessions waiting for a lock to be granted. Performance problems could also be because of a lock escalation issue or increased memory pressure that causes increased I/O. The greater I/O can cause locks to be held longer and transaction time to go up as well. Transaction duration should be as short as possible. You can see more information about currently active lock manager resources in the `sys.dm_tran_locks` DMV and whether a lock has been granted or is waiting to be granted. You can set up the Lock wait time (ms) Perfmon counter and check the isolation level for shared locks.

Find All Locks Being Held by a Running Batch Process

The following query uses `sys.dm_exec_requests` to find the batch process in question and get its `transaction_id` from the results:

```
SELECT * FROM sys.dm_exec_requests;
GO
```

Then, use the `transaction_id` from the previous query output using the DMV `sys.dm_tran_locks` to find the lock information.

```
SELECT * FROM sys.dm_tran_locks
WHERE request_owner_type = N'TRANSACTION'
    AND request_owner_id = < your transaction_id >;
GO
```

Find All Currently Blocked Requests

The old-school way was to run a quick `sp_who2` and check whether there is an SPID entry in the `BlkBy` column in one or more of the rows. Another quick way was to query the `sys.sysprocesses` view, which would return only rows of sessions that are blocked.

```
SELECT * FROM sys.sysprocesses WHERE blocked > 0
```

Once you obtained the session or SPID for the blocked processes, you could find the statement text associated with it by running this:

```
DBCC INPUTBUFFER (SPID)
```

The following example is a more elegant and modern method that queries the `sys.dm_exec_requests` view to find information about blocked requests and also returns the statements involved in the blocking and related wait stats.

```
SELECT sqltext.TEXT,
xr.session_id,
xr.status,
xr.blocking_session_id,
xr.command,
xr.cpu_time,
xr.total_elapsed_time,
xr.wait_resource
FROM sys.dm_exec_requests xr
CROSS APPLY sys.dm_exec_sql_text(sql_handle) AS sqltext
WHERE status='suspended'
```

Summary

This was quite a technical and detailed chapter, introducing you to the waits and queues performance-tuning methodology, as well as demonstrating other useful DMVs that you will use in the upcoming chapters. Now that you understand the methodology and the DMVs and performance counters you need in order to implement your performance-tuning strategy, you will move on to the tools of the trade, where you build upon this knowledge and set of DMVs and counters and leverage them for further automated analysis. Always remember in your DBA travels that when performance is slow, and it will be at some point, look at wait statistics first as the quickest way to identify your performance bottlenecks. Mining, collating, comparing, and compiling this data will allow you to build your data repository, enable you to create comprehensive reporting, and give you a clear path toward a certifiably healthy SQL Server.

CHAPTER 4

■ ■ ■

Much Ado About Indexes

The keys to a healthy SQL Server are healthy indexes, and therefore I'll cover indexes in this chapter. This chapter is an introduction to indexes and does not deep dive into index internals. Instead, the goal of this chapter is to provide you with some useful index analysis scripts and methods so you can understand how indexes affect the performance of your SQL Server. The primary things you need to look at in terms of having a healthy index strategy and therefore a high-performing SQL Server are as follows: missing indexes, too many indexes, duplicate indexes, and fragmented indexes. You'll look at index usage statistics and how queries are affected, and I'll discuss page splitting and fill factor. These are some of the highlights of this chapter:

- Index basics

- Reviewing available index DMVs

- Providing insightful scripts for index analysis

- Correlating worst-performing queries with missing indexes

Often at a client's site, I am called in to do an analysis on indexes and make recommendations on improving performance. There are different categories of index issues to analyze such as whether indexes are used, unused, missing, duplicates, fragmented, and so on. I have all these neat little scripts that I will share with you here in this chapter. As always, all DMV cumulative stats are persisted only until SQL Server is restarted or the statistics are manually cleared.

■ **Note** The traditional plural form of index is *indices*, but I will stick with the common vernacular *indexes*.

Some of the demos you will see in this chapter will require the AdventureWorks2012 database that can be downloaded from CodePlex. (See Figure 4-1). Because there are several options for download, I recommend you download the full database backup file and restore the database. This way, the database, data, objects, and so on, are ready to go and sufficient for the purposes in this book. Please download the AdventureWorks2012 database from `http://msftdbprodsamples.codeplex.com/releases/view/55330`.

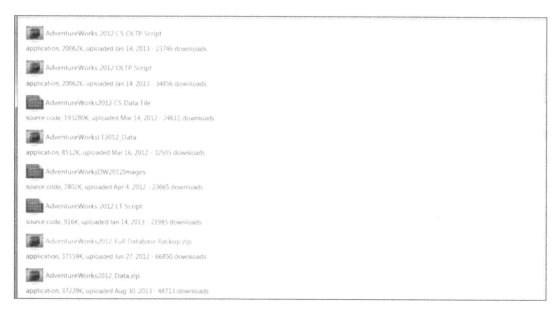

Figure 4-1. Download options for AdventureWorks2012 database at CodePlex.com

Indexes 101

I'll review the basics of indexes in this section. You will first be introduced to what indexes are and the terminology that you need to know to understand indexes.

What Are Indexes?

Indexes are all about finding data quickly. The quicker SQL Server can find the information when you execute a query, the better the performance will be. Rather than looking at every single row in the table, essentially what's known as a *table scan*, you can place indexes on one or a number of columns using index keys (pointers) that enable SQL Server to know how to quickly get the row or rows associated with the values in the keys. Indexes are basically storage items or data structures within a database that contain these keys.

In the instance that there are no clustered indexes, the data structure is known as a *heap*, which is a big pile of unstructured pages with no order. To track the data pages, SQL Server uses an index allocation map (IAM) for both heaps and indexes. Indexes have keys, unlike heaps, that uniquely identify a record and its location.

A great analogy to help understand what indexes are is to compare them to how books in a library are stored, categorized, and searched on. Indexes in a library are similar to indexes in a database, which allow the information you are seeking to be retrieved quickly. If, for example, you want to locate a book about SQL Server, then finding it should be rather quick and easy. First, you can look up and find the section it is stored in, which is the technical book section. This section is analogous to the nonclustered index, serving as a pointer to where the book is located. Now assuming the books in the library are stored by book name (title), a formal library catalog sorts the books alphabetically, by title, and serves as the index. This is like a clustered index in that the books are physically stored in the order of the catalog index. Rather than starting your search for the book at letter *A*, you would go right to the shelf that begins with the letter *S*.

Index Types and Terminology

The following are different types of indexes:

- *Clustered indexes*: These sort and store data in order based on the clustered index key. By default, the primary key is the clustering key of a clustered index. Each entry represents one row in a table. You may have only one clustered index on a table. Therefore, the clustered index should be the most common column that is in your WHERE clauses for queries against the table.

- *Nonclustered indexes*: These can be defined on tables or views having a clustered index (primary key) or on tables or views (heap) not having a clustered index defined. Nonclustered indexes have a structure separate from the data rows. The nonclustered index has a key and row locator pointing to the data row. SQL Server 2005 allows up to 249 nonclustered indexes on a table, and SQL Server versions 2008 through 2014 allow up to 999.

- *Unique index*: This is an index that ensures the uniqueness of each value in the indexed column. If the index is a composite, the uniqueness is enforced across the columns as a whole, not on the individual columns. For example, if you were to create an index on the FirstName and LastName columns in a table, the names together must be unique, but the individual names can be duplicated. You can set the property of clustered and nonclustered indexes to be a unique index. A unique index is automatically created when you define a primary key or unique constraint.

- *Composite index*: This is an index that contains more than one column. In versions of SQL Server 2005 through 2014, you can include up to 16 columns in an index, as long as the index key doesn't exceed the 900-byte limit. Both clustered and nonclustered indexes can be composite indexes.

- *Index with included columns or covering index*: An index with included columns is a nonclustered index that has other column values included in the index to cover queries that the key columns cannot cover themselves.

- *Covering index*: A covering index is one that includes all the columns that are needed to process a particular query. For example, your query might retrieve the FirstName and LastName columns from a table, based on a value in the ContactID column. You can create a covering index that includes all three columns.

- *Full-text index*: This is an index you apply on a database to text fields that you plan to run a full-text search on. A full-text index can be created on tables or indexed views. This type of index is primarily used for word and natural-language search. To use full-text indexes, you must install the component and set up the full-text engine with SQL server.

- *Spatial indexes*: These are special indexes specific to spatial data stored geometry data type columns, such as geometry and geography. This index is available only in SQL Server 2008 and later versions.

- *Filtered index*: This is used to cover queries selecting from a defined subset of data. This is an index with a WHERE clause that indexes only the portion of the data that meets the WHERE criteria. Therefore, not all rows are indexed. Using a filtered index, you can improve performance, reduce maintenance, and index storage as an advantage over a traditional table index.

With filtered index criteria, you can limit the search to a particular value or set of values or exclude NULLs. Here's an example:

```
-- Creating a nonclustered Filtered index on DOJ column
CREATE NONCLUSTERED INDEX FI_Employee_DOJ ON Employee(DOJ)
WHERE DOJ IS NOT NULL
```

Notice here the filter criteria for the index which is the condition WHERE DOJ IS NOT NULL. Therefore, only rows that meet this criteria will be indexed.

- *XML index*: An XML index is used on XML data type columns. These indexes cover tags, values, and paths within your XML data and can improve performance.

- *Primary key*: When you define a primary key constraint on one or more columns, SQL Server creates a unique, clustered index, by default, if a clustered index does not already exist on the table or view. Sometimes the primary key is not the best or natural choice for a clustered index, so the user can override this default and define a primary key on a nonclustered index as well.

- *Unique constraint*: When you define a unique constraint, SQL Server automatically creates a unique, nonclustered index. You can specify that a unique clustered index be created if a clustered index does not already exist on the table.

- *Columnstore index*: This feature was introduced in SQL Server 2012. Unlike the traditional row-based indexes, columnstore data is stored physically in columns. This was a revolutionary way to store data by column, rather than row. In SQL Server 2012, you could have a columnstore index only on a nonclustered index; however, now in SQL Server 2014, you can have columnstore indexes on a clustered or nonclustered index. A common usage scenario benefitting from columnstore indexes is a data warehouse. You can use a columnstore index on OLTP or OLAP systems, for any type of query.

  Executing queries with columnstore indexes in place can potentially increase query performance by 10 to 100 times. According to Microsoft, the columnstore index can achieve up to 10x query performance gains over traditional row-oriented storage and up to 7x data compression over the uncompressed data size. Because data is physically stored in a columnar format, query processing is much faster where columstore data is compressed, stored, and managed as a collection of partial columns called *column segments.* Data is only logically organized as a table with rows and columns, where data is physically stored in columns. Compression of the data is also determined by fill factor.

Memory is a big factor in creating and managing these indexes. You can create a columstore by using similar T-SQL as with traditional indexes. Here are two examples:

```
CREATE NONCLUSTERED COLUMNSTORE INDEX mycolumnstoreindex ON mytable (col1, col2, col3);
CREATE CLUSTERED COLUMNSTORE INDEX myclstrindex ON mytable WITH (DROP_EXISTING = ON);
```

Columnstore indexes can be your answer to solving performance problems and increasing gains in performance. Complex queries on large volume data sets, such as data warehouses, will benefit from columnstore indexes. The in-depth details on this new feature are out of scope for this book but worth further exploration. You can start with columnstore indexes described on MSDN here:

```
http://msdn.microsoft.com/en-us/library/gg492088.aspx
```

Index Advantages vs. Disadvantages

Properly placed indexes on tables can increase performance dramatically, but if indexes are not optimally designed or not well maintained, there can be a significant negative performance impact. Even too few or too many indexes can affect performance. Let's talk about the advantages and disadvantages of having indexes. Certainly, the advantages far outweigh the disadvantages. The disadvantages listed are intended to make DBAs aware of the need to maintain healthy indexes and keep them optimized, not to discard the use of indexes altogether. Indexes are an absolute necessity for high-performance data retrieval. You just need to be mindful of the behavior of indexes over time as data is inserted, updated, and deleted.

Advantages

When thinking about indexes, you need to be aware of what you gain by using indexes. In a nutshell, indexes speed up retrieval of data. If used properly, indexes can reduce disk I/O operations, reduce the resources needed, and improve overall query performance. When you are doing a health check and looking to identify areas of improvement, analyzing indexes and ensuring that indexes are properly designed and implemented can be a giant win for optimizing database performance. Indexes are one of the key areas that should be focused on to achieve a healthy SQL database.

Indexes on tables can dramatically improve performance when selecting data from a table because SQL Server does not need to look at every row. The behavior without an index would cause SQL Server to start at the beginning until it finds the row it is looking for. In terms of SQL Server performance, you want to ensure there is a clustered index and avoid heaps at all costs. A table or view not having a clustered index defined is known as a heap. If SQL Server is searching the entire table for a row, by actually traversing the table row by row, this is called a *table scan*. To find the rows requested needed to satisfy the query would be a slow process and expensive query cost.

The table scan operation is very I/O intensive because SQL Server may need to retrieve the data from disk. That is why if you have an index on the table, SQL Server will use the index as a pointer to all the rows that the query is looking for. In summary, the advantages of having an index are as follows:

- Reduces disk I/O

- Improves query performance (faster SELECTs/reads)

- Scans smaller range of data (index) vs. a larger one (table scan)

- Provides efficient data retrieval operations

Disadvantages

Over time indexes get fragmented, and page splitting occurs. The disadvantages of indexes therefore are fragmentation and the excessive page splitting that can result from fragmentation. For example, when you update a record and change the value of an indexed column in a clustered or nonclustered index, the database might need to move the entire row into a new position to keep the rows in sorted order and can cause a performance penalty. This behavior essentially turns an update query into a DELETE followed by an INSERT, with an obvious decrease in performance. Indexes are intended for quick data retrieval, that is, SELECT statements, and slow the performance of INSERT, UPDATE, and DELETE operations. Any time these Data Manipulation Language (DML) operations occur, it results in the reorganization of rows in the tables, causing fragmentation and page splitting. This is expected behavior but becomes an issue when fragmentation and page splitting are excessive. I'll talk more page splitting and fragmentation later in the chapter.

Another disadvantage is that using too many indexes can actually slow down your database. If your tables have indexes on every column, which index will the query optimizer choose? It may choose the less efficient index and less efficient execution plan and therefore result in poor query response time. A common misconception is that indexes will solve all performance issues. This is not true, and I discussed various causes of poor SQL Server performance in the previous chapter (for example, blocking). Keep in mind that each time a page or database row is updated or removed, the reference or index also has to be updated, and this can slow overall performance because SQL Server has to work harder to complete these operations on all the existing indexes. Therefore, tables should not be overindexed, such as placing an index on every table column, which can lead to slow database performance. Therefore, too many indexes on a table can yield diminishing returns.

In addition, another issue can be with the size of an index. If you take an encyclopedia, for example, and include the words *the*, *and*, or *at* in the index, the index would cease being useful. Imagine if every *the*, *and*, or *at* was included in the index. In this case, an index would cease being useful and can grow as big as the text itself. In addition, indexes themselves take up space, which in and of itself has a storage cost attached to it. With respect to the number of indexes and size, if you have too many unnecessary indexes, covering too many columns, their usefulness is decreased and can become too big to serve a beneficial purpose.

Indexes are automatically updated when the data rows themselves are updated, which can lead to additional overhead and can impact performance. Ultimately, you must assess whether the performance gains on selects via using indexes are worth the additional overhead that updates and deletes incur when needing to update indexes. There is a delicate balancing act to consider when determining the right indexes for your tables in terms of performance. In sum, the disadvantages of indexes are as follows:

- Slows inserts, updates, and deletes
- Reorganization of rows
- Too many indexes
- Page splits
- Fragmentation

B-Tree Index Structure

The traditional internal index structure is known as a *B-tree*. An index consists of a set of pages (index nodes) organized in a B-tree structure. This structure is hierarchical in nature, with the root node at the top of the hierarchy and the leaf nodes at the bottom, as shown in Figure 4-2.

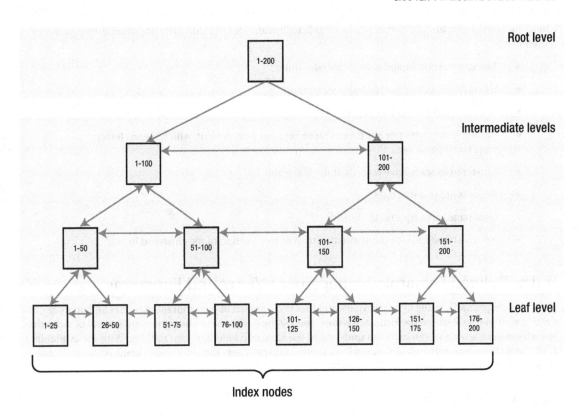

Figure 4-2. *Model of index B-tree structure*

Let's briefly discuss the elementary B-tree structure of a SQL Server index. When a query is issued against an indexed column, the query engine starts at the root node and navigates down through the intermediate nodes, with each layer of the intermediate level more granular than the one above. The query engine continues down through the index nodes until it reaches the leaf node.

For example, if you're searching for the value 123 in an indexed column, the query engine would first look in the root level to determine which page to reference at the top intermediate level. In this example, the first page points to the values 1 to 100, and the second page point to the values 101 to 200, so the query engine would go to the second page on that level. The query engine would then determine that it must go to the third page at the next intermediate level. From there, the query engine would navigate to the leaf node for value 123. The leaf node will contain either the entire row of data or a pointer to that row, depending on whether the index is clustered or nonclustered. You can visualize and follow this example by referring to Figure 4-2, showing a B-tree model.

The *leaf* nodes of a clustered index contain the data pages, whereas the leaf nodes of a nonclustered index contain only the values from the indexed columns and row locators that point to the actual data rows, rather than contain the data rows themselves. This means the query engine must take an additional step in order to locate the actual data.

A row locator's structure depends on whether it points to a clustered table or to a heap. If referencing a clustered table, the row locator points to the clustered index, using the key value or primary key from the clustered index to navigate to the correct data row. If referencing a heap, the row locator points to the actual data row. As mentioned earlier when talking about heaps, the only way to track and locate the data pages where the row exists is for SQL Server to use an index allocation map (IAM). Here are some B-tree points to remember:

- The tree portion includes key attributes only.

- It is ordered like a `create index` statement.

- Keys are packed in index pages.

- Having fewer bytes per key means more keys per page/extent, which means fewer page faults per access.

- Clustered indexes have records at the leaf level.

- Records are in data pages.

- Data pages are sequentially linked.

- Nonclustered indexes point into the heap or tree portion of the clustered index.

Index-Related Dynamic Management Views and Functions

Since you are primarily using dynamic views and functions as part of your tool set to collect and analyze data, as well as troubleshoot performance issues, you will be delighted to know there are several of these that are related to indexes and can help you understand the state and health of your indexes. With the available DMVs and DMFs, you can look at indexes from several perspectives. Table 4-1 shows some of the available system views and functions specific to indexes.

Table 4-1. *Index-Related DMVs and DMFs*

sys.indexes	sysindexes
sys.dm_db_index_operational_stats	sys.index_columns
sys.dm_db_index_usage_stats	sys.dm_db_index_physical_stats
sys.dm_db_missing_index_groups	sys.dm_db_missing_index_details
sys.dm_db_missing_index_group_stats	sys.dm_db_missing_index_columns

If you want a full description of these index-related DMVs and DMFs, refer to the following MSDN page that contains links to each of the objects in Table 4-1.

`http://msdn.microsoft.com/en-us/library/ms187974`

Let's define these dynamic management views and functions in context of what scripts you will be running and the types of information you can derive from these useful index views and functions. Please visit the MSDN link listed previously to learn about the specific column definitions. Here I will list them in terms of the valuable information DBAs need to know about the health of their indexes:

- `sys.indexes` vs. `sys.sysindexes`: Essentially, they both return the same information about all the indexes on a database. However, from SQL Server version 2005 on, the recommendation is to use only `sys.indexes` because `sysindexes` is deprecated and provided for backward compatibility.

The information that is returned from sys.indexes is the index metadata, which consists of the properties of each index on a table. This view will return information such as the name and type of index, whether the index is unique (not to allow duplicate keys), whether it is part of a primary key constraint, what the fill factor is, whether it is a filtered index, what locking scheme it has, and finally whether the index is enabled or disabled.

- sys.index_columns: The index_columns view basically returns one row per column that is part of a sys.indexes index or unordered table (heap). It includes ordering of columns and whether they are included in the index.

- sys.dm_db_index_operational_stats: This is rich with operational stats about your indexes and partitions and keeps track of data such as allocation, latching, locking, and I/O-related statistics. Data returned here is granular, starting at the database level and drilling down to the object, index, and partition. There are 44 columns of information in this DMV treasure trove, and you'll need the right scripts to mine the data. The scripts provided in this chapter will allow you to identify issues and capture pertinent information related to indexes on page splits, lock escalations, and locking and blocking. In addition, statistics about singleton lookups and range scans are exposed to help with advanced index analysis.

- sys.dm_db_index_usage_stats: This system view simply returns counts of different types of index operations along with the date and time each type of operation was last performed in SQL Server. The data derived here will be valuable in some cases where you want to decide how useful the indexes you have on your database are, what type of operation the index is performing, and when is the last time they were used. So, if, for example, you were looking for inactive indexes that are no longer used or perhaps you can drop, sys.dm_db_index_usage_stats view will tell you this.

- sys.dm_db_index_physical_stats: Primarily, if you want to know how fragmented your indexes are, you can query this system index view. Size and fragmentation information for the data and indexes of the specified table or view is exposed. Using some key columns in this view, as discussed in the upcoming section on index fragmentation, you will be able to analyze and pinpoint fragmented indexes and decide whether you should rebuild the indexes or simply perform what's called an *index reorg*. The sys.dm_db_index_physical_stats DMV runs in three modes: LIMITED, SAMPLED, and DETAILED. The min_record_size_in_bytes and max_record_size_in_bytes columns are available only in SAMPLED or DETAILED mode.

The data about missing indexes is stored in the following collection of dynamic management views (DMVs); they all exclude information about spatial indexes. Let's list and then provide details about each of them.

- sys.dm_db_missing_index_details
- sys.dm_db_missing_index_groups
- sys.dm_db_missing_index_groups_stats
- sys.dm_db_missing_index_columns
- sys.dm_db_missing_index_groups
- sys.dm_db_missing_index_group_stats

- `sys.dm_db_missing_index_details`: SQL Server keeps track of what the optimizer thinks could use certain indexes, and detailed information about a missing index is exposed in this view. Assumptions about missing indexes are based on the query execution plans stored in the cache and the number of times a query is executed. This DMV can suggest which columns would benefit from the index.

- `sys.dm_db_missing_index_groups`: This exposes data about missing indexes contained in a specific missing index group. This is usually joined with `sys.dm_db_missing_index_details` for analysis. This DMV returns only two columns with information about which indexes are in which group.

- `sys.dm_db_missing_index_group_stats`: This has summary information about groups of missing indexes, such as how many times SQL Server could have used that index and how great an impact it would have had on the query. Useful column data such as `avg_total_user_cost` and `avg_user_impact` are key in determining the potential benefits and cost of adding an index. Whereas `sys.dm_db_index_usage_stats` gives you actual usage statistics of existing indexes, `sys.dm_db_missing_index_group_stats` provides you with potential use statistics of missing indexes, had they been available at the time of query execution. This view is usually joined with `sys.dm_db_missing_index_details` for complete index analysis.

- `sys.dm_db_missing_index_columns`: This DMF accepts an `index_handle` parameter. It returns columns that should be in the suggested index identified with the `index_handle` that can be obtained from `sys.dm_db_missing_index_details` and `sys.dm_db_missing_index_groups`. It does not include spatial indexes.

■ **Note**   Spatial indexes are not included in the missing index system views.

Where to Place Indexes

The question of which tables and columns to add indexes to is a most essential question when designing a database for optimal performance. Moreover, you want to implement an index strategy for quick data retrieval. There are several things you need to consider when creating proper indexes. First, the most important decision is where to place the clustered index. Oftentimes the answer is on the primary key. Remember, you can create only one clustered index per table, so make it count! The clustered index, as you recall, will place the data in the physical order of the clustered key. Clustered indexes are the foundation of good database design, and therefore, a poorly chosen clustered index can lead to high execution times, wasted disk space, poor I/O, and heavy fragmentation and can drag down the performance of your entire SQL Server.

Consider which attributes the most efficient clustered index key should have, in terms of storage, how often it is updated, and whether it is continuously incrementing. By continuously incrementing, the key can improve write performance and help avoid fragmentation. Therefore, a clustered index key should be as narrow as possible, it should be unique to avoid duplicate key values, it should essentially be static, and it should continuously increase to improve write performance and limit fragmentation. Since a clustered index key is in the physical order of the rows, you don't really want to have a key column that is wide, frequently updated, and not unique. All these factors play into optimal performance, and choosing a clustered index is one of those things you should endeavor to do early on. To review, the ideal attributes of a clustered index key are as follows:

- Narrow

- Unique

- Static

- Ever-increasing

Data grows over time, and so the indexes you plan for may not be the most efficient indexes later. It may be that you will need to add indexes later, based on the use of the system, types of queries, and reporting. Indexes speed access to table data but are costly to maintain. One thing to keep in mind is that almost every update to the table requires altering both data pages and every index and will affect nonclustered indexes. All inserts and deletions affect all indexes.

As mentioned earlier under some of the index disadvantages, you don't want to overindex. Therefore, sometimes less is more, so not creating an index may be best.

When developing your T-SQL coding, statements, and transactions, you'll want to ask yourself whether they have a WHERE clause, what columns are used, and do they require sort operations. The answers can lead you to make the right indexing decisions.

To ensure that an index will be most effective, you should consider the selectivity of the data (which will be indexed) or the infrequency of the data. The query optimizer will use the selectivity to figure out whether it is actually worth using an index to find certain rows in a table.

Indexes, particularly nonclustered indexes, are primarily beneficial in situations where there is a reasonably high level of selectivity within the index. In terms of percentages, the higher percentage of unique values, the higher the selectivity. You want a high percentage of values in columns that are unique. The query engine loves highly selective key columns, especially if those columns are referenced in the WHERE clause of your frequently run queries. The higher the selectivity, the faster the query engine can reduce the size of the result set. The flipside, of course, is that a column with relatively few unique values is seldom a good candidate to be indexed.

Let's say, for example, you have an M&M manufacturing table, representing a bag of M&Ms, with values of red, green, and pink. From your M&M experience, you assume there is a large number of reds and greens. If 80 percent of the table values are either red or green, this is not very selective, and therefore, using an index may not be very efficient. The low selectivity here indicates there is not much variety of the column values. If a query is looking to select all the rows based on the red or green value, the query engine might, in fact, resort to a table scan to find all the requested rows. However, I have rarely seen a pink M&M, and if it represents a selective or rare value, then the rows I will query based on pink M&Ms have a high selectivity and will likely use an index to find the matching rows. Therefore, the higher the selectivity, the more likely an index will be used. Moreover, you can now see that an index is most efficient when searching for a smaller number of unique rows in relation to a table with a large number of total rows.

Fill Factor and Page Splitting

When creating or optimizing indexes or considering how updates, inserts, and deletes may be affecting performance, fill factor and page splitting come into play. I will discuss both in this section and their importance.

Fill Factor

Generally speaking, the read performance of an index is directly proportional to the fill factor, and write performance is inversely proportional to the fill factor. An index's fill factor specifies the percentage that the index data pages on disk are filled when the index is first created. An index fill factor set to 0 or 100 percent will cause each index data page to be completely filled up. This is ideal from a disk capacity standpoint because there is no wasted space with data pages that are not fully allocated. However, this is not ideal from a SQL Server performance perspective regarding data updates (inserts, updates, and deletes). If you create a clustered index that has a fill factor of 100 percent, every time a record is inserted, deleted, or even modified, page splits can occur because there is likely no room on the existing index data page to write the change. Page splits increase I/O and can dramatically degrade SQL Server performance.

A lower fill factor will reduce the number of page splits. However, it is easy to react by simply applying a fill factor of, say, 50 percent to reduce page splits in a highly transactional system. The problem with this approach is that by doing this, you have in effect doubled the amount of data required to read and cache index information for a table. So, in improving write performance, you have potentially degraded read performance. The trick is to find the right balance between read and write performance by optimizing the fill factor settings for each index.

So, what should your fill factors be set to? It is a question that can be answered only by the continuous monitoring of performance, as discussed when setting baselines and watching for deviations in performance, and tuning your indexes as needed. By understanding the initial workload and purpose of SQL Server, such as whether you anticipate heavy reads, writes, or a mixture of both, you can use the following numbers as a general starting point:

- If your database is read-only (low number of updates), use a fill factor of 100 percent or 0 percent.

- If your database is write-intensive (writes greatly exceed reads), use a fill factor somewhere between 50 percent and 70 percent.

- If your database is both read- and write-intensive, start with a fill factor of 80 percent to 90 percent.

As you can tell, the fill factor settings depend on the use of the table. Even where SQL Server is update intensive, if a specific table is used only for lookups, for example, then its clustered index can have a fill factor of 100 percent. Furthermore, for indexes that consume fewer than 100 pages, the fill factor settings are likely to yield insignificant results.

Get fill factor information about your indexes as follows:

```
SELECT
  db_name() AS DbName
, B.name AS TableName
, C.name AS IndexName
, C.fill_factor AS IndexFillFactor
, D.rows AS RowsCount
, A.avg_fragmentation_in_percent
, A.page_count
, GetDate() as [TimeStamp]
FROM sys.dm_db_index_physical_stats(DB_ID(),NULL,NULL,NULL,NULL) A
INNER JOIN sys.objects B
  ON A.object_id = B.object_id
INNER JOIN sys.indexes C
  ON B.object_id = C.object_id AND A.index_id = C.index_id
```

```
INNER JOIN sys.partitions D
  ON B.object_id = D.object_id AND A.index_id = D.index_id
WHERE C.index_id > 0
```

Page Split Tracking

What exactly is a page split? When there is no space left on a data page for more inserts or updates, SQL Server moves some data from the current data page and moves it to another data page. So, if a new row is inserted onto an already full page, moving data to another page is done in order to make space for the new rows, and the data now spans multiple data pages. So, to hammer this concept home, the page split is moving the data from one page to a new one, and the span is the result. Although page splits are a normally occurring process in an OLTP system, too many page splits can cause performance issues that will slow down your system because of fragmentation. Page splits are an expensive operation; therefore, the fewer page splits you have, the better your system will perform.

The traditional way to monitor and evaluate page splitting activity is using the Performance Monitor counter Page Splits/sec. The Page Splits/sec counter is likely to increase proportionately as workload activity on the server increases. The Page Splits/sec counter measures the number of times SQL Server had to split a page when updating or inserting data, per second. This counter is cumulative of all databases and objects in that server. It does not have any breakdown. From this counter, there is no way of identifying the database, table, or index where the page split has occurred. The other scripts will have more details. The page_io_latch_wait_count and page_io_latch_wait_in_ms columns indicate whether physical I/Os were issued to bring the index or heap pages into memory and how many I/Os were issued.

You can find the page splits/sec counter in the sys.dm_os_performance_counters DMV with the following query:

```
Select *
from sys.dm_os_performance_counters
where counter_name = 'page splits/sec'
```

Because the counter is a per-second counter, in order to calculate the actual per-second rate, you need to capture the per-second cntr_value twice and then calculate the per-second amount based on the two cntr_value values and the number of seconds between the two samplings.

Here is an example of how to calculate the per-second counter value for Page Splits/sec:

```
-- Collect first sample
DECLARE @old_cntr_value INT;
DECLARE @first_sample_date DATETIME;
SELECT @old_cntr_value = cntr_value,
@first_sample_date = getdate()
FROM sys.dm_os_performance_counters
where counter_name = 'page splits/sec'

-- Time frame to wait before collecting second sample
WAITFOR DELAY '00:00:10'
-- Collect second sample and calculate per-second counter
SELECT (cntr_value - @old_cntr_value) /
DATEDIFF(ss,@first_sample_date, GETDATE()) as PageSplitsPerSec
FROM sys.dm_os_performance_counters
WHERE counter_name = 'page splits/sec'
```

To track page splits per second, you would have to insert this into an archive table for historical trending. How many page splits are too many? It is recommended to set up these counters to capture this information on a regularly scheduled interval in order to establish a baseline for normal operating workloads. This way, when the workload increases and transactions are pounding away at the server, you can analyze the trends and understand what is too high, too many, and too much for your particular system. You may need to correlate other metrics, such as the leaf and nonleaf allocation counts, as well as with certain resource wait types, discussed next.

Although recognizing a higher number of page splits per second on the system may indicate an I/O bottleneck, it doesn't give you a good indication of where the splits are coming from. For an index, a page allocation corresponds to a page split, and therefore you can use the sys.dm_db_index_operational_stats system view to pinpoint the objects and indexes associated with page splitting. Excessive page splitting can have a significant effect on performance. The following query identifies the top ten objects involved with page splits (ordering by leaf_allocation_count and referencing both the leaf_allocation_count and nonleaf_allocation_count columns). The leaf_allocation_count column represents page splits at the leaf, and the nonleaf_allocation_count column represents splits at the nonleaf levels of an index:

```
SELECT      TOP 10
            OBJECT_NAME(object_id, database_id) object_nm,
            index_id,
            partition_number,
            leaf_allocation_count,
            nonleaf_allocation_count
FROM sys.dm_db_index_operational_stats
      (db_id(), NULL, NULL, NULL)
ORDER BY leaf_allocation_count DESC
```

The reason why too many page splits can decrease the performance of SQL Server is because of the large number of I/O operations. One solution is to deploy a faster I/O subsystem, where page splits would be less of an issue. Of course, throwing hardware at the problem can be an expensive and temporary Band-Aid.

Page splits can also show up as a resource wait when pages highly in demand during page splitting can cause in-memory contention and show up as page latches. So, by examining waits as well, you can identify one of the common symptoms of excessive page splitting.

During data modifications where access to the specific data page is requested, SQL Server will take a short latch on the page to add the data. However, once there is not enough space on a data page, a new page is allocated, data is copied from the old page to the new page, and then new data is added. Taking into account whether there is a clustered index on the table, SQL Server must take and hold the latch for a longer period of time. This is where the end user begins to see a performance slowdown. All the user is hoping to do is add new data, not realizing or understanding the internals of the data engine.

Therefore, one way to tell whether excessive page splits exist on the system is to look at wait stats. High wait times for latch-wait statistics is one possible indication of too many page splits. The latches are held in EX (exclusive) mode and therefore will show up in the waiting queue as PageLatch_EX.

Contrary to many folks' confusion, PageLatch_EX is *not* an I/O request. Rather, it occurs when a task is waiting on a latch for a buffer and can cause contention of access to the in-memory pages. In other words, while page split operations are occurring, the latches will hold the pages in memory and not release them until the operation is complete. You can first look at the cumulative wait stats view by running a simple query.

```
select * from
sys.dm_os_wait_stats
WHERE wait_type LIKE 'PAGELATCH%'
AND waiting_tasks_count >0
```

You might get results similar to the results shown here and then see whether the wait times are extremely high for PageLatch_* wait types. The chief way to reduce the excessive number of page splits is to lower the fill factor on an index. You were introduced to fill factor in the previous section, as well as the relation between fill factor and page splits. You can refer to the section on fill factor for some general guidance.

wait_type	waiting_tasks_count	wait_time_ms	max_wait_time_ms	signal_wait_time_ms
PAGELATCH_SH	390	185	51	22
PAGELATCH_UP	273	679	69	9
PAGELATCH_EX	3070	608	101	106

If the top waits with high wait times show up for PAGELATCH_* in the sys.dm_os_wait_stats view, you can query the sys.dm_os_waiting_tasks DMV. This system view shows you what's happening now on the system and shows the queue of waiting tasks waiting on a resource. To search for a task waiting for PAGELATCH, you can run the following query, which will identify the associated session and the resource_description column that tells you the actual database_id, file_id, and page_id:

```
SELECT session_id, wait_type, resource_description
FROM sys.dm_os_waiting_tasks
WHERE wait_type LIKE 'PAGELATCH%'
```

Recall the hierarchal B-tree structure in which index nodes are a set of pages. Latches are held on a page that is being split, on the existing next page in the index, and on the parent page in the index tree, all for the duration of the split. Any attempts to access any of these pages during the split are blocked, including read access. Because the operation does not occur instantly, performance bottlenecks arise.

By using sys.dm_db_index_opertational_stats with the sys.dm_db_missing index_details DMV, you can see whether any blocking or locking is happening. You can identify the top ten objects associated with waits on page locks by running the following queries:

```
SELECT TOP 10
OBJECT_NAME(o.object_id, o.database_id) object_nm,
o.index_id,
partition_number,
page_lock_wait_count,
page_lock_wait_in_ms,
case when mid.database_id is null then 'N' else 'Y' end as missing_index_identified
FROM sys.dm_db_index_operational_stats (db_id(), NULL, NULL, NULL) o
LEFT OUTER JOIN (SELECT DISTINCT database_id, object_id
FROM sys.dm_db_missing_index_details) as mid
ON mid.database_id = o.database_id and mid.object_id = o.object_id
ORDER BY page_lock_wait_count DESC
```

Furthermore, you can specifically identify the top ten objects involved with page splits. Page splits at the leaf level are shown in the leaf_allocation_count column, and the nonleaf levels of an index split are shown in the nonleaf_allocation_count columns. The results here will lead you to the indexes associated with page splitting and thus point out which indexes you should consider applying a low fill factor to, potentially reducing page splits.

```
SELECT TOP 10
OBJECT_NAME(object_id, database_id) object_nm,
index_id,
partition_number,
```

```
leaf_allocation_count,
nonleaf_allocation_count
FROM sys.dm_db_index_operational_stats
(db_id(), NULL, NULL, NULL)
ORDER BY leaf_allocation_count DESC
```

Common Index Issues

Let's define the common issues that occur with indexes that affect performance and how you can diagnose and detect these problems.

Index Usage

How can you tell whether an index is being used? Obviously, you want to ensure that SQL Server is in fact utilizing the indexes that are created on a table. Information on index usage can give you a look into how effective the existing indexes are and how often they are used. This section discusses index usage and provides some DMV queries to assist you with index usage analysis.

You can use both sys.dm_db_index_operational_stats and sys.dm_db_index_usage_stats to analyze the way in which indexes are being used on the system. They return different sets of data, but unlike sys.dm_db_index_operational_stats, which depicts the number of index operations that have actually occurred in an execution plan, sys.dm_db_index_usage_stats returns results based on the number of plans that have been executed that utilize an index.

Most interesting in using the sys.dm_db_index_usage_stats DMV, you can see the count of various index operations broken down by user and system queries. User queries will often be more important in index analysis, and you can see the individual counts including the number of seeks, scans, lookups, and updates along with the associated time for this index that was last accessed. For example, you can see the number of user_updates and the date and time of the last_user_update, answering the common question of when a table was last used or touched. So, not only can this DMV tell you the most active and inactive indexes but when the table or even database was last accessed altogether. Then you can make some intelligent assumptions and drop indexes, tables, or databases based on this information. The simplest way to quickly see index usage is to query the sys.dm_db_index_usage_stats view using the following GetIndexUsageSimple script:

```
SELECT
DB_NAME(database_id) As DBName,
Object_Name(object_id,database_id) As ObjectName,
database_id,
object_id,
Index_id,
user_seeks,
user_scans,
user_lookups,
user_updates,
last_user_seek,
last_user_scan,
last_user_lookup,
last_user_update
FROM sys.dm_db_index_usage_stats
order by DB_NAME(database_id)
GO
```

The return results show the database name, object name, and user-related index operations. To derive the database name and object name, you need to invoke the built-in metadata functions, DB_Name() and Object_Name(), respectively. You would need to pass the database_id parameter to DB_Name(database_id) and Object_Name(object_id, database_id).

DBName	ObjectName	database_id	object_id	Index_id
AdventureWorks2012	Person	12	1765581328	1
MDW_HealthySQL	smo_servers_internal	10	452196661	1
MDW_HealthySQL	volumes_internal	10	404196490	1
MDW_HealthySQL	os_schedulers	10	551673013	1
MDW_HealthySQL	disk_usage	10	919674324	1

user_seeks	user_scans	user_lookups	user_updates	last_user_seek
0	3	0	0	NULL
1	0	0	24	NULL
72	0	0	24	2014-12-02 16:15:00.303
0	0	0	24	NULL
0	0	0	1	NULL

last_user_scan	last_user_lookup	last_user_update
2014-12-02 16:18:57.183	NULL	NULL
NULL	NULL	2014-12-02 16:15:00.303
NULL	NULL	2014-12-02 16:15:00.303
NULL	NULL	2014-12-02 16:15:02.153
NULL	NULL	2014-12-02 12:00:04.417

Singleton lookups, as the name implies, search for a single record using unique indexes. This is not apparent even in the execution plans because there is no property that indicates "singleton lookup" or "range scan," although such information is readily available in the operational stats system view. You can specifically look at the range_scan_count and singleton_lookup_count values in the DMV. range_scan_count displays the cumulative number of range and table scans, while singleton_lookup_count shows the cumulative count of single row retrievals, started on or from the index or heap, respectively. If you join the sys.dm_db_index_operational_stats system view with sys.indexes, you can also capture the singleton lookup count, with the range scan count, along with the table and index name, by using the following query (singleton lookup count):

```
SELECT OBJECT_SCHEMA_NAME(idxos.object_id) + '.' + OBJECT_NAME(idxos.object_id) as
table_name
,idx.name as index_name
,idxos.range_scan_count
,idxos.singleton_lookup_count
FROM sys.dm_db_index_operational_stats(DB_ID(),NULL,NULL,NULL) idxos
INNER JOIN sys.indexes idx ON idx.object_id = idxos.object_id AND idx.index_id =
idxos.index_id
WHERE OBJECTPROPERTY(idxos.object_id,'IsUserTable') = 1
ORDER BY idxos.range_scan_count DESC
GO
```

If there are any such range scans or single record "singleton lookup," you would see similar output such as `table_name index_name range_scan_count singleton_lookup_count`:

```
Person.Person IX_Person_LastName_FirstName_MiddleName 2 0
Person.Person PK_Person_BusinessEntityID 1 3
Person.BusinessEntityContact PK_BusinessEntityContact_BusinessEntityID_PersonID_
ContactTypeID 1 0
Person.BusinessEntityContact AK_BusinessEntityContact_rowguid 0 0
Person.BusinessEntityContact IX_BusinessEntityContact_PersonID 0 0
```

Even with indexes, there is a balance and a cost to optimizing indexes for performance. One thing you need to do is look at how often the index is used for seeking and compare it to how often the index is updated. As such, optimal seek performance comes at the cost of update performance. Moreover, when indexes are frequently updated, as mentioned, the indexes become fragmented, and the statistics become out of date. You'll learn more about index fragmentation later.

Conversely, a range scan, essentially a seek plus range scan operation, searches the index structure for the first qualifying leaf row and does a scan on the range of values at that level, both backward and forward, until the end of the range. In that a range scan is more desireable than a singleton lookup, you can use `sys.dm_db_index_operational_stats` to compare `range_scan_count` to `singleton_lookup_count`. An index seek and a key lookup operation may be caused by a singleton lookup, where SQL Server will look up the data page in the clustered index for every row found in the index seek. As far as performance is concerned, this type of operation might suffice for a few thousand records but would be fairly expensive for millions of rows.

Index Fragmentation

Ever wonder why when you first deploy your SQL Server with perfectly designed indexes, performance couldn't be better, but after some time in operation, the database performance begins to get slower and slower? This could be because of heavily fragmented indexes, which can degrade query performance and cause your application to respond slowly. Over time as the database grows, pages split, and data is inserted, updated, and deleted, indexes become fragmented.

Index fragmentation should not be confused with OS or disk fragmentation. Such fragmentation can be referred to as *external* fragmentation, while index fragmentation is *internal*. Index fragmentation is when the pages are not contiguous, and thus the disk access requires more operations. This internal fragmentation occurs when inside the data file the logical ordering no longer matches the physical ordering of the index pages. Sometimes when the pages are out of order, this can result in wasted space, with even one entire extent containing one record on a page. Data can be spread out over many extents without any order to them. Imagine searching for records when they're all over the place and how much longer that search would take.

There can be numerous hits to disk (Reads per Sec, where the data is stored) when there are many extents, resulting in disk thrashing and the process of moving data into and out of virtual memory (a process also called swapping pages). Because data has to be transferred back and forth from the hard drive to the physical memory, disk thrashing considerably slows down the performance of a system.

Fragmentation is an expected condition, however, of a normal OLTP system. Fortunately, moving away from the cumbersome and legacy `DBCC SHOWCONTIG`, which helped diagnose fragmentation and page splitting, the `sys.dm_db_index_physical_stats` DMV can help you more accurately detect and analyze index fragmentation. Table 4-2 describes some of the key columns in thi view.

Table 4-2. *Key Columns for Index Fragmentation (sys.dm_db_index_physical_stats)*

Column	Description
avg_fragmentation_in_percent	The percent of logical fragmentation (out-of-order pages) in the index
fragment_count	The number of fragments (physically consecutive leaf pages) in the index
avg_fragment_size_in_pages	Average number of pages in one fragment in an index

Here is a quick way to view the most fragmentation on your indexes by querying the sys.dm_db_index_ physical_stats system function using the QuickIdxFrag script. The statement Drop Table dbo.INDEX_ FRAG_STATS will drop all the information after it's displayed onscreen. If you want to preserve the data in this table, simply comment out or delete the Drop Table statement.

```
SELECT * INTO dbo.INDEX_FRAG_STATS FROM sys.dm_db_index_physical_stats (5, NULL, NULL,
NULL , 'LIMITED')

SELECT t.database_id, s.name, s.type,t.object_id, t.index_type_desc,
t.avg_fragmentation_in_percent, t.page_count
FROM dbo.INDEX_FRAG_STATS t inner join sysobjects s on t.[OBJECT_ID]  = s.id
order by t.avg_fragmentation_in_percent desc

Drop Table dbo.INDEX_FRAG_STATS
```

database_id	name	type	object_id
5	StateProvince	U	462624691
5	StateProvince	U	462624691
5	StateProvince	U	462624691
5	DF_StateProvince_ModifiedDate	D	510624862
5	DF_StateProvince_ModifiedDate	D	510624862

index_type_desc	avg_fragmentation_in_percent	page_count
CLUSTERED INDEX	50	2
CLUSTERED INDEX	0	2
NONCLUSTERED INDEX	0	1
CLUSTERED INDEX	0	1
NONCLUSTERED INDEX	0	1

The previous script uses SAMPLED mode), but you can also do a more intensive index scan by using DETAILED mode. DETAILED implies a full scan of every single page in the index (or heap). In essence, if you are running a detailed mode scan for every table and every secondary index, you are doing a full database scan. As you can infer, a sampled or detailed scan can take a certain amount of time to complete because of the following factors:

- How big your database is
- How fast your I/O subsystem is to read the entire database
- Additional concurrent load competing for the I/O throughput

■ **Caution**   Beware running this DMV in production or on large tables because SAMPLED mode scans 1 percent of pages and DETAILED mode scans all pages.

With `avg_fragmentation_in_percent` in descending order, the indexes reporting the highest fragmentation percentages will be at the top of the results. Once you run the script, by looking at the `avg_fragmentation_in_percent` column value returned for each index, you can determine your next action to defragment the indexes. Here is another one of those areas where you need to see what works best, but some general guidelines will be provided for you. The thresholds vary.

Based on the results, you will want to decide whether you should do any of the following:

- Rebuild indexes

- Reorganize indexes

- Do nothing

Rebuilding indexes completely drops and re-creates the database indexes. Technically, rebuilding consists of copying, renaming, and dropping the old one, internally. This is one of the operations you will perform to defragment your indexes since you are rebuilding them and realigning the physical and logical order of the index rows in contiguous pages from scratch. Fragmentation is eliminated, pages are compacted together, and disk space is reclaimed. The fill factor, as discussed earlier, determines how the data in the pages is allocated. By specifying "ALL", all the indexes on a table are dropped and rebuilt in a single transaction. In addition, this operation requires lots of disk space. You should be OK if you have 1.5 to 2 times the space of the largest index as an initial guideline. For more on disk space requirements for index DDL operations, you can refer to the MSDN article here:

`https://msdn.microsoft.com/en-us/library/ms179542.aspx`

The command you will use, since SQL Server version 2005, is `ALTER INDEX REBUILD`. In addition, you may want to specify `ALTER INDEX REBUILD WITH (ONLINE = ON)` for rebuilding indexes, as an `ONLINE` operation, which will be defined in a moment.

You can use your AdventureWorks2012 sample database to run an example rebuild index statement, which will rebuild all the indexes on the `Production.Product` table.

```
USE AdventureWorks2012;
GO
ALTER INDEX ALL ON Production.Product REBUILD
GO
```

▪ **Note**   You cannot stop this operation partway; otherwise, the entire transaction will be rolled back before any indexes are rebuilt.

Keep in mind when running rebuild indexes on your database and tables in production, it is an I/O and resource-intensive operation and should typically be scheduled during off-peak business hours or during scheduled maintenance/outage windows. Online indexing, however, can take place without affecting normal database operations because this feature does not lock the tables, as with traditional index rebuilds. Of course, this feature is available only in Enterprise Edition and comes with the cost that online indexing will take longer to complete and require sufficient tempdb space. The following MSDN article will provide an example of calculating disk space for index operations:

`https://msdn.microsoft.com/en-us/library/ms179542.aspx`

Index Reorganization

The index reorganization process physically reorganizes the leaf nodes of the index. Reorganizing an index uses minimal system resources. It defragments the leaf level of clustered and nonclustered indexes on tables and views by physically reordering the leaf-level pages to match the logical, left to right, order of the leaf nodes. Reorganizing also compacts the index pages, and the syntax is shown here:

```
USE AdventureWorks2012;
GO
ALTER INDEX ALL ON Production.Product REORGANIZE
GO
```

Unlike rebuilding indexes, reorganizing indexes does *not* require any additional disk space but requires log space. Because reorganizing indexes is a fully logged transaction, the log can potentially grow substantially. Log usage for a reorganize could be way more than the size of the index, which depends on how much reorganizing and compaction is done, as well as the level of fragmentation distributed through the index.

To learn more about how to reorganize and rebuild indexes, visit the official MSDN article here:

http://msdn.microsoft.com/en-us/library/ms189858.aspx

The next question you might ask is, "How do I know if I should reorganize or rebuild my indexes?" As always in the SQL Server world, it depends.

You might consider doing both operations at different maintenance intervals where you would get some performance benefit out of a reorganization during a smaller maintenance window and then just perform rebuild indexes during a larger maintenance window. For example, you can run a nightly reorganization and then a weekly rebuild on the weekends. Moreover, you can also build some intelligence into your index maintenance jobs, based on whether you rebuild or reorganize indexes on the percentage of fragmentation on the index. Do note that it makes no sense to run both operations on a particular index at the same interval. Some folks set up maintenance routines that both rebuild and reorganize the same indexes in the same job. It's totally redundant to run these both at the same time and yield the same result to achieve the same objective, which is defragmenting your indexes. Do not get confused in that you can run both reorg and rebuild in the same job, just not against the same index.

Looking at the results of your `QuickIdxFrag` script, you can determine to rebuild or reorganize based on the results in the `avg_fragmentation_in_percent` column for each index. You don't need to rebuild every index in the entire database every time, especially in light of the time it takes to complete an index rebuild, especially on larger databases. You can apply certain logic to each index on a table, based on its own individual fragmentation. For example, just as a rough guideline, you may want to do a reorg when the percentage of fragmentation is between 5 and 30 percent and do a complete rebuild of the index when the percentage is higher than 30 percent. Or, you can choose to do nothing if fragmentation levels are below 5 to 10 percent.

In addition, you can build an intelligent index maintenance script that excludes certain large tables and/or partitions or stagger the rebuilds at varying intervals, such as rebuild all small tables on Monday through Thursday and rebuild only your largest tables beginning Friday night, or even exclude certain tables on certain days. Parameters to set the fill factor or pad the index are available as well. Furthermore, defrag a single database, a list of databases, or all databases on SQL Server. It is possible to even log the results of your index operations to a table.

There are so many possibilities and parameters you can use when addressing index fragmentation, and there are several scripts out there. In fact, one of my favorite index defrag maintenance script that I have used was created by SQL MVP colleague Michelle Ufford, aka SQLFool. Her Index Defrag Script v.4.1 is fully deployable, scalable, and compiled as a stored procedure (called `dba_sp_indexDefrag`) and has its own centralized repository for runtime statistics and logging. This index optimization process gives the user the ability to control its behavior and offers several parameters and runtime options. You can download the code and documentation here:

http://sqlfool.com/2011/06/index-defrag-script-v4-1/

One particular commonplace operation you should be aware of that causes index fragmentation is running shrink database and data file operations. First, running the DBCC ShrinkDB operation will itself cause index fragmentation and incur significant overhead in performance. As there are data and log files that could potentially be shrunk in size, DBCC Shrinkfile can individually shrink the data or log files, depending on the specified parameters.

Having said that, shrinking your log files is more acceptable than shrinking your data files. I would definitely try to avoid running a shrink on your data files. Since the operations to the transaction log are transient, you might very well decide to shrink the transaction log and attempt to reclaim unused space. The transaction log, if not properly managed, can and will grow out of control, often resulting in an out-of-disk-space error and stopping database transactions in its tracks. You can use the command DBCC SQLPERF(LOGSPACE) to specifically return the log size and the percentage of space used. Your log space report results will look like the following:

```
Database Name    Log Size (MB)   Log Space Used (%)   Status
ReportServer        6.867188           15.48635          0
ReportServerTempDB  1.054688           50.64815          0
TEST                0.9921875          48.96653          0
```

■ **Caution**   Avoid using ShrinkDB operations on your database!

The overall analysis is to minimize use of shrink operations on the database, unless you have to, in which case you can plan for some downtime and then remember to rebuild your indexes and leave sufficient space in the file after the shrink to allow for the rebuild, as well as to eliminate any fragmentation caused by shrink operations.

Missing Indexes

One of the most obvious reasons for poor SQL Server performance should be the fact that certain indexes are not available, or "missing," to the SQL Server query engine during query execution. The SQL Server optimizer looks for the best execution path it thinks will execute queries and return the selected data as fast as possible. Therefore, the optimizer will decide whether to use available indexes to retrieve the selected data. On the flip side, SQL Server even keeps track of queries that would perform a whole lot better if it had certain indexes on the tables being queried. Indexes that "could have been" used and suggested by the missing index features are known as missing indexes, and SQL Server keeps metadata about these possible missing indexes, exposing these index suggestions through specific DMVs, which makes finding missing indexes easier than before. Based on the queries stored in the plan cache and the number of executions, SQL Server can make valid suggestions for the structure of the indexes and creating the indexes.

You must be careful, though, not to completely rely on these missing index suggestions to create every single index suggested. Based on your SQL Server's actual index usage over time and by observing the same recurring queries, a missing index suggestion will be more valid. This means you must do an analysis of your workload over time and see whether the most frequently executed queries may benefit from the missing index suggestions. If you observe the top most expensive queries that are running against your SQL Server and correlate this with query execution counts, you might take advantage of missing index suggestions. However, if you are running a particular set of queries once a month, say for end-of-the-month reporting, a missing index suggestion here might be in vain since the index may be used infrequently.

I will now use the AdventureWorks2012 sample database to explain and demonstrate your missing index scripts.

I will demonstrate how the missing index feature works by using a simple SELECT statement from the Person.Address table: Where StateProvinceID=1. In your query window, use the AdventureWorks2012 database context and select the option Include Actual Execution Plan. You can do this from the menu bar by selecting Query and then Include Actual Execution Plan from the pop-up menu. You can also click the Execution Plan symbol; both are shown in Figure 4-3.

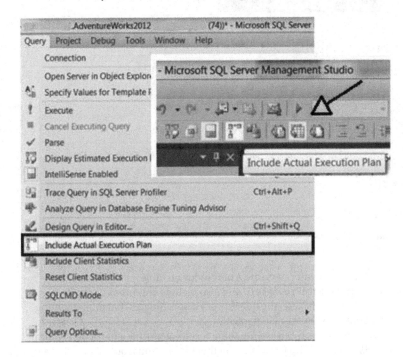

Figure 4-3. *Setting an include actual execution plan*

Now run the SELECT statement with the AW_StateProvinceID=1 script:

```
USE AdventureWorks2012;
GO
SELECT City, StateProvinceID, PostalCode FROM Person.Address
WHERE StateProvinceID = 1;
GO
```

As you will observe that with the Include Actual Execution Plan option turned on, when running a query, any missing indexes that the query optimizer thinks would have made the query faster, or would have chosen to use, are displayed there. In addition, the impact on performance and the CREATE statement for the suggested "missing" index are also shown. You can get the same information from the missing index views, which will be demonstrated in this section. If you were to run this query over and over again, you would likely need another index, a nonclustered index, to cover the columns that the clustered index does not have, in this case StateProvinceID. In addition, because the query also selects City and PostalCode, the optimizer suggests creating an index with these columns included.

In examining the first execution plan for this query, as shown in Figure 4-4, you will observe that the query engine is using a Clustered Index Scan operation to locate the fields of City, StateProvinceID, and PostalCode, where StateProvinceID=1. This means that every row in the table was searched to find all the records matching the WHERE clause, otherwise known as the *predicate*. Obviously, you want to narrow your search by limiting or filtering the results to a particularly parameter value. You predicate your query on the WHERE clause. In addition, the execution plan is also suggesting an index it could have used, based on this execution.

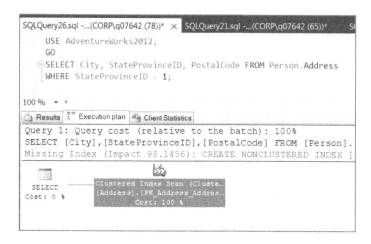

Figure 4-4. *Execution plan details clustered index scan*

Based on this one example, you can see that you can create a new index on table AdventureWorks.Person.Address on column StateProvinceID and also include columns City and PostalCode. According to the missing index details here, the query processor estimates that implementing the following index could improve the query cost by 98.1456 percent.

If you directly use your missing index views, you can see the same results as to how a particular column would benefit for a particular index. EQUALITY and INEQUALITY mean that the column would be used in a WHERE clause predicate. Predicates, as defined by Microsoft, are used in the search condition of WHERE clauses and HAVING clauses and also the join conditions of FROM clauses. So, for example, Equality_columns displays columns using equality predicates.

```
"Select * from employee where id = 2"
```

Inequality_columns displays columns using inequality predicates, as shown here:

```
"Select * from employee where id > 2"
```

INCLUDE means that the column should be an included column on an existing nonclustered index. I discussed this in the "Index Types and Terminology" section, with respect to indexes with included columns.

Using the missing index views, from where this missing index data is exposed, you can determine which ones to create, as well as other useful information such as a combination of avg_total_user_cost, avg_user_impact, user_seeks, and user_scans. You can run the following GetMissingIdxCreate script:

```
-- GetMissingIdxCreate script - Missing indexes with CREATE statement
SELECT MID.[statement] AS ObjectName
      ,MID.equality_columns AS EqualityColumns
      ,MID.inequality_columns AS InequalityColms
      ,MID.included_columns AS IncludedColumns
      ,MIGS.user_seeks
```

```
        ,MIGS.last_user_seek AS LastUserSeek
        ,MIGS.avg_total_user_cost
        ,MIGS.avg_user_impact
        ,N'CREATE NONCLUSTERED INDEX <Add Index Name here> ' +
        N'ON ' + MID.[statement] +
        N' (' + MID.equality_columns
             + ISNULL(', ' + MID.inequality_columns, N'') +
        N') ' + ISNULL(N'INCLUDE (' + MID.included_columns + N');', ';')
        AS CreateStatement
FROM sys.dm_db_missing_index_group_stats AS MIGS
    INNER JOIN sys.dm_db_missing_index_groups AS MIG
        ON MIGS.group_handle = MIG.index_group_handle
    INNER JOIN sys.dm_db_missing_index_details AS MID
        ON MIG.index_handle = MID.index_handle
WHERE database_id = DB_ID()
    AND MIGS.last_user_seek >= DATEDIFF(month, GetDate(), -1)
ORDER BY MIGS.avg_user_impact DESC;
```

Confirming the missing index data shown in the execution plan results, the output of the GetMissingIdxCreate shows you the following:

```
ObjectName     EqualityColumns      InequalityColms      IncludedColumns
1    [AdventureWorks2012].[Person].[Address]    [StateProvinceID]    NULL    [City],
[PostalCode]

user_seeks    LastUserSeek             avg_total_user_cost    avg_user_impact
1    2014-12-04 14:36:04.930    0.189827675555556      98.15

CreateStatement
CREATE NONCLUSTERED INDEX <Add Index Name here> ON [AdventureWorks2012].[Person].[Address]
([StateProvinceID]) INCLUDE ([City], [PostalCode]);
```

So, go ahead and run the CreateStProvID_NC_IDX script to create the index.

```
USE [AdventureWorks2012]
GO
CREATE NONCLUSTERED INDEX [<StProvID_NC_IDX, sysname,>]
ON [Person].[Address] ([StateProvinceID])
INCLUDE ([City],[PostalCode]);



SELECT mig.*, statement AS table_name,
column_id, column_name, column_usage
FROM sys.dm_db_missing_index_details AS mid
CROSS APPLY sys.dm_db_missing_index_columns (mid.index_handle)
INNER JOIN sys.dm_db_missing_index_groups AS mig
ON mig.index_handle = mid.index_handle
ORDER BY mig.index_group_handle, mig.index_handle, column_id;
```

Now check the execution plan again as shown in Figure 4-5. This time the plan uses the nonclustered index.

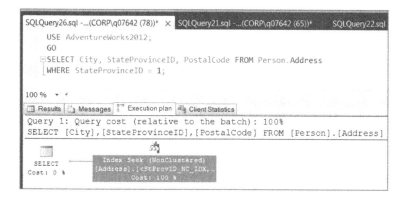

Figure 4-5. *Execution plan details index seek using the nonclustered index*

Making suggestions on what indexes should be added to a table has become somewhat easier with the missing index DMVs, as outlined in the section "Index-Related Dynamic Management Views and Functions." Even so, they do have their limitations; see this MSDN article:

```
http://msdn.microsoft.com/en-us/library/ms345485.aspx
```

For example, some limitations of the missing index features are that they do not suggest filtered indexes or even clustered indexes. They are definitely a good place to start and can be quite helpful in analyzing and adding necessary indexes, after the workload has been running a while to populate the table. Using the Database Tuning Advisor, based on server and query workload, as a supplement in your analysis is also recommended. You will be shown how to invoke and use the DTA later in this chapter.

Throughout my DBA travels, I have seen scripts for the top most expensive queries, and I have seen, as here, scripts to identify missing indexes. Wouldn't it be great if you could identify the top expensive queries as well as certain suggested missing indexes? I have searched high and wide for this solution and even tried to hack together a comprehensive T-SQL statement that would somehow join sys.dm_db_missing_index_ details and sys.dm_exec_query_plan together so I could correlate the missing index suggestions with the queries involved in those suggestions. I began working on this solution that involves joining an XML element to one of the regular T-SQL columns and blends both the use of T-SQL and XQuery.

While the topic of XQuery is beyond the scope for this book, since I make use of it here, you should have a rudimentary understanding of what it is. Basically, XQuery is to XML what SQL is to database tables. XQuery is designed to query XML data, not just XML files but anything that can appear as XML, including databases. XQuery is useful in finding and extracting elements and attributes from XML documents. Here is an MSDN article that is an XQuery language reference for SQL Server:

```
https://msdn.microsoft.com/en-us/library/ms189075.aspx
```

Essentially the key here is to join all the query/plan stat DMVs to the missing index DMVs, on the OBJECT_ID from sys.dm_db_missing_index_details, and the OBJECT_ID derived from the shredded XML. By concatenating these elements (the database, schema, and table) and passing them into the function Object_Id(), you are able to join all the DMVs and extract the information you're looking for.

At the same time I published my solution, my colleague SQL MVP Jason Brimhall published his as well. For completeness, I will include the link to his blog, and the script will be included in the e-book for download. Version 2 of the Missing Index Script, making use of T-SQL and XQuery, can be found here:

```
http://jasonbrimhall.info/2014/05/15/missing-indexes-script-v2/
```

Duplicate Indexes

Another performance penalty that frequently occurs is because of duplicate indexes, which can cause performance overhead such as slow inserts, updates, and deletes. There are several scenarios in which a duplicate index can occur, and the occurance of one is more often than not because of nonskilled developers or DBAs trying to increase the performance of a particular query by placing a new index on the target table based on their current query search parameters.

What is not understood is that without properly examining the existing indexes, such a devolper or DBA may cause more harm than good, at the cost of more I/O, CPU, and memory resources. This seems counterintuitive because the intention of placing an index on a table is to speed up performance and make your queries run faster.

So, the thinking often is that if a particular query or statement is running slow, then the solution must be to automatically add some indexes so the queries will run faster. After they create some indexes, their particular query does run faster for a while but quite likely at the expense of other, perhaps more critical queries.

Queries may be transient. In other words, it could be a one-time request, an ad hoc report, or something that is run fairly infrequently. What happens is that as database usage continues over time, indexes become less effective. This could simply be because of fragmentation, which you now know can be rebuilt. Queries will also get pushed out of cache, and then indexes that remain are not used. When this happens, a simple lack of knowledge may lead the DBA or developer to simply add another index, covering the same columns.

Indeed, nonclustered indexes are essential to query performance in SQL Server. Properly implemented nonclustered indexes can speed up your queries significantly and actually reduce I/O, CPU, and memory usage. However, duplicate indexes waste space and take resources during inserts, updates, and deletes. SQL Server may try to use all of the duplicate indexes or avoid them altogether.

The common scenarios that cause duplicate indexes are as follows:

- Creating a nonclustered covering index on the primary key

- Two indexes with the same fields but different included columns

- Another index with the same indexed columns, with a different name

In the case of creating a nonclustered index on the primary key, what happens is if the index doesn't get used, it still has to be maintained. That means, as discussed earlier, every insert, update, and delete requires updating both data pages and indexes, affecting the nonclustered index as well. When two indexes have the same fields with different included columns, this is redundant because the query optimizer will use only one of these indexes or may even ignore them altogether. So, there is no advantage of duplicate indexes; they just take up additional space. In the second scenario, you have an index with additional columns defined. This case is perhaps a bit more subtle but very common, where you have an index on columns A and B and then create another index on columns A, B, and C. Finally, in the third scenario, a second index covers the same fields with a different name. So, you create an index on columns A, B, and C called ABCIndex and then inadvertently, perhaps without observing an existing index, create another second index with columns A, B, and C, calling it IndexABC.

You can find duplicate indexes by identifying the common scenarios as described in the previous paragraph and using the following FindDupIdx script. This script will provide you with the database, table, index, and included column names, as well as the index type and whether the index key is unique or a primary key. You are also provided with the page count, size of the index, and fragmentation percent to help you determine further what the impact of the duplicate indexes might have on the database.

```
IF OBJECT_ID (N'tempdb.dbo.#GetDupIdx') IS NOT NULL
    DROP TABLE #GetDupIdx

CREATE TABLE #GetDupIdx
(
      [Database Name] varchar(500),
      [Table Name] varchar(1000),
      [Index Name] varchar(1000),
      [Indexed Column Names] varchar(1000),
      [Index Type]  varchar(50),
      [Unique] char(1),
      [Primary Key] char(1),
      [Page Count] int,
      [Size (MB)] int,
      [Fragment %] int

)

Declare @db_name sysname
DECLARE c_db_names CURSOR FOR
SELECT name
FROM sys.databases
WHERE name NOT IN('tempdb') --can exclude other databases

OPEN c_db_names

FETCH c_db_names INTO @db_name

WHILE @@Fetch_Status = 0
BEGIN
  EXEC('Use ' + @db_name + ';
WITH FindDupIdx AS
(

SELECT DISTINCT sys.objects.name AS [Table Name],
    sys.indexes.name AS [Index Name],
    sys.indexes.type_desc AS [Index Type],
    Case sys.indexes.is_unique
        When 1 then ''Y''
        When 0 then ''N'' End AS [Unique],
    Case sys.indexes.is_primary_key
        When 1 then ''Y''
        When 0 then ''N'' End AS [Primary Key],
    SUBSTRING((SELECT '', '' + sys.columns.Name as [text()]
            FROM sys.columns
            INNER JOIN sys.index_columns
                ON sys.index_columns.column_id = sys.columns.column_id
                AND sys.index_columns.object_id = sys.columns.object_id
        WHERE sys.index_columns.index_id = sys.indexes.index_id
            AND sys.index_columns.object_id = sys.indexes.object_id
            AND sys.index_columns.is_included_column = 0
```

```
            ORDER BY sys.columns.name
        FOR XML Path('''')), 2, 10000) AS [Indexed Column Names],
        ISNULL(SUBSTRING((SELECT '', '' + sys.columns.Name as [text()]
            FROM sys.columns
                INNER JOIN sys.index_columns
                ON sys.index_columns.column_id = sys.columns.column_id
                AND sys.index_columns.object_id = sys.columns.object_id
            WHERE sys.index_columns.index_id = sys.indexes.index_id
                AND sys.index_columns.object_id = sys.indexes.object_id
                AND sys.index_columns.is_included_column = 1
            ORDER BY sys.columns.name
            FOR XML Path('''')), 2, 10000), '''') AS [Included Column Names],
        sys.indexes.index_id, sys.indexes.object_id
FROM sys.indexes
    INNER JOIN SYS.index_columns
        ON sys.indexes.index_id = SYS.index_columns.index_id
        AND sys.indexes.object_id = sys.index_columns.object_id
    INNER JOIN sys.objects
        ON sys.OBJECTS.object_id = SYS.indexes.object_id
    WHERE sys.objects.type = ''U''
)
 INSERT INTO #GetDupIdx (
 [Database Name],[Table Name],[Index Name],[Indexed Column Names],
 [Index Type],[Unique], [Primary Key],
 [Page Count],[Size (MB)],[Fragment %]
 )
  SELECT DB_NAME(),FindDupIdx.[Table Name],
     FindDupIdx.[Index Name],
     FindDupIdx.[Indexed Column Names],
     FindDupIdx.[Index Type],
     FindDupIdx.[Unique],
     FindDupIdx.[Primary Key],
     PhysicalStats.page_count as [Page Count],
     CONVERT(decimal(18,2), PhysicalStats.page_count * 8 / 1024.0) AS [Size (MB)],
     CONVERT(decimal(18,2), PhysicalStats.avg_fragmentation_in_percent) AS [Fragment %]
FROM FindDupIdx
    INNER JOIN sys.dm_db_index_physical_stats (DB_ID(), NULL, NULL, NULL, NULL)
        AS PhysicalStats
        ON PhysicalStats.index_id = FindDupIdx.index_id
            AND PhysicalStats.object_id = FindDupIdx.object_id
WHERE (SELECT COUNT(*) as Computed
        FROM FindDupIdx Summary2
        WHERE Summary2.[Table Name] = FindDupIdx.[Table Name]
            AND Summary2.[Indexed Column Names] = FindDupIdx.[Indexed Column Names]) > 1
            AND FindDupIdx.[Index Type] <> ''XML''
ORDER BY [Table Name], [Index Name], [Indexed Column Names], [Included Column Names]
  ')
  FETCH c_db_names INTO @db_name
END
```

```
CLOSE c_db_names
DEALLOCATE c_db_names

SELECT * FROM #GetDupIdx
```

Here is a subset of the results for the AdventureWorks2012 database:

```
Database Name           Table Name   Index Name                     Indexed Column Names
AdventureWorks2012      Address      <StProvID_NC_IDX, sysname,>    StateProvinceID
AdventureWorks2012      Address      NC_STPROV_CITY_ADD_1_2_PC      StateProvinceID
Included Column Names
City, PostalCode
AddressID, AddressLine1, AddressLine2, City, PostalCode
Index Type      Unique     Primary Key
NONCLUSTERED    N     N
NONCLUSTERED    N     N
Page Count    Size (MB)      Fragment %
    116          0          0
    211          1          22
```

Sometimes the missing index feature or even the Database Tuning Advisor (discussed in the next section) could make a duplicate index suggestion. However, none of these are 100 percent accurate, and it depends on your sample workload. Identifying and removing duplicate indexes will actually increase your query performance. Remember, it's more art than science!

Database Engine Tuning Advisor

The Database Engine Tuning Advisor (DTA) can analyze your workload, whether it's a T-SQL statement from a file, a table, or the queries in the plan cache, and can make recommendations about creating the best possible indexes and indexed views and partitions. Specifically, the DTA can make recommendations such as the best mix of indexes for databases by using the query optimizer to analyze queries in a workload. The DTA will recommend aligned or nonaligned partitions for databases referenced in a workload, as well as recommend indexed views for databases referenced in a workload. The DTA can make recommendations to tune the database for a small set of most costly and problematic queries.

In addition, the DTA will analyze the effects of the proposed changes, including index usage, query distribution among tables, and query performance in the workload. The DTA can even customize the recommendation by specifying advanced options such as disk space constraints. It can provide reports that summarize the effects of implementing the recommendations for a given workload. Consider alternatives in which you supply possible design choices in the form of hypothetical configurations for the Database Engine Tuning Advisor to evaluate.

To launch the DTA, from SQL Server Management Studio, go to the menu bar and select Tools and then Database Engine Tuning Advisor from the pop-up menu, as shown in Figure 4-6.

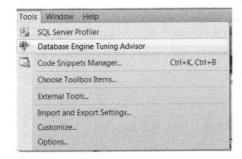

Figure 4-6. *Launching the Database Engine Tuning Advisor*

You will be prompted with a screen, as shown in Figure 4-7, to connect to the SQL Server instance you will be running the DTA against. Provide your credentials that you use for that SQL Server and click Connect.

Figure 4-7. *Connecting to the server for the DTA*

The DTA will be launched, and the General tab will be displayed, as in Figure 4-8; all the databases on the server for which you can select for tuning recommendations will be shown. You can also drill down on the databases and select individual tables to tune. You can give a session name and select databases that the DTA will analyze the workload. For the workload, you can choose to use a file or table or analyze the workload based on the queries residing in the plan cache. For more independent learning about the DTA, visit the following MSDN article on the Database Engine Tuning Advisor:

```
http://msdn.microsoft.com/en-us/library/ms166575.aspx
```

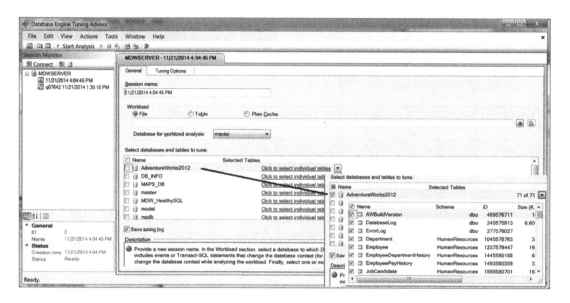

Figure 4-8. *DTA choosing workload analysis and database/tables*

If you click the Tuning Options tabs, as shown in Figure 4-9, you can provide more specific parameters to make recommendations on, including additional index structures, a partitioning strategy, and whether to keep the existing physical design structure (PDS) in the database. Moreover, you should limit the tuning time to a specific period and provide a stop date and time. You can explore any advanced options as well.

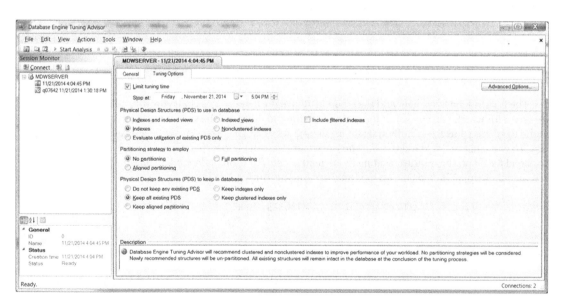

Figure 4-9. *DTA Tuning Options tab*

Once you have provided enough information for the DTA to analyze a workload, you are ready to start the analysis. You can do this by clicking the Start Analysis button on the top just below the menu bar. Starting the analysis, as in Figure 4-10, will show the progress of submitting the configuration options you selected, consume the workload, begin the analysis, and finally generate reports with its recommendations.

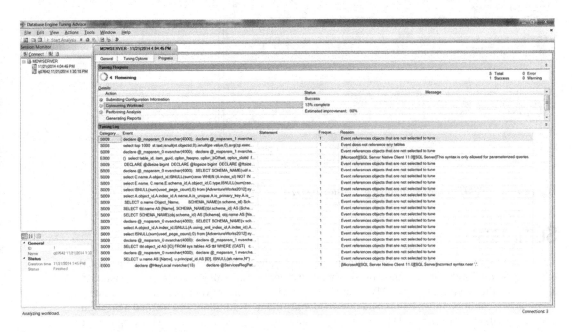

Figure 4-10. *DTA showing analysis in progress*

As the analysis proceeds, you will see details appear in the tuning log, showing the statements being analyzed, how often they are being executed, and a reason code.

When the DTA analysis completes, you will see additional tabs appear, such as the Recommendations tab, as shown Figure 4-11, with an improvement estimate, partition, and/or index recommendation. Since the workload that was analyzed for this book was based on queries in plan cache, the DTA is making a similar "missing index" suggestion to what you saw earlier when using the related DMVs. The advantage to using the DTA is that the analysis is more thorough.

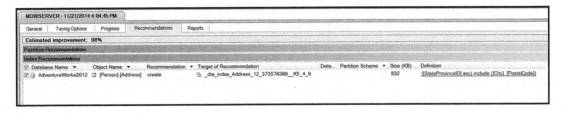

Figure 4-11. *DTA recommendations and improvement estimate*

If you click the metadata in the Definition column, you can get the CREATE INDEX statement that is recommended for performance. Figure 4-12 shows an example. You can copy that statement to the clipboard and execute the script via SSMS.

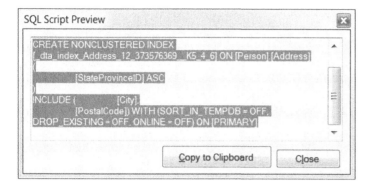

Figure 4-12. CREATE INDEX *statement generated by DTA*

Summary

You should now be intimately familiar with the basics of indexes, including the types of indexes, their advantages and disadvantages, and how they affect the performance of your SQL Server instances. You also learned the essential system DMVs available to provide all sorts of valuable index metadata usage and analysis, common index issues, and how to identify them. In addition, you learned a bit about index internals and structure, fill factors, and page splitting. You were informed of the importance of where to place indexes, having a proper index strategy, and how this impacts the overall system performance. Moreover, you learned to use the Database Tuning Advisor to analyze workloads and make recommendations for adding indexes and improving performance.

Finally, you looked at an industry-known downloadable free tool called the Index Defrag Script, which every DBA responsible for database performance optimization and maintenance should have their toolbox. In Chapters 5 and 6, you will be given many more tools and scripts to better manage your DBA work.

CHAPTER 5

Tools of the Trade: Basic Training

This chapter will discuss some key tools, utilities, and scripts provided by Microsoft SQL MVPs; these are people who are continuously in the field with their clients and have created tools that offer a better way to collect and analyze data, helping the SQL community and users of SQL Server worldwide. MVPs are indeed a charitable bunch, which makes their dedication and loyalty to the Microsoft SQL Server stack a unique character trait that has earned them MVP status. I have used these tools throughout my own DBA career and will direct you to where you can acquire and learn more about them.

In addition, Microsoft engineers have provided many tools and methodologies to mine, monitor, and troubleshoot performance issues. (Remember, you just spent a whole chapter diving into waits and queues.) For example, system views expose SQL Server's health metadata via dynamic management objects (views and functions), and with each new version, you can benefit from the available tool sets in the native SQL Server product. This chapter will demonstrate how to leverage these native tools out of the box, as well as improve upon them with your own customizations.

Build a Better Mousetrap

There is a saying that "if you build a better mousetrap, the world will beat a path to your door." I always interpreted this as if you build a good invention, folks will take notice and use it. So, in that context, let's talk about tools of the trade. The best part about this chapter is that if you have already purchased this book, there will be no additional costs to learn about and obtain the excellent *free* tools available that you should be using in your daily DBA life.

Indeed, you will see that with respect to capturing performance data and doing health checks there is more than one way to skin a cat, meaning there are several solutions and tools that get the job done. I will discuss an array of available tools, scripts, and features that will assist you in getting to and achieving a healthy SQL environment. In the end, you will choose the tools that are right for you and your own comfort level, your SQL Server environment, and your company's needs.

Once you know all the available options, you'll be able to decide which works best for the situation and use the tools effortlessly in managing, monitoring, and reporting on SQL Server health and performance. You will be well armed using the various tools, scripts, and automated methods discussed in this chapter. Once you understand how to use them, you will be on your way to a healthy SQL Server environment and to ensuring SQL fitness.

Sometimes, the available tools are just not sufficient for what you need, and in those cases, you can extend the functionality (or, simply put, build a better mousetrap). I will provide some examples of a do-it-yourself performance package and leverage the available DMOs and other features in SQL Server to show how to create a custom automated health-check system. I already spoke about what information you should collect, and now I will show you how.

As a DBA, you know how monotonous some daily DBA tasks can be, especially when you are responsible for supporting dozens and even hundreds of SQL Server systems. How can you possibly keep track of all them, all the time? Are there a handful of SQL Server instances running slowly? Wouldn't it be great to automate these routines as much as possible? The following are some of the most routine and essential DBA tasks:

- Review the OS event and SQL Server logs for atypical events and errors.

- Make sure that all the SQL Server services are online, up and running, and that there are no cluster failovers.

- Make sure that all databases are online, accessible, and not corrupt.

- Verify that all backup and scheduled maintenance and batch jobs have actually started, completed, and run successfully. That is, make sure they are not hanging.

- Validate the backups and ensure they are successfully saved to a secure location.

- Make sure that none of your SQL Server drives have run out of disk space or that space is too low.

- Check database sizes and growth, also making sure transaction logs didn't run out of space.

- Check to see whether there are any blocking issues or deadlocks that have occurred.

- Analyze any available performance data for any deviations from your baseline.

- Maintain a record of any changes made to SQL Server, including recent code deployments, schema changes, new indexes, and configurations.

Monday Morning Mania (Busiest DBA Day)

Indeed, the morning is one of the busiest times for a DBA, especially when there have been recent change deployments or overnight events that users are just becoming aware of. Often, because of the law of averages and poor planning for code releases, the morning after the weekend causes chaos for the production DBA. Monday mornings are tough enough to get things off the ground, but throw an unorganized, barely tested new code fix or enhancement into the mix on Friday evening or over the weekend, and Mondays can be the most dreaded day of the week for DBAs. Beware, this is the "blame game" in the making!

The last thing you want to happen when coming in to the office, maybe even just getting off 24/7 support rotation, is that users and managers are lined up at your desk with complaints of failed jobs, missing or corrupt data, down servers, or slow performance. Such is the life of a DBA, and this puts you firmly in reactive mode. What I aim to do here is get you into proactive mode. Once you implement the healthy SQL health-check tools and processes, you will be on your way to being a proactive DBA.

In most cases, performing regular health checks as well as monitoring will prevent most surprises, ensure that your SQL Server environment is performing optimally, and allow you as the DBA to get in front of any potentially serious issues. By being proactive, like I am advocating in this book, the DBA will often discover issues, through automated health checks and performance monitoring, before anyone else does and, most importantly, before escalation. That is the goal here, which will put you, the DBA, in a position of strength and create real value perception.

■ **Note** By being proactive, the DBA will often discover issues before anyone else and before escalation and potentially resolve it.

As I've mentioned, in this chapter I will empower you with tools of the trade so you can perform your own health checks. In Chapter 7, I will talk about monitoring solutions in-depth and leveraging available SQL Server features to help do the job. You will learn how to create SQL Server alerts to notify you of potential problems, via e-mail, which will enable you to decide which action to take as necessary. In the meantime, let's get to the hardware store and pick up some of our DBA tools and get to work.

The best part about Microsoft SQL Server is that it is no longer a simple database engine that sits by itself and uses Transact-SQL (T-SQL) to query its data. SQL Server is a fully featured end-to-end business intelligence database platform with a rich set of tools. Many of them stand alone and are intuitive GUI tools that make it easy for anyone managing the databases to see current and historical activity and monitor SQL Server. Other lesser-known features are just as powerful but need some scripting for maximum data exposure and user-friendly output.

If the number of SQL Server instances you manage are few, then using a spreadsheet is probably the easiest and quickest way to store the data you collect. If you have many SQL Server instances, then you need to automate the health-check process and store the data in a database. However, if you don't have the time to automate your health checks, then doing it manually with a spreadsheet is better than doing nothing at all.

The following are the available features in SQL Server to help monitor the health of your database infrastructure:

- Activity Monitor

- Out of the box: activity and performance reports from SSMS

- T-SQL, DMOs: System views and functions, system stored procedures

- SQL Trace/Profiler/X-Events

- PowerShell

- Management data warehouse (MDW): SQL Server 2008

Here are some of the Windows OS and Microsoft tools that can assist with your health check:

- System and event logs

- Performance Monitor

- SQL Server Performance Monitor (Data Collector)

- Performance Analysis of Logs (PAL)

- SQL Server Best Practices Analyzer (through 2012)

Let's briefly discuss these so that you can learn your way around the product and some ways to view useful performance and usage statistics.

Activity Monitor

The quickest and interactive way to view current activity and performance reports on your SQL Server instance is by using SQL Server Management Studio. Let's wade into the kiddie pool and talk about Activity Monitor. Then you'll take a look at the available built-in reports at both the server and database levels. Once you have your feet wet, you will dive into more challenging and technical techniques to not only capture raw performance data but to trend, archive, and report on it.

You can access Activity Monitor via Object Explorer. Select and right-click your desired SQL Server instance at the top-level folder and then select Activity Monitor from the pop-up menu, as displayed in Figure 5-1. You can also open Activity Monitor by pressing Ctrl+Alt+A. Activity Monitor will show you server-level information.

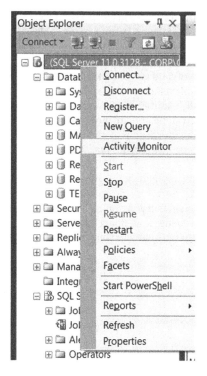

Figure 5-1. *Accessing Activity Monitor from SSMS*

On the Activity Monitor tab, you will see in the Overview section some graphs, including Percentage Processor Time, Waiting Tasks, Database I/O (MB/sec), and Batch Requests/sec. By default, Activity Monitor refreshes every ten seconds, but you can change this interval by right-clicking Overview and selecting the desired refresh interval. You will also see in the Overview section four expandable sections, showing live performance and activity data for current processes, resource waits, data file I/O, and recently captured expensive queries.

Activity Monitor, as shown in Figure 5-2, is a graphical user interface that visually represents the data exposed in the many DMOs discussed in this book. Because information is derived from underlying DMOs, Activity Monitor requires at least VIEW SERVER STATE permissions to view the data if you are not a member of the sysadmin role. Please note, in addition to VIEW SERVER STATE, you'll need to also have CREATE DATABASE, ALTER ANY DATABASE, or VIEW ANY DEFINITION permission to be able to view the Data File I/O section of Activity Monitor.

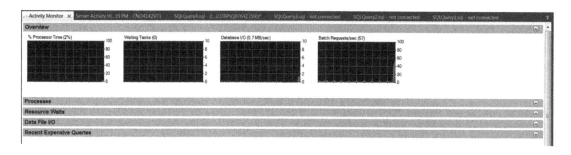

Figure 5-2. *Activity Monitor tab's Overview section with unexpanded sections*

In the Processes section, as shown in Figure 5-3, you can see detailed data for active users/current processes, including the session ID, database, task status, wait stats for each process, blocking, and memory.

Session ID	U...	L...	D...	Task...	Command	Application	Wait Time (ms)	Wait Type	Wait Resource	Blocked By	Head Blocker	H...	Memory Use (...	Workload Group
56	1	CORP...	master			Microsoft SQL ...	0					CND4...	16	default
60	1	CORP...	tempdb	RUNNING	SELECT	Microsoft SQL ...	0					CND4...	24	default
59	1	CORP...	MAPS...			Microsoft SQL ...	0					CND4...	16	default
58	1	NT S...	Repor...			Report Server	0					CND4...	16	default
66	1	NT S...	Repor...			Report Server	0					CND4...	16	default
55	1	NT S...	msdb			SQL Server Da...	0					CND4...	16	default
62	1	NT S...	msdb			SQL Server Da...	0					CND4...	16	default
63	1	NT S...	msdb			SQL Server Da...	0					CND4...	16	default
65	1	NT S...	msdb			SQL Server Da...	0					CND4...	16	default

Figure 5-3. *Output of current processes via Activity Monitor*

The information in Figure 5-3 is similar to the sp_who2 output and to a combination of the DMVs sys.dm_exec_sessions and sys.dm_exec_requests. You can right-click this section for more options to get the statement details associated with a session, to "kill" the process, and to trace it in SQL Profiler, which will open a separate Profiler window.

In the Resource Waits section (in Figure 5-4), you can view the actual wait stats, based on the sys.dm_os_wait_stats DMO, as discussed in the previous chapter, along with the wait category, wait time, cumulative wait time, and so on. You can sort and filter out wait categories and types, as well as sort by the different column data, by clicking the arrows on each column.

Resource Waits

Wait Category	Wait Time (ms/sec)	Recent Wait Time...	Average Waiter Count	Cumulative Wait Time (sec)
Buffer I/O	0	0	0.0	11
Buffer Latch	0	0	0.0	0
Latch	0	0	0.0	0
Lock	0	0	0.0	25
Logging	0	0	0.0	245
Memory	0	0	0.0	0
Network I/O	0	0	0.0	8
Other	0	0	0.0	9

Figure 5-4. *Resource waits displayed via Activity Monitor*

In this section (Figure 5-5), you can see I/O usage statistics, per file, based on the sys.dm_io_virtual_file_stats view as well as sys.master_files. I discussed this in Chapter 3.

Data File I/O

Database	File Name	MB/sec Read	MB/sec Written	Response Time (ms)
tempdb	C:\Program Files\Microsoft SQL Server\MSSQL11.MS...	0.0	0.0	1
Corp...	C:\Program Files\Microsoft SQL Server\MSSQL11.MS...	0.0	0.0	0
Corp...	C:\Program Files\Microsoft SQL Server\MSSQL11.MS...	0.0	0.0	0
MAPS_DB	C:\Program Files\Microsoft SQL Server\MSSQL11.MS...	0.0	0.0	0
MAPS_DB	C:\Program Files\Microsoft SQL Server\MSSQL11.MS...	0.0	0.0	0
master	C:\Program Files\Microsoft SQL Server\MSSQL11.MS...	0.0	0.0	0
master	C:\Program Files\Microsoft SQL Server\MSSQL11.MS...	0.0	0.0	0
model	C:\Program Files\Microsoft SQL Server\MSSQL11.MS...	0.0	0.0	0
model	C:\Program Files\Microsoft SQL Server\MSSQL11.MS...	0.0	0.0	0

Figure 5-5. *Data file I/O stats via Activity Monitor view*

Finally, in the Recent Expensive Queries section (Figure 5-6), you can have a quick view of the recent expensive queries running on the system. The information is derived from the union of `sys.dm_exec_requests` and `sys.dm_exec_query_stats` and includes queries in process and queries that finished over the last 30 seconds. You can further view the execution plan for each query by right-clicking the desired query and selecting Show Execution Plan or the query text Edit Query Text.

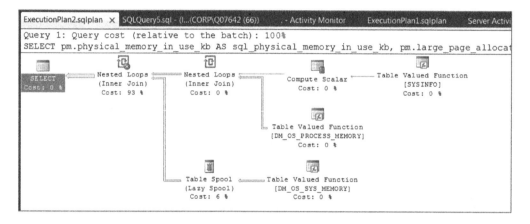

Figure 5-6. *Top expensive queries and stats via Activity Monitor*

Figure 5-7 is an example of the execution plan for an individual query, launched from Activity Monitor.

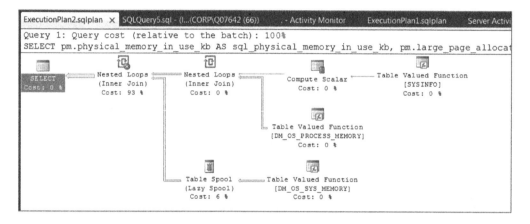

Figure 5-7. *Execution plan for an individual query, launched from Activity Monitor*

■ **Caution**   Because Activity Monitor is a GUI that continuously pulls metadata from the DMOs, you don't want to leave it open indefinitely. It is used for immediate short-term analysis and can itself cause potential performance overhead on the server.

---

sp_whoisactive

If you're looking for something a little bit more advanced and definitely GUI-free, the terrific T-SQL custom stored procedure `sp_whoisactive` might interest you. Intended to be a way to instantly see all of the current active sessions and user activity on the server, the award-winning `sp_whoisactive` (from SQL MVP Adam Machanic) can show you what is happening right now on the server. This neat stored procedure is well-coded, well-documented, well-maintained, and well-reviewed, and it is a popular download among the SQL Server DBA community. It is the T-SQL equivalent of the current Activity Monitor, and I consider sp_whoisactiveto besp_who and sp_who2 on steroids. It allows you to identify immediate issues such as blocking, locking, waits, and so on. Also, it can correlate execution plans, find the open transactions and queries involved, and allow you to quickly triage and troubleshoot performance bottlenecks and resource contention.

If you go to http://sqlblog.com/tags/Who+is+Active/default.aspx, the site founded by Adam Machanic, you will find the latest download links, bug fixes, enhancements, and discussion blogs on this T-SQL utility. Adam even has a 30-part blog series called "Twenty Nine Days of Activity Monitoring," primarily discussing sp_whoisactive design, development, and usage. The latest version as of this writing is v.11.11, compatible with SQL Server 2005 and 2008, although I've run it on SQL Server 2012. Nonetheless, it's something easily deployed and runnable as a single T-SQL script to create the stored procedure and execute.

```
Exec dbo.sp_WhoIsActive
```

■ **Note** The sp_WhoIsActive stored procedure is created in the master database and may be deleted during SQL Server upgrades or migration. You need to re-create it if that happens.

SSMS Standard Reports

For the DBA, there are also a set of standard reports straight out of the box and accessible through SQL Server Management Studio (SSMS).

The SQL Server Reporting Services development framework allows you to create custom reports and import them into SQL Server. The available canned reports are at the server and database levels. There are a host of ready-to-run configuration, activity, and performance reports.

Server-Level Reports

The reports discussed in this section will report on activity at the server level. To access the server-level reports available in SSMS, connect to the SQL Server node, right-click it, select Reports, click Standard Reports, and pick any report (see Figure 5-8).

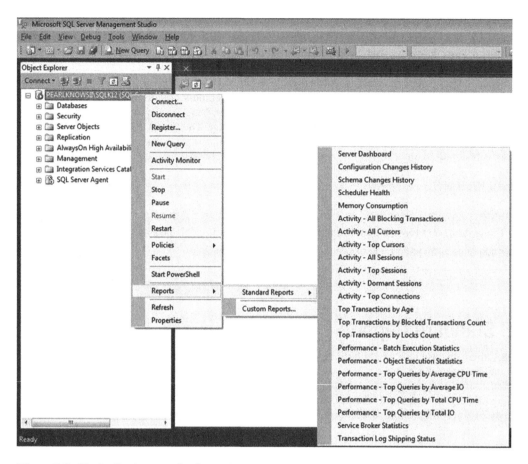

Figure 5-8. *Navigating to server-level reports*

Database Reports

The reports in the Databases section refer to the reports generated for activity at the database level. To access the database-level reports, connect to the SQL Server node, navigate to the Databases folder, select and right-click Database, select Reports, click Standard Reports, and pick any report (see Figure 5-9).

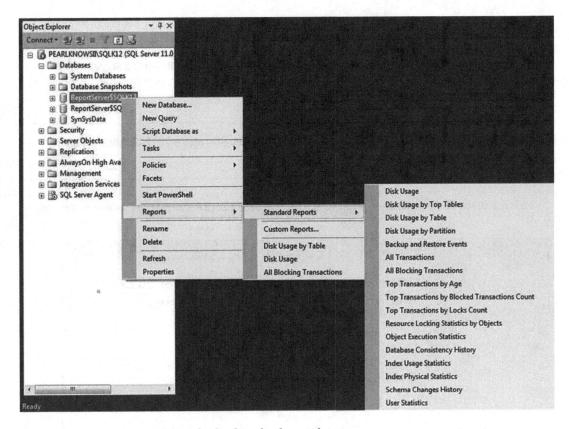

Figure 5-9. *Navigating in SSMS to the database-level canned reports*

As you can see, there are many available SSMS standard reports; this is just a short list. Buck Woody, a well-known senior Microsoft technologist, has cataloged the full list of SQL Server performance and activity reports, along with complete documentation, aptly titled "SQL Server Management Studio Standard Reports – The Full List." You can access this list at http://bit.ly/SSMS_ReportList.

SQL Server 2012 Performance Dashboard

In addition to the standard reports, you can take a look at the SQL Server 2012 Performance Dashboard Reports. Any DBA can use these reports to quickly identify whether their SQL Server instance has any current bottlenecks and report on and capture additional diagnostic data to triage and resolve the problem.

Common performance problems that the dashboard reports may help to resolve include the following:

- CPU bottlenecks (and what queries are consuming the most CPU)

- I/O bottlenecks (and what queries are performing the most I/O)

- Index recommendations generated by the query optimizer (missing indexes)

- Blocking

- Latch contention

123

The information captured in the reports is retrieved from SQL Server's dynamic management views. There is no additional tracing or data capture required, which means the information is always available; this is an inexpensive means of monitoring your server.

The good thing, even with these Performance Dashboard Reports, is that Reporting Services is not required to be installed to use them. Even though they are Reporting Services report files, they are designed to be used with SQL Server Management Studio's Custom Reports feature.

■ **Note**   Before you proceed with this section, please download the SQL Server 2012 dashboard from www.microsoft.com/en-us/download/details.aspx?id=29063.

Figure 5-10 shows the installation setup screen for SQL Server 2012 Performance Dashboard Reports.

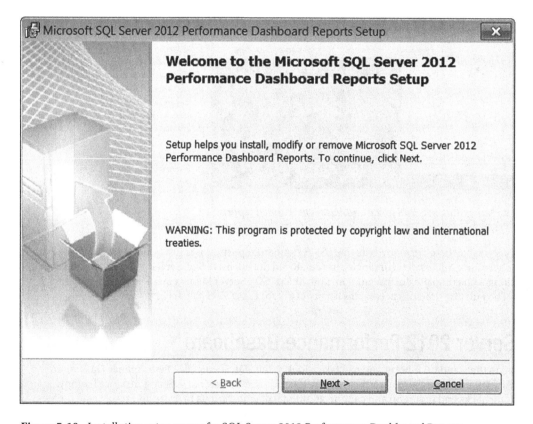

Figure 5-10.   Installation setup screen for SQL Server 2012 Performance Dashboard Reports

Once you download and install them using a simple installation wizard, where you just follow all the prompts, all the .rdl report files and scripts will be deployed for you in the Tools folder of your default SQL Server installation path. To get to the reporting dashboard, you navigate via SSMS to the instance level, right-click Reports, and select Custom Reports. Then, you need to browse to the path of your SQL Server installation and Performance Dashboard folder (for example, C:\Program Files (x86)\Microsoft SQL Server\110\Tools\Performance Dashboard) and select the performance_dashboard_main.rdl file, as shown in Figure 5-11.

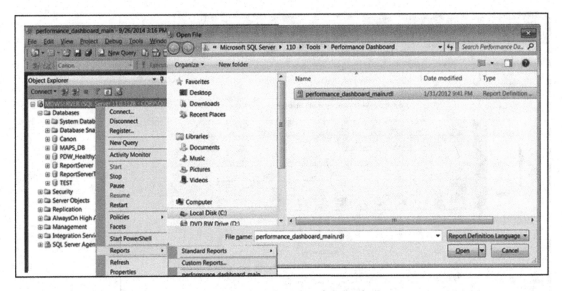

Figure 5-11. *A combo of the Custom Reports pop-up menu and dialog box*

When you launch `performance_dashboard_main.rdl`, the main landing screen will look like Figure 5-12, and you can drill down to the other detail reports.

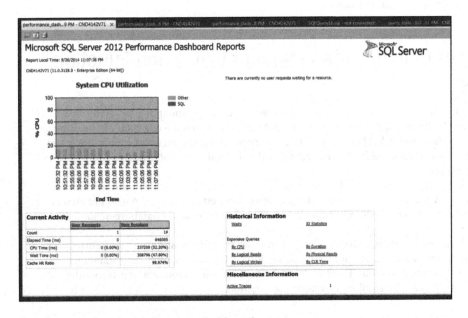

Figure 5-12. *The main performance dashboard*

The dashboard has links that you can follow to get further details. Figure 5-13 shows an example of the Historical Waits by wait category and graph.

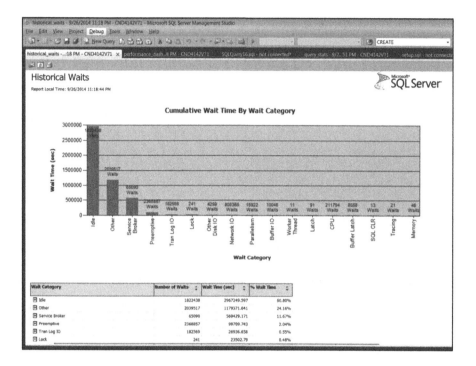

Figure 5-13. *Sample report of historical waits*

The Power of Dynamic Management Views and Function Categories

I have already mentioned and showed how to use various dynamic management objects (DMO views and functions), but now I'll break them down a bit, categorize them, and discuss the ones you will be using to create your automated health check. They are an extremely useful and powerful set of system views and functions that give information in the form of metadata, in-depth details, and internals about the state and health of your SQL Server.

There are available views at the both the server and database levels. As mentioned earlier in the book, they require VIEW SERVER STATE permission for server-scoped dynamic management views and functions and require VIEW DATABASE STATE permission on the database for database-scoped dynamic views and functions.

This rich and invaluable metadata gives you insight into server (SQLOS) and database information, index-related information, processes, connections, transactions, I/O statistics, query and statement execution data, wait statistics, and more. These DMOs have naming conventions each corresponding to their inherent purpose. Table 5-1 describes the naming convention.

Table 5-1. *Internal Naming Convention of DMOs*

Naming Convention	Description
Db	Database-related information
Exec	Query execution–related information
Io	I/O statistics
Os	SQL Server Operating System (SQLOS) information
tran	Transaction-related information

As of SQL Server 2014, there are more than 200 DMOs, prefixed with sys.dm _ stored in the master database. You can see them via SSMS by drilling down in the master database. For views, go to databases ➤ system databases ➤ views ➤ system views and functions under master ➤ programmability ➤ functions ➤ system functions ➤ table-valued functions. Using T-SQL, you can see all the available views and functions on the server, as well as distinguish each type of dynamic management view or function from sys.sysobjects.

```
SELECT [name] ,
CASE [type]
WHEN 'V' THEN 'DMV'
WHEN 'IF' THEN 'DMF'
END AS [DMO Type]
FROM [sys].[sysobjects]
WHERE [name] LIKE 'dm_%'
ORDER BY [name] ;
```

The T-SQL query language makes it easy to join various DMOs as well as sort and filter data, which could not be done with Activity Monitor. I have already provided a number of scripts that allow you to derive useful results and user-friendly output.

If you want to find out details on each DMO, you can consult http://msdn.microsoft.com/en-us/library/ms188754.aspx, which is an MSDN article that sorts them by category and allows you to drill down on them. Definitely bookmark any dynamic management views and functions you want to know about for your future and ongoing reference (because they are updated with each version release of SQL Server).

sys.dm_os_performance_counters (How to Read and Calculate Them)

An extremely useful DMV that I use frequently while monitoring performance is sys.dm_os_performance_counters. This view exposes the raw data from the Perfmon counters. It collects and updates the SQL Server–related counters with this view when queried, returning a row for each performance counter. By default, it stores raw value data that is not very useful for analysis, unless it is interpreted in the right way. This means you need to have the right formula to calculate some of the values and also get the deltas between two time periods for other values. First run the select ALL statement on the view to ensure your counters are enabled. If no values are returned, then you need to enable them using lodctr, which is a Windows command-line utility that updates registry values related to performance counters.

```
Select * from sys.dm_os_performance_counters
```

If you select directly from sys.dm_os_performance_counters, some of the values you find in the cntr_value column might not make much sense, especially if you compare them with the performance counter values you get from Performance Monitor. The reason for this is that sys.dm_os_performance_counters doesn't give you completely calculated performance counter values, like Performance Monitor does.

Therefore, the way you calculate the values depend on the type of counter, specified by an integer value in the cntr_type column. The cntr_type column identifies the type of counter in that row and dictates how the counter is calculated. The cntr_type column in sys.dm_os_performance_counters has these distinct values, as of SQL Server 2005 and higher: 65792, 272696576, 537003264, 1073939712, and 1073874176. So, to categorize the counter types, you have the following:

- Point-in-time counters
- Ratio counters
- Delta counters
- Delta ratio counters

The point-in-time counters correlate to the raw data current value. Ratio counters are the ones that must be calculated by comparing the base counters. Delta counters are the ones you need to sample by calculating the changes in value from one point-in-time interval to the next and are the per-second counters. Finally, the delta ratio counters are a cross between the two previously described counter types, where you calculate a ratio between the delta values. The delta ratio counters come in the form of the "average counters" such as Average Latch Wait Time (ms) and Average Wait Time (ms).

How it all works is like this: Based on the Windows Performance Monitor documentation, counter type 65792 is named PERF_COUNTER_LARGE_RAWCOUNT. A counter of this type (such as the Buffer Manager's Free pages counter) shows the last value measured from the source. Type 272696576 is named PERF_COUNTER_BULK_COUNT. A counter of this type (such as the Buffer Manager's Page reads/sec counter) shows the average number of operations completed per second during the sample interval. These are distinguished as the "per-second" counters in which the delta is calculated. SQL Server already calculates the values of these two counter types for you: counter type 537003264 (called PERF_LARGE_RAW_FRACTION) and type 1073939712 (called PERF_LARGE_RAW_BASE).Counter type 1073874176 is for PERF_AVERAGE_BULK, which displays a ratio of the items processed to the number of operations completed and requires a base property with PERF_LARGE_RAW_BASE.

Prominent examples are the Buffer Cache Hit Ratio (BCHR) and Buffer Cache Hit Ratio Base (BCHRB) counters. In this scenario for Buffer Cache Hit Ratio, the cntr_type with a value of 537003264 tells you that the counter is expressed as a ratio and needs to be calculated between the counter as a ratio and the correlating counter, Buffer Cache Hit Ratio Base, as the base.

If you're querying the sys.dm_os_performance_counters view for information about the Buffer Cache Hit Ratio counter, you would get a raw number value, such as 54678, for example, which by itself doesn't tell you anything meaningful for analysis. However, when the values are completely calculated, you get a value of, say, 90 percent, which is a useful metric. Therefore, to get the coveted value for your Buffer Cache Hit Ratio counter, you would need to select the BCHR value divided by the BCHRB value and multiply it by 100; this gives you the percentage. Here is an example of this type of ratio/base*100 calculation:

```
SELECT (a.cntr_value * 1.0 / b.cntr_value) * 100 [BufferCacheHitRatio]
FROM (SELECT * FROM sys.dm_os_performance_counters
WHERE counter_name = 'Buffer cache hit ratio'
AND object_name = CASE WHEN @@SERVICENAME = 'MSSQLSERVER'
THEN 'SQLServer:Buffer Manager'
ELSE 'MSSQL$' + rtrim(@@SERVICENAME) +
':Buffer Manager' END ) a
CROSS JOIN
(SELECT * from sys.dm_os_performance_counters
WHERE counter_name = 'Buffer cache hit ratio base'
and object_name = CASE WHEN @@SERVICENAME = 'MSSQLSERVER'
THEN 'SQLServer:Buffer Manager'
ELSE 'MSSQL$' + rtrim(@@SERVICENAME) +
':Buffer Manager' END ) b;
```

Because the two values are the same, the ratio\base*100 is 100 percent. For example, if the values are 5645 and 5645, you would do 5645/5645 * 100=100 percent. This calculation method would work for all the counters, where cntr_type has a value of 537003264. Here is the result you would get from the previous query, where the BufferCacheHitRatio value calculated here is 100 percent:

BufferCacheHitRatio
100

The following is a T-SQL query that calculates all SQL Server performance counter values from sys.dm_os_performance_counters based on the counter type. If you look at the results of the value column, you will see the ratio (the *delta*), which is the point-in-time raw value, already calculated.

```
SELECT
perf1.[object_name],
perf1.counter_name,
perf1.instance_name,
perf1.cntr_type,
'value' = CASE perf1.cntr_type
WHEN 537003008 -- This counter is expressed as a ratio and requires calculation. (Sql 2000)
THEN CONVERT(FLOAT,
perf1.cntr_value) /
(SELECT CASE perf2.cntr_value
WHEN 0 THEN 1
ELSE perf2.cntr_value
END
FROM sys.dm_os_performance_counters perf2
WHERE (perf1.counter_name + ' '
= SUBSTRING(perf2.counter_name,
1,
PATINDEX('% Base%', perf2.counter_name)))
AND perf1.[object_name] = perf2.[object_name]
AND perf1.instance_name = perf2.instance_name
AND perf2.cntr_type in (1073939459,1073939712)
)
WHEN 537003264 -- This counter is expressed as a ratio and requires calculation. >=SQL2005
THEN CONVERT(FLOAT,
perf1.cntr_value) /
(SELECT CASE perf2.cntr_value
WHEN 0 THEN 1
ELSE perf2.cntr_value
END
FROM sys.dm_os_performance_counters perf2
WHERE (perf1.counter_name + ' '
= SUBSTRING(perf2.counter_name,
1,
PATINDEX('% Base%', perf2.counter_name)))
AND perf1.[object_name] = perf2.[object_name]
AND perf1.instance_name = perf2.instance_name
AND perf2.cntr_type in (1073939712)
)
ELSE perf1.cntr_value -- The values of the other counter types are
-- already calculated.
END
```

```
FROM sys.dm_os_performance_counters perf1
WHERE perf1.cntr_type not in (1073939712) -- Don't display the divisors.
ORDER BY 1,2,3,4
```

sys.dm_os_performance_counters is an excellent way to collect performance metrics and baseline and trend the historical performance data overtime. However, this can't happen on its own because it stores only the most current values and is not persisted once the instance is restarted or the statistics are cleared. I will be mentioning this DMV again and show you ways to persist and collect this data for performance monitoring and reporting.

Diagnostic DMOs

There are several DMOs (DMVs and DMFs) available in SQL Server that you can use to format, sort, filter, create common table expressions, join, and cross apply with other DMOs to derive the most relevant statistics and useful metadata results. You did a lot of that in the previous chapter. Thanks to SQL Server MVP Glenn Berry, aka Doctor DMV, the hard work has already been done for you. Berry has put together a wide variety of awesome T-SQL queries that you can use to diagnose the health and performance of your SQL Server instances. I have used Berry's queries at several of my client and project sites as part of performing an initial health check. His scripts have proved invaluable throughout my DBA career and will be in yours as well.

Berry has been blogging, organizing, cataloging, and updating all of his diagnostic DMV queries since SQL Server 2005, all the way through SQL Server 2014. They are available on his blog and are updated as frequently as each month. You should bookmark his blog at https://sqlserverperformance.wordpress.com/; *all* his scripts should be in everyone's DBA toolbox. You can also download scripts as one script file.

■ **Caution**   Although Berry's DMV diagnostic scripts can be downloaded as one large script file, do not run them all at once! Run only the relevant queries for the desired data.

With each version of SQL Server, Berry has created new diagnostic queries based on new DMOs and features. Table 5-2 is the current count of diagnostic queries for each version. Many of them are backward compatible for earlier versions, but Berry makes adequate notation for which queries work on which version.

Table 5-2. *Number of DMV Queries in Glen Berry DIQ Collection for Each SQL Version*

SQL Server Version	No. of DMV Diagnostic Queries
SQL Server 2005	51
SQL Server 2008	59
SQL Server 2008 R2	65
SQL Server 2012	69
SQL Server 2014	72

It would probably be best to Google *SQL Server diagnostic information queries* and *Glenn Berry* to get the latest ones, but you can start at this URL: http://sqlserverperformance.wordpress.com/2014/09/17/sql-server-diagnostic-information-queries-for-september-2014/.

Figure 5-14 shows how the diagnostic queries are organized by link to each version's scripts. He also provides a blank spreadsheet template for you to cut and paste the query results for each set, and it comes with a tab for each of the metadata categories reported on.

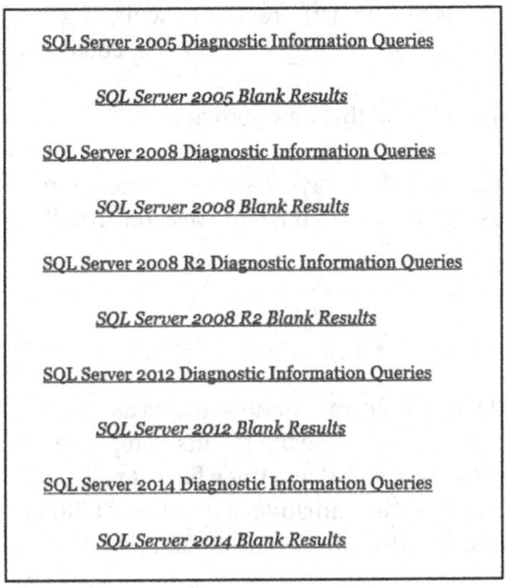

SQL Server 2005 Diagnostic Information Queries

SQL Server 2005 Blank Results

SQL Server 2008 Diagnostic Information Queries

SQL Server 2008 Blank Results

SQL Server 2008 R2 Diagnostic Information Queries

SQL Server 2008 R2 Blank Results

SQL Server 2012 Diagnostic Information Queries

SQL Server 2012 Blank Results

SQL Server 2014 Diagnostic Information Queries

SQL Server 2014 Blank Results

Figure 5-14. *Glenn Berry's blog links to DMV queries for each SQL Server version*

I am particularly partial to the query Get CPU Utilization by Database. (I say this in jest, as I am honored to be in Berry's collection of DMV diagnostics.)This is a script adapted from one I wrote. I have also created several similar types of queries for memory and I/O to get the usage as a percentage of each database out of the total resource usage of all the databases in a SQL Server instance.

Even with all these wonderful diagnostic queries and blank spreadsheets Berry has provided, it can still be a bit tedious to execute each query and then cut and paste the results into a spreadsheet. The innovative SQLDiagCmd program, a stand-alone .NET program by developer Mitch Wheat, can save you the time and trouble of doing this manually. Wheat calls the program a stand-alone runner for Berry's SQL Server diagnostic scripts.

To get the utility, go to http://mitch-wheat.blogspot.com.au/2013/01/sqldiagcmd-standalone-runner-for-glenn.html. You will see a download button and all the instructions you need to set it up and run it. Once installed, you execute it via a command line pointing to the Glenn's downloaded diagnostic query script files (.sql), which should reside in the same directory as SQLDiagCmd. The command-line syntax, as demonstrated by Mitch Wheat on his site, is as follows:

```
SQLDiagCmd -E -S URSERVER -i queries.sql -o C:\outputfolder -d databaselist –A
SQLDiagCmd -S URSERVER -U username -P password -i queries.sql -o C:\outputfolder -d databaselist –A
```

The SQLDiagCmd command allows you to run these queries and capture the results automatically into a neatly formatted Excel spreadsheet. In fact, this is a great little applet that should be considered a companion tool for Berry's SQL diagnostic information queries.

Bonus: sys.dm_exec_query_profiles DMO (SQL Server 2014 Only)

I've been discussing ways to capture real-time performance data using DMOs, so I should mention a new DMV, introduced in SQL Server 2014, which can track the progress of your query at any point in time at a granular level. In other words, if a long-running query presented itself on your server, it certainly would be useful if you could see exactly where the query is taking the longest to execute, what percentage of it is complete, the number of rows returned so far, the estimated row count (for comparison), the number of threads, and what it is doing now at the physical operator level (in other words, what operation the query is performing such as clustered index scan, hash match, merge join) just like the execution statistics in an execution plan. These statistics report on the actual number of reads, writes, CPU time, and so on.

The `sys.dm_exec_query_profiles` DMV can monitor the progress of a query in real time, while it is executing. For detailed analysis, you can join it with other DMVs such as `sys.dm_os_performance_counters`, `sys.dm_os_tasks`, `sys.dm_os_waiting_tasks`, and so on.

You can whet your appetite for this by viewing the MSDN description on this new gem at `http://msdn.microsoft.com/en-us/library/dn223301.aspx`.

In the meantime, if you're not quite at SQL Server 2014 yet, there are other ways to get real-time query performance data, such as by using a server-side profiler trace or using an Extended Events session. You'll learn more about this in the next section.

SQL Profiler/Trace

You can use SQL Profiler to capture all events on SQL Server in order to create and manage traces as well as analyze and replay trace results. You can later examine the file output or use the results to replay a specific series of steps when trying to diagnose a problem. These events are saved in a trace file (`.trc`). You can define and select several event classes, categories, and data columns to include, as well as set filters, to narrow down the desired output. The more events that are defined and the more column data that is collected, the bigger the performance penalty will be.

The problem with Profiler is that it is a client-side tool that creates performance overhead. Therefore, while useful, it should be used only for short-term analysis and not continuously run on the server. To minimize the impact of performance overhead, you can use server-side traces, which can be set to automatically run in the background; they are lightweight processes and collect information about various events on the server. Server-side traces are more efficient than Profiler, which essentially is a visual GUI built on top of some system stored procedures. By scripting these traces, you can eliminate the need for Profiler, extend its functionality to more efficiently to capture metadata on the server, and deploy it more easily to multiple SQL Servers.

There are about 180 events and event categories and columns that exist with traces. You can examine the trace framework and see all this information by running the following statements:

```
select * from sys.trace_events;
```

```
select * from sys.trace_categories;
```

```
select * from sys.trace_columns;
```

You need to know about some key trace-related system stored procedures that are needed to set up and manage the traces. Each performs a specific function to create the trace and specify file output path and parameters, add events and columns, set filters to the trace data capture, and set the status by turning trace on/off. They are as follows:

- `sp_trace_create` is used to define a trace and specify an output file location as well as other parameters and returns a `trace_ID`.

- `sp_trace_setevent` is used to add event/column combinations to traces based on the trace ID, as well as to remove them, if necessary, from traces in which they have already been defined.

- `sp_trace_setfilter` is used to define event filters based on trace columns.

- `sp_trace_setstatus` is called to turn on a trace, stop a trace, and delete a trace definition once you're done with it. Traces are reusable and can be started and stopped multiple times until they are deleted off the server.

In this book, you will use traces to audit some functions. In case you aren't familiar with the SQL Server default trace, I'll talk about it next briefly.

Default Trace

As of SQL Server 2005, the default trace was introduced, which is a lightweight server-side trace running continuously in the background.

The default trace records a handful of useful events to a trace file that can be loaded and reviewed in SQL Profiler or queried using the fn_trace_gettable(@trcpath) function. With this process you should be able to capture when a change is made, who made the change, and which option was changed. It will trace data for the event class 22, which is the ErrorLog event. I will show you how to use the default trace along with Extended Events for auditing purposes later in Chapter 9.

Ensure Default Trace Is On

Even though the default trace is enabled by default, you should ensure it is enabled by running the following query. Basically, if it's enabled, leave it because it might come in handy one day.

```
SELECT name, CASE WHEN value_in_use=1 THEN 'ENABLED'
WHEN value_in_use=0 THEN 'DISABLED'
END AS [status]
FROM sys.configurations
WHERE name='default trace enabled'
```

You can also see all the events captured by the default trace (or any trace for that matter) using T-SQL function fn_tracegeteventinfo and joining it with sys.trace_events, as shown with this query:

```
declare @handle int = (select id from sys.traces where is_default = 1);
-- or use where id=@traceid
select distinct e.eventid, n.name from
    fn_trace_geteventinfo(@handle) e
    join sys.trace_events n
    on e.eventid = n.trace_event_id
    order by n.name asc
```

In the following code, the top 15 events are displayed, along with the event IDs:

```
        eventidname
1109Audit Add DB User Event
2108Audit Add Login to Server Role Event
3110Audit Add Member to DB Role Event
4111Audit Add Role Event
5104Audit Addlogin Event
6115Audit Backup/Restore Event
7117Audit Change Audit Event
8152Audit Change Database Owner
9102Audit Database Scope GDR Event
10116Audit DBCC Event
11106Audit Login Change Property Event
1220Audit Login Failed
13105Audit Login GDR Event
14103Audit Schema Object GDR Event
15153Audit Schema Object Take Ownership Event
```

Finally, if you want to read the trace files (.trc) in SQL Server, via a T-SQL query, you can use the functions fn_trace_getinfo, fn_trace_gettable, and sys.trace_events to return the active default trace data capture. You first use fn_trace_getinfo to get the current file path of the default trace. Then you use fn_trace_gettable to read the raw trace data, joining it to sys.trace_events to get the name of the event, the category ID, and the trace_event ID.

The script you use to do this in one shot will dynamically get the current path and read it into fn_trace_gettable, with the associated event metadata. As you can see, I select a handful of columns that are relevant and display sample output. You of course can use select * to expand your query.

```
declare @trcpath varchar(255)

select @trcpath=convert(varchar(255),value) from [fn_trace_getinfo](NULL)
where [property] = 2 AND traceid=1

select @trcpath As ActiveDefaultTracePath

SELECT name, EventClass, category_id, substring(TextData,1,50), Error, DatabaseName,
ApplicationName,LoginName,SPID,StartTime,ObjectName
FROM [fn_trace_gettable]('' + @trcpath + '', DEFAULT) t
inner join sys.trace_events te
on t.EventClass=te.trace_event_id
ORDER BY StartTime;
```

This is the output of select @trcpath As ActiveDefaultTracePath:

The actual path of the default trace may vary by system. ActiveDefaultTracePath C:\Program Files\Microsoft SQL Server\MSSQL11.MSSQLSERVER\MSSQL\Log\log_50.trc

Figure 5-15 shows the output of the previous fn_trace_gettable for the first ten rows returned and highlights some key trace data.

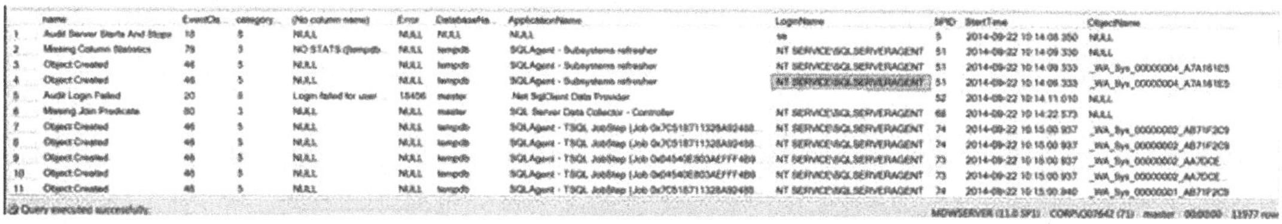

	name	EventCls	category	(No column name)	Error	DatabaseN...	ApplicationName	LoginName	SPID	StartTime	ObjectName
1	Audit Server Starts And Stops	18	8	NULL	NULL	NULL	NULL	sa	8	2014-09-22 10:14:08.350	NULL
2	Missing Column Statistics	79	3	NO STATS:([tempdb...	NULL	tempdb	SQLAgent - Subsystems refresher	NT SERVICE\SQLSERVERAGENT	51	2014-09-22 10:14:09.330	NULL
3	Object:Created	46	5	NULL	NULL	tempdb	SQLAgent - Subsystems refresher	NT SERVICE\SQLSERVERAGENT	51	2014-09-22 10:14:09.333	_WA_Sys_00000004_A7A161E5
4	Object:Created	46	5	NULL	NULL	tempdb	SQLAgent - Subsystems refresher	NT SERVICE\SQLSERVERAGENT	51	2014-09-22 10:14:09.333	_WA_Sys_00000004_A7A161E5
5	Audit Login Failed	20	8	Login failed for user...	18456	master	.Net SqlClient Data Provider		52	2014-09-22 10:14:11.010	NULL
6	Missing Join Predicate	80	3	NULL	NULL	master	SQL Server Data Collector - Controller		68	2014-09-22 10:14:22.573	NULL
7	Object:Created	46	5	NULL	NULL	tempdb	SQLAgent - TSQL JobStep (Job 0x7C518771329A82488...	NT SERVICE\SQLSERVERAGENT	74	2014-09-22 10:15:00.937	_WA_Sys_00000002_AB71F2C9
8	Object:Created	46	5	NULL	NULL	tempdb	SQLAgent - TSQL JobStep (Job 0x7C518771329A82488...	NT SERVICE\SQLSERVERAGENT	74	2014-09-22 10:15:00.937	_WA_Sys_00000002_AB71F2C9
9	Object:Created	46	5	NULL	NULL	tempdb	SQLAgent - TSQL JobStep (Job 0x04540E803AEFFF4B9...	NT SERVICE\SQLSERVERAGENT	73	2014-09-22 10:15:00.937	_WA_Sys_00000002_AA3DCE
10	Object:Created	46	5	NULL	NULL	tempdb	SQLAgent - TSQL JobStep (Job 0x04540E803AEFFF4B9...	NT SERVICE\SQLSERVERAGENT	73	2014-09-22 10:15:00.937	_WA_Sys_00000002_AA3DCE
11	Object:Created	46	5	NULL	NULL	tempdb	SQLAgent - TSQL JobStep (Job 0x7C518771329A82488...	NT SERVICE\SQLSERVERAGENT	74	2014-09-22 10:15:00.940	_WA_Sys_00000001_AB71F2C9

Query executed successfully. MDWSERVER (11.0 SP1) CORP\007642 (71) master 00:00:00 11977 rows

Figure 5-15. *Output of the default trace using fn_trace_gettable*

Performance Monitor

In Chapter 3, I touched upon specific SQL Server–related counters you can set up to continue investigating what you found out with respect to wait statistics. Let's expand this discussion and see how a new concept in the data collection of performance data can lead to ways of building a repository.

First, let's talk about the traditional Performance Monitor tool with all its selected counters running live on the system. Performance Monitor resides at Control Panel ➤ System &Security ➤ Administrative Tools. The easiest way to launch Performance Monitor is to click Start, click in the Start Search box, type **perfmon**, and press Enter. Select Performance and drill down to Monitoring Tools (see Figure 5-16). You can see current activity, add and delete counters, freeze the frame display, and change the appearance. Of course, unless something is happening on the server at that moment in time, it's not really the best way to identify and resolve a performance issue.

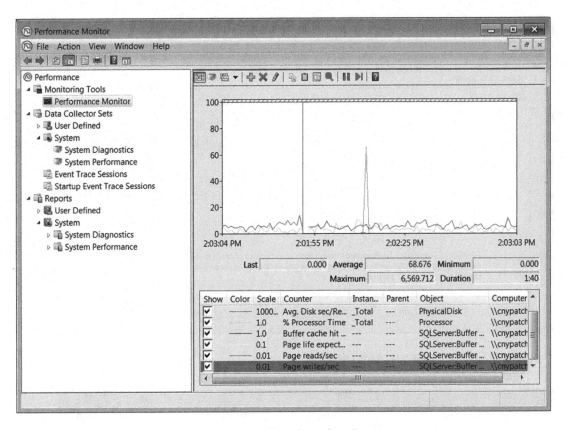

Figure 5-16. *Performance Monitor: current activity based on selected counters*

Data Collector

Let's say you need an automated process to collect or log your data and store it for further troubleshooting or even postmortem analysis. The Performance Data Collector, introduced in SQL Server 2008, works in tandem with another gem called the *management data warehouse* (MDW). The purpose of Data Collector, as its name sounds, is to collect data. You can store this data in a central repository and generate performance reports from it. The data collection can run continuously or be scheduled, and you can set up predefined templates or a custom collection.

There are three default templates when setting up Data Collector: Basic, System Diagnostics, and System Performance. However, you can customize these templates. Data Collector gives you the option of storing performance data to a log file or a SQL Server database. Here I will walk you through setting up a custom collection set and storing the data in SQL Server.

The first thing you need to do when directing Data Collector to log to a SQL Server database is to set up an ODBC connection and create a system DSN to your SQL Server. To do this, open the ODBC Data Source Administrator dialog by selecting Start ➤ Run and typing **odbc**.

Select the System DSN tab and click Add; you will see the available ODBC drivers for selection, as shown in Figure 5-17. Select the SQL Server driver (not the native driver), as shown in Figure 5-18.

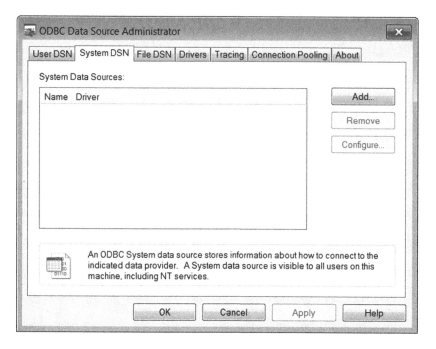

Figure 5-17. *Configuring the system DSN data source*

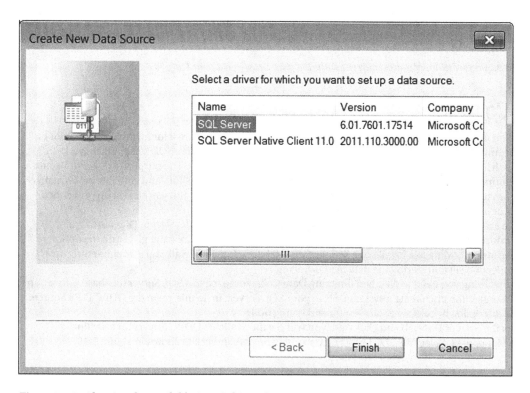

Figure 5-18. *Showing the available ODBC drivers for SQL*

Click Finish, and now you will create the DSN. Most important, select or enter the destination of your server where you want to collect and store the data, as shown in Figure 5-19.

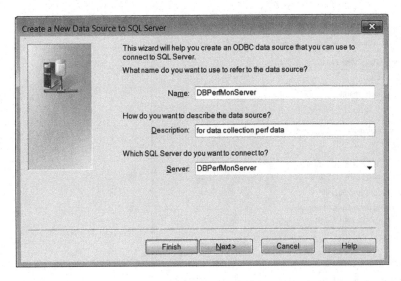

Figure 5-19. *Creating a new data source for Perfmon data collection to SQL Server*

Select your preferred authentication mode that ODBC will use to connect to SQL Server. Click Next to proceed, as shown in Figure 5-20.

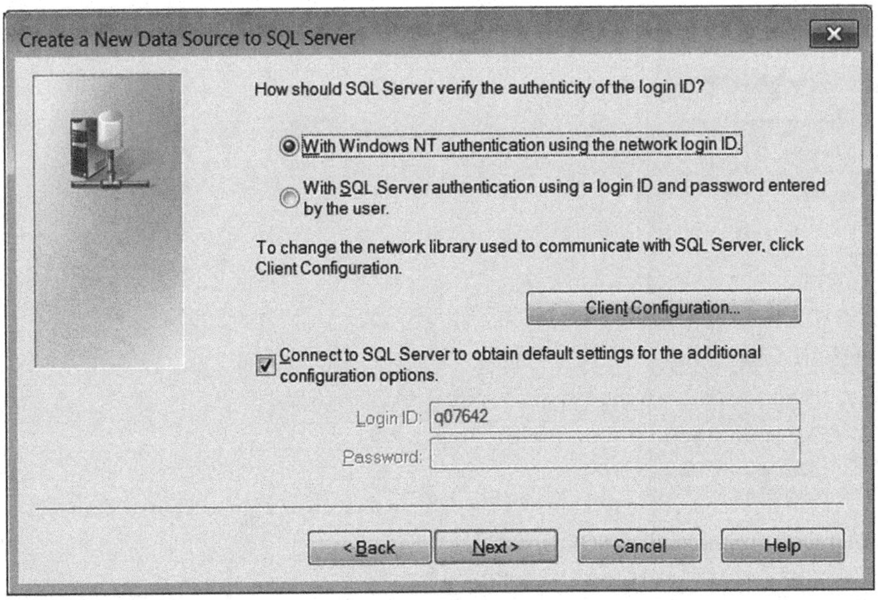

Figure 5-20. *Choosing the authentication method*

Here you will check the "Change the default database" checkbox and select the target database you want to store the performance data to. (You need to select an existing database or create a new one on the server before you do this step.) Click Next and then Finish on the next screen, as shown in Figure 5-21.

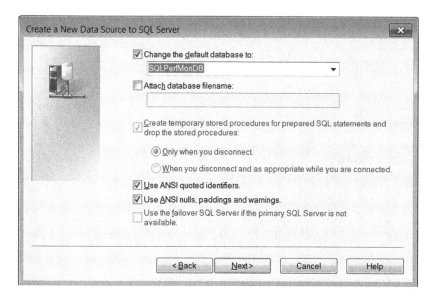

Figure 5-21. *Selecting the database for Perfmon data collection and storage*

Review ODBC setup selections, and click TEST Data Source to confirm successful connectivity to SQL Server. The screen will display SUCCESS or FAILED. If it was successful, click OK and then OK, as shown in Figure 5-22.

Figure 5-22. *Testing data source connectivity to SQL Server*

Once the ODBC data source is created, go to Performance Monitor, expand the item called Data Collector Sets, right-click User Defined, and select New ➤ Data Collector Set, as shown in Figure 5-23.

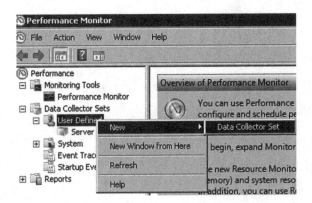

Figure 5-23. *Launching the data collector creation wizard*

Enter the desired name and select the "Create manually" option, as shown in Figure 5-24. Click Next.

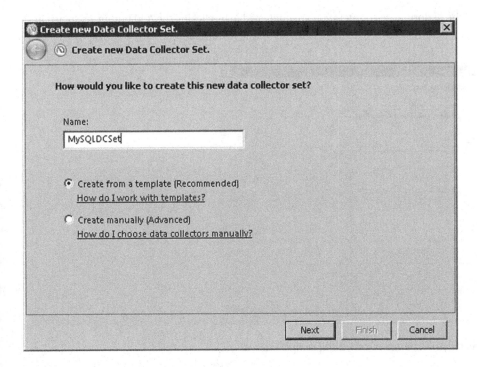

Figure 5-24. *Creating a new data collector set*

Now select Performance Counters under the "Create Data logs" radio button, as shown in Figure 5-25, and click Next.

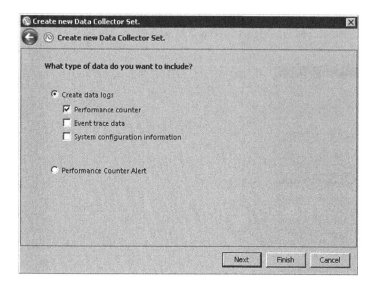

Figure 5-25. *Selecting the type of data for the data collector set*

Select and add the performance counters you are interested in by clicking the Add button, as shown in Figure 5-26.

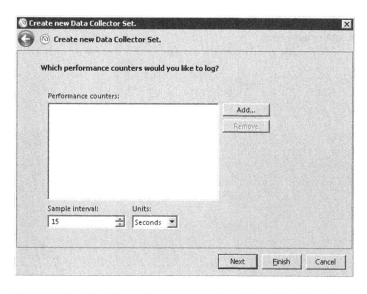

Figure 5-26. *Select the performance counters and sample interval*

The Available Counters screen will appear. After your desired counters are selected, click OK. Some common counters that you may want to look at for ongoing performance monitoring are shown in Figure 5-27.

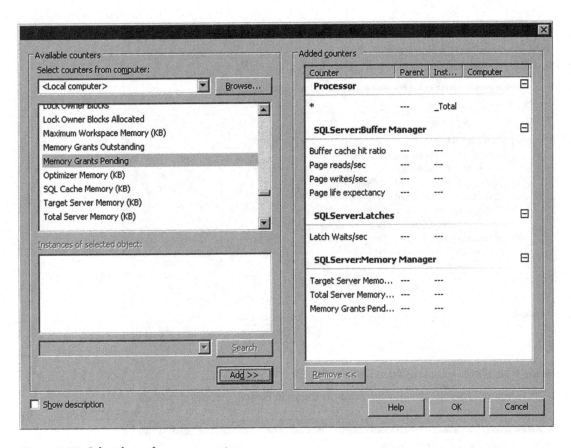

Figure 5-27. *Select the performance counters*

You will see the screen in Figure 5-28 populated with the selected Perfmon counters.

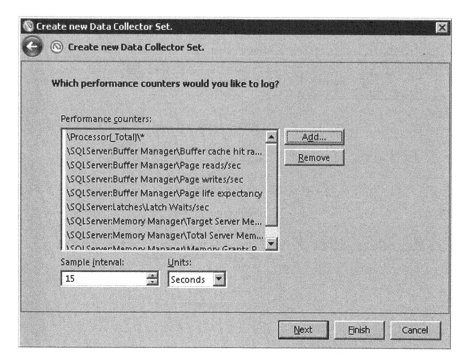

Figure 5-28. *All the selected counters returned*

Click Next. Leave the root directory as is, as shown in Figure 5-29, and click Next.

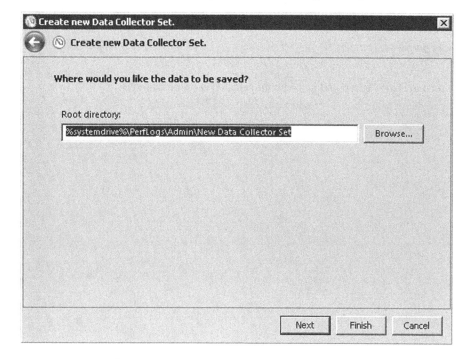

Figure 5-29. *Root directory where data collector set information is saved*

At this point, leave the "Save and close" radio button selected, as shown in Figure 5-30, and then click Finish.

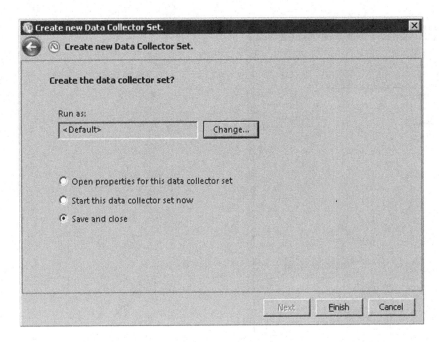

Figure 5-30. *Last step in creating data collector set*

Now you should have your PerfDataToSql data collector set listed under the User Defined node, and it should be in the Stopped state.

Select the MySQLDC set node; this should list DataCollector01 in the right pane, as shown in Figure 5-31.

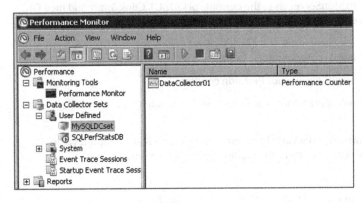

Figure 5-31. *Custom-defined collector set*

Right-click DataCollector01, select Properties, and then select the Performance Counters tab. Change the "Log format" drop-down to SQL, which should enable the "Data Source name" drop-down, as shown in Figure 5-32.

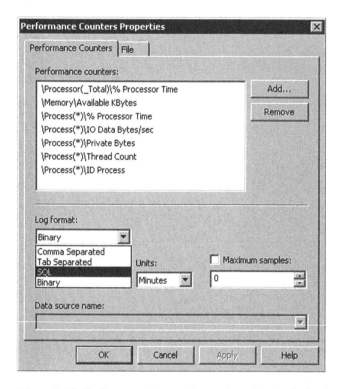

Figure 5-32. *Performance Counter Properties: selecting the log format*

Now, select your ODBC DSN (DBPerfMonServer, as in the example of ODBC). Click Apply and then OK.

Once the collection is started, if you go to your destination SQL Server database, you will see three tables created:

- CounterData: Contains the actual counter data

- CounterDetails: Contains details about your Perfmon counters

- DisplayToID: Contains the metadata about your collection, like when it was started and stopped

You can query your collected performance data and the average, maximum, and minimum values by datetime, as shown in Figure 5-33. Here is a query you can use, along with sample output:

```
SELECT MachineName,
   CONVERT(DATETIME, CONVERT(VARCHAR(16), CounterDateTime)) as [Date],
   AVG(CounterValue) as Average,
   MIN(CounterValue) as Minimum,
   MAX(CounterValue) as Maximum
FROM CounterDetails
   JOIN CounterData ON CounterData.CounterID = CounterDetails.CounterID
```

```
    JOIN DisplayToID ON DisplayToID.GUID = CounterData.GUID/*WHERE CounterName = 'Context
Switches/sec'—uncomment to filter for specific counter */
GROUP BY MachineName,
    CONVERT(DATETIME, CONVERT(VARCHAR(16), CounterDateTime))


MachineNameDateAverageMinimumMaximum
\\MYSQLDCServer2014-10-09 04:41:00.0001485849.26291826021820272
\\MYSQLDCServer2014-10-08 15:40:00.0001334575.08208145022137872
\\MYSQLDCServer2014-10-08 19:16:00.0001336348.08461437022169680
\\MYSQLDCServer2014-10-08 16:22:00.0001332025.22097522022091728
\\MYSQLDCServer2014-10-08 20:49:00.0001365055.99575651022830576
\\MYSQLDCServer2014-10-08 17:31:00.0001321601.78722734021869664
\\MYSQLDCServer2014-10-09 14:48:00.0001535508.80525481021498800
\\MYSQLDCServer2014-10-08 12:29:00.0001331626.7249187022195680
\\MYSQLDCServer2014-10-08 21:09:00.0001359797.48193571022656256
\\MYSQLDCServer2014-10-09 07:25:00.0001480279.89914166021691616
```

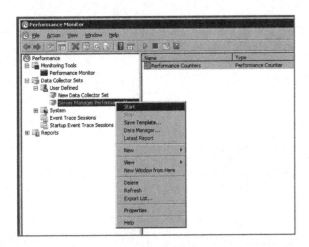

Figure 5-33. *Starting the data collection*

■ **Note** If you receive the error "Call to SQLExecDirect failed with %1," the most likely cause is that the data collection is set to SYSTEM. Right-click, go to the data collection set properties, and modify the account to one that has access to SQL Server.

Management Data Warehouse: SQL Server 2008 and Higher

Data Collector stores the collected data in a relational database, called the *management data warehouse* (MDW). Introduced in SQL Server 2008, the data management and collection strategy includes all these components for performance monitoring, troubleshooting, and historical baseline comparisons.

The MDW is a great out-of-the box tool, for versions SQL Server 2008 and higher, that will allow you to collect and report on historical performance data and store it in a central database repository. I briefly mention this golden native nugget here because I will cover it more extensively as a jump-start to creating a repository of performance metadata that can be easily set up and deployed on multiple SQL Server instances. In this case, it is part of the existing SQL Server product stack, and there is no need to download anything! If you are using SQL Server 2008 or higher, you already have MDW at your fingertips.

To set up and configure the MDW, in SSMS simply right-click the Data Collection item, located under the Management folder and select Configure Management Data Warehouse to launch an intuitive wizard to step you through the process (shown in Figures 5-34 and 5-35). You'll see more in-depth how to use this feature in later chapters; for instance, I will show one way to create a simple but powerful repository that will enable you to create a baseline of performance data and analyze and troubleshoot issues.

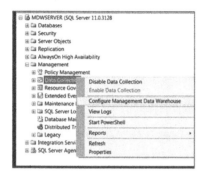

Figure 5-34. *Launching the MDW in SSMS*

Figure 5-35. *The MDW wizard*

As soon as you select Configure Management Data Warehouse from the pop-up menu, the welcome screen will appear to take you through the wizard steps, as shown in Figure 5-35.

That's as far as you are going to go with MDW in this chapter! Now that you know about its existence, purpose, and where to go to configure MDW, you will come back to it later in the book. I will use MDW to show you how to create a simple repository of database health metrics, as well as show you the reports that come with it. Here I discussed Data Collector, the core engine that MDW is built on top of, to perform the task of collecting performance metadata.

Basic Training Completed

In this first of two chapters about tools of the trade, I introduced you to the basic tools of SQL Server Management Studio. The features don't have a steep learning curve, so anyone who has just taken on the role of managing the SQL Server infrastructure can quickly know what's going on with SQL Server. You learned about the Activity Monitor GUI, as well as out-of-the-box server and database reports. Then you learned how to add some custom reports, in the form of the SQL Server 2012 Performance Dashboard, and how to access them via SSMS.

Then, you continued to focus on the dynamic management objects, views, and functions that are super-useful and a must-know for all database professionals managing SQL Server. These views and functions provide invaluable metadata that offers insight into the performance, health, and state of SQL Server. As part of the ongoing discussion, I talked about ways to monitor and capture data by using SQL Profiler traces, as discussed in this chapter, and Extended Events, discussed in the next chapter.SQL Server traces and Extended Events are powerful native tools at your disposal and should be part of your DBA arsenal.

These are the foundation for other tools and utilities, and it's important to understand how they work and how to use them so you can build upon them to collect and store data that you can use later. The elements of a healthy SQL Server environment will consist of a central repository of data that you can use for historical trend analysis, reporting, monitoring, performance tuning, documentation, and auditing. In the next chapter, you will expand your toolset and learn about some more advanced tools, including some first released with SQL Server 2012.

CHAPTER 6

■ ■ ■

Expanding Your Tool Set

The native tools that Microsoft provides to you become more flexible with each version released, adding more functionality to help database professionals leverage them and put them to use in practical ways. By enhancing your DBA tool set, you can rapidly deploy these techniques without much of a learning curve. I will expand your DBA tool set here and discuss the new tools and features in SQL Server version 2012, as well as other free and downloadable tools you should be aware of.

New Tools

With respect to performance monitoring and system health, there are some new neat features in SQL Server, many introduced in SQL Server 2012, that will come in handy when solving common challenges. I will discuss these tools and show you how to utilize them for your own SQL health and SQL fitness! The following are the new tools I will discuss:

- Extended Events

- The New Session Wizard for Extended Events

- The `system_health` session

- The `sp_server_diagnostics` system stored procedure and the 2012 System Health Reporting Dashboard

Extended Events

Extended Events, otherwise known as XE or X-events, was introduced in SQL Server 2008 as a lightweight system that allows users to collect data to identify and troubleshoot performance issues. It is a highly configurable and scalable architecture that uses few resources and little overhead. Extended Events is something that all DBAs should know about and learn how to use because it will replace SQL Profiler and Trace. In fact, to the surprise of many, SQL Profiler and Trace has already been deprecated. That does not mean they are not still available, but folks should start getting familiar and comfortable using Extended Events. Luckily, all the previous functionality of SQL Profiler is available with Extended Events. Although similar to SQL Profiler, Extended Events definitely has its advantages.

Extended Events is intended as a performance and health-monitoring system that can be configured to capture information about all server activity. I will introduce Extended Events here but will cover more advanced topics in Chapter 8.

Indeed, Extended Events, using XML and XPath query syntax (XQuery), is something that most DBAs may find difficult to learn, but you don't necessarily need to master Extended Events in order to use it for performance monitoring and system health. It seems that XML and XQuery intimidate the ordinary production DBA, but there are many scripts out there to help. There is no shame in cutting and pasting when it comes to XQuery. In fact, I'll provide some samples later in this chapter.

■ **Note** You don't have to master Extended Events to use it. When it comes to XML and XQuery, there is no shame in cutting and pasting!

It is to the good fortune of the database professional that with SQL Server 2012, an easy-to-use graphical interface was introduced as a way to create, modify, display, and analyze your data. Microsoft has given you the New Session Wizard to set this all up for you.

If you want to take a quick look and see which Extended Events sessions are active on your server, you can run the following simple query:

```
select * from sys.dm_xe_sessions
```

Figure 6-1 shows the output from this query as it appears in the Results grid in SQL Server Management Studio.

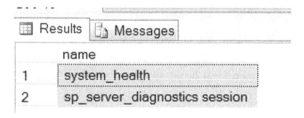

Figure 6-1. *Showing active Extended Events sessions*

The New Session Wizard

With the New Session Wizard, you can create the event session to set session properties, choose a template (or create your own), select events to capture, set session event filters, and specify where the session data is to be stored. The wizard is a helpful feature to allow you to create a session to select the events you want to capture on your SQL Server instance.

To launch the New Session Wizard, from SSMS, navigate to the Management folder, expand it, and drill down to Extended Events. Once there, then drill down to the Sessions folder. At this point, you will see the default sessions, AlwaysOn_Health and system_health. I will cover system_health shortly. AlwaysOn_Health, which is beyond the scope of this book, is simply to monitor and help with troubleshooting an availability group issue.

If you right-click the Sessions folder, you will see the pop-up menu option to launch the New Session Wizard, as shown in Figure 6-2. I'll take you through this wizard as a means to quickly deploy event monitoring and collection.

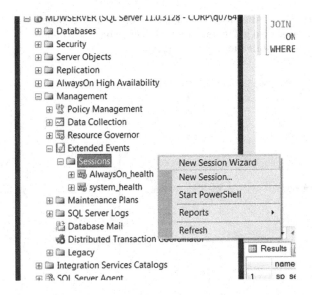

Figure 6-2. *The navigation tree in SSMS to launch the New Session Wizard*

Once you click New Session Wizard, the Introduction screen will appear, describing its use and taking you through all the steps to configure it, as shown in Figure 6-3. Click Next to go to the next screen.

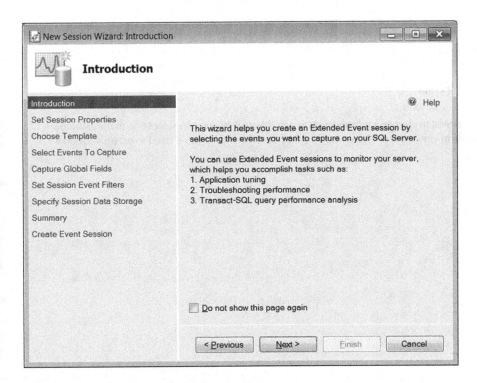

Figure 6-3. *New Session Wizard Introduction screen*

In this step, you simply set the session properties by giving the session a name. You can also choose the checkbox "Start the event session at server startup," as shown in Figure 6-4. This is a great option, whereas with SQL Trace, it was more difficult to get tracing to autostart after a service restart.

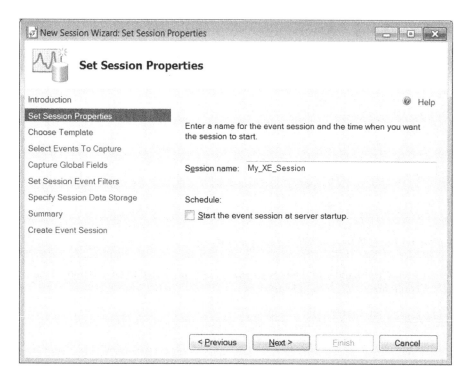

Figure 6-4. *Set Session Properties screen*

Click Next to proceed to choose a template, shown in Figure 6-5. You can select one of the available templates from the drop-down list or choose no template (in which case you'll need to set up your own collection).

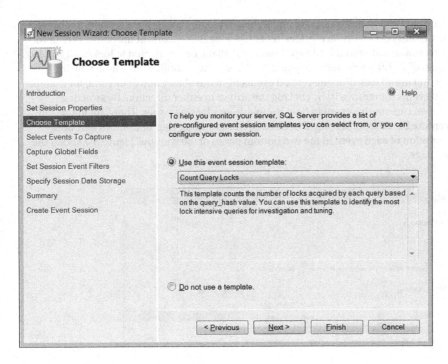

Figure 6-5. *Choosing a session template*

The list of available built-in templates will be displayed for your desired selection. In the dialog box below the selection, a detailed description of each template functionality is displayed, as shown in Figure 6-6.

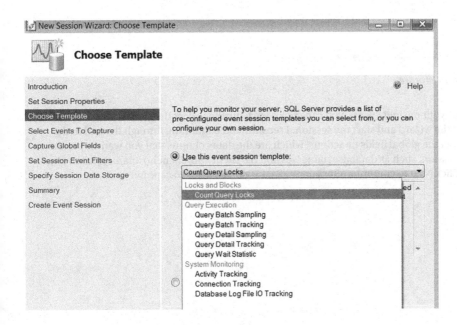

Figure 6-6. *Some of the available event session template*

When selecting the Count Query Locks template under the Locks and Blocks event session, as shown in the example, you can monitor and report on any locking or blocking that occurs. In the Select Events To Capture window, you can browse and search the Event Library for all the events related to locks and blocks. By default, the "lock acquired" event is selected, but you can add or remove multiple events at will. In Figure 6-6, I searched for and found lock timeout–related events from the library and could add, for example, a lock timeout to selected events (or remove it) by clicking the arrows in either direction. By selecting the "lock timeout" event, you can use this event to help troubleshoot blocking issues. There are many mechanisms that can capture blocking, and using Extended Events is among your options. In addition, you can see a detail description of each event in the two bottom panes of the window. Figure 6-7 shows the Select Events To Capture page.

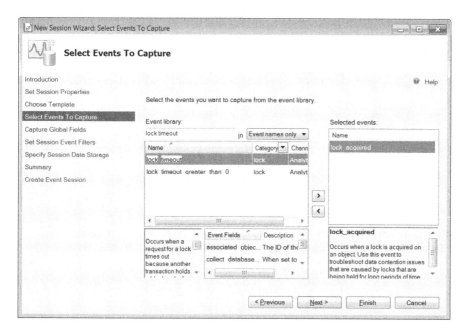

Figure 6-7. *The events to capture*

Once you select all your desired events, you can click Next to further select the global fields, or you can click Finish to end the wizard and start the session. I recommend continuing through the end of the wizard. Then you can set the global fields or actions, which are the data columns that you want captured and included in your session, such as database name, session ID, client app, client hostname, and so on, as shown in Figure 6-8. Click Next to continue, after you select the globals fields to capture.

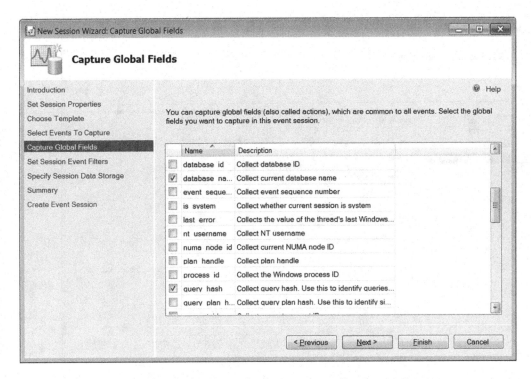

Figure 6-8. *All the available global fields to capture common to all events*

Set Session Event Filters is an important step that will help narrow down the pertinent information. You will be prompted to set session event filters for this session. Applying filters allows you to limit the data captured by the event session, which can streamline performance tuning and analysis.

By default here, you can see in the predicate column that the lock acquired event is filtered for database id > 4 and sqlserver.is system =false. This predicate or filter tells the event session to ignore system databases and all SQL Server system processes. Therefore, only session data for user databases and processes, respectively, will be returned. You can add additional filters to further limit the data set. When you are done defining filters, click Next to proceed. Figure 6-9 shows how to set session filters.

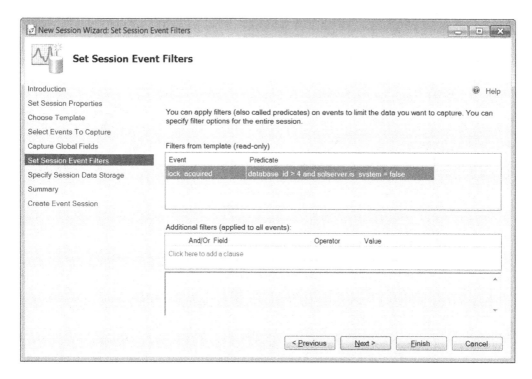

Figure 6-9. *Set Session Event Filters allows you to limit the vast data returned*

Now you need to tell the wizard how you want to collect and store your data for later analysis. In the Specify Session Data Storage step, shown in Figure 6-10, you can choose to save data to a file/location, as well as the maximum file size, number of files, and whether to enable file rollover, similar to defining a SQL Server Profiler trace. Extended Events data is stored in .xel files, which stands for Extended Events logs.

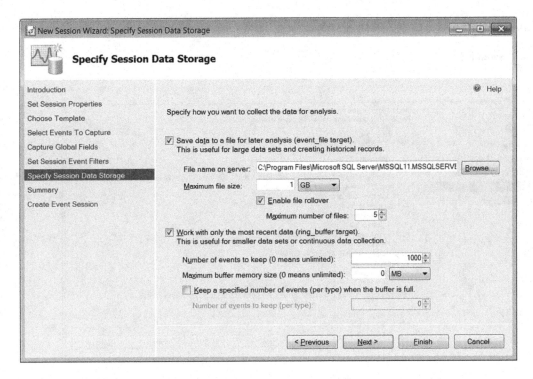

Figure 6-10. *Specify Session Data Storage page*

However, with the Extended Events, you can also tell the session to use the most recent data stored in memory with `ring_buffer_target`. You can set the number of events to keep, the maximum buffer memory, and how many events to keep if the buffer memory is full. Therefore, you can use both targets here.

It is recommended that you use this option for smaller data sets or continuous data collection, as opposed to saving data to a file, which is suggested for large data sets and historical recording.

Click Next for the Summary page, displayed in Figure 6-11, and verify your selections are correct. Expand each line to review. You can also click the Script button to copy your defined event session to the query window.

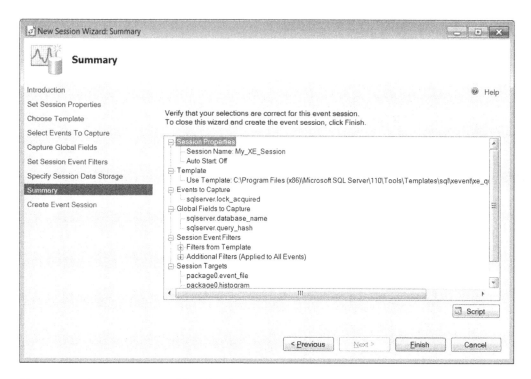

Figure 6-11. *Summary screen of the wizard*

Finally, click Finish to accept your selections and create the event session.

If you reach this screen and see the "SUCCESS" message like in Figure 6-12, then you are in good shape and have successfully completed the wizard and created an Extended Events session.

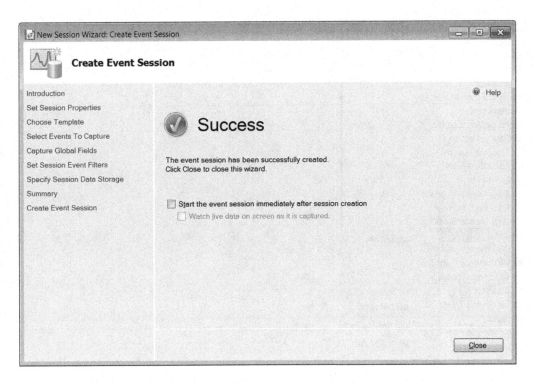

Figure 6-12. *The success of creating an event session*

Now you will want to navigate in SSMS to your created session; under the folders, the path is Management ➤ Extended Events ➤ Sessions. Highlight My_XE_Session, right-click, and select Start Session from the pop-up menu, as shown in Figure 6-13. Here you can check to start the event session immediately after it's created and even watch live data onscreen as it is captured. I want you to start the event session but do not suggest selecting watching live data onscreen for continuous monitoring. You may want to watch the data live for immediate analysis and short-term troubleshooting, such as testing code or capturing an errant statement.

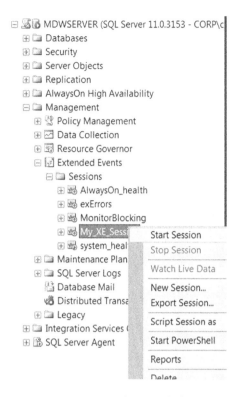

Figure 6-13. *Starting the Extended Events session*

The system_health Session

Similar to the default trace, the system health session, which is on by default, is the equivalent of Extended Events and automatically starts when the SQL Server database engine starts. As part of this lightweight architecture, the session starts and runs without any noticeable performance impact. Like with the default trace, it is recommend that you do not stop or delete the system health session because it will collect valuable performance data that can later help troubleshoot performance issues.

If you want to see all the events captured by the system_health Extended Events session, simply run the query joining sys_dm_xe_session_events and sys.dm_xe_session, specifying the name of the session you want data returned for. In the following query example, you are getting the information for system_health:

```
select event_name,name from sys.dm_xe_session_events e
    inner join sys.dm_xe_sessions s
    on e.event_session_address = s.address
    where name='system_health'
```

Output from this query shows the list of events captured by the system health session.

```
event_name
xml_deadlock_report
wait_info_external
wait_info
scheduler_monitor_system_health_ring_buffer_recorded
```

```
scheduler_monitor_stalled_dispatcher_ring_buffer_recorded
scheduler_monitor_non_yielding_rm_ring_buffer_recorded
scheduler_monitor_non_yielding_ring_buffer_recorded
scheduler_monitor_non_yielding_iocp_ring_buffer_recorded
scheduler_monitor_deadlock_ring_buffer_recorded
memory_node_oom_ring_buffer_recorded
memory_broker_ring_buffer_recorded
clr_virtual_alloc_failure
clr_allocation_failure
sp_server_diagnostics_component_result
security_error_ring_buffer_recorded
error_reported
connectivity_ring_buffer_recorded
```

When the system_health session was introduced in SQL Server 2008, its event information was not persisted to disk; it collects to a ring buffer in memory that is available only while the SQL Server is running. Information in the ring buffer target is not persisted once the SQL Server instance is restarted. When storing data to the ring_buffer (in any version), the events will get overwritten as necessary. In SQL Server 2012, this event data is stored and written to disk, as well as the ring_buffer. Now the session data is written to both ring_buffer and file as the default behavior. However, if you are still to SQL 2008, it is recommended that you modify the 2008 system_health session to also write to file.

As you can see from the list of events available in the system_health session, there are several of them having the appended text _ring_buffer_recorded. This naming convention in SQL Server 2012 now lets pertinent historical performance information stored in the SQLOS ring buffers persist beyond in-memory ring counts and after the instance restarts.

To simply view all currently active event sessions running on your SQL Server instance and the target or storage area the data is being captured to, you can query the sys.server_event_sessions view and join it with sys.server_event_session_targets. For each of the configured targets defined for an event session, one row exists in the _session_targets view. Session targets, as defined in the Specify Session Data Storage step of the wizard, can be as follows: ring buffer, event file, histogram, event counter, event pairing, or event tracing for Windows (ETW). Moreover, data can be processed synchronously or asynchronously by a target. The most common targets, of course, are ring buffer and event file, but I will briefly describe each of the SQL Server Extended events target in the following list:

- *Event file*: With this asynchronous target, all event session data is written to disk, from the data in the memory buffers.

- *Ring buffer*: Ring buffer is another asynchronous target where event data is held in memory while the SQL Server instance is running. The data here is per event on a first-in first-out (FIFO) basis, which means the oldest events recorded here are flushed out and replaced by new events.

- *Event counter*: All specified events that occur during an Extended Events session are counted, and information about the workload details is captured without full event collection overhead. The event counter target is synchronous.

- *Event pairing*: When events such as lock acquires and lock releases occur, they do so in pairs. There are several paired events, and when a specified paired event does not occur together, this asynchronous target will store this data.

- *Event Tracing for Windows (ETW)*: This particular target is synchronous and is for associating SQL Server events with Windows operating system or application events.

- *Histogram*: The histogram asynchronous target is based on a specified event column or action and is used to count the number of times an event occurs.

The following query will give you the event session name and target information:

```
SELECT
        es.name AS session_name,
        tg.name AS target_name
    FROM sys.server_event_sessions AS es
    JOIN sys.server_event_session_targets AS tg
            ON es.event_session_id = tg.event_session_id
```

The results will be similar to the following:

```
session_name      target_name
system_health     event_file
system_health     ring_buffer
AlwaysOn_health     event_file
My_XE_Session     event_file
My_XE_Session     histogram
My_XE_Session     ring_buffer
```

The previous output shows the two default sessions, system_health and AlwaysOn_health, as well as the session I used to walk you through the New Session Data Wizard earlier, My_XE_Session. Because the server used for validating and running all the scripts in this book is a SQL Server 2012 instance, you can see the system_health session's target is now both to a file and to the ring_buffer.

If you want to read the raw output using a T-SQL query, you can use the system function sys.fn_xe_file_target_read_file (similar to the function of fn_trace_gettable()), but beware the results are generated in XEL and XEM format. The key data information that you would be interested in is in the event_data column, and it is suggested that you use SSMS to review the XEL output.

```
select * from
sys.fn_xe_file_target_read_file ('C:\Program Files\Microsoft SQL Server\MSSQL11.MSSQLSERVER\
MSSQL\Log\*.xel',null,null,null)
system_health_0_130558688483430000.xel
```

There is good amount of documentation out there about the system health session, so I will just scratch the surface in this book. I will also show you how to set up and create your own sessions to capture relevant health check performance data. In this introductory section about Extended Events, you learned how to use the New Session Wizard to graphically set up event sessions and took a look at the Extended Events metadata. Later in the book, I will focus more on customizing your own event sessions for reporting on system health and show you some neat X-Query scripts to view the data in a user-friendly way.

The sp_server_diagnostics Procedure

Along with the default system_health session, the system stored procedure sp_server_diagnostics was introduced in SQL Server 2012 to provide you with SQL Server instance health information in five-minute intervals. The advantage of this system stored procedure is that it is lightweight with minimal impact, but also it allows you to have a point-in-time snapshot of data about the health of your SQL Server, even if you had no existing data collection going on. Because it exposes useful data about queries, I/O, memory, CPU, resources, waits, and events, it is considered and referred to as the true black-box recorder. Here is a description of the type of performance data that is collected and reported on, by using sp_server_diagnostics:

- *System*: This captures information with respect to CPU usage, page faults, nonyielding tasks, latches, access violations, dumps, and spinlock activity.

- *Resource*: This captures data such as physical and virtual memory, page faults, cache, buffer pools, and other relevant memory-related objects.

- *Query processing*: This captures data with respect to query processing such as wait types, tasks, worker threads, CPU-intensive requests, blocking tasks, and so on.

- *I/O subsystems*: This captures data with respect to I/O such as I/O latch timeouts, longest pending requests, and so on. It also produces a clean or warning health state on the I/O subsystem.

- *Events*: This captures data such as ring buffer exceptions, ring buffer events memory broker, buffer pool, spinlocks, security, out of memory exceptions, scheduler monitor events, and so on.

The sp_server_diagnostics stored procedure has a single parameter that it accepts, which is @repeat_interval. This parameter tells the procedure to run continuously at this time interval, so you would set the value in seconds, as this standard syntax demonstrates:

```
sp_server_diagnostics [@repeat_interval =] 'repeat_interval_in_seconds'
```

The default value is 0. If it's run without a parameter value, it will run one time and stop. To return complete data, it must run at least five seconds to return useful health information. To get a feel for the data exposed, when I run Exec sp_server_diagnostics, I get the raw output shown in Figure 6-14.

create_time	component_type	component_name	state	state_desc	data
2014-09-24 14:25:31.527	instance	system	1	clean	<system spinlockBackoffs="0" sickSpinlockType="none" sickSpinlockT...
2014-09-24 14:25:31.527	instance	resource	1	clean	<resource lastNotification="RESOURCE_MEMPHYSICAL_HIGH" outOf...
2014-09-24 14:25:31.527	instance	query_processing	1	clean	<queryProcessing maxWorkers="576" workersCreated="61" workersIdl...
2014-09-24 14:25:31.527	instance	io_subsystem	1	clean	<ioSubsystem ioLatchTimeouts="0" intervalLonglos="0" totalLonglos="...
2014-09-24 14:25:31.527	instance	events	0	unknown	<events><session startTime="2014-09-22T10:14:08.353" droppedEve...

Figure 6-14. *Raw output of* sp_server_diagnostics

As you can see, you get the create_time, component_type, state, and state_desc information. However, the most important health information is returned in the data column field, which is stored as XML. Now I know if you're a DBA, that look of excitement just turned into disappointment when pondering how to read XML. Well, I told you before and will do so again, I will give you some script foundations to help translate this XML data into understandable and actionable performance data. I hereby introduce you to XQuery.

XQuery

Basically, XQuery is to XML what T-SQL is to relational database tables. It is designed to query anything that is returned as XML data, such as XML files and databases. XQuery is useful in finding, parsing, and extracting elements and attributes from XML data, and that is what I will demonstrate here, using sp_server_diagnostics XML.

Now I will take you through some sample queries and XQuery queries that help analyze the health data returned by sp_server_diagnostics. First, let's create a temp table and load the results of sp_server_diagnostics.

```
create table #diagdata
(
create_time datetime,
component_type sysname,
component_name sysname,
[state] int,
state_desc sysname,
data varchar(max)
)
insert into #diagdata
exec sp_server_diagnostics
```

Once you execute the previous statement and dump all the sp_server_diagnostics data into the temp table, you can look at the result, with a simple select statement. So far, you see the same data as executing the system stored procedure itself, but now you have a table to work with for the next step. You can take a quick look at the results by running this select statement:

```
select * from #diagdata
```

To further analyze and parse the data field, you can convert it and cast the data as XML. Once you run the following query, you can see the data in XML format.

```
select cast(data as xml) as xml_data
from #diagdata for xml auto,elements
```

So, now that you have your performance data in XML format, here are some queries against the temp table you created. For example, let's get some metrics about memory by extracting the elements and data related to memory resources. Basically, the next query returns content similar to the DBCC MemoryStatus output. You can reformat the output, which was originally XML data, and store it to a history table for point-in-time data collection and further analysis.

```
declare @x varchar(max)
declare @dochandle int

select @x = data
from #diagdata
where component_name = 'resource'

exec sp_xml_preparedocument @dochandle output, @x

select *
from openxml(@dochandle, '/resource/memoryReport/entry', 3)
with (description varchar(255), value bigint)

exec sp_xml_removedocument @dochandle
```

The following is the output from this T-SQL block:

Description	value
Available Physical Memory	24826863616
Available Virtual Memory	8742456905728
Available Paging File	57586995200
Working Set	1703915520
Percent of Committed Memory in WS	100
Page Faults	640618
System physical memory high	1
System physical memory low	0
Process physical memory low	0
Process virtual memory low	0
VM Reserved	52011684
VM Committed	1646180
Locked Pages Allocated	0
Large Pages Allocated	0
Emergency Memory	1024
Emergency Memory In Use	16
Target Committed	24055368
Current Committed	1646184
Pages Allocated	1346872
Pages Reserved	0
Pages Free	11688
Pages In Use	527584
Page Alloc Potential	30626448
NUMA Growth Phase	0
Last OOM Factor	0
Last OS Error	0

Furthermore, if you want to get the top ten waits on the server, you can extract that information as well and show wait statistics by count and duration with the next two XML queries, respectively. You can see there is an attribute embedded in the XML, that is, /byCount and /byDuration. The following are the queries, each in its own T-SQL block, with each block followed by its output:

```
--Top 10 waits by count:

declare @x varchar(max)
declare @dochandle int

select @x = data
from #diagdata
where component_name = 'query_processing'

exec sp_xml_preparedocument @dochandle output, @x

select *
from openxml(@dochandle, '/queryProcessing/topWaits/nonPreemptive/byCount/wait', 3)
with (waitType varchar(255), waits bigint, averageWaitTime bigint, maxWaitTime bigint)

exec sp_xml_removedocument @dochandle
```

waitType	waits	averageWaitTime	maxWaitTime
ASYNC_NETWORK_IO	579234	0	331
HADR_FILESTREAM_IOMGR_IOCOMPLETION	153827	1229	37490921
WRITELOG	114160	2	1603
SLEEP_BPOOL_FLUSH	57258	0	40
CXPACKET	15922	3	33816
LOGBUFFER	7877	0	259
PAGEIOLATCH_SH	6132	0	34
PAGELATCH_EX	5764	0	16
IO_COMPLETION	3816	3617	13803302
PAGEIOLATCH_EX	1816	2	124

```
-- Top 10 waits by duration:

declare @x varchar(max)
declare @dochandle int

select @x = data
from #diagdata
where component_name = 'query_processing'

exec sp_xml_preparedocument @dochandle output, @x
```

```
select *
from openxml(@dochandle, '/queryProcessing/topWaits/nonPreemptive/byDuration/wait', 3)
with (waitType varchar(255), waits bigint, averageWaitTime bigint, maxWaitTime bigint)

exec sp_xml_removedocument @dochandle

--Waits Output by Duration:
```

waitType	waits	averageWaitTime	maxWaitTime
HADR_FILESTREAM_IOMGR_IOCOMPLETION	153827	1229	37490921
IO_COMPLETION	3816	3617	13803302
XE_LIVE_TARGET_TVF	37	36581	60000
ASYNC_NETWORK_IO	579234	0	331
WRITELOG	114160	2	1603
LCK_M_S	59	1457	70411
CXPACKET	15922	3	33816
ASYNC_IO_COMPLETION	102	405	10624
SLEEP_BPOOL_FLUSH	57258	0	40
LOGBUFFER	7877	0	259

```
--Drop the temp table when you've finished:

drop table #diagdata
```

So, is XML spinning you on your head yet? Do you wish there was some neat graphical user interface Microsoft would give you for sp_server_diagnostics? You already know where this is going. With the SQL Server 2012 System Health Reporting Dashboard, Microsoft has put this rich GUI and collection of reports on top of this system stored procedure to allow you to visualize sp_server_diagnostics, as well as the system_health session.

SQL Server 2012 System Health Reporting Dashboard

For a default SQL Server 2012 installation, you will always see two active XEvent sessions as it imports the data from sys.dm_xe_sessions output, which shows the system_health session and the sp_server_diagnostics session. The SQL Server 2012 System Health Reporting Dashboard displays the information graphically of the combined output in a visually intuitive manner. The SQL Server 2012 Health Reporting Dashboard was created by Denzil Ribeiro, a senior SQL premier field engineer at Microsoft, and is downloadable from Microsoft's TechNet.

You can download the SQL Server 2012 System Health Reporting Dashboard from the following URL:

http://gallery.technet.microsoft.com/scriptcenter/SQL-2012-System-Health-eb753bb6

Once at the site, you will download the SystemHealthSessionReports.zip file. Within the .zip file, you will find all the components you need to get started. When you download the dashboard reports from Microsoft, there will be three components in the package, including the script to create the database and schema, the .rdl report files, and the readme file that walks you through the deployment and setup. These components are represented graphically in Figure 6-15.

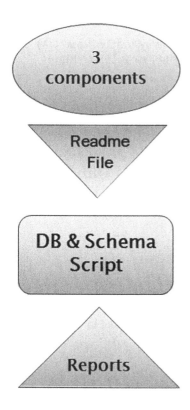

Figure 6-15. *A graphical overview of the SQL Server 2012 Performance Dashboard Reports components*

When you are finished installing and configuring all the components of the system health dashboard, you will have created and deployed the objects shown in Table 6-1.

Table 6-1. *All the Objects in the SQL Server 2012 System Health Dashboard: Tables, Sprocs, and Reports*

Tables	Stored Procedures	Reports (.rdl Files)
tbl_ServerDiagnostics		
tbl_ImportStatus	spLoadSystemHealthSession	ImportSessionStatus
tbl_BlockingXeOutput	SpLoadQueryProcessingComponent _Blocking	Blocking
tbl_connectivity_ring_buffer	spLoadConnectivity_ring_buffer	ConnectivityRingBuffer
tbl_DeadlockReport	spLoadDeadlockReport	DeadlockReport
tbl_errors	SpLoadErrorRecorded	Errors_reported
tbl_IO_SUBSYSTEM	SpLoadIO_SUBSYSTEMComponent	IO_Subsystem

(continued)

Table 6-1. (*continued*)

Tables	Stored Procedures	Reports (.rdl Files)
tbl_OS_WAIT_STATS_byDuration	SpLoadQueryProcessingComponent _TopWaits	TopWaits
tbl_QUERY_PROCESSING	SpLoadQueryProcessing	Query_Processing
tbl_Resource	SpLoadResourceComponent	Resource
tbl_scheduler_monitor	spLoadSchedulerMonitor	DashBoard
tbl_security_ring_buffer	SpLoadSecurityRingBuffer	SecurityRingBuffer
tbl_Summary	SpLoadComponentSummary	
tbl_SYSTEM	SpLoadSYSTEMComponent	System
tbl_waitqueries	spLoadWaitQueries	WaitQueries
tbl_XEImport	sp_ImportXML	
tblQryProcessingXmlOutput	SpLoadQueryProcessingComponent	

There are about 15 .rdl reports including the main dashboard.rdl, which acts as a landing page for the rest of the reports. As you know, SQL Server 2012 provides an array of diagnostic data collected by the system health Extended Events session as well as the sp_server_Diagnostics system stored procedure. Information collected and reported on by the server dashboard includes the following:

- CPU utilization

- Memory resource utilization

- Blocking events longer than 30 seconds

- Queries that were waiting more than 30 seconds for some wait_types and more than 15 seconds for others

- The status of all the sp_server_diagnostics subsystems and their underlying data

- Other ring buffer data such as security and connectivity ring buffers

The System Health Dashboard does require the SQL Server Reporting Services component to be installed and configured. Because the dashboard relies on the system_health Extended Events session, it is highly recommended that you increase the size and number of the rollover files. (The documentation tells you to increase it to five rollover files, from four, and to 25MB each, from 5MB. This is to prevent excessive rollover and allow it to capture more data, especially if there are significant issues that occur.)

Full deployment instructions are in the downloaded documentation, which has you create the XEvents_ ImportSystemHealth repository database where data is imported and stored procedures are created. All these stored procedures are unencrypted, so you can further optimize them and modify the code to your own needs. There are two ways to import the session data to the database. The first is to manually run or schedule a SQLAgent job to execute the spLoadSystemHealthSession on a routine or daily basis. The spLoadSystemHealthSession will import the data into the tables by invoking a number of specific other stored procedures that collect the data for the various performance health metrics, querying the current instance for the system health XEvent session data.

The behavior is such that it will import from the current active default system_health session, as well as the datetime format. The date from the system_health.xel files is stored as Coordinated Universal Time (UTC), and that's how the date will be stored in the import tables, unless you specify the UTC offset to your local time zone. The following example shows how to initialize the parameters. Of course, you can always use T-SQL to format the UTC date, but it's best to store the date in your current time zone so you can accurately choose the time frames for reporting. In the following query, you specify the UTC offset in the @UTDDateDif-6.

```
exec spLoadSystemHealthSession @path_to_health_session='D:\XELFiles\system_health*.xel',
@UTDDateDiff=-6
```

Each time the spLoadSystemHealthSession is run, the import will update and store each step of the process, along with the date and time. This is helpful so you know the current and last status of the import. To get that information, just query from the tbl_ImportStatus table.

```
select * from tbl_ImportStatus
```

Your output will appear as follows:

```
StepName      Status      Starttime
Load System Health Session    Processing     2014-09-29 10:45:13.357
Importing XEL file    Processing    2014-09-29 10:45:13.407
Load Scheduler Monitor    Processing    2014-09-29 10:45:14.510
Load Resource Server Health Component    Processing    2014-09-29 10:45:15.193
Load IO_Subsystem Server Health Component    Processing    2014-09-29 10:45:18.330
Load System Server Health Component    Processing    2014-09-29 10:45:18.697
Load System Health Summary    Processing    2014-09-29 10:45:19.220
Load Query_Processing Server Health Component    Processing    2014-09-29 10:45:19.633
Load Security Ring Buffer    Processing    2014-09-29 10:45:26.293
Load Errors Recorded    Processing    2014-09-29 10:45:26.380
Wait Queries    Processing    2014-09-29 10:45:26.420
Connectivity Ring Buffer    Processing    2014-09-29 10:45:26.510
Deadlock Report    Processing    2014-09-29 10:45:27.650
Import Finished    Done    2014-09-29 10:45:27.653
```

The second method for importing the session is using the ImportSessionStatus.rdl report via SQL Server Reporting Services, and you can select relevant parameters such as the server name and whether to import or process the system_health from a file share location. This approach makes it possible to import data from .xel files from another SQL instance stored on a UNC file share and initializes the @path_to_health_session input parameter. You can also set the UTC offset here and select the destination database directly from this report.

To use the reports, you must deploy them to your SQL Server Report Server and configure their path. After you extract the report files, project, and solution from XEventReporting.zip, you'll need to open, as the administrator, the XEventReporting.sln file in Visual Studio and set the TargetServerUrl property, as shown in Figure 6-16.

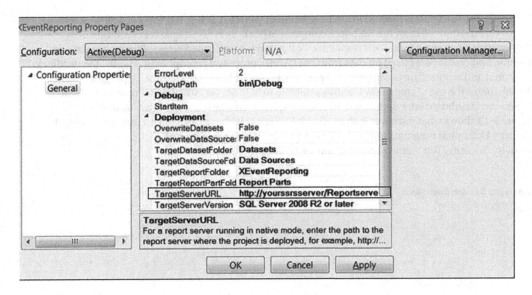

Figure 6-16. *The TargetServerURL property for SSRS deployment*

Once the reports are successfully deployed, you can navigate to the main System Health Session Dashboard (dashboard.rdl) and enter your input parameters for the server you want to report on, the database repository (XEvents_ImportSystemHealth) name, and the start and end date and time. You can see the report parameters in Figure 6-17 . Once you select the desired parameters, you will click View Report.

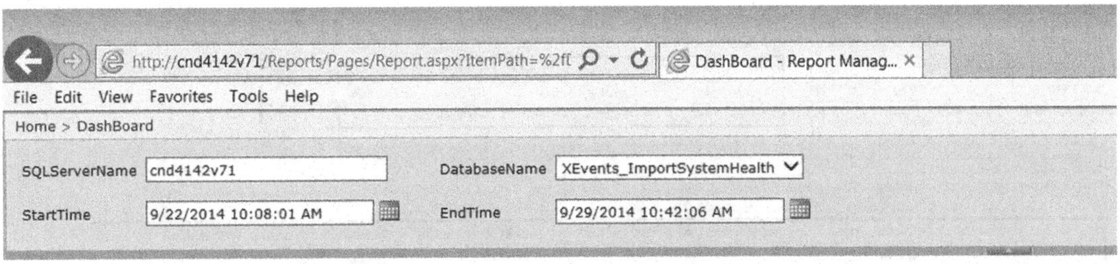

Figure 6-17. *Report parameters for user selection for the dashboard*

The System Health Session Dashboard was made possible with the new features introduced in SQL Server 2012, including the system_health session, _ring_buffer_recorded, sp_serverdiagnostics, and xml_deadlock_graph. xml_deadlock_graph is a great new feature in that you no longer need to set any trace flags because all historical deadlock information is now captured by default! Previously, to capture deadlock details, you needed to enable the right global trace flags, by either using a startup parameter option (in other words, T1222) or using the command DBCC TRACEON(1222,-1) once SQL was started. Trace flag 1222 shows the deadlock victim, each process involved in the deadlock. TF 1204 zooms in on the nodes involved in the deadlock, each having its own section with the last one about deadlock details of the victim. In addition, you can use TF 3605 (DBCC TRACEON(3605)) with the previous ones to write the output of the deadlock information to the error log.

Internally, the CPU data is derived from the `scheduler_monitor_ring_buffer_recorded` target, the memory data is derived from the Resource component of `sp_server_diagnostics`, and security and connectivity are derived from their respective `_ring_buffer_recorded` events. Blocking tasks, wait information, and queries are based on data from the QUERY processing component. Finally, the deadlocks are monitored and reported on using the `xml_deadlock` graph. Indeed, it is a simple, deployable package that demonstrates the use of some new features available in SQL Server 2012. I will return to the System Health Session Dashboard later in the book to discuss more about the reports that are available.

Figure 6-18 shows what the main System Health Session Dashboard looks like, complete with CPU and Memory Utilization timeline graphs and drill-down activity to other reports such as Errors, Blocking, Connectivity, Security, Top Waiting Queries, and Deadlocks.

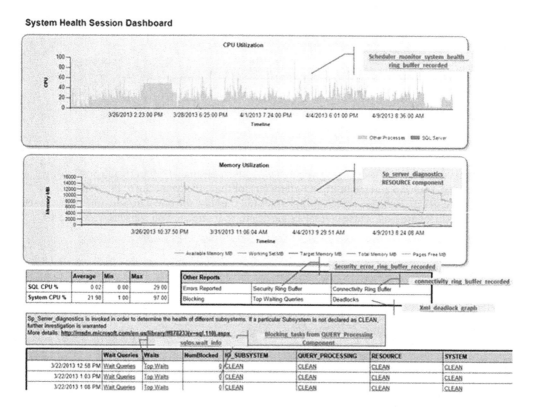

Figure 6-18. Graphic display of the main System Health Session Dashboard for SQL Server 2012

SQL Profiler, Trace, and Extended Events allow you to capture performance data and monitor, troubleshoot, and even audit your environment. I will show you some simple methods to capture and audit your environment using the default trace, as well as Extended Events in Chapters 7 and 9.

Other Free and Downloadable Tools

In this section, you will learn about some other useful tools that are free and available for download that can help you in your efforts to manage and document your SQL Servers, measure SQL Server performance, and analyze best practices. Although there are several tools out there, I mention these few as examples that have helped me throughout my DBA travels.

PowerShell

Any book on tools of the trade to assist with your SQL Server health check would not be complete without at least mentioning a powerful scripting language called PowerShell. It is also an advanced language, with a bit of a learning curve. There is a wealth of information out there on PowerShell and several resources that range from beginner to advanced. There is much to learn on this topic, and therefore I can't do it much justice here. A complete introductory course on PowerShell is in order but out of scope for this book. One important thing to note about PowerShell is that it is often a required component of many of the tools, including the ones discussed here.

Even though PowerShell is increasingly popular for use with SQL Server, it is essentially a Windows language. With SQL Server 2008, a PowerShell executable program was provided and can be invoked by launching sqlps.exe. A set of cmdlets specific to using PowerShell with SQL Server is incorporated in the sqlps.exe executable. A cmdlet is used in the Windows PowerShell environment as a lightweight command that is invoked by automation scripts from the command line. In addition, you can navigate through SQL Server as if it were a file system by adding a PowerShell drive (PSDrive). You can open a SQL PowerShell session by typing the command sqlps.exe. The window, similar to a DOS command window, shown in Figure 6-19 will open.

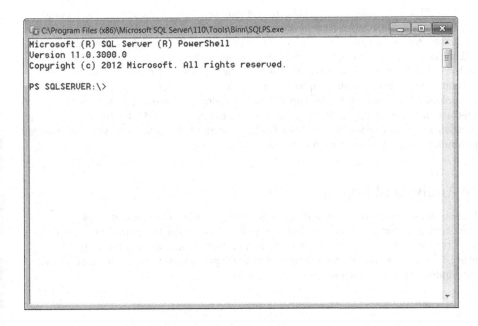

Figure 6-19. SQL PowerShell window in DOS

You can see that this applet is included in SQL Server Tools path. A PS SQLServer:\> prompt appears. You can start by typing help, or the simple command Get-Process will list all the currently running processes on Windows and other related information.

Since PowerShell is an advanced topic and this book is more beginner to intermediate, I will make you aware of its potential usages and point you to some PowerShell resources. For your own further investigation and learning on this topic, you can start out with these MSDN links:

> SQL Server PowerShell: http://msdn.microsoft.com/en-us/library/hh245198.aspx

> Windows PowerShell scripting: http://technet.microsoft.com/en-us/ scriptcenter/powershell.aspx

Indeed, there is much about PowerShell you can learn, and it is one more powerful tool in the DBA shed of tools of the trade to assist you in your SQL Server health checks. One of the important steps I discussed in establishing a healthy SQL Server environment is to first take an inventory and document your servers. Here is where PowerShell scripting can help.

SQLPowerDoc

As inventory collection and documentation is a big part of the healthy SQL solution, I want to mention a great documentation and inventory system that uses PowerShell called SQLPowerDoc. This comprehensive utility was compiled, written, and created by SQL Server MVP Kendyl Van Dyke and is available on CodePlex.com for free download. You can access the tool directly by going to this URL:

https://sqlpowerdoc.codeplex.com/

As described on CodePlex, SQL PowerDoc is a collection of Windows PowerShell scripts and modules that discover, document, and diagnose SQL Server instances and their underlying Windows OS and machine configurations. SQL Power Doc works with all versions of SQL Server from SQL Server 2000 through 2012 and all versions of Windows Server and consumer Windows operating systems from Windows 2000 and Windows XP through Windows Server 2012 and Windows 8. SQL PowerDoc is also capable of documenting Windows Azure SQL databases. It comes with complete instructions on how to set this up and install the modules. At first it may look a little tricky to get it set up, but once you do, the scope and breadth of the information captured are amazing. All the output is captured to and neatly formatted into multiple tabs on a Microsoft Excel spreadsheet for your review and analysis. It is a pretty comprehensive tool, as far as free ones go, and a great contribution to the SQL Server community and DBAs at large.

Performance Analysis of Logs

I spoke extensively about performance counters and how to read and calculate them from the sys.dm_os_ sqlperformance_counters view earlier in this book. I also discussed some of the key counters to set up through Windows Performance Monitor in Chapter 3. Performance Analysis of Logs (PAL) is another free downloadable tool available on CodePlex that draws upon the data exposed in sys.dm_os_sqlperformance_ counters and other Windows counters. You can get your PAL here:

https://pal.codeplex.com/

PAL helps you visualize and collect all the needed counters and analyzes the performance counter logs using industry-known thresholds. It is a powerful tool essentially created using PowerShell, with various user parameters available.

The tool requires three components that should be installed on the server that will be running PAL. All the links to download these components are available on the PAL CodePlex home page.

- PowerShell v2.0 or greater

- Microsoft .NET Framework 3.5 Service Pack 1

- Microsoft Chart Controls for Microsoft .NET Framework 3.5

The installation is quite simple. Once you see the PAL Setup Wizard, as displayed in Figure 6-20, follow the prompts.

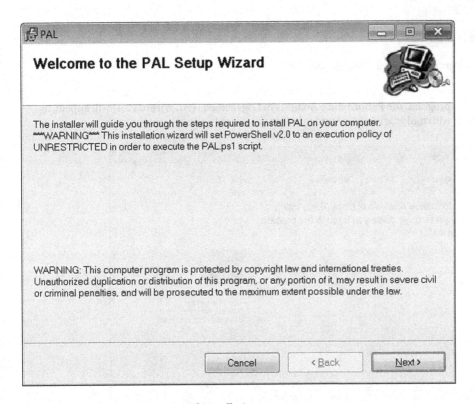

Figure 6-20. *The PAL Setup Wizard installation screen*

The wizard will ask for an installation folder. You can accept the default path or browse for desired install location. Once path is selected, continue with the install by clicking Next.

You will see at the end that updates for the Microsoft Chart controls and .NET Framework SP1 will be applied. Any more recent updates must be manually downloaded and installed. After PAL is successfully installed, you should see a program icon or shortcut that looks like the one in Figure 6-21.

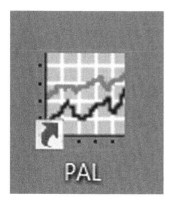

Figure 6-21. *The program icon created for PAL tool*

If you launch the program, the Performance Analysis of Logs screen (PAL Wizard v2.4) will appear, as shown in Figure 6-22, with multiple configuration tabs that the wizard will walk you through.

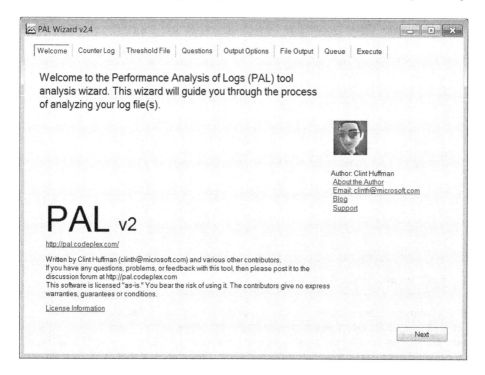

Figure 6-22. *PAL wizard configuration*

If you select the Counter Log tab, shown in Figure 6-23, or click Next, this screen will allow you to choose a performance counter log file and path. You can also select a specific time frame by restricting the data analysis to a datetime range. You set the begin and end time. There is a sample included to help you understand how to use the tool. You can also select your performance data stored in a .csv file. Click Next.

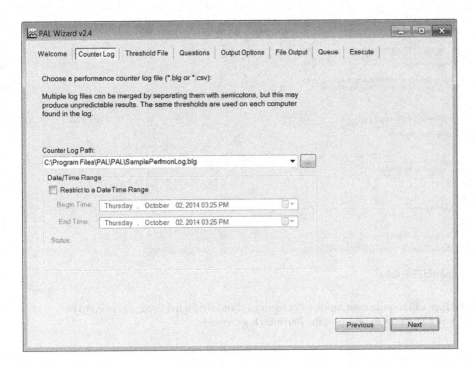

Figure 6-23. *Counter Log tab*

On the Threshold File tab, you can choose from several templates for the appropriate thresholds, as shown in Figure 6-24.

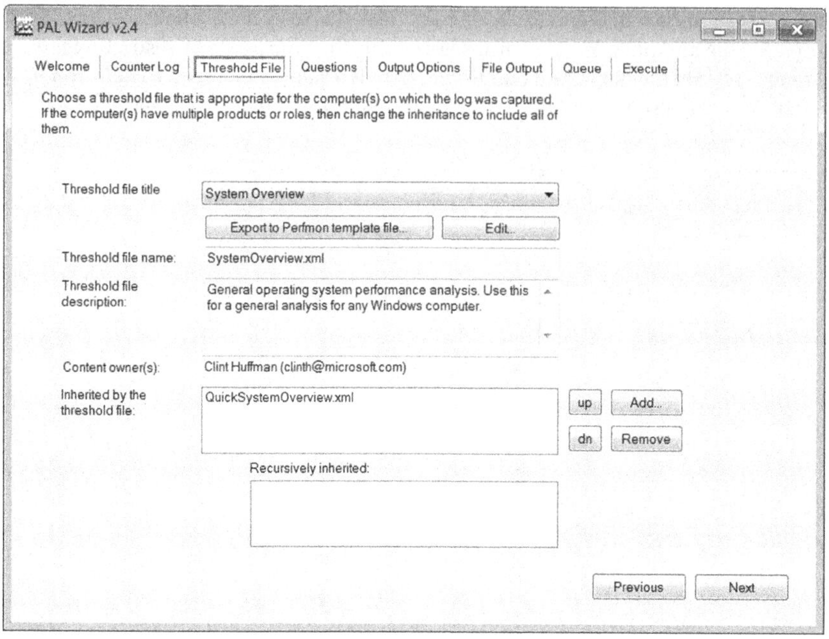

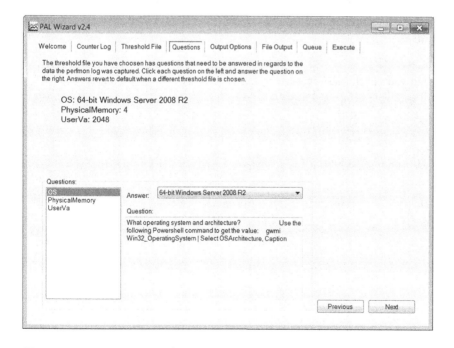

Figure 6-24. PAL Threshold File tab

Certain threshold files will require user input, or questions, shown in Figure 6-25, will need to be answered so that PAL will know how to interpret the Perfmon log properly.

Figure 6-25. PAL Questions tab

Next, you will want to specify the output options, as in Figure 6-26, which set the time intervals and divide the counter log data into equal time slices for easy analysis. The default Auto analysis interval specifies that the logs be cut automatically into 30 time slices. You can also enable the option to process all of the counters in the counter logs, though doing this is sure to increase resource usage.

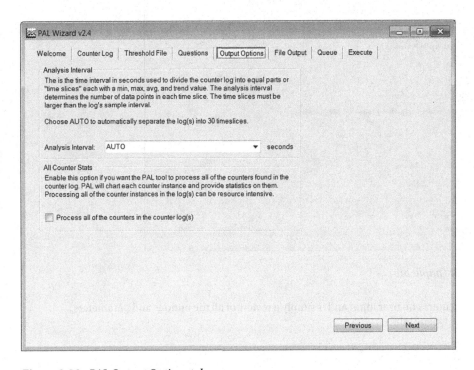

Figure 6-26. *PAL Output Options tab*

Once you configure the output options, you then specify the actual file output directory and path for the PAL reports, specified as in Figure 6-27, that will be generated (based on all your selected parameters). You have the option of formatting the PAL reports as HTML or XML documents.

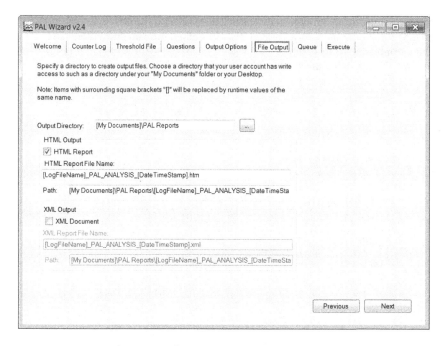

Figure 6-27. *PAL File Output tab*

The Queue tab requires no user input and is simply a review of all the options and parameters. Figure 6-28 shows the Queue tab.

Figure 6-28. *PAL Queue review tab*

Once you review and are satisfied, click Next or select the Execute tab.

The analysis can begin now that you have provided all the relevant information and selected parameters. Review the option here and set the execution priority and threading, as shown in Figure 6-29. Clicking Finish will launch the program and begin the analysis.

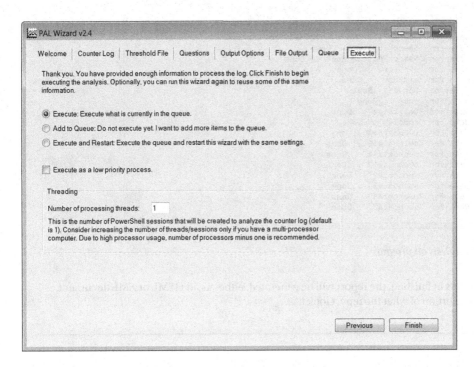

Figure 6-29. PAL Execute tab

After the wizard is complete, the app will launch in a command window and begin to process the analysis of the log (.blg or .csv file) provided by the user. It will show the inspection of the counter data, as well as the progress, as shown in Figure 6-30.

```
C:\Windows\System32\cmd.exe - C:\Users\Q07642\AppData\Local\Temp\{8cc51885-b16d-4bac-93...

        Counter data for "mmc"...Done
        Counter data for "MSASCui"...Done

Analysis of SamplePerfmonLog.blg...
    Progress: 11% (Analysis 9 of 80)
    [ooooooo                                                              ]

        Counter data for "SearchFilterHost"...Done
        Counter data for "SearchIndexer"...Done
        Counter data for "SearchProtocolHost"...Done
        Counter data for "services"...Done
        Counter data for "sidebar"...Done
        Counter data for "SLsvc"...Done
        Counter data for "smss"...Done
        Counter data for "Solitaire"...Done
        Counter data for "spoolsv"...Done
        Counter data for "svchost#1"...Done
        Counter data for "svchost#10"...Done
        Counter data for "svchost#11"...Done
        Counter data for "svchost#12"...Done
        Counter data for "svchost#2"...Done
        Counter data for "svchost#3"...Done
        Counter data for "svchost#4"...Done
        Counter data for "svchost#5"...Done
```

Figure 6-30. *PAL analysis on progress*

Once the progress in finished, the report will be generated, either as an HTML or XML document. Figure 6-31 shows a portion of what the report look like.

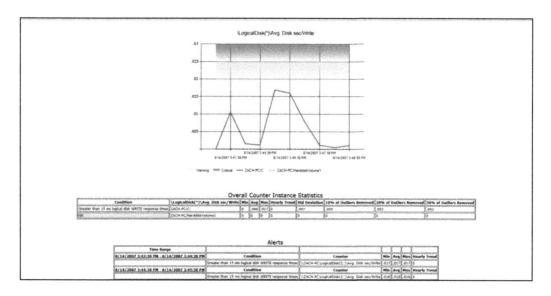

Figure 6-31. *Sample HTML PAL report*

SQL Server Best Practice Analyzer (Through 2012)

If you're not sure your SQL Server instances are configured properly and following Microsoft's best practices, you may want to get hold of the SQL Server Best Practice Analyzer (BPA). This diagnostic tool provides a quick overview and evaluation of your SQL Server. As the name implies, it will help identify various issues on your server and ensure it's up-to-date with the latest service packs. The BPA, as per the details on its download page, can perform the following functions:

- Gather information about a server and a Microsoft SQL Server 2012 instance installed on that server

- Determine whether the configurations are set according to the recommended best practices

- Report on all configurations, indicating settings that differ from recommendations

- Indicate potential problems in the installed instance of SQL Server

- Recommend solutions to potential problems

For SQL Server 2012, you can download it here:

`www.microsoft.com/en-us/download/details.aspx?id=29302`

SQL Server BPA for 2012 runs on any edition of SQL Server 2012, but it's not backward compatible. You'll need to download the SQL BPA for each respective version. In addition, you'll need to consider the following prerequisites:

- PowerShell V2.0

- Microsoft Baseline Configuration Analyzer (BCA) V2.0

As you see, PowerShell is the base requirement for many tools of the trade. Microsoft BCA allows you to analyze multiple configurations of your servers against a predefined set of best practices and reports results of the analyses. Since with BPA you can scan both local computer and remote computers, the setup will prompt you to enable remoting using `Enable-PSRemoting`, which is required on each machine you want to run the analysis against remotely. To run the SQL Server BPA, you must launch the Microsoft BCA and select it from the "Select a product" drop-down menu, as in Figure 6-32.

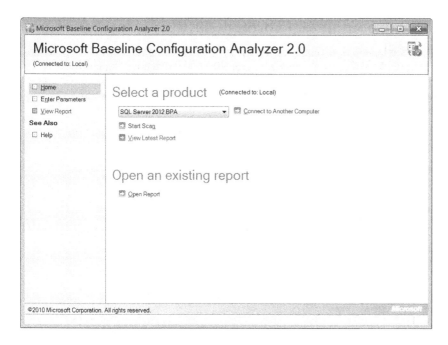

Figure 6-32. *Microsoft Baseline Configuration Analyzer (BCA)*

Then you need to enter the parameters of which server/instance to scan, represented in Figure 6-33. Please note if you are running this locally or as a default instance, you'll need to enter **MSSQLServer**. Check off one or more of the components you would like checked. Then click Start Scan, as shown in Figure 6-33. After the analysis is done, you can view the report and export it into XML format.

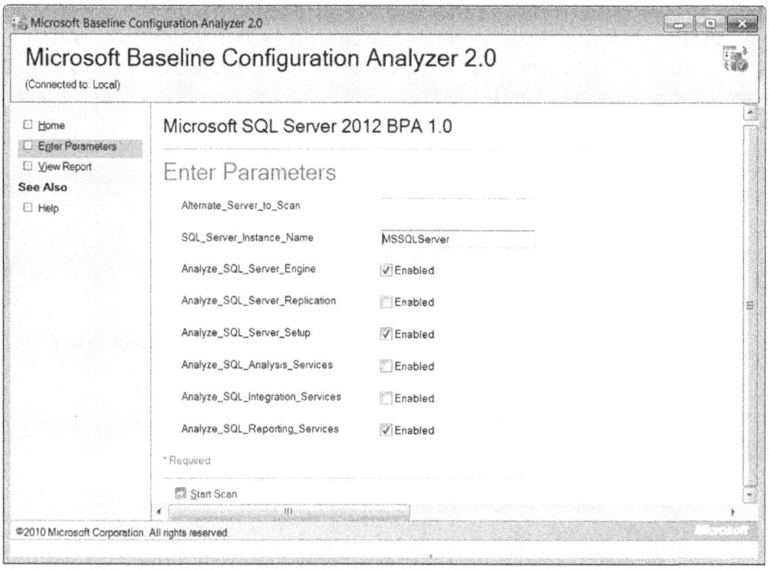

Figure 6-33. *Select the server and instance, plus the components to scan*

Closing the Tool Shed

Well, this chapter has covered a lot of material and introduced you to the wide array of valuable tools and information available that you as a database professional can easily get started using. Indeed, there are more out there than I can possibly cover in this book. However, these tools, though some of them quite simple to use, give you the ability to manage, monitor, triage, and troubleshoot performance issues. They will help you ensure that your SQL Server environments are healthy by getting familiar with the basic features and facets to collect, analyze, and interpret performance data.

The greatest aspect of all the tools and features I discussed here is that beyond the initial cost of SQL Server licensing they won't cost you or your organization a single extra penny to use them. This is the return on investment that this book is providing. All you need is the knowledge and desire to excel in your DBA career, which you have shown with the good fortune of reading this book. Now that you are armed with an awesome arsenal of database tools and weapons, I will build upon these concepts and take what you have learned to show you how to create a repository to collect and store your SQL Server performance data. This repository will allow you to persist performance data beyond restarts, create baselines, do historical trend analysis and reporting, and serve as a documentation and audit-proof trail. The healthy SQL plan continues to come together!

CHAPTER 7

■ ■ ■

Creating a SQL Health Repository

You now have enough knowledge and technical foundation to put together all you know so far to create and build a DBA and SQL health repository. In this chapter, I will expand on the tools and scripts I have been discussing.

Laying the Repository Groundwork

Since you will be collecting a whole host of metadata, performance measures, and statistics regarding the health of your SQL Server on a continuous basis, you will need a place to store and review this information. One readily available place to store and review collected data is an Excel spreadsheet. Here you can create a tab for each set of specific metadata. For example, one tab can store results for top expensive queries by memory, another can store top expensive queries by CPU, and so forth. You can label each tab accordingly. In addition, you can format the spreadsheet so that ultimately you can import this data into a database.

The preferred method of data collection and archiving historical data is, of course, the database. Ironically, I have seen many DBAs dump raw information into a spreadsheet or even Microsoft Word for review, even though a relational database is the perfect place to store, sort, query, filter, and secure your data. Of course, if you have no time or place to create a database repository, collecting information in a spreadsheet is better than nothing. You can count, sort, and filter the data, as well as create separate tabs for various performance metrics. In fact, this is what Glenn Berry and Mitch Wheat sought to do with the Diagnostic Information Queries and the .NET app SQLDiagCmd.

However, if you have your performance, configuration, and inventory metadata in a database, you can create several T-SQL statements to query the data and pinpoint where a potential issue lies. With a database repository, the possibilities are endless. Moreover, besides just troubleshooting, you can create simple and complex SQL performance, configuration, and inventory reports with graphs and charts.

There's nothing like a colorful pie chart to show your managers when they come to you and say, "Hey, how many SQL Server instances do we have, and which versions are they?" This question has come up at many of the companies I have worked with. Usually, it's in the context of an audit, which I will discuss in Chapter 10, or a true-up. A *true-up* as related to the SQL Server world is when Microsoft, in accordance with a company's enterprise agreement (EA), reconciles the number of SQL Server engine installations with the number of actual licenses purchased. In fact, recently I imported an inventory spreadsheet in a database repository, created some data mining queries for the existing data set, and generated a 3D pie graph showing the total number of SQL Server instances by version, physical vs. virtual, and by edition.

Before I get to the details of the management data warehouse (MDW), which will serve as your database repository in this chapter, I'll discuss a little background. Then you will be walked through the setup and implementation of the repository. SQL Server 2005 shipped with new dynamic management views and functions that exposed metadata to help you in analyzing and troubleshooting internals and performance issues, but there was no native way or existing feature set that would collect, store, and persist these performance statistics from the set of DMVs available. Therefore, you needed to purchase third-party software or come up with your own solution.

Then, based upon the framework of SQL Server 2005, members of the Microsoft Custom Advisory Team (M-CAT) came up with a utility that is essentially a SQL Server 2005 Performance Data Warehouse. You can download it from CodePlex by searching for SQL DMVstats v1.0. DMVstats 1.0 is an application that can collect, analyze, and report on SQL Server 2005 DMV performance data. This system will install all the components including the DMV data collection (scheduled via SQL Agent jobs), database repository, and SSRS reports. If you are working on version 2005, you can find the complete code project and full documentation here:

http://sqldmvstats.codeplex.com

I will not drill down on this tool any further because all the information you need to know about DMVstats is at the aforementioned URL. I mention it because I believe it was the early basis for the development and inclusion of the ability to collect, store, analyze, and report on performance stats in SQL Server 2008, retitled as the SQL Server *management data warehouse* (MDW). This functionality is now packaged with the core database product in versions SQL Server 2008 and newer.

Deploying the Management Data Warehouse

You can use MDW to baseline the performance of your SQL Server instances, trend the performance over time, and monitor and report on the state of the health of the SQL Server instances. In this chapter, you will set up a central MDW database repository, run the MDW wizard on each SQL Server instance, and point each data collection to the target MDW. Each local instance will have its own local cache directory that will stage the data for upload into your centralized MDW database repository. The collection agent job will collect and store the data locally and then at some scheduled time load it to the central MDW. By default, server activity and query statistics are cached on the server, while disk usage uploads in real time (on a schedule).

You will also need to map logins and define users so that each instance can connect and upload the data. The MDW is deployable in a few clicks of a wizard and creates a new database named MDW, as well as the corresponding SQL Server Agent jobs, SSIS packages, and SSRS reports, which makes monitoring and performance analysis easy.

I introduced you to one of the out-of-the-box features to create a management data warehouse in Chapter 5; here I'll discuss how this works and the simplicity of rapidly deploying such a performance warehouse. To reiterate, once you navigate to the Management folder in SSMS, you right-click the Data Collection item and launch the Configure Management Data Warehouse Wizard. Click Next on the Welcome screen to proceed.

On this first screen, you are offered two choices, as shown in Figure 7-1. Choose the first option.

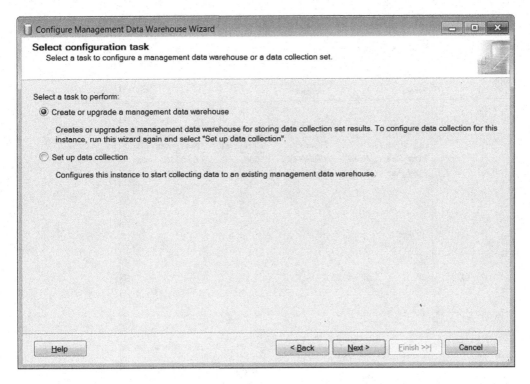

Figure 7-1. *Selecting a configuration task for MDW*

The wizard prompts you to create a new database, as in Figure 7-2, that will serve as the SQL Server MDW data repository. Enter the desired database name and specify an initial size of at least 100MB. As you can see, all the create database options are available like when creating any new database via SSMS. Click OK when done.

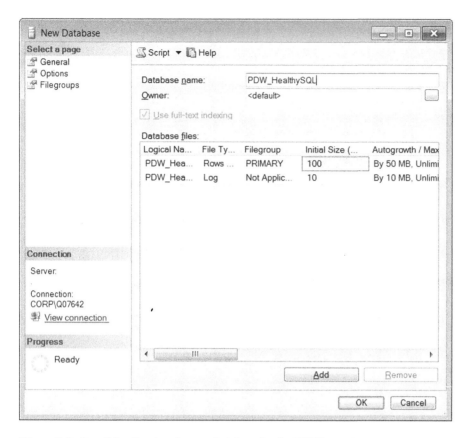

Figure 7-2. *Specifying the size of a new database for the MDW repository*

After you create the new MDW database, the next screen will prompt you to select the server and database that will be the host for the MDW repository, as shown in Figure 7-3. To continue, make your selections and click Next.

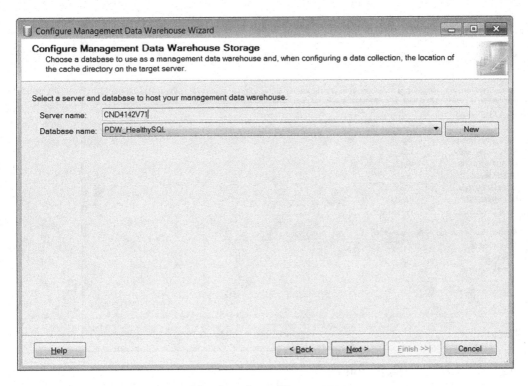

Figure 7-3. Selecting the server and database that will host MDW

Now you'll need to map logins and users to the proper MDW roles, as shown in Figure 7-4. Choose the logins/users to add to these roles accordingly and then click Next. There are three distinct roles for MDW.

- mdw_admin: This is the highest level of rights on the MDW database. Members of this role have both read and write permissions for uploading data and reports.

- mdw_writer: This role allows users to upload the data to the MDW database.

- mdw_reader: This is the lowest level of rights and used for reports.

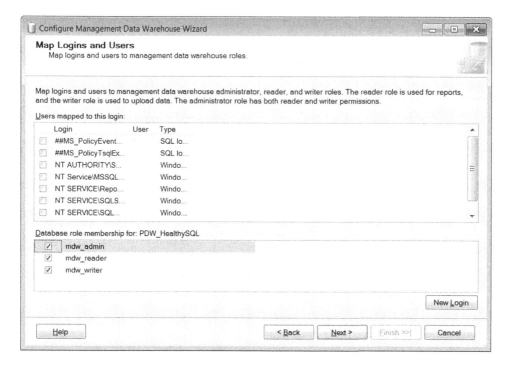

Figure 7-4. Mapping logins/users to MDW roles

The MDW wizard summarizes your selections. Review and click Finish to complete the wizard, as shown in Figure 7-5.

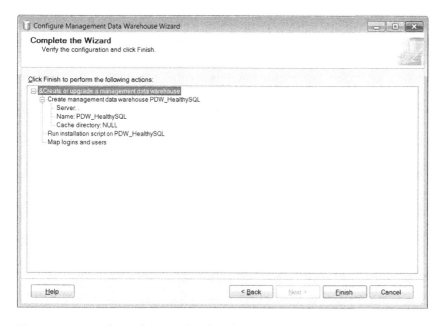

Figure 7-5. Completing the wizard and confirming your selections

Once all your input parameters are collected, the wizard will execute the steps to set up the MDW and display its progress, success or failure, as shown in Figure 7-6. The wizard will then perform the following actions:

- Create the MDW database

- Run the installation script against the database

- Map logins and users to the MDW roles

Once the wizard completes, ensure that the status messages display success for all actions. Your results should appear as in Figure 7-6.

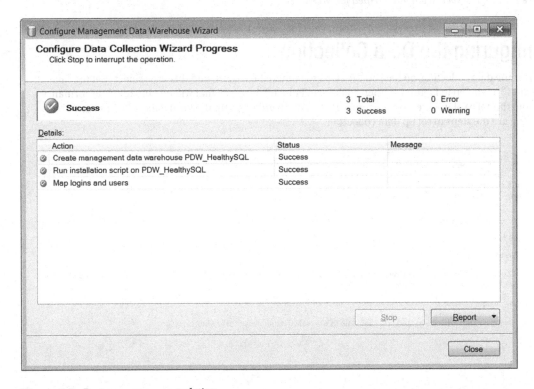

Figure 7-6. *Progress screen: completion*

Under the SQL Server Agent ➤ Jobs folder, there are some jobs created, as shown in Figure 7-7. One job added is called mdw_purge_data_[MDW_HealthySQL], which is used to clean up the data over time. To actually collect data, you need to enable collection. You are ready to proceed and set up the data collection process.

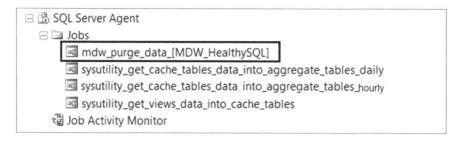

Figure 7-7. *SQL Server Agent jobs created for MDW*

Configuring the Data Collection

Now, for the data collection, go back to the steps to launch the wizard, and this time select "Set up data collection," as shown in Figure 7-8; then click Next. For each instance that will be uploading performance data into the MDW database, you must run the MDW wizard to set up the local data collection set. The following are the steps to set up data collection.

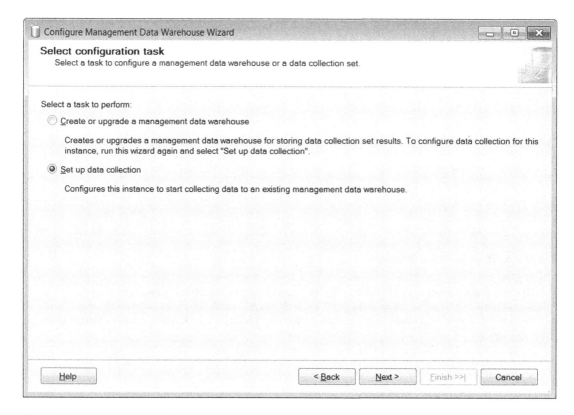

Figure 7-8. *Setting up data collection*

Here you select the MDW storage, which is the database repository you created the first time you ran the wizard. This step will have you specify a local cache directory for collection data, which will be uploaded to the MDW database at scheduled intervals. If you do not specify a custom path or leave it blank, it will use the default path or temp directory of the collector for the service account that your SQL Server Agent service is using.

It is important to note that when choosing a location for the cache directory, you should select a path that will have the least potential impact on SQL Server. Since there are many writes being performed to the cache directory, the directory should ideally be in a separate location from the actual SQL Server data and log files. Since the cache files can grow rapidly, you want to ensure that space is sufficient, and certainly you do not want to fill up the drives containing your SQL Server database files. In addition, the SQL Server Agent account should have privileges to the cache location, which I will discuss more in the upcoming section "Accounts, Privileges, Rights, and Credentials." Figure 7-9 shows this storage configuration step.

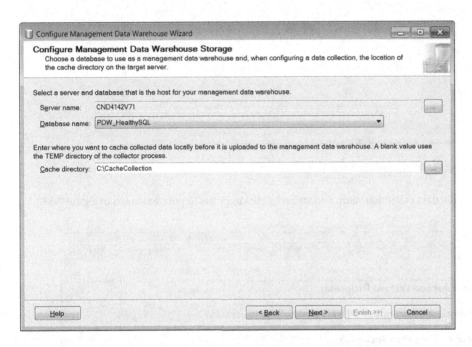

Figure 7-9. *Configuring MDW data storage and repository database*

View the summary of selections, shown in Figure 7-10, and click Finish to start the system collection sets and enable the data collection.

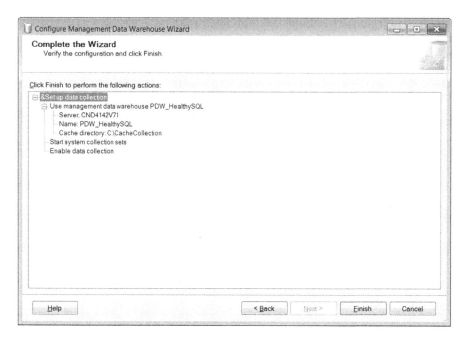

Figure 7-10. *Verifying the configuration and finishing*

You can review the data collection setup and status by clicking View Report, as shown in Figure 7-11.

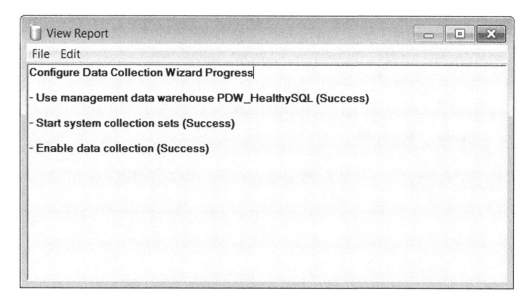

Figure 7-11. *Viewing the report for data collection setup*

Post-Configuration Tasks

If you go to the SQL Server Agent and peek into the All Jobs folder a illustrated in Figure 7-12, you will see, in addition to the original jobs setup with the MDW creation, that additional "collection set" jobs were also created. These are the MDW jobs that work together to gather all the performance data, at various scheduled intervals, and upload the data into your MDW database repository. To keep your MDW process running smoothly, do not delete or modify any of the job specifications for the data collection and upload jobs within SQL Server Agent.

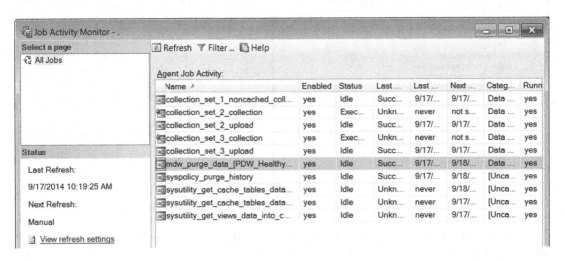

Figure 7-12. *The MDW-related SQL Server Agent jobs*

■ **Caution** Be careful not to delete or modify any of the MDW-related SQL Server Agent jobs.

Now that you have successfully set up and enabled your data collection, you can see that in your target MDW database, several objects were created. You can observe the multiple schemas, tables, views, stored procedures, and table-valued and scalar-valued functions in the database. You can see some of tables in Figure 7-13. If you want to see all the objects, you can drill down into the database object folders in SSMS and view them there.

Figure 7-13. *SSMS tables of some of the 44 tables created for MDW database*

If you go back to SSMS ➤ Management ➤ Data Collection ➤ System Data Collection, you will see all the created default data collection sets that will be used by MDW. You can see these data sets in Figure 7-14. They are Disk Usage, Query Statistics, Server Activity, and Utility Information. Let's define their purpose.

- *Disk Usage*: Collects data about the disk and log usage for all databases.

- *Query Statistics*: Collects query statistics, T-SQL text, and query plans of most of the statements that affect performance. Enables analysis of poorly performing queries in relation to overall SQL Server Database Engine activity.

- *Server Activity*: Collects top-level performance indicators for the computer and the database engine. Enables analysis of resource use, resource bottlenecks, and database engine activity.

- *Utility Information*: Collects data about instances of SQL Server that are managed in SMSS.

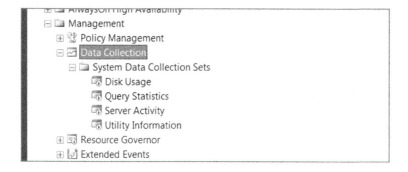

Figure 7-14. *System data collection sets, to be used for MDW*

Let's now take a look at the collection set properties, which will help you understand how they work, and build a foundation for setting up your own custom collections.

If you right-click any of the system data collection sets and select Properties from the pop-up menu, the Properties window will appear. Figure 7-15 shows the Properties window for Disk Usage.

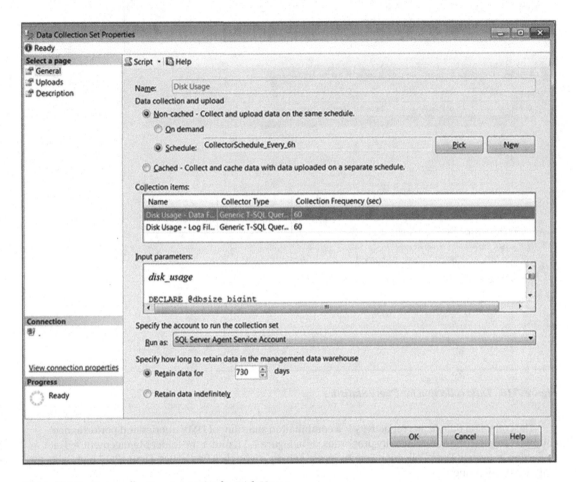

Figure 7-15. *Data collection properties for Disk Usage*

To see the properties of query statistics, under Management ➤ Data Collection ➤ System Data Collection Sets ➤ Query Statistics, right-click that collection and select Properties. You will now see the properties of this collection, as displayed in Figure 7-16.

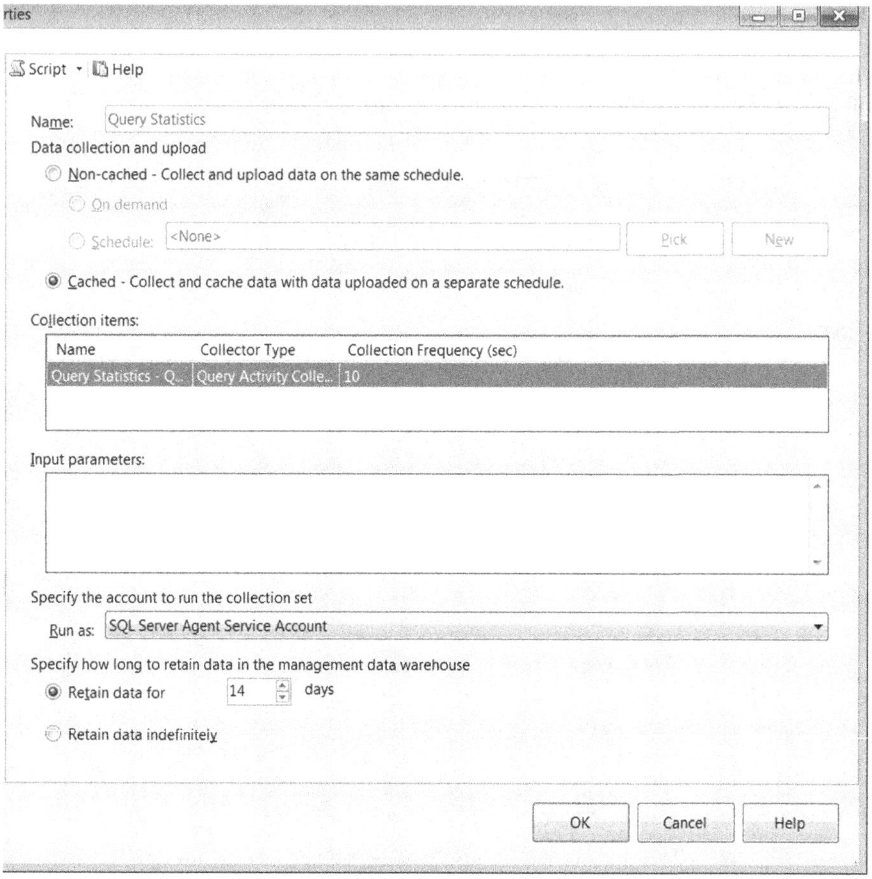

Figure 7-16. *Data collection for Query Statistics*

The collection data for server activity is a combination snapshot of DMV queries and performance counters. To get to the Server Activity properties, as in Figure 7-17, under the folder Management ➤ Data Collection ➤ System Data Collection Sets ➤ Server Activity, right-click Properties. Figure 7-17 highlights the DMV snapshot properties.

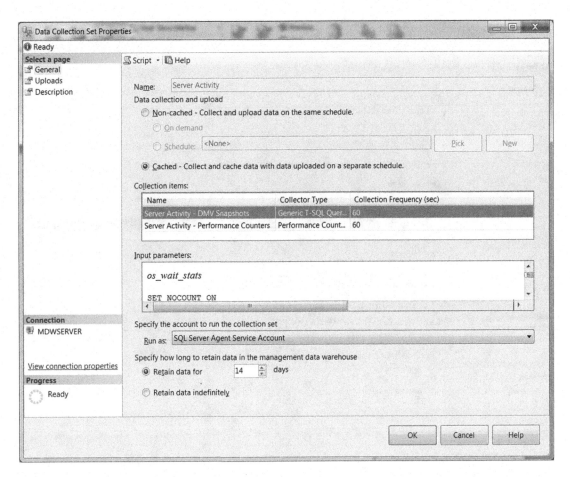

Figure 7-17. *Data collection properties for Server Activity: DMVs*

Now, if you click and select the Server Activity – Performance Counters item under Collection Items, the properties for the performance counters will be displayed, as shown in Figure 7-18. You can scroll through the performance counters in the Input Parameters field.

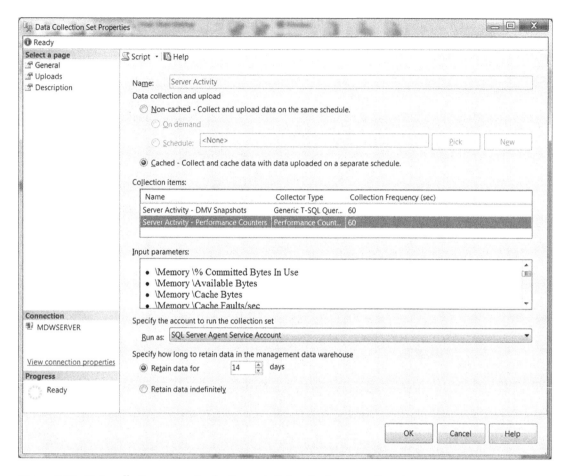

Figure 7-18. *Data collection properties for Server Activity – Performance Counters*

Now let's take a look at the Utility Information collection; navigate to the properties screen under the Data Collection folder, and right-click Properties, as in Figure 7-19.

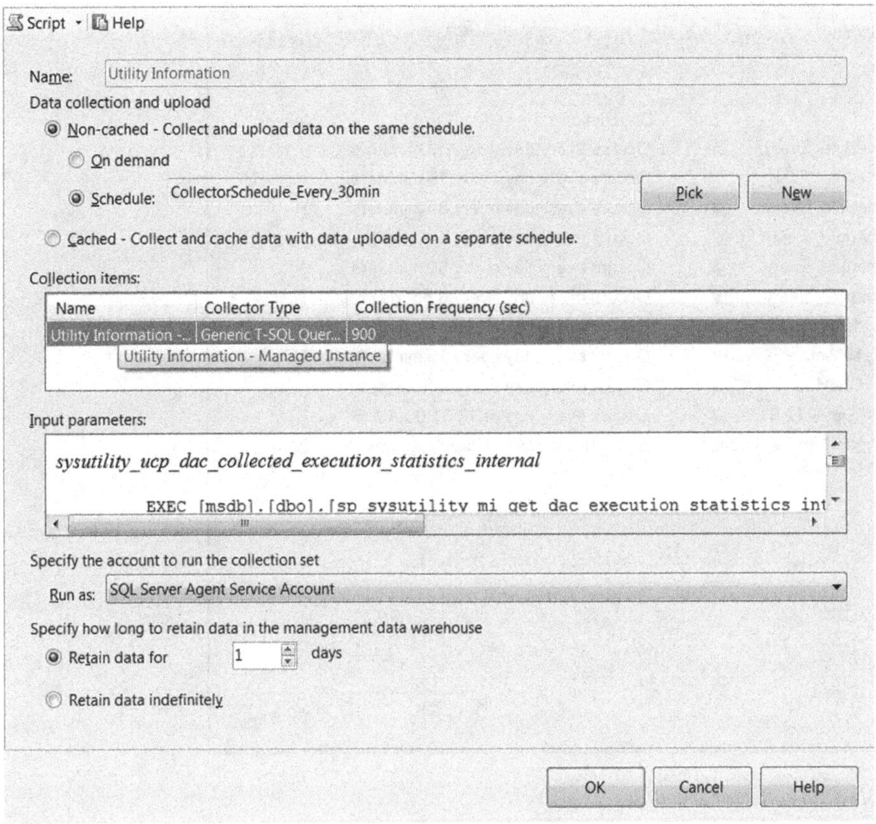

Figure 7-19. *Data collection for Utility Information*

With respect to the Non-cached option of collecting and uploading data on the same schedule, shown in Figure 7-19, you can pick from a list of predefined schedules, which comes with the collector, or you can choose a new one. The predefined ones pretty much cover most recommended collection scenarios. By clicking Pick, you will get a list of available schedules, as shown in Figure 7-20.

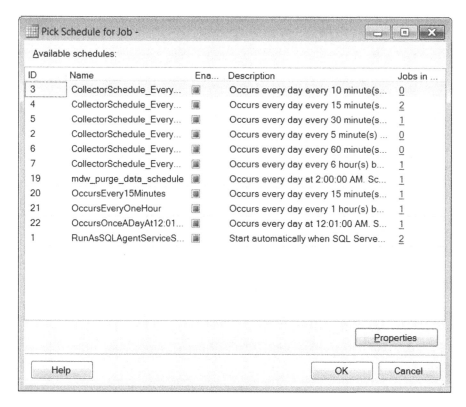

Figure 7-20. *Available data collector schedules*

If you click Properties here, you can launch the Job Schedule Properties box, as shown in Figure 7-21.

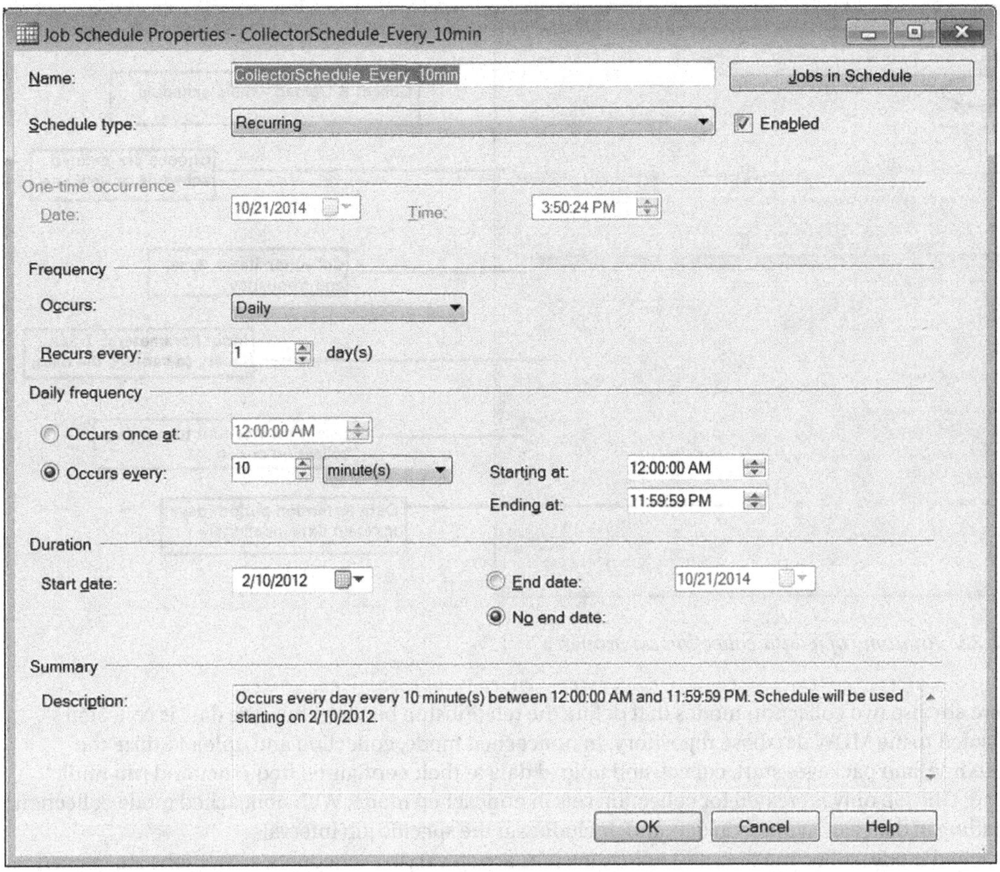

Figure 7-21. *Job Schedule Properties box*

Now that you've seen how each data collection set looks and have examined their properties, let's break one of them down so you can prepare your custom data collection set to be integrated with the MDW. Figure 7-22 shows the anatomy of a data collection set. You will use the Disk Usage collection set as your template.

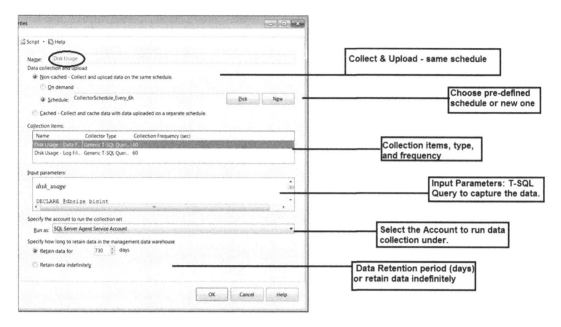

Figure 7-22. *Anatomy of a data collection set property*

There are also two collection modes that define the relationship between how the data is collected and uploaded to the MDW database repository. In noncached mode, collection and upload utilize the same schedule, and packages start, collect, and upload data at their configured frequency and run until completed. One job only is created for collection sets in noncached mode. With noncached mode collection, the uploading of data can happen on demand, including at the specific job intervals.

In cached mode, collecting data and uploading jobs are on varying schedules, so two jobs are created for each collection set. The continuous collection of data is supported with cached mode, but uploads are less frequent. For example, the default Server Activity collection set uploads data by default every 15 minutes, while the collection items are collected every 60 seconds. You can examine Figure 7-22 for an anatomy of a data collection set property that identifies each section of the Properties window.

Viewing the logs for each data collection set will show you the job status of each one, whether each run is successful or failed. Right-click the collection set and select View Logs from the pop-up menu to view the job history, along with dates and times. Figure 7-23 shows the Log File Viewer, accessible from the Data Collection menu.

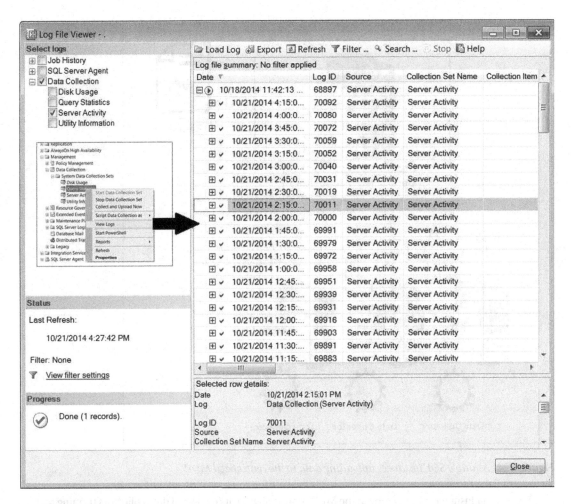

Figure 7-23. *Viewing logs*

Now that you have set up your MDW database repository, configured your data collection sets, and set your schedules, let's take a high-level architectural view of how this all works. As MDW is intended to be a central repository or performance data warehouse, with other SQL instances reporting in and uploading its own metadata performance stats, Figure 7-24 demonstrates the logic flow of a centralized MDW with multiple SQL instances uploading its data.

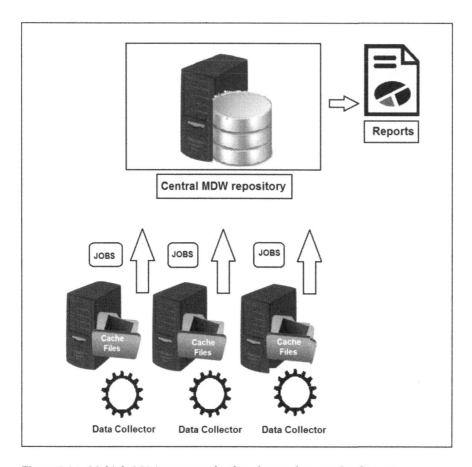

Figure 7-24. Multiple SQL instances uploading data to the centralized MDW

Each server instance participating in the MDW setup will have its own local data collectors running and scheduled jobs. The collection data will be stored at the user-specified (or default) location in the local path cache directory. This step was completed earlier in this chapter, as shown in Figure 7-9. Additionally, you can see in Figure 7-24 the graphical representation of the process of the data collectors uploading data to the central MDW repository. Moreover, you can generate reports from the central MDW database, which is something I will discuss more at length in Chapter 8; here I will demonstrate how to generate the MDW reports.

Accounts, Privileges, Rights, and Credentials

In this section, let's discuss the rights you will need to implement remote clients. There is little detail written on the subject of configuring the proper privileges needed for running the MDW with multiple SQL Server client instances uploading to the central MDW database repository. This is an essential body of knowledge that you must be aware of to ensure that data is being successfully uploaded and the SQL Agent jobs succeed.

The critical step in the MDW architecture is the ability to upload the collected data from the remote clients into the MDW central database repository. The upload process requires connectivity and access between the servers. By default the data collection upload job step will run as the SQL Agent account. If your SQL Agent is using the Local System account, then you'll need to give the computer account (domain\servername$) a login and permission on the MDW database server.

For example, let's use the following scenario where you have two servers (called MDWSERVER, the MDW central repository, and CLIENTCOLLECTOR, the remote client) on the same AD domain. The simplest solution is to take the AD login used to run SQL Agent on CLIENTCOLLECTOR and create a Windows login in SQL Server on MDWSERVER. Then create a user inside your MDW database on MDWSERVER and grant this user the mdw_writer role inside the MDW database.

My recommendation is to use a centralized server for the MDW database so that you will have a central location to run and view reports on all instances participating in the data collection. All participating MDW SQL Server instances must be in the same domain. Enable client collectors on other remote machines, and use a single service account for the SQL Server Agent that will have rights to log in to the MDW Database. Or, if using separate accounts, ensure that each account will have access to the MDW database.

In reality, not all shops have an individual service account for their SQL Server Agents, if even at all. The SQL Server Agent may simply rely on Local System. If your SQL Server Agent service is running under Local System, the cache will be in the temp directory for the user who is running the wizard.

As mentioned earlier, while discussing choosing the cache location, I stated that you must make sure that the SQL Server Agent account has read-write privileges to the cache location. Because you will be configuring the data collection from a remote server, the SQL Server Agent account must have access to the MDW database for the data upload.

Because of the practical security precautions and policy considerations, you can work around this requirement by setting up a SQL Server Agent proxy account to ensure the access it needs to run. If you have 25 instances where each SQL Agent instance runs under a different AD account (or a local account not on the domain), then creating the proxy will avoid you having to create 25 logins on the MDW server. Let's briefly step through the process of creating a proxy, and I'll describe the proper minimal rights needed.

Configuring Account Privileges for MDW Server

Ideally, you want to ask your AD admin to create a new domain user account in Active Directory for the purposes of uploading MDW data to the central repository. In this example, you'll use a domain account called UPL_MDW (upload to MDW) to connect to the MDW server. Then, on the MDWSERVER create a login for this account (DOMAIN\UPL_MDW), grant access to the MDW database, and grant the mdw_writer role. Figure 7-25 shows the login mapped to the MDW database and mdw_writer role.

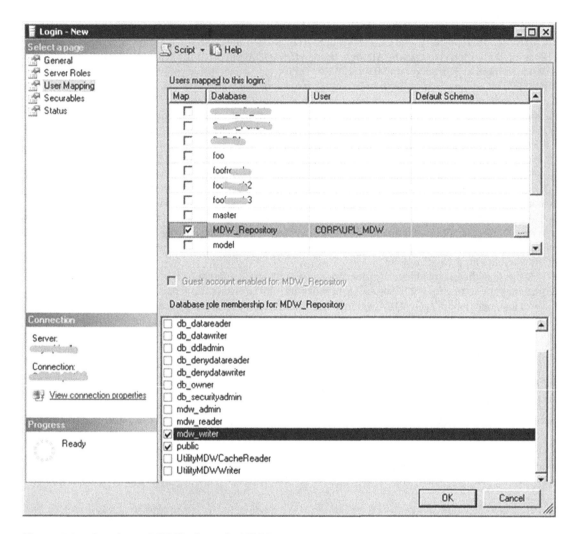

Figure 7-25. *Creating an MDW login on the MDW server*

Configuring Account Privileges for the MDW Client

You are going to create a login, a credential, and then an agent proxy (to point to that credential) on the MDW client, all with the same name and password. When you are done, you will configure your collection agent upload job to use this proxy. The login will be mapped to a user on the msdb database and given the dc_proxy role. (Also, there are the dc_operater and dc_admin database roles, all related to the data collector.) Members of these database roles can administer and use the data collector.

▪ **Note** You will need to do all the following steps for the proxy configuration on each MDW client you want to upload performance data to the repository.

On the MDW client (CLIENTCOLLECTOR), first create and add the login for the AD account and map it to the msdb database, adding the account to the msdb database role dc_proxy as one of the proxy account principals. Click OK. You can see this demonstrated in Figure 7-26 on the User Mapping page.

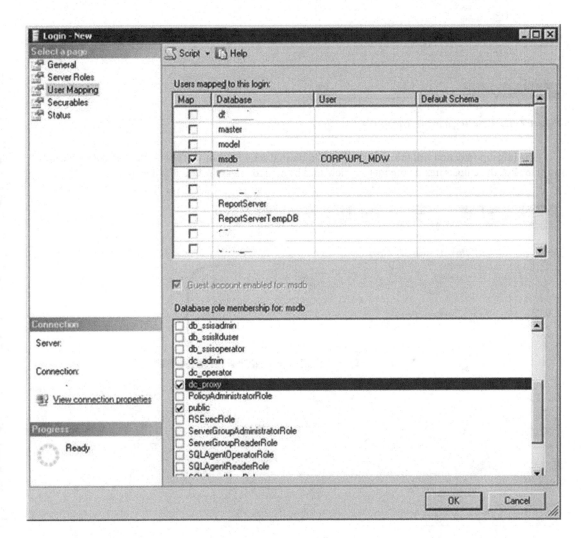

Figure 7-26. *Adding MDW login to the dc_proxy role on msdb*

The next thing you want to do is create a new credential for the UPL_MDW AD account you created. You will do this through SSMS by navigating the Security folder, right-clicking Credentials, and selecting New Credential from the pop-up menu, as shown in Figure 7-27.

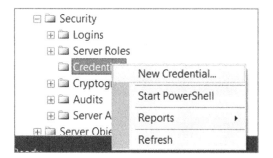

Figure 7-27. *Creating a new credential*

The pop-up selection will bring up the New Credential screen, as shown in Figure 7-28. Here you will want to click the ellipsis next to the Identity field and browse to select the UPL_MDW account.

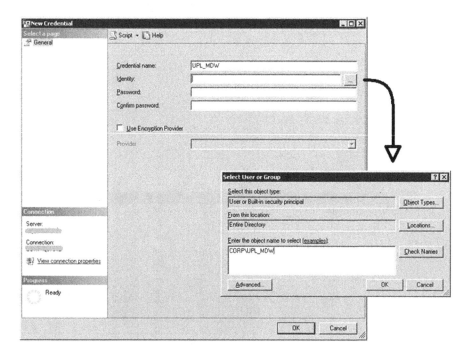

Figure 7-28. *Creating the credential/identity*

Click "Check names" to resolve the account and then OK. Now, be sure to enter the same password for the AD (UPL_MDW) account and confirm. Click OK.

Once you create the credential, you will then create a proxy to use this credential. You create the proxy via SSMS in the Proxies folder under the SQL Server Agent drill-down. Right-click Proxies, as in Figure 7-29.

Figure 7-29. Creating a new proxy

The New Proxy Account screen will be displayed as in Figure 7-30. Here enter the name of the proxy (name it the same as the credential) and click the ellipsis button to browse for the credential (UPL_MDW) that you created in the previous steps. In addition, you want to check the appropriate subsystems that the SQL Server Agent will use for the upload job. In this case, the upload job uses the operating system subsystem (CmdExec) to invoke the dcexec executable. DCEXEC.EXE is the data collector run-time component that manages data collection based on the definitions provided in a collection set and can accept any collection set as input.

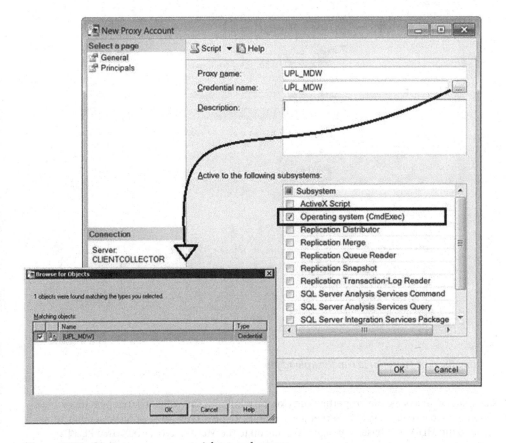

Figure 7-30. Giving proxy account rights to subsytems

Finally, now that you have your proxy account and credentials set up properly, you will need to set the SQL Agent upload jobs to use the proxy account. Navigate SSMS to the SQL Server Agent jobs and drill down to view all the jobs under the Jobs folder, specifically the upload collector jobs named `collection_set_X_upload`, where X represents a number.

Double-click or right-click the job to bring up the Job Properties window of the collection upload job. Go to Steps. In the job step list, select job step 2 and double-click or click Edit. In the Job Step Properties window, click the drop-down menu under Run As, and select your proxy account (UPL_MDW). This is visually demonstrated in Figure 7-31.

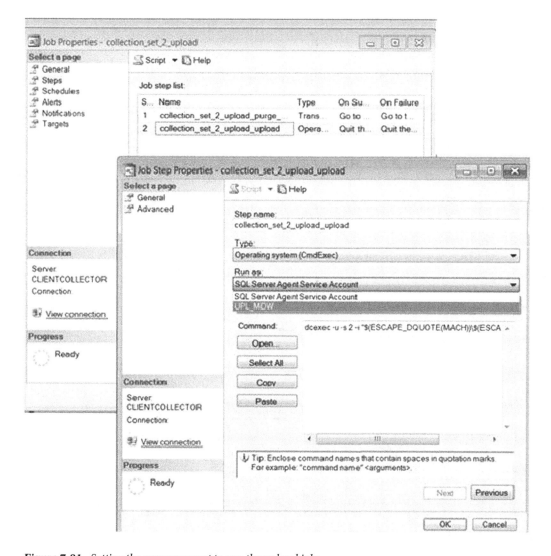

Figure 7-31. *Setting the proxy account to run the upload jobs*

Click OK and OK again to save the properties and exit the windows. You will need to repeat these steps for each collection upload job on every SQL Server participating in the MDW. Now, when your collectors attempt to upload to the MDW database, SQL Agent will log on to the MDW server as DOMAIN\UPL_MDW.

MDW Caveats

Here are some MDW caveats.

Difficult to Remove

Although the MDW is a great feature, providing a rapidly deployable and configurable performance data collection tool out of the box, you need to be aware of some of the limitations that I will discuss here. The main limitations (at least as of SQL 2008) are that you couldn't remove the data collections or drop or change the MDW database name. The jobs cannot easily be deleted because there are constraints as well.

In SQL Server 2012, a system stored procedure called `msdb.dbo.sp_syscollector_cleanup_collector` was added to help with this, but even though it removed some of the MDW components, it didn't remove them all. This stored procedure needs to be run in the `msdb` database and takes no parameters. It should be used only if the intention is to completely remove the data collections. Here is an article on Microsoft TechNet that talks about removing MDW:

```
http://social.technet.microsoft.com/wiki/contents/articles/27572.removing-sql-server-
management-data-warehouse-data-collector.aspx
```

Performance Overhead

You should be aware of latency and performance overhead with multiple collection sets and servers participating. The data collection queries are resource-intensive queries running on the system. Sometimes the collector job schedules can cause deadlocks. Even the MDW database can grow pretty large, depending on your configuration.

Furthermore, files in the cached collection directory can grow rather large and stress disk space. The collector kicks off an EXE in a separate memory space, so multiple collectors can stress memory.

Some of these caveats are ones to be mindful of, when deploying MDW, but not necessarily prevent you from using it. Many of these issues can have workarounds and strategies employed to manage resources just like any other database process. I think the benefits outweigh the liabilities, but if you want an alternative, skip to the "Roll Your Own" section for a custom process.

Defining a Custom Data Collection

There may be additional information you want to capture on a continuing basis that the MDW collector does not do by default. In this case, it is possible to create a custom data collection, but you'll need to do a little manual work. Since there is no wizard or user interface to do this, you will need to use a T-SQL script and bit of reverse engineering.

There are a couple of ways to define a custom data collection. Whichever method you choose, I believe it is a good idea to understand both because they show you internally how the data collection process works. You can create a custom collection set with collection items that use the Generic T-SQL Query collector type. You can employ the use of two specific system stored procedures to create a new custom data collection set and collection items, defining the T-SQL statement to capture the performance data. These stored procedures are the ones you would use to define the collection sets:

```
sp_syscollector_create_collection_set
```

```
sp_syscollector_create_collection_item
```

Using the sp_syscollector_create_collection_set stored procedure, you will define the name of the collection set, a description, the logging level, the expiration in days, the schedule name, and the interval. The logging level correlates to the execution information and SSIS events that track errors, stop/start status, statistics and warnings, and level of detailed logging. You can view complete information about the sp_syscollector_create_collection_set stored procedure on MSDN, at this link:

http://msdn.microsoft.com/en-us/library/bb677291.aspx

You will create a custom collection set as the first step. Then you will need to create the collection item by defining its type, which is the Generic T-SQL Query Collector type, give it a name, and add your desired T-SQL statement to capture the data you want to collect on a continuous basis. In the following example, you collect the query stats from the sys.dm_exec_query_stats DMV and use the following T-SQL code to create the collection set:

```
USE msdb
DECLARE @collection_set_id int
DECLARE @collection_set_uid uniqueidentifier
EXEC sp_syscollector_create_collection_set
@name=N'QueryExecStatsDMV',
@collection_mode=0,
@description=N'HealthySQL sample collection set',
@logging_level=1,
@days_until_expiration=14,
@schedule_name=N'CollectorSchedule_Every_15min',
@collection_set_id=@collection_set_id OUTPUT,
@collection_set_uid=@collection_set_uid OUTPUT
DECLARE @collector_type_uid uniqueidentifier
SELECT @collector_type_uid = collector_type_uid FROM [msdb].[dbo].[syscollector_collector_
types]
WHERE name = N'Generic T-SQL Query Collector Type';
DECLARE @collection_item_id int

EXEC sp_syscollector_create_collection_item
@name=N'Query Stats - Test 1',
@parameters=N'
<ns:TSQLQueryCollector xmlns:ns="DataCollectorType">
<Query>
<Value>SELECT * FROM sys.dm_exec_query_stats</Value>
<OutputTable>dm_exec_query_stats</OutputTable>
</Query>
</ns:TSQLQueryCollector>',
@collection_item_id=@collection_item_id OUTPUT,
@frequency=5,
@collection_set_id=@collection_set_id,
@collector_type_uid=@collector_type_uid
SELECT @collection_set_id as Collection_Set_ID, @collection_set_uid as Collection_Set_UID,
@collection_item_id as Collection_Item_ID
```

Once you run the previous script, some identifying information about the data collection will be displayed.

```
Collection_Set_ID Collection_Set_UID Collection_Item_ID
17 166D9F8C-4F23-4B7A-9326-21F81AE15526 13
```

Now, you can go to the Data Collection view under the Management folder and see the manually created custom collection set, as shown in Figure 7-32. To enable this new data collection, right-click QueryExecStatsDMV and select Start Data Collection Set.

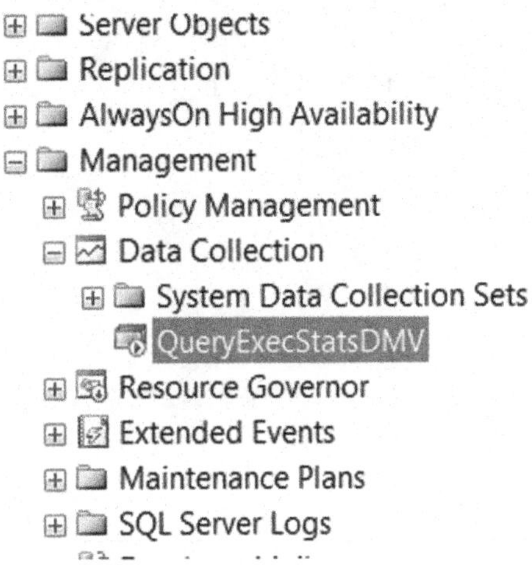

⊞ ▢ Server Objects
⊞ ▢ Replication
⊞ ▢ AlwaysOn High Availability
⊟ ▢ Management
    ⊞ ▢ Policy Management
    ⊟ ▢ Data Collection
        ⊞ ▢ System Data Collection Sets
            ▢ QueryExecStatsDMV
    ⊞ ▢ Resource Governor
    ⊞ ▢ Extended Events
    ⊞ ▢ Maintenance Plans
    ⊞ ▢ SQL Server Logs

Figure 7-32. *Custom collection set displayed*

Because MDW runs via SQL Agent scheduled jobs, you can view the collector information by querying the syscollector_ tables in the msdb database. These tables correspond to the aforementioned stored procedures. You can examine them and see the collector metadata stored there with the following queries:

```
USE msdb
Go
SELECT * FROM syscollector_collection_sets
GO
```

Table 7-1 describes some of the data returned by this query.

Table 7-1. *Metadata About the Collection Sets Stored in MSDB*

Name	Description	is_running	is_system	collection_mode
Disk Usage	Collects data about the disk and log usage for all databases.	1	1	1
Server Activity	Collects top-level performance indicators for the computer and the database engine. Enables analysis of resource use, resource bottlenecks, and database engine activity.	1	1	0
Query Statistics	Collects query statistics, T-SQL text, and query plans of most of the statements that affect performance. Enables analysis of poorly performing queries in relation to overall SQL Server database engine activity.	1	1	0
Utility Information	Collects data about instances of SQL Server that are managed in the SQL Server Utility.	0	1	1
QueryExecStatsDMV	The custom DMV data collection set created earlier.	1	0	0

While in the msdb, you can also see the collection items using the following T-SQL:

```
SELECT name, frequency, parameters FROM syscollector_collection_items
```

This returns the output shown in Figure 7-33, and the parameters column is XML. You can click the XML column data to expand the XML output in another window.

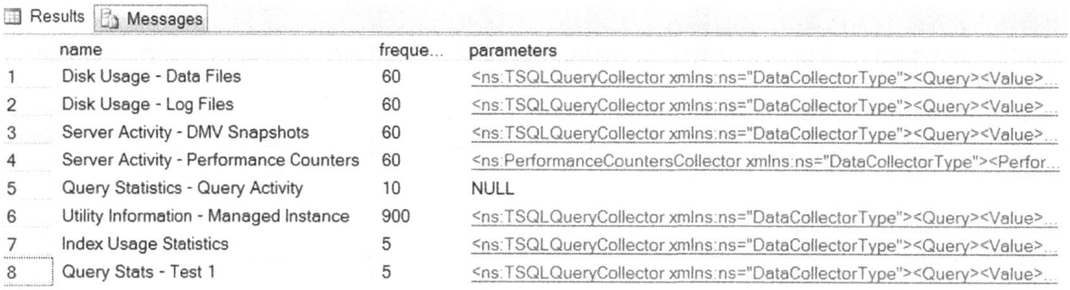

	name	freque...	parameters
1	Disk Usage - Data Files	60	<ns:TSQLQueryCollector xmlns:ns="DataCollectorType"><Query><Value>...
2	Disk Usage - Log Files	60	<ns:TSQLQueryCollector xmlns:ns="DataCollectorType"><Query><Value>...
3	Server Activity - DMV Snapshots	60	<ns:TSQLQueryCollector xmlns:ns="DataCollectorType"><Query><Value>...
4	Server Activity - Performance Counters	60	<ns:PerformanceCountersCollector xmlns:ns="DataCollectorType"><Perfor...
5	Query Statistics - Query Activity	10	NULL
6	Utility Information - Managed Instance	900	<ns:TSQLQueryCollector xmlns:ns="DataCollectorType"><Query><Value>...
7	Index Usage Statistics	5	<ns:TSQLQueryCollector xmlns:ns="DataCollectorType"><Query><Value>...
8	Query Stats - Test 1	5	<ns:TSQLQueryCollector xmlns:ns="DataCollectorType"><Query><Value>...

Figure 7-33. *Output from syscollector_collection_items*

You can create a T-SQL script manually to define your custom data collection using the previous stored procedure code, or you can generate and modify the script from one of the system data collections. This latter method is a lot simpler than scripting it manually. It is also a lot more accessible to beginner DBAs.

To build a custom data collection using this method, you first want to determine what data to collect. In this example, let's use the sys.dm_db_index_usage_stats DMV to collect some index usage statistics on your SQL Server, which do not have a default collector. As I discussed, index use and health are indicative of a healthy SQL Server system. You can track index usage over time, which will help determine the most used and unused indexes. You can use the following Index_Usage_Stats script for the custom collection:

```
SELECT o.name Object_Name,
       SCHEMA_NAME(o.schema_id) Schema_name,
       i.name Index_name,
       i.Type_Desc,
       s.user_seeks,
       s.user_scans,
       s.user_lookups,
       s.user_updates,
       s.system_seeks,
       s.system_scans,
       s.system_lookups,
       getdate() Capture_Date
 FROM sys.objects AS o
    JOIN sys.indexes AS i
 ON o.object_id = i.object_id
    JOIN
  sys.dm_db_index_usage_stats AS s
 ON i.object_id = s.object_id
  AND i.index_id = s.index_id
  AND DB_ID() = s.database_id
 WHERE  o.type = 'u'
   AND i.type IN (1, 2)
   AND(s.user_seeks > 0 OR s.user_scans > 0 OR s.user_lookups > 0
   OR s.system_seeks > 0 OR s.system_scans > 0
   OR s.system_lookups > 0)
```

Results based on your database schema definitions would look similar if you simply executed the previous query via the query editor:

Object_Name	Schema_name	Index_name	Type_Desc	user_seeks	user_scans	user_lookups	user_updates	system_seeks	system_scans	system_lookups	Capture_Date
tblCalender	dbo	PK_tblCalender	NONCLUSTERED	13605	0	0	0	0	0	0	2014-11-14 16:10:49.743
tblOrder	dbo	PK_tblOrder	CLUSTERED	10449	10986	26910	15849	0	0	0	2014-11-14 16:10:49.743
tblOrder	dbo	IX_tblOrder_1	NONCLUSTERED	980119	2621	0	1347	0	0	0	2014-11-14 16:10:49.743

You can capture and store index usage information in the MDW repository so you can have historical index usage and determine the indexes that can be dropped. The previous T-SQL script Index Usage Stats will be used to list the index usage statistics for a database. This script will be incorporated into a custom data collection using the T-SQL collector type that will capture index usage statistics on a daily basis for one or more user databases.

The first thing you need to do is go to the Disk Usage system data collection set, which you are using as the custom template. Right-click and select Script Data Collection as ➤ Create To ➤ New Query Editor Window, as shown in Figure 7-34.

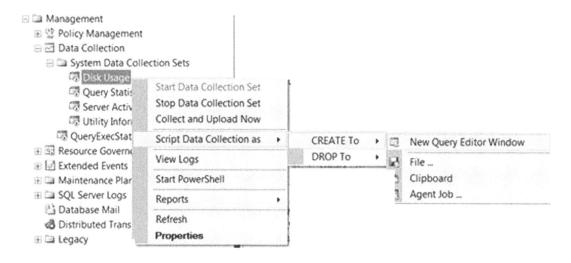

Figure 7-34. *Scripting data collections*

Once you have your script created and visible in the query editor window, you will make some modifications to the script parameters, modifying it for your custom code. Here is the sample script, Create Custom Index Usage Collector:

```
Begin Transaction
Begin Try
Declare @collection_set_id_1 int
Declare @collection_set_uid_2 uniqueidentifier
EXEC [msdb].[dbo].[sp_syscollector_create_collection_set] @name=N'Index Usage',
@collection_mode=1,
 @description=N'Collects data about index usage for all databases.',
@logging_level=0,
@days_until_expiration=730,
@schedule_name=N'OccursOnceADayAt12:01AM',
@collection_set_id=@collection_set_id_1 OUTPUT,
 @collection_set_uid=@collection_set_uid_2 OUTPUT
Select @collection_set_id_1, @collection_set_uid_2

Declare @collector_type_uid_3 uniqueidentifier
Select @collector_type_uid_3 = collector_type_uid From [msdb].[dbo].[syscollector_collector_
types] Where name = N'Generic T-SQL Query Collector Type';
Declare @collection_item_id_4 int
EXEC [msdb].[dbo].[sp_syscollector_create_collection_item] @name=N'Index Usage Statistics',
```

```sql
@parameters=N'<ns:TSQLQueryCollector xmlns:ns="DataCollectorType"><Query><Value>
SELECT o.name Object_Name,
       SCHEMA_NAME(o.schema_id) Schema_name,
       i.name Index_name,
       i.Type_Desc,
       s.user_seeks,
       s.user_scans,
       s.user_lookups,
       s.user_updates,
       s.system_seeks,
       s.system_scans,
       s.system_lookups,
       getdate() Capture_Date
 FROM sys.objects AS o
     JOIN sys.indexes AS i
 ON o.object_id = i.object_id
     JOIN
  sys.dm_db_index_usage_stats AS s
 ON i.object_id = s.object_id
  AND i.index_id = s.index_id
  AND DB_ID() = s.database_id
 WHERE  o.type = ''u''
   AND i.type IN (1, 2)
   AND(s.user_seeks > 0 OR s.user_scans > 0 OR s.user_lookups > 0
   OR s.system_seeks > 0 OR s.system_scans > 0
   OR s.system_lookups > 0)
</Value><OutputTable>index_usage</OutputTable></Query><Databases UseSystemDatabases="true"
UseUserDatabases="true" /></ns:TSQLQueryCollector>',
 @collection_item_id=@collection_item_id_4 OUTPUT,
     @collection_set_id=@collection_set_id_1,
     @collector_type_uid=@collector_type_uid_3

Commit Transaction;
End Try
Begin Catch
Rollback Transaction;
DECLARE @ErrorMessage NVARCHAR(4000);
DECLARE @ErrorSeverity INT;
DECLARE @ErrorState INT;
DECLARE @ErrorNumber INT;
DECLARE @ErrorLine INT;
DECLARE @ErrorProcedure NVARCHAR(200);
SELECT @ErrorLine = ERROR_LINE(),
       @ErrorSeverity = ERROR_SEVERITY(),
       @ErrorState = ERROR_STATE(),
       @ErrorNumber = ERROR_NUMBER(),
       @ErrorMessage = ERROR_MESSAGE(),
       @ErrorProcedure = ISNULL(ERROR_PROCEDURE(), '-');
RAISERROR (14684, @ErrorSeverity, 1 , @ErrorNumber, @ErrorSeverity, @ErrorState, @
ErrorProcedure, @ErrorLine, @ErrorMessage);

End Catch;
GO
```

The table that will be created in the MDW database repository is identified by the <OutputTable> element. The table, which is named IndexUsage, will be used to store statistics being collected. You may also want to limit the collection of these index stats to a handful of databases. By default it will run against *all* databases, but you can use the <Databases> element to specify one or more databases in this collection. There are various attributes that instruct the data collector as to which databases to collect from. For example, when set to true, the attribute UseUserDatabases tells SQL Server to collect statistics for user databases only, excluding system databases.

Note that there are a number of different ways to specify this last element, <Databases>.

Specify only the UseSystemDatabases parameter to collect only from the system databases. If you want to collect statistics for specific databases, you can use the following parameters:

```
<Databases>
  <Database>DatabaseABC</Database>
  <Database>DatabaseXYZ</Database>
</Databases>
```

In the previous example, the data collection process will collect statistics for only the databases specified, DatabaseABC and DatabaseXYZ. As you can see, there are a number of different ways to identify the databases from which you want to collect statistics.

Once I have run the data collection script shown earlier, my custom data collection will be created, but this doesn't mean SQL Server will be start collecting my statistics. I must first start the collection in order for it to start collecting information. To start it, I can run the following command or right-click the Data Collection item in SSMS under the data collection folder and then choose Start Data Collection Set from the pop-up menu:

```
EXEC msdb.dbo.sp_syscollector_start_collection_set @name = 'Index Usage'
```

After the collection runs for some time, you can query the custom table that was created in the MDW repository database. In this case, the table would be called custom_snapshots.index_usage. If you right-click the table in SSMS or query the table and run the query select top 5 * from custom_snapshots.index_usage, you will see the following output data in the table:

```
Object_Name    Schema_name    Index_name    Type_Desc    user_seeks    user_scans    user_
lookups    user_updates    system_seeks    system_scans    system_lookups    Capture_Date
database_name    collection_time    snapshot_id
sysutility_ucp_cpu_memory_configurations_internal    snapshots    PK_sysutility_cpu_memory_
related_info_internal_clustered    CLUSTERED    32    64    0    0    0    0    0    2014-
11-10 23:10:46.310    MDW_HealthySQL    2014-11-11 04:10:46.0000000 +00:00    2866
performance_counter_values    snapshots    IDX_performance_counter_values1    NONCLUSTERED
3    0    0    16316    0    5    0    2014-11-10 23:10:46.310    MDW_HealthySQL    2014-11-
11 04:10:46.0000000 +00:00    2866
performance_counter_values    snapshots    PK_performance_counter_values    CLUSTERED    4
0    0    16316    0    5    0    2014-11-10 23:10:46.310    MDW_HealthySQL    2014-11-11
04:10:46.0000000 +00:00    2866
```

Rolling Your Own

Sometimes there isn't always a one-size-fits-all solution, and you'll just want to create your own customized system. It does not have to be overly complex as long as you are collecting the data you are interested in and persisting this data in stored historical tables for baselining, trending, and analysis. The idea is something that I worked on at a client site, where I created and implemented a custom automated health-check system that draws on the concepts discussed in this book. The Automated Health Check System consists of components already available to you, leveraging native SQL Server native features out of the box including various system DMVs, SQL Server Agent, custom stored procedures, T-SQL, and SSRS.

The purpose of this system is to have a fully deployable package of DMV statistics, performance metrics collection, and reports that will be supportable for the entire SQL Server infrastructure. With it you can establish a baseline for such metrics for each server allow the capacity to collect ongoing statistics, query archive data (get point-in-time historical data) and create on-demand reports. The information derived from this system will enable further and more in-depth analysis of deeper performance issues. While the system itself is quite comprehensive, touching all aspects of the Pearl Knowledge Solution's proprietary 15-point health check, I will cover only a sample here to demonstrate how it was built and give you an idea of how to build your own.

Let's take some of the examples from Chapter 3 using the sys.dm_os_wait_stats DMV. You already know how to query this DMV and what its output looks like. Now it's time to get a delta (that is< compare wait statistics at two points in time). The following is the PIT WaitType Script; it is a good diagnostic script that you can run when there is a high level of server activity and want to capture the wait statistics for two points in time and compare them with the delta as the final result for the waits on the system. For sample purposes, the WAITFOR DELAY parameter is ten seconds. You may want to change this and leave it running for a number of minutes.

```
--Capture point in time (PIT) - Baseline
Select wait_type,
       waiting_tasks_count,
       wait_time_ms/1000 as WaitTimeSec,
       (wait_time_ms - signal_wait_time_ms) / 1000 AS ResourceWaitTimeSec,
signal_wait_time_ms / 1000 AS SignalWaitTimeSec,
       max_wait_time_ms,
       signal_wait_time_ms,
       100.0 * wait_time_ms / SUM (wait_time_ms) OVER() AS Percentage,
       ROW_NUMBER() OVER(ORDER BY wait_time_ms DESC) AS RowNum
into    #WaitStatSnapshotPIT1
from sys.dm_os_wait_stats

-- Wait for x amount of time
WAITFOR DELAY '00:00:10';

--Collect again - Trend
Select  wait_type,
       waiting_tasks_count,
       wait_time_ms/1000 as WaitTimeSec,
       (wait_time_ms - signal_wait_time_ms) / 1000.0 AS ResourceWaitTimeSec,
signal_wait_time_ms / 1000.0 AS SignalWaitTimeSec,
       max_wait_time_ms,
       signal_wait_time_ms,
        100.0 * wait_time_ms / SUM (wait_time_ms) OVER() AS Percentage,
       ROW_NUMBER() OVER(ORDER BY wait_time_ms DESC) AS RowNum
```

```
into    #WaitStatSnapshotPIT2
from sys.dm_os_wait_stats

--select * from #WaitStatSnapshotPIT1

-- Compare Results - Delta
Select pit1.wait_type,
        (pit2.WaitTimeSec-pit1.WaitTimeSec) CumWaitTimeSecDelta,
        (pit2.ResourceWaitTimeSec -pit1.ResourceWaitTimeSec) ResourceWaitTimeDelta,
        (pit2.SignalWaitTimeSec -pit1.SignalWaitTimeSec) SignalWaitTimeDelta,
         CAST (pit1.Percentage AS DECIMAL(4, 2)) AS Percentage,
        GETDATE() as CaptureDateTime
from #WaitStatSnapshotPIT1 pit1
inner join #WaitStatSnapshotPIT2 pit2 on
    pit1.wait_type=pit2.wait_type
where pit2.WaitTimeSec > pit1.WaitTimeSec
    GROUP BY pit2.RowNum, pit2.wait_type, pit2.WaitTimeSec, pit2.WaitTimeSec, pit2.
ResourceWaitTimeSec,
pit2.SignalWaitTimeSec, pit2.waiting_tasks_count, pit2.Percentage,
    pit1.RowNum, pit1.wait_type, pit1.WaitTimeSec, pit1.WaitTimeSec, pit1.
ResourceWaitTimeSec,
pit1.SignalWaitTimeSec, pit1.waiting_tasks_count, pit1.Percentage
HAVING SUM (pit2.Percentage) - pit1.Percentage < 95; -- percentage threshold
--order by pit2.WaitTimeSec DESC

drop table #WaitStatSnapshotPIT1
drop table #WaitStatSnapshotPIT2
```

Here are some sample results of what the output looks like:

```
wait_type    CumWaitTimeSecDelta    ResourceWaitTimeDelta    SignalWaitTimeDelta
Percentage    CaptureDateTime
CXPACKET    19    17.830000    2.910000    23.03    2014-11-12 00:24:53.180
SOS_SCHEDULER_YIELD    9    0.690000    9.230000    17.71    2014-11-12 00:24:53.180
BACKUPIO    5    4.734000    0.739000    13.01    2014-11-12 00:24:53.180
OLEDB    20    20.505000    0.000000    10.53    2014-11-12 00:24:53.180
BACKUPBUFFER    4    3.223000    1.840000    7.16    2014-11-12 00:24:53.180
ASYNC_NETWORK_IO    1    1.785000    0.924000    5.25    2014-11-12 00:24:53.180
PAGEIOLATCH_SH    3    2.885000    0.582000    0.64    2014-11-12
00:24:53.180
```

In a slight variation of the previous script, you can simply take all the wait time column stats and average them by wait count, using the `waiting_task_counts` values, which are incremented at the start of each wait type. `waiting_tasks_counts` is a key counter that is the number of waits for each wait type. The average wait times, including cumulative wait times, resource wait times, and signal wait times will be calculated by dividing this temporal number by the `waiting_tasks_counts`, such as `wait_time_ms/ waiting_tasks_count`. In addition, as the raw numbers are displayed and stored in milliseconds (ms), you will divide each by 1,000 to derive the wait times in seconds, which is a more tangible and readable format for end users.

First, since there are so many wait types that exist and that list is growing with each new version of SQL Server (a link to the wait-type repository was referenced in Chapter 3), you will build a table of existing wait types and flag them to be ignored. These are the waits that are harmless and can be safely ignored, so you won't bother capturing information about these here. Rather than updating the script each time you want to add or modify a wait type, you can add them to the table and flag them on and off (1=on/2=off (or ignore)). The advantage here is you can even limit your wait stat analysis to a handful of particular waits and filter out the harmless waits.

The following is the Create MonitoredWaitTypes script to create the schema and wait-type repository. In addition, the script will create a clustered index on the wait_type and a filtered index where track = 1 for faster retrieval performance. The track predicate indicates that these are the only waits that will be tracked or reported on.

```
-- Create Schema
IF SCHEMA_ID('Monitor') IS NULL EXECUTE ('CREATE SCHEMA Monitor');

-- Create WaitType repository for wait types
IF OBJECT_ID('Monitor.WaitTypes','U') IS NULL
 CREATE TABLE Monitor.WaitTypes (wait_type varchar(50),track bit default (1));
GO


-- Build the repository of available waits from the sys.dm_os_wait_stats DMW
Insert Into Monitor.WaitTypes (wait_type)
 Select distinct s.wait_type
  From sys.dm_os_wait_stats s;

-- Create clustered and filtered indices
Create Clustered Index CX_waittype on Monitor.WaitTypes(wait_type);

Create Index IX_waittype on Monitor.WaitTypes(wait_type)
 Where track = 1;
```

Now, you will update the Monitor.WaitTypes table to flag waits to ignore. Again, these are harmless system waits that aren't essential to performance analysis and tuning. This script will set the track flag to 0.

```
-- Set WaitsToIgnore
Update Monitor.WaitTypes
 Set track = 0
 Where wait_type in (
        'CLR_SEMAPHORE', 'LAZYWRITER_SLEEP', 'RESOURCE_QUEUE', 'SLEEP_TASK','SP_SERVER_
DIAGNOSTICS_SLEEP',
        'SLEEP_SYSTEMTASK', 'SQLTRACE_BUFFER_FLUSH', 'WAITFOR', 'LOGMGR_QUEUE',
        'CHECKPOINT_QUEUE', 'REQUEST_FOR_DEADLOCK_SEARCH', 'XE_TIMER_EVENT', 'BROKER_TO_
FLUSH',
        'BROKER_TASK_STOP', 'CLR_MANUAL_EVENT', 'CLR_AUTO_EVENT', 'DISPATCHER_QUEUE_
SEMAPHORE',
        'FT_IFTS_SCHEDULER_IDLE_WAIT', 'XE_DISPATCHER_WAIT', 'XE_DISPATCHER_JOIN', 'BROKER_
EVENTHANDLER',
        'TRACEWRITE', 'FT_IFTSHC_MUTEX', 'SQLTRACE_INCREMENTAL_FLUSH_SLEEP', 'DIRTY_PAGE_
POLL',
```

```
      'BROKER_RECEIVE_WAITFOR', 'ONDEMAND_TASK_QUEUE', 'DBMIRROR_EVENTS_QUEUE',
      'DBMIRRORING_CMD', 'BROKER_TRANSMITTER', 'SQLTRACE_WAIT_ENTRIES',
      'SLEEP_BPOOL_FLUSH', 'SQLTRACE_LOCK', 'HADR_FILESTREAM_IOMGR_IOCOMPLETION');

      SET ANSI_NULLS ON
GO
```

Next go ahead and create the table that will store historical wait statistics, with the following T-SQL:

```
CREATE TABLE [dbo].[waitstats](
    [wait_type] [nvarchar](60) NOT NULL,
    [WaitSec] [numeric](26, 6) NULL,
    [ResourceSec] [numeric](26, 6) NULL,
    [SignalSec] [numeric](26, 6) NULL,
    [WaitCount] [bigint] NOT NULL,
    [AvgWait_Sec] [numeric](26, 6) NULL,
    [AvgRes_Sec] [numeric](26, 6) NULL,
    [AvgSig_Sec] [numeric](26, 6) NULL,
    [Percentage] [numeric](38, 15) NULL,
    [CaptureDate] [datetime] NULL
) ON [PRIMARY]

GO
```

The waitstats table that was created must now be populated with metadata. To do this, you must calculate the wait times, along with capturing the associated wait types, and insert this data into the table. Since you want to automate this collection process, let's wrap this code into a stored procedure. Using the following T-SQL script, you can create this custom stored proc and call it usp_DailyWaitStats, which you will later schedule via the SQL Server Job Agent, to run once a day every day.

```
/****** Object:  StoredProcedure [dbo].[usp_DailyWaitStats]******/
SET ANSI_NULLS ON
GO
SET QUOTED_IDENTIFIER ON
GO
CREATE PROC [dbo].[usp_DailyWaitStats] AS

INSERT  INTO dbo.WaitStats
        (
        [CaptureDate],
        [wait_type] ,
           [WaitSec] ,
           [ResourceSec] ,
           [SignalSec] ,
           [WaitCount] ,
           [Percentage] ,
           [AvgWait_Sec] ,
           [AvgRes_Sec] ,
           [AvgSig_Sec]
         )
        EXEC
```

```
        ( '
    WITH [Waits] AS
      (SELECT
        s.[wait_type],
        [wait_time_ms] / 1000.0 AS [WaitSec],
        ([wait_time_ms] - [signal_wait_time_ms]) / 1000.0 AS [ResourceSec],
        [signal_wait_time_ms] / 1000.0 AS [SignalSec],
        [waiting_tasks_count] AS [WaitCount],
        100.0 * [wait_time_ms] / SUM ([wait_time_ms]) OVER() AS [Percentage],
        ROW_NUMBER() OVER(ORDER BY [wait_time_ms] DESC) AS [RowNum]
      FROM sys.dm_os_wait_stats s
INNER JOIN Monitor.waittypes w
  On s.wait_type = w.wait_type
WHERE w.track = 1
      )
    SELECT
      GETDATE(),
      [W1].[wait_type] AS [Wait_Type],
      CAST ([W1].[WaitSec] AS DECIMAL(14, 2)) AS [Wait_Sec],
      CAST ([W1].[ResourceSec] AS DECIMAL(14, 2)) AS [Resource_Sec],
      CAST ([W1].[SignalSec] AS DECIMAL(14, 2)) AS [Signal_Sec],
      [W1].[WaitCount] AS [WaitCount],
      CAST ([W1].[Percentage] AS DECIMAL(4, 2)) AS [Percentage],
      CAST (([W1].[WaitSec] / [W1].[WaitCount]) AS DECIMAL (14, 4)) AS [AvgWait_Sec],
      CAST (([W1].[ResourceSec] / [W1].[WaitCount]) AS DECIMAL (14, 4)) AS [AvgRes_Sec],
      CAST (([W1].[SignalSec] / [W1].[WaitCount]) AS DECIMAL (14, 4)) AS [AvgSig_Sec]
    FROM [Waits] AS [W1]
    INNER JOIN [Waits] AS [W2]
      ON [W2].[RowNum] <= [W1].[RowNum]
    GROUP BY [W1].[RowNum], [W1].[wait_type], [W1].[WaitSec],
      [W1].[ResourceSec], [W1].[SignalSec], [W1].[WaitCount], [W1].[Percentage]
    HAVING SUM ([W2].[Percentage]) - [W1].[Percentage] < 95;'
        );
```

Finally, to test this process, you can now simply run the following statement to execute the stored procedure, which can now be scheduled to run daily as a new job, under the SQL Server Agent. You can see how the job is configured in Figure 7-35.

```
Exec usp_DailyWaitStats
Go
```

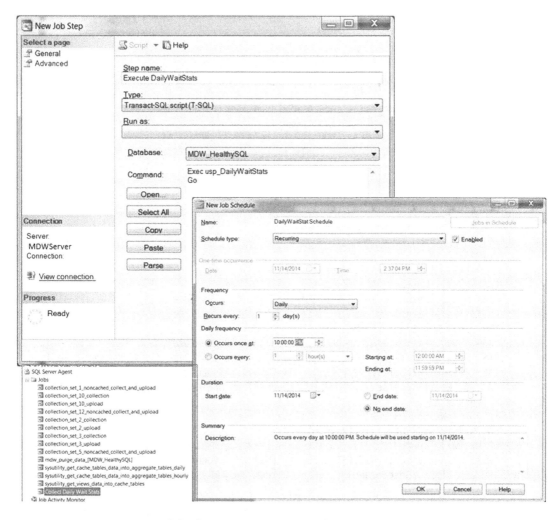

Figure 7-35. *Creating a SQL job for the custom wait stats stored proc*

There you have it now. This is the blueprint on how to roll your own custom wait stat collection process and repository. As you have observed, creating this process doesn't have to be overly complicated. All of this chapter was spent on the basics of creating a SQL health repository, totally leveraging all of the existing features in the SQL Server product. With respect to this custom collection process, you used the following simple components:

- DMV script, appending a capture date field

- Created a WaitType lookup table and wait stats historical table

- Created a stored procedure wrapping the previous code

- Used the SQL Server Agent to create a scheduled job

Here is some sample output of the results from the data in the table generated by the custom stored procedure:

```
wait_type     WaitSec     ResourceSec     SignalSec     WaitCount     AvgWait_Sec     AvgRes_Sec
AvgSig_Sec     Percentage     CaptureDate
CX_PACKET     15927.760000     15927.250000     0.510000     31817     0.500600     0.500600
0.000000     48.480000000000000     2014-11-14 13:59:03.200
SOS_SCHEDULER_YIELD     16047.700000     16047.060000     0.640000     158995     0.100900
0.100900     0.000000     93.680000000000000     2014-11-14 14:00:58.697
LCK_M_U     529.250000     529.150000     0.100000     446     1.186700     1.186400     0.000200
3.090000000000000     2014-11-14 14:00:58.697
DIRTY_PAGE_POLL     16849.970000     16849.300000     0.680000     166950     0.100900
0.100900     0.000000     93.940000000000000     2014-11-14 14:14:21.050
LCK_M_U     529.250000     529.150000     0.100000     446     1.186700     1.186400     0.000200
2.950000000000000     2014-11-14 14:14:21.050
```

You now have a historical wait stats table that will be persisted beyond any instance restarts. This table can be part of your repository, along with other key DMV statistics. You have top waits information from the sys.dm_os_wait_stats DMV in a readable format where you have all wait times as seconds and an average of all wait times, saved with the capture datetime, which will allow you to report on historical waits and choose the period to select. As a user, you can now report on historical waits as they occurred between some start and end time. The usefulness will become quite apparent when you build a custom report, as shown in Chapter 8.

Summary

In this detailed chapter, you learned how to create a central database repository to collect various data sets for performance analysis, baselines, and historical trends. The tool of choice in this chapter was SQL Server's management data warehouse, an easily deployable tool for such purposes. You also were shown an alternative method of designing your own simple solution.

Using the information in this chapter, you will continue to build your healthy SQL environment in the next chapter. By using the available MDW reports and creating a custom report, you will be able to see the fruits of your labor. Furthermore, the next chapter discusses the DBA need for proactive monitoring and shows you how to leverage the out-of-the-box features for monitoring and alerting.

CHAPTER 8

■ ■ ■

Monitoring and Reporting

Proactive, continuous monitoring and alerting are essential to managing multiple SQL Server instances. By setting up automated monitoring, you ensure that you are being proactive and not reactive to a potential technical issue or outage before escalation. With targeted monitoring, you can get in front of and resolve a situation before it becomes known to the general user population and management. There are a number of out-of-the-box solutions, as well as established third-party vendors. I will talk about and recommend some in this chapter.

In Chapter 2, I discussed what data to collect, such CPU, memory, I/O, locking, and blocking information. You will primarily want to monitor resource usage to see whether any locking or blocking occurs that potentially impacts the overall performance of SQL Server. In addition, frequently checking the error log is essential to ensure your SQL Server is performing smoothly without any serious errors that could bring your server to a complete halt. Therefore, you can set up SQL Server to monitor various errors, conditions, and thresholds that affect SQL Server health and performance.

In addition to monitoring and alerting, you will also want to frequently report on the state of your SQL Server infrastructure. With the ability to produce and generate ad hoc reports upon request, you will be able to analyze patterns and trends, stay abreast of what's happening in your SQL Server environment, and impress the honchos. Once you have gathered baselines and have started monitoring the server, what happens to all of that information? There needs to be a means of consuming that data. This is done through targeted reporting. Using SQL Server Reporting Services, you can create simple yet elegant reports and graphs that are easy to understand and often desirable to management. I will discuss this more as you proceed on your journey of learning about healthy SQL and how to perform a comprehensive health check.

I will demonstrate how to report on your server health (specifically the data collected from monitoring via XE). Here I will discuss proactive and preventative monitoring using DMVs and XE to monitor server health.

Beyond the default health check that comes with SQL Server, I will explore a means to monitor the server and report on various health symptoms. This is designed to go deeper than the default health check and provide greater flexibility for monitoring and ensuring good server health.

I will also be using SSRS to create simple reports and cover the following:

- Pointing to the data via data sources

- Setting up user-defined parameters

- Using searchable parameters

- Inserting charts and graphs

- Sending the reports on a schedule

SQL Server Agent Alerts, Operators, and Notifications

In this section, you will learn about how to configure alerts, operators and notifications, and Database Mail. All these components used together will allow you to use these native SQL Server features to monitor for and alert on specific events and errors that occur. Alerts, operators, and notifications are all managed under the SQL Server Agent. The Database Mail profile must be enabled and configured to be used by the SQL Server Agent. You will learn how to leverage all these features and set them up for your SQL Server instances.

Configure Database Mail

Because a lot of the native ability to monitor and alert the DBA when there is an issue or even to send status reports depends on Database Mail, let's set this up first. Whether it's low disk space, failed backups/jobs, or a server or database is offline, you'll definitely want to know about it ASAP! Leveraging Database Mail will allow you to address and ideally resolve the issue before it's escalated up the chain of command.

You'll want to configure Database Mail in order to be able to send any alerts and e-mails to get automatic notification. To do that, launch SQL Server Management Studio and open a query window. Run the following T-SQL code to enable advanced options and Database Mail extended stored procedures (XPs):

```
sp_configure 'show advanced options', 1
GO
RECONFIGURE WITH OVERRIDE
GO
sp_configure 'Database Mail XPs', 1
GO
RECONFIGURE WITH OVERRIDE
GO
```

The step to enable the Service Broker on the msdb database are as follows:

1. Connect to SQL Server.

2. Stop the SQL Agent services.

3. Run the query ALTER DATABASE MSDB SET ENABLE_BROKER.

    3.1. If the query takes long, add WITH ROLLBACK IMMEDIATE after ENABLE_BROKER.

4. Check that the service broker is enabled by executing the following query:

    4.1. select is_broker_enabled from sys.databases where name = 'MSDB'

    4.2. The output value 1 means the service broker is successfully enabled.

5. Start the SQL Agent services.

Then, navigate to Object Explorer. Expand the Management folder and right-click Database Mail, as shown in Figure 8-1. Then click Configure Database Mail. The Database Mail configuration wizard will be launched; click Next.

Figure 8-1. *Launching the Configure Database Mail Wizard*

You will be presented with the Select Configuration Task screen, which has three options. The first time, select "Set up Database Mail by performing the following tasks." These tasks are as follows:

1. Create a new e-mail profile and specify its SMTP accounts.

2. Specify a profile security.

3. Configure system parameters.

Click Next, and you should see something similar to Figure 8-2.

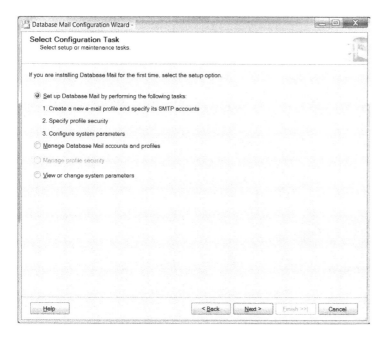

Figure 8-2. *Select Configuration Task page*

Create a profile name, as shown in Figure 8-3, and click Add. This will bring up the new Database Mail account window.

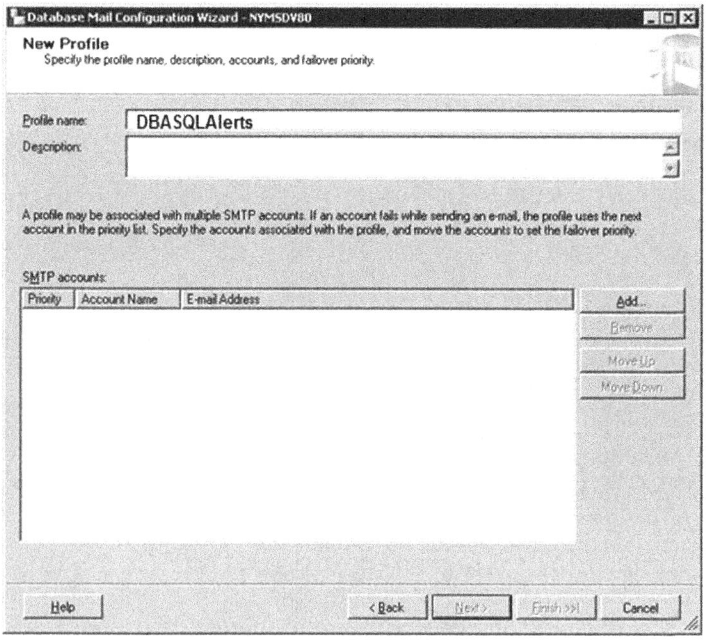

Figure 8-3. *Creating a profile name*

234

The next step for setting up your Database Mail is specifying the name and attributes for your SMTP account. This is also demonstrated in Figure 8-4. Enter an account name, and for the Outgoing Mail Server (SMTP) box, which is in essence the From e-mail, specify an e-mail address that should be set up by your mail administrator. Give a display name, and use the same e-mail address for the reply e-mail. For the server name, you will have to find out from your system administrator the SMTP address to use for outgoing mail. The default SMTP port is usually 25, but confirm that and whether it requires a secure connection.

Under SMTP authentication, I tend to use the first option of Windows Authentication using Database Engine service credentials. Here are all the authentication options explained:

- *Windows authentication*: Database Mail uses the credentials of the SQL Server Database Engine Windows service account for authentication on the SMTP server.

- *Basic authentication*: Database Mail uses the username and password specified to authenticate on the SMTP server.

- *Anonymous authentication*: The SMTP server does not require any authentication. Database Mail will not use any credentials to authenticate on the SMTP server.

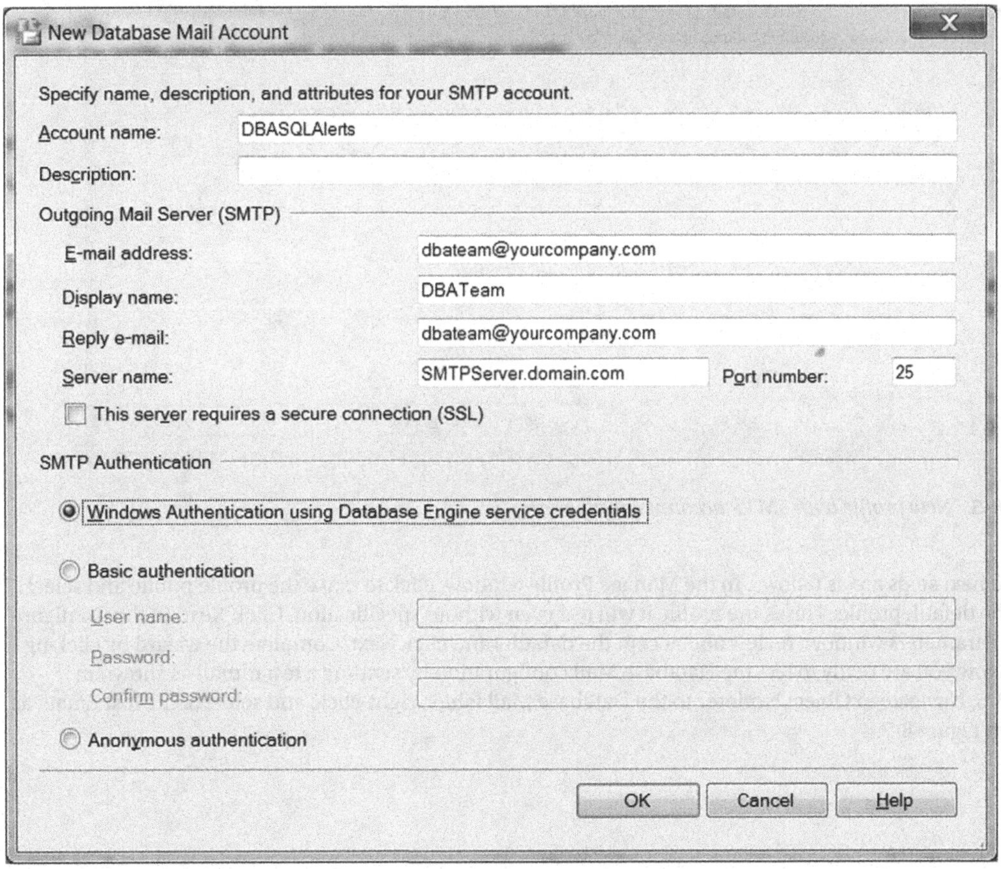

Figure 8-4. *Configuring the database mail account*

Once you see the New Profile screen with the SMTP account visible, as in Figure 8-5, click Next to proceed.

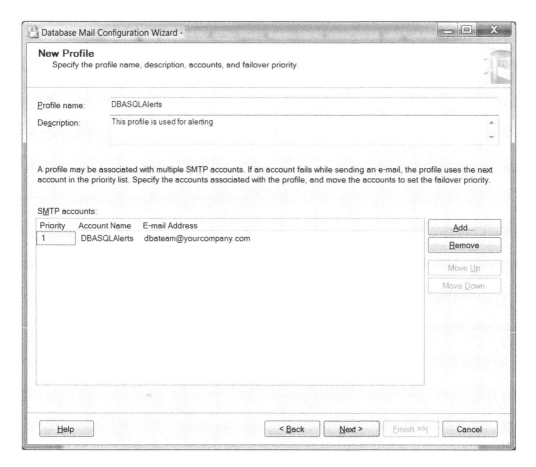

Figure 8-5. *New profile with SMTP account configured*

The next steps are as follows. In the Manage Profile window, click to make the profile public and select Yes as the default profile. This is the profile it will use even without specification. Click Next. In the Configure System Parameters window, review and accept the defaults and click Next. Complete the wizard by clicking Finish. Now you are ready to test the Database Mail configuration by sending a test e-mail as shown in Figure 8-6. Navigate in Object Explorer to the Database Mail folder, right-click, and select Send Test Email, as shown in Figure 8-7.

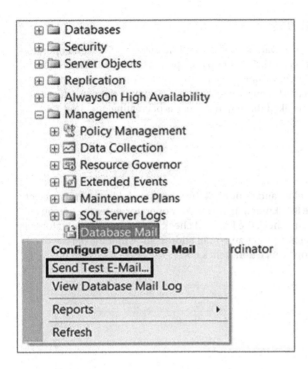

Figure 8-6. *Sending a test e-mail*

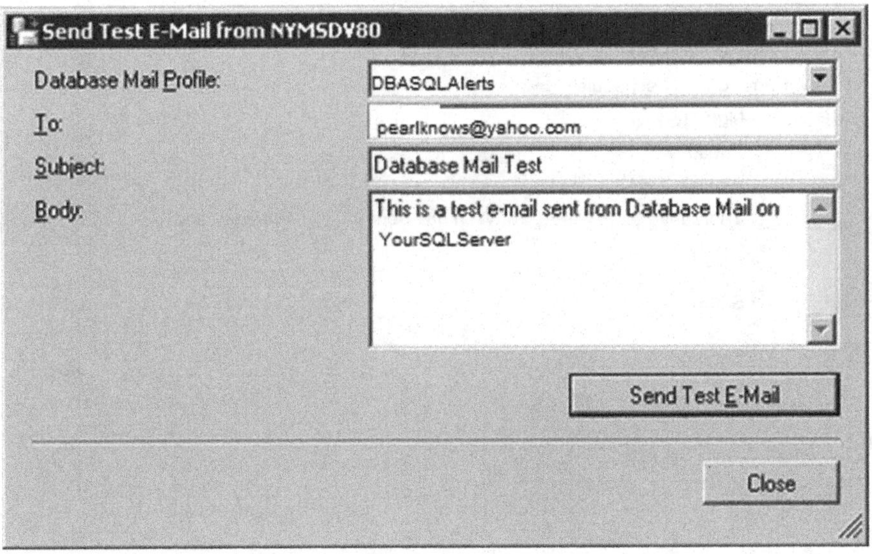

Figure 8-7. *Writing the e-mail to verify the Database Mail profile*

Configuring SQL Server Agent Alerts

Once you have successfully configured and tested your Database Mail, it's time to set up alerts and operators by configuring SQL Server Agent alerts and operators. Let's first set up the operator and then discuss how to create alerts. Error log checking on multiple SQL Server instances is an essential but monotonous task that DBAs can do manually, but with SQL Server Agent alerts you can pretty much automate them and receive notification if a particular error occurs. You will be walked through the process of creating operators and alerts using SQL Server Agent.

Create a New Operator

From SSMS under the SQL Server Agent, you can select and right-click the Operators folder and then select New Operator to open the next screen, as in Figure 8-8. Enter a name for your operator, enter the person or e-mail group name that will receive notifications, and check the Enabled check box so that this operator will receive notifications. In the Notification options section, enter an e-mail address for either the person or e-mail group/distribution list to send all notifications. Once done, click OK.

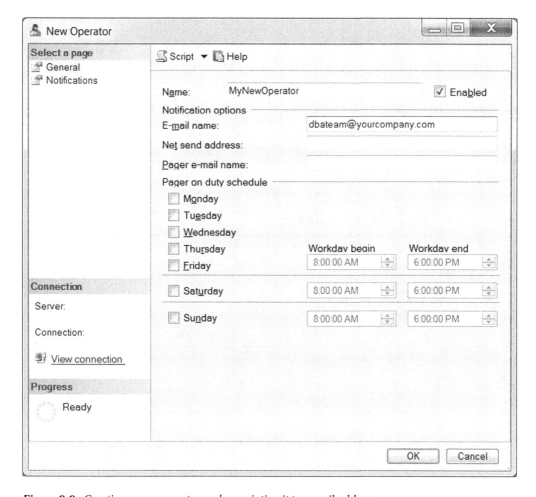

Figure 8-8. *Creating a new operator and associating it to e-mail address*

Some things to note in the New Operator dialog is that the pager and net send options have been deprecated, and it is suggested that you do not use these features because they will be removed from future versions of SQL Server. If you still use pagers, you can simple set pager alerts using e-mail because most pagers are reachable through e-mail. Most providers allow for sending an e-mail message to alphanumeric pagers. For example, you might use something like 9417228135@pageme.net.

You can also use T-SQL to accomplish the same task with the system stored proc sp_add_operator. Using T-SQL and the alerts will allow you to easily deploy them across multiple servers. The following is how you create an operator for alert notification. To notify multiple e-mail recipients, you should specify an e-mail distribution list, instead of individual e-mail addresses.

```
EXEC msdb.dbo.sp_add_operator @name = N'MyNewOperator',
  @enabled = 1,
  @email_address = N'dbateam@yourcompany.com';
```

Create a New Alert

You will want to specifically set up the SQL Server Agent alerts for severity 17 through 25, which will capture the most critical errors, including insufficient resources and fatal errors. In addition, you will want to set up alerts for specific errors 823, 824, and 825. These errors relate to database corruption and potential I/O subsystem errors that threaten database integrity. Early detection is key to avoiding corrupt databases and consistency errors. Errors 823 and 824 are severity 24 level errors. Error 823 is an I/O error where the OS cannot read the data, and error 824 is an I/O error where SQL Server cannot read the data and indicates a bad checksum or torn page. Error 825 is also an I/O error. These are severe system-level error conditions that threaten database integrity and must be corrected immediately. It is recommended that you complete a full database consistency check (DBCC CHECKDB) on your database. I will talk about database corruption in Chapter 8.

When first creating a new alert, you have the choice of the type of alert to set up. This can be an alert for a particular SQL Server event, a SQL Server performance condition, or even a Windows Management Instrumentation (WMI) event. The most common alert type that the DBA will set up is SQL Server events, which happens when a certain error or severity level of an error occurs on the server.

SQL Server Agent alerts work as follows. SQL Server generates events that are then logged to the Microsoft Windows application log, which is the same log that you see through Event Viewer. The application log is read by the SQL Server agent, comparing events written there to alerts that you have defined. When SQL Server Agent finds a match, it fires an alert, which is an automated response to an event.

Examples of a SQL Server event that can occur are when a transaction log has run out of space or a database cannot be recovered or there is insufficient system memory to run a query. There are too numerous to mention events here, but you'll be able to browse the error messages, which you can associate with a SQL Server Agent alert, with a simple query. All the SQL Server logged error messages can be viewed with the sys.sysmessages view. The view returns the error number, associated severity level, and description (and error messages in other languages).

Select * from sys.sysmessages

A SQL Server performance condition is where you can set an alert to be fired when a certain threshold is reached based on a performance counter and object. So, for example, you can even monitor CPU usage by defining the Processor: % Processor Time counter.

Now, to create the actual alert, in this example for a SQL Server event, go to SSMS and navigate to and expand SQL Server Agent. You will see the folder Alerts. Highlight Alerts, right-click to bring the pop-up menu, and select New Alert. The following screen, Figure 8-9, will appear. Here you give it a name, choose the type, select individual database or all databases, and select the specific error message or severity level.

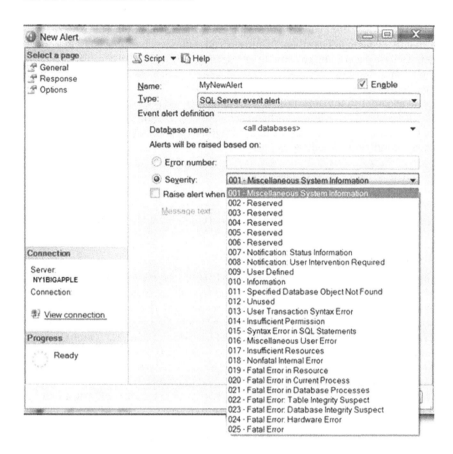

Figure 8-9. *Creating alerts and selecting errors to be notified*

You can use the following T-SQL script (CreateAgentAlerts) to set up alerts on all the recommended severity levels 17–25 and for errors 823, 824, and 825. You should also set up an alert for another common error, 833, which means SQL Server has encountered an occurrence of I/O requests taking longer than 15 seconds to complete on a specific file in a specific database.

This error was discussed in detail in Chapter 3. To reiterate, the error tells you that SQL Server has issued a read or write request from disk, which has taken longer than 15 seconds to return. You can do a find and replace to modify the @operator_name parameter for your specified operator e-mail address. As you'll see, this script will come in handy when creating the multiple alert conditions, rather than manually creating each one.

Once you have both your operators and alerts created, the next step is to assign alerts to operators and add notification e-mail for the various alerts. For @notification_method, you will set @notification_method = 1, for e-mail only. The T-SQL example you would use to do this is as follows:

```
USE msdb ;
GO
EXEC dbo.sp_add_notification
 @alert_name = N'Alert Tester',
 @operator_name = N'MyNewOperator',
 @notification_method = 1 ;
GO
```

```
USE [msdb]
    GO
    EXEC msdb.dbo.sp_add_alert @name=N'Severity 017',
    @message_id=0,
    @severity=17,
    @enabled=1,
    @delay_between_responses=60,
    @include_event_description_in=1;
    GO
    EXEC msdb.dbo.sp_add_notification @alert_name=N'Severity 017',
    @operator_name=N'MyNewOperator', @notification_method = 1;
    GO
    EXEC msdb.dbo.sp_add_alert @name=N'Severity 018',
    @message_id=0,
    @severity=18,
    @enabled=1,
    @delay_between_responses=60,
    @include_event_description_in=1;
    GO
    EXEC msdb.dbo.sp_add_notification @alert_name=N'Severity 018',
    @operator_name=N'MyNewOperator', @notification_method = 1;
    GO
    EXEC msdb.dbo.sp_add_alert @name=N'Severity 019',
    @message_id=0,
    @severity=19,
    @enabled=1,
    @delay_between_responses=60,
    @include_event_description_in=1;
    GO
    EXEC msdb.dbo.sp_add_notification @alert_name=N'Severity 019',
    @operator_name=N'MyNewOperator', @notification_method = 1;
    GO
    EXEC msdb.dbo.sp_add_alert @name=N'Severity 020',
    @message_id=0,
    @severity=20,
    @enabled=1,
    @delay_between_responses=60,
    @include_event_description_in=1;
    GO
    EXEC msdb.dbo.sp_add_notification @alert_name=N'Severity 020',
    @operator_name=N'MyNewOperator', @notification_method = 1;
    GO
    EXEC msdb.dbo.sp_add_alert @name=N'Severity 021',
    @message_id=0,
    @severity=21,
    @enabled=1,
    @delay_between_responses=60,
    @include_event_description_in=1;
    GO
    EXEC msdb.dbo.sp_add_notification @alert_name=N'Severity 021',
    @operator_name=N'MyNewOperator', @notification_method = 1;
```

241

```
GO
EXEC msdb.dbo.sp_add_alert @name=N'Severity 022',
@message_id=0,
@severity=22,
@enabled=1,
@delay_between_responses=60,
@include_event_description_in=1;
GO
EXEC msdb.dbo.sp_add_notification @alert_name=N'Severity 022',
@operator_name=N'MyNewOperator', @notification_method = 1;
GO
EXEC msdb.dbo.sp_add_alert @name=N'Severity 023',
@message_id=0,
@severity=23,
@enabled=1,
@delay_between_responses=60,
@include_event_description_in=1;
GO
EXEC msdb.dbo.sp_add_notification @alert_name=N'Severity 023',
@operator_name=N'MyNewOperator', @notification_method = 1;
GO
EXEC msdb.dbo.sp_add_alert @name=N'Severity 024',
@message_id=0,
@severity=24,
@enabled=1,
@delay_between_responses=60,
@include_event_description_in=1;
GO
EXEC msdb.dbo.sp_add_notification @alert_name=N'Severity 024',
@operator_name=N'MyNewOperator', @notification_method = 1;
GO
EXEC msdb.dbo.sp_add_alert @name=N'Severity 025',
@message_id=0,
@severity=25,
@enabled=1,
@delay_between_responses=60,
@include_event_description_in=1;
GO
EXEC msdb.dbo.sp_add_notification @alert_name=N'Severity 025',
@operator_name=N'MyNewOperator', @notification_method = 1;
GO
EXEC msdb.dbo.sp_add_alert @name=N'Error Number 823',
@message_id=823,
@severity=0,
@enabled=1,
@delay_between_responses=60,
@include_event_description_in=1;
GO
EXEC msdb.dbo.sp_add_notification @alert_name=N'Error Number 823',
@operator_name=N'MyNewOperator', @notification_method = 1;
```

```
GO
EXEC msdb.dbo.sp_add_alert @name=N'Error Number 824',
@message_id=824,
@severity=0,
@enabled=1,
@delay_between_responses=60,
@include_event_description_in=1;
GO
EXEC msdb.dbo.sp_add_notification @alert_name=N'Error Number 824',
@operator_name=N'MyNewOperator', @notification_method = 1;
GO
EXEC msdb.dbo.sp_add_alert @name=N'Error Number 825',
@message_id=825,
@severity=0,
@enabled=1,
@delay_between_responses=60,
@include_event_description_in=1;
GO
EXEC msdb.dbo.sp_add_notification @alert_name=N'Error Number 825',
@operator_name=N'MyNewOperator', @notification_method = 1;
GO
EXEC msdb.dbo.sp_add_alert @name=N'Error Number 833',
@message_id=833,
@severity=0,
@enabled=1,
@delay_between_responses=60,
@include_event_description_in=1;
GO
EXEC msdb.dbo.sp_add_notification @alert_name=N'Error Number 833',
@operator_name=N'MyNewOperator', @notification_method = 1;
```

Now that you have run the previous script to set the alerts and notifications, you can visually see them created in SSMS. Navigate to SQL Server Agent and drill down to Alerts and Operators, respectively, as shown in Figure 8-10.

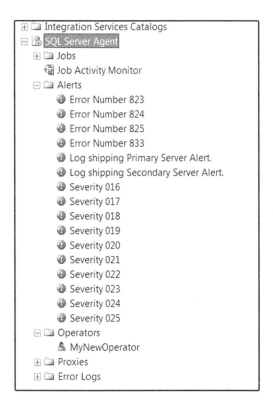

Figure 8-10. *Alerts and operators created*

Once you run the previous script, or just for reference, you can go back to the operators properties screen (SQL Server Agent Operators) and select the Notifications page to observe that all the alerts you created are now assigned to your operator, as shown in Figure 8-11. All the alerts that the operator will receive are checked. You can manage this and manually unselect or select more alerts for this operator here.

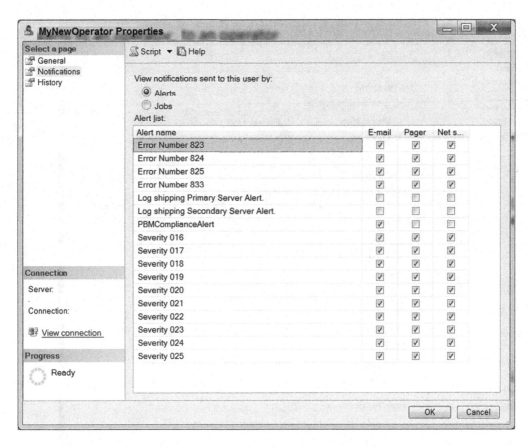

Figure 8-11. *Operator notifications properties for alert assignment*

Finally, you want to ensure that you actually get notified by e-mail, once all the previous information is configured. If you're not getting notified, chances are if you look in the SQL Server Agent log in SSMS, under SQL Server Agent ➤ Error Logs ➤ Current, you may see an error such as the following:

```
[476] Database Mail is not enabled for agent notifications. Cannot send e-mail to 'myemail@
company.com'.
```

This is because you have to tell SQL Server Agent which profiles you'd like to enable. You may need to restart SQL Agent. To set up SQL Server Agent mail to use Database Mail, follow these steps, as shown in Figure 8-12:

1. In SSMS Object Explorer, expand a server.

2. Right-click SQL Server Agent and then click Properties.

3. Click Alert System.

4. Select Enable Mail Profile.

5. In the Mail system list, choose Database Mail.

6. In the Mail profile list, select a mail profile for Database Mail.

7. Click OK.

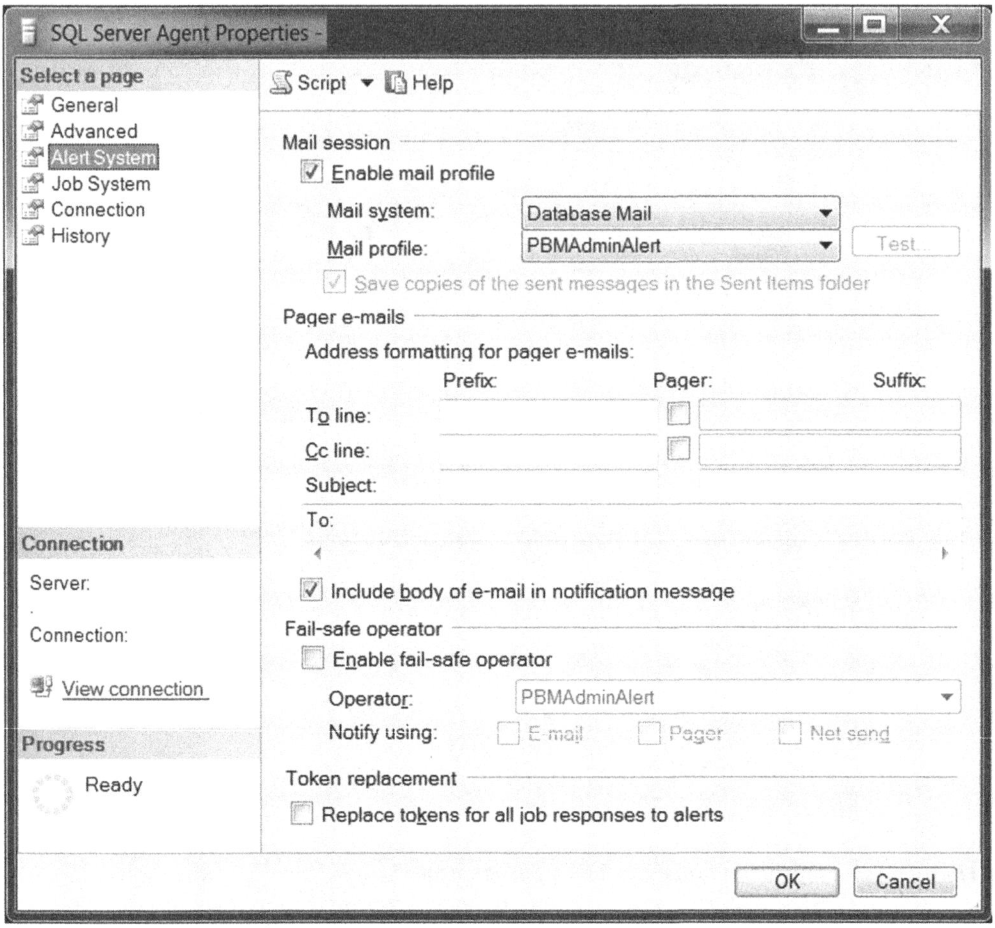

Figure 8-12. SQL Server Agent enabling e-mail profile for Alert System

Monitoring with Extended Events

In Chapter 6, I introduced Extended Events in the context of the New Session Wizard for Extended Events from SQL Server 2012. This intuitive GUI allows the user to easily set up and use Extended Events to create sessions without touching the XML behind them. Included with SQL Server by default, the system_health session is an Extended Events session that starts automatically when the SQL Server Database Engine starts. This session collects system data that is used for troubleshooting performance issues and runs without minimal performance effects on your SQL Server. Therefore, you should not stop or delete the session.

In this chapter, I will show you how to query and report on the default system_health session and show you some additional ways to monitor your SQL Server using Extended Events. The health status information of the SQL Server instance is gathered by the scheduler_monitor_system_health_ring_buffer_recorded event and also by the output collected from sp_server_diagnostics system stored procedure. To reiterate, among the things that the system_health session will show you are any deadlocks that are detected, any sessions that have waited on latches for 15 seconds, and any sessions waiting for locks for 30 seconds. Preemptive waits, which are where SQL Server is waiting on external API calls, are also captured. Other information stored in the ring_buffer, such as memory broker, scheduler monitor, security, connectivity, and out-of-memory (OOM) errors, is also available.

To see a summary report of the events being captured and stored in the ring buffer, with the last reported event time and oldest recorded event time, as well as the number of occurrences for each event, use this query:

```
SET NOCOUNT ON

--Store the XML data in a temp table
SELECT CAST(xet.target_data as xml) as XMLDATA
INTO #SystemHealthSessionData
FROM sys.dm_xe_session_targets xet
JOIN sys.dm_xe_sessions xe
ON (xe.address = xet.event_session_address)
WHERE xe.name = 'system_health'

-- Group the events by type
;WITH CTE_HealthSession AS
(
SELECT C.query('.').value('(/event/@name)[1]', 'varchar(255)') as EventName,
C.query('.').value('(/event/@timestamp)[1]', 'datetime') as EventTime
FROM #SystemHealthSessionData a
CROSS APPLY a.XMLDATA.nodes('/RingBufferTarget/event') as T(C))
SELECT EventName,
COUNT(*) as Occurrences,
MAX(EventTime) as LastReportedEventTime,
MIN(EventTime) as OldestRecordedEventTime
FROM CTE_HealthSession
GROUP BY EventName
ORDER BY 2 DESC

--Drop the temporary table
DROP TABLE #SystemHealthSessionData
```

If there is anything to report, you will see the output results similar to the following:

```
EventName      Occurrences    LastReportedEventTime      OldestRecordedEventTime
scheduler_monitor_system_health_ring_buffer_recorded      124     2015-02-17 15:33:51.120
2015-02-17 13:30:49.647
sp_server_diagnostics_component_result      100      2015-02-17 15:29:52.303      2015-02-17
13:29:51.943
xml_deadlock_report      1      2015-02-17 15:34:31.330      2015-02-17 15:34:31.330
security_error_ring_buffer_recorded      1      2015-02-17 13:29:51.950      2015-02-17
13:29:51.950
```

Deadlocks

Deadlocks, not to be confused with blocking, occur when multiple connections to your SQL database are trying to read and write data at the same time, blocking each other's requests and forcing SQL Server to kill one of the requests as the "deadlock victim."

Deadlocking occurs when two user processes have locks on separate objects and each process is trying to acquire a lock on the object that the other process has. When this happens, SQL Server identifies the problem and ends the deadlock by automatically choosing one process and aborting the other process, allowing the other process to continue. The aborted transaction is rolled back, and an error message is sent to the user of the aborted process. If the application code is not handling the deadlock and resubmitting the transaction, it could result in the front-end application aborting as well.

In Chapter 6, I demonstrate some of the available reports, including the deadlock report available with the SQL 2012 System Health Reporting Dashboard.

In the past, capturing deadlock events was hit-or-miss. Deadlock monitoring was not set up by default. To capture this information, you needed to enable a trace flag that is active in advance. If you ran into a deadlock and the flags were not started, nothing was logged. I can't remember how many times early in my DBA career that users would ask to retrieve information on the deadlock, the cause, and the competing statements that caused the deadlock. In SQL Server version 2005 and newer, you would run DBCC TRACEON and DBCC TRACEOFF or use the trace flag -T1222 option as a startup parameter in SQL Server service properties. These will turn global deadlock tracing on and off.

```
-- SQL 2005 version and above:
DBCC TRACEON (1222, -1)
```

If you're using SQL Server 2008 and newer, you can use Extended Events to monitor deadlocks by capturing and analyze its output. You no longer have to enable any trace flags. You can select the xml_ deadlock_report event, which is retrieved from the ring_buffer from the system_health session. From the system_health session, the deadlock graph is returned, which shows you the sessions and resources that were involved with the deadlock. The ring buffer target holds event data in memory and stores tons of useful troubleshooting and performance metadata. As also mentioned, as of SQL Server 2012, the session data was also written to a file target of .xel by default. This would ensure that all events get captured because there is a known issue where many deadlocks are missed by the ring_buffer target.

To actually return deadlock data output, you would need to have a deadlock occur so you can simulate one, by using the following create deadlock code. To create a deadlock, use the following steps so that you can observe deadlock behavior:

```
-- 1) Create Tables for Deadlock Simulation
USE TEMPDB

CREATE TABLE dbo.tab1 (col1 INT)
INSERT dbo.tab1 SELECT 1

CREATE TABLE dbo.tab2 (col1 INT)
INSERT dbo.tab2 SELECT 1

-- 2) Run in first connection
BEGIN TRAN
UPDATE tempdb.dbo.tab1 SET col1 = 1

-- 3) Run in second connection
BEGIN TRAN
```

```
UPDATE tempdb.dbo.tab2 SET col1 = 1
UPDATE tempdb.dbo.tab1 SET col1 = 1

-- 4) Run in first connection
UPDATE tempdb.dbo.tab2 SET col1 = 1
```

The second connection will be chosen as the deadlock victim, and you should receive a deadlock error message.

```
Msg 1205, Level 13, State 45, Line 4
Transaction (Process ID 57) was deadlocked on lock resources with another process and has
been chosen as the deadlock victim. Rerun the transaction.
```

The following is a query to find the deadlock XML details using Extended Events:

```
SELECT XEvent.query('(event/data/value/deadlock)[1]') AS DeadlockGraph
FROM ( SELECT XEvent.query('.') AS XEvent
        FROM ( SELECT CAST(target_data AS XML) AS TargetData
                FROM sys.dm_xe_session_targets st
                    JOIN sys.dm_xe_sessions s
                    ON s.address = st.event_session_address
                WHERE s.name = 'system_health'
                    AND st.target_name = 'ring_buffer'
                ) AS Data
                CROSS APPLY
                    TargetData.nodes                    ('RingBufferTarget/event[@name="xml_
deadlock_report"]')
                AS XEventData ( XEvent )
        ) AS src;
```

Here is a partial sample of the XML output, from the previous query, of the deadlock graph showing the process section. The full output would show the resource section, including the file ID, page ID, database ID, object ID, request type, and mode.

```
<deadlock>
  <victim-list>
    <victimProcess id="process307acf8" />
  </victim-list>
  <process-list>
    <process id="process307acf8" taskpriority="0" logused="144" waitresource="RID:
2:1:295:0" waittime="1905" ownerId="381403" transactionname="user_transaction"
lasttranstarted="2015-02-16T12:06:03.060" XDES="0x8cc074d28" lockMode="U" schedulerid="7"
kpid="48364" status="suspended" spid="56" sbid="0" ecid="0" priority="0" trancount="2"
lastbatchstarted="2015-02-16T12:06:24.960" lastbatchcompleted="2015-02-16T12:06:03.060"
lastattention="1900-01-01T00:00:00.060" clientapp="Microsoft SQL Server Management
Studio - Query" hostname="MyServer" hostpid="51432" loginname="DOMAIN\MYLOGIN"
isolationlevel="read committed (2)" xactid="381403" currentdb="2" lockTimeout="4294967295"
clientoption1="671090784" clientoption2="390200">
        <executionStack>
            <frame procname="adhoc" line="3" stmtstart="16" sqlhandle="0x02000000f33afb2a0a0c265
98467cb1bbfb9cc19c1b2518e00000000000000000000000000000000000000000">
```

```
UPDATE [tempdb].[dbo].[tab2] set [col1] = @1     </frame>
        <frame procname="adhoc" line="3" stmtstart="66" sqlhandle="0x02000000041c1905c630e27
82bbbb0247a377622469b4e97000000000000000000000000000000000000000000">
UPDATE tempdb.dbo.tab2r SET col1 = 1      </frame>
      </executionStack>
      <inputbuf>
-- 4) Run in first connection
UPDATE tempdb.dbo.tab2 SET col1 = 1
   </inputbuf>
    </process>
```

Using the following T-SQL, you can examine the Deadlock Graph, and you can also return details of the statements involved in the deadlock.

```
;WITH SystemHealth
AS (
SELECT CAST(target_data AS xml) AS SessionXML
FROM sys.dm_xe_session_targets st
INNER JOIN sys.dm_xe_sessions s ON s.address = st.event_session_address
WHERE name = 'system_health'
)
SELECT Deadlock.value('@timestamp', 'datetime') AS DeadlockDateTime
,CAST(Deadlock.value('(data/value)[1]', 'varchar(max)') as xml) as DeadlockGraph
FROM SystemHealth s
CROSS APPLY SessionXML.nodes ('//RingBufferTarget/event') AS t (Deadlock)
WHERE Deadlock.value('@name', 'nvarchar(128)') = 'xml_deadlock_report';
```

By using the SQL Server 2012 GUI and invoking the system_health live data session, you can see a graphical representation of the Deadlock Graph report, as displayed in Figure 8-13.

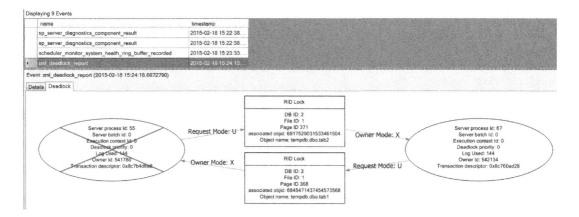

Figure 8-13. *Deadlock report as shown through XE session GUI*

To get the full xml_deadlock_report details returned as neat query results, you will need a comprehensive script to parse the XML and return it as user-friendly data. I recommend a great script for this, shown next, which is based on SQL Server MCM, Wayne Sheffield's XML Shred Deadlock script, which can be accessed in its original form at http://bit.ly/ShredDL. The original allows you to specify different targets, but here you use the one that gets the data more reliably from the current event file target.

```
DECLARE @deadlock TABLE (
        DeadlockID INT IDENTITY PRIMARY KEY CLUSTERED,
        DeadlockGraph XML
        );
WITH cte1 AS
(
SELECT    target_data = convert(XML, target_data)
FROM      sys.dm_xe_session_targets t
          JOIN sys.dm_xe_sessions s
            ON t.event_session_address = s.address
WHERE     t.target_name = 'event_file'
AND          s.name = 'system_health'
), cte2 AS
(
SELECT    [FileName] = FileEvent.FileTarget.value('@name', 'varchar(1000)')
FROM      cte1
          CROSS APPLY cte1.target_data.nodes('//EventFileTarget/File') FileEvent(FileTarget)
), cte3 AS
(
SELECT    event_data = CONVERT(XML, t2.event_data)
FROM      cte2
          CROSS APPLY sys.fn_xe_file_target_read_file(cte2.[FileName], NULL, NULL, NULL) t2
WHERE     t2.object_name = 'xml_deadlock_report'
)
INSERT INTO @deadlock(DeadlockGraph)
SELECT  Deadlock = Deadlock.Report.query('.')
FROM    cte3
        CROSS APPLY cte3.event_data.nodes('//event/data/value/deadlock') Deadlock(Report);

        -- use below to load individual deadlocks.
INSERT INTO @deadlock VALUES ('');
-- Insert the deadlock XML in the above line!
-- Duplicate as necessary for additional graphs.

WITH CTE AS
(
SELECT  DeadlockID,
        DeadlockGraph
FROM    @deadlock
), Victims AS
(
SELECT    ID = Victims.List.value('@id', 'varchar(50)')
FROM      CTE
```

```
            CROSS APPLY CTE.DeadlockGraph.nodes('//deadlock/victim-list/victimProcess') AS
Victims (List)
), Locks AS
(
-- Merge all of the lock information together.
SELECT  CTE.DeadlockID,
        MainLock.Process.value('@id', 'varchar(100)') AS LockID,
        OwnerList.Owner.value('@id', 'varchar(200)') AS LockProcessId,
        REPLACE(MainLock.Process.value('local-name(.)', 'varchar(100)'), 'lock', '') AS
LockEvent,
        MainLock.Process.value('@objectname', 'sysname') AS ObjectName,
        OwnerList.Owner.value('@mode', 'varchar(10)') AS LockMode,
        MainLock.Process.value('@dbid', 'INTEGER') AS Database_id,
        MainLock.Process.value('@associatedObjectId', 'BIGINT') AS AssociatedObjectId,
        MainLock.Process.value('@WaitType', 'varchar(100)') AS WaitType,
        WaiterList.Owner.value('@id', 'varchar(200)') AS WaitProcessId,
        WaiterList.Owner.value('@mode', 'varchar(10)') AS WaitMode
FROM    CTE
        CROSS APPLY CTE.DeadlockGraph.nodes('//deadlock/resource-list') AS Lock (list)
        CROSS APPLY Lock.list.nodes('*') AS MainLock (Process)
        OUTER APPLY MainLock.Process.nodes('owner-list/owner') AS OwnerList (Owner)
        CROSS APPLY MainLock.Process.nodes('waiter-list/waiter') AS WaiterList (Owner)
), Process AS
(
-- get the data from the process node
SELECT  CTE.DeadlockID,
        [Victim] = CONVERT(BIT, CASE WHEN Deadlock.Process.value('@id', 'varchar(50)') =
ISNULL(Deadlock.Process.value('../../@victim', 'varchar(50)'), v.ID)
                                THEN 1
                                ELSE 0
                        END),
        [LockMode] = Deadlock.Process.value('@lockMode', 'varchar(10)'), -- how is this
different from in the resource-list section?
        [ProcessID] = Process.ID, --Deadlock.Process.value('@id', 'varchar(50)'),
        [KPID] = Deadlock.Process.value('@kpid', 'int'), -- kernel-process id / thread ID
number
        [SPID] = Deadlock.Process.value('@spid', 'int'), -- system process id (connection to sql)
        [SBID] = Deadlock.Process.value('@sbid', 'int'), -- system batch id / request_id (a
query that a SPID is running)
        [ECID] = Deadlock.Process.value('@ecid', 'int'), -- execution context ID (a worker
thread running part of a query)
        [IsolationLevel] = Deadlock.Process.value('@isolationlevel', 'varchar(200)'),
        [WaitResource] = Deadlock.Process.value('@waitresource', 'varchar(200)'),
        [LogUsed] = Deadlock.Process.value('@logused', 'int'),
        [ClientApp] = Deadlock.Process.value('@clientapp', 'varchar(100)'),
        [HostName] = Deadlock.Process.value('@hostname', 'varchar(20)'),
        [LoginName] = Deadlock.Process.value('@loginname', 'varchar(20)'),
        [TransactionTime] = Deadlock.Process.value('@lasttranstarted', 'datetime'),
        [BatchStarted] = Deadlock.Process.value('@lastbatchstarted', 'datetime'),
        [BatchCompleted] = Deadlock.Process.value('@lastbatchcompleted', 'datetime'),
```

```
        [InputBuffer] = Input.Buffer.query('.'),
        CTE.[DeadlockGraph],
        es.ExecutionStack,
        [QueryStatement] = Execution.Frame.value('.', 'varchar(max)'),
        ProcessQty = SUM(1) OVER (PARTITION BY CTE.DeadlockID),
        TranCount = Deadlock.Process.value('@trancount', 'int')
FROM    CTE
        CROSS APPLY CTE.DeadlockGraph.nodes('//deadlock/process-list/process') AS Deadlock
(Process)
        CROSS APPLY (SELECT Deadlock.Process.value('@id', 'varchar(50)') ) AS Process (ID)
        LEFT JOIN Victims v ON Process.ID = v.ID
        CROSS APPLY Deadlock.Process.nodes('inputbuf') AS Input (Buffer)
        CROSS APPLY Deadlock.Process.nodes('executionStack') AS Execution (Frame)
-- get the data from the executionStack node as XML
        CROSS APPLY (SELECT ExecutionStack = (SELECT   ProcNumber = ROW_NUMBER()
                                                OVER (PARTITION BY CTE.DeadlockID,
                                                Deadlock.Process.value('@id', 'varchar(50)'),
                                                Execution.Stack.value('@procname', 'sysname'),
                                                Execution.Stack.value('@code', 'varchar(MAX)')
                                                ORDER BY (SELECT 1)),
                                        ProcName = Execution.Stack.value('@procname', 'sysname'),
                                        Line = Execution.Stack.value('@line', 'int'),
                                        SQLHandle = Execution.Stack.value('@sqlhandle', 'varchar(64)'),
                                        Code = LTRIM(RTRIM(Execution.Stack.value('.', 'varchar(MAX)')))
                                        FROM Execution.Frame.nodes('frame') AS Execution (Stack)
                                        ORDER BY ProcNumber
                                        FOR XML PATH('frame'), ROOT('executionStack'), TYPE )
) es
)
    -- get the columns in the desired order

SELECT  p.DeadlockID,
        p.Victim,
        p.ProcessQty,
        ProcessNbr = DENSE_RANK()
                    OVER (PARTITION BY p.DeadlockId
                            ORDER BY p.ProcessID),
        p.LockMode,
        LockedObject = NULLIF(l.ObjectName, ''),
        l.database_id,
        l.AssociatedObjectId,
        LockProcess = p.ProcessID,
        p.KPID,
        p.SPID,
        p.SBID,
        p.ECID,
        p.TranCount,
        l.LockEvent,
        LockedMode = l.LockMode,
        l.WaitProcessID,
        l.WaitMode,
```

```
        p.WaitResource,
        l.WaitType,
        p.IsolationLevel,
        p.LogUsed,
        p.ClientApp,
        p.HostName,
        p.LoginName,
        p.TransactionTime,
        p.BatchStarted,
        p.BatchCompleted,
        p.QueryStatement,
        p.InputBuffer,
        p.DeadlockGraph,
        p.ExecutionStack
FROM    Process p
        LEFT JOIN Locks l
            ON p.DeadlockID = l.DeadlockID
               AND p.ProcessID = l.LockProcessID
ORDER BY p.DeadlockId,
        p.Victim DESC,
        p.ProcessId;
```

Tips to Minimize Deadlocks

In this section, I will discuss some tips for how to reduce deadlocking on your SQL Server. Database design is key to minimizing the occurrences of deadlocks. The database should be fairly normalized, but not overly normalized, because transactions that involve multiple joins can hold locks on multiple tables, which increases the chances of deadlocks.

When server objects are accessed by transactions in an application, they should consistently access them in same order each time. Make sure that the application collects all user input before transactions begin, not during transaction processing. If a transaction is waiting on the user, this will most certainly hold up processing and hold locks until the transaction is committed or rolled back. Transactions should be kept as short as possible by reducing the number of round-trips between SQL Server and the application. One way to do this is to rely on stored procedures that are stored and compiled code on SQL Server and only need to be invoked by the application. The actual processing occurs on the back end. Additionally, it does this by optimizing T-SQL code to avoid cursors and ensures that transactions are executed in a single batch. SQL Server should also avoid reading the same data again from disk, when it can be stored to a temporary variable and read from there. Furthermore, shortening transactions can have the effect of reducing the time a table has a lock and will therefore reduce the chances of deadlock. The application should release a lock as soon as possible. You can also consider reducing lock escalation and control locking in SQL Server by using hints, such as PAGLOCK and ROWLOCK. PAGLOCK locks the table, while ROWLOCK locks the data at the row level. Another hint you can use to prevent locking is NOLOCK, when you are reading data and data is not often modified.

Finally, with respect to deadlocks, you can use a low isolation level where possible, which can minimize the lock level. One such option is to use a row versioning–based isolation level, where read operations do not request shared locks on the data. These are just some practical ways to reduce the potential for deadlocks to occur.

Blocking and Locking

I discussed the concepts of blocking and locking in terms of resource waits in Chapter 3. I also talked about monitoring blocking and locking as part of the default system_health session introducing Extended Events, in Chapter 6. Let's set the "blocked process threshold" configuration option. This option allows you to capture blocking on system tasks and tasks waiting for resources by setting a threshold, in seconds, for blocked processes. Because it is an advanced option, you will first need to enable advanced configuration options. You can enable advanced options and set the threshold for blocked processes with the following T-SQL code:

```
sp_configure 'show advanced options',1 ;
GO
RECONFIGURE;
GO
sp_configure 'blocked process threshold',5 ;
GO
RECONFIGURE;
GO
```

You can also use an XQuery script to retrieve the blocking processes and information from the blocked_process_report event session. Now that you configured the blocked process threshold, using the previous code, you need to create the event blocking session and then start the session as follows. The following blocking script is based on SQL MVP Jonathan Kehayias code. He is a trusted authority on Extended Events.

```
CREATE EVENT SESSION MonitorBlocking
ON SERVER
ADD EVENT sqlserver.blocked_process_report
ADD TARGET package0.ring_buffer(SET MAX_MEMORY=2048)
WITH (MAX_DISPATCH_LATENCY = 5SECONDS)
GO

ALTER EVENT SESSION MonitorBlocking
ON SERVER
STATE=START
```

Once the session is created and started, you can test the Monitor_Blocking script by creating a blocking chain. Do this against the AdventureWorks2012 example database.

Open your SQL Server instance and open two query windows. In the first query window, run the following code (CauseBlocking):

```
USE AdventureWorks2012;
GO
BEGIN TRANSACTION
SELECT * FROM Person.Person WITH (TABLOCKX, HOLDLOCK);
WAITFOR DELAY '00:00:30' ---Wait 30 seconds!
ROLLBACK TRANSACTION
--Release the lock
```

In the second query window, run the following code:

```
USE AdventureWorks2012;
GO
SELECT * FROM Person.Person;
```

Once you create the blocking condition, in a new query window run the `Monitoring_Blocking` session script, shown here:

```
SELECT
    n.value('(event/@name)[1]', 'varchar(50)') AS event_name,
    n.value('(event/@package)[1]', 'varchar(50)') AS package_name,
    DATEADD(hh,
            DATEDIFF(hh, GETUTCDATE(), CURRENT_TIMESTAMP),
            n.value('(event/@timestamp)[1]', 'datetime2')) AS [timestamp],
    ISNULL(n.value('(event/data[@name="database_id"]/value)[1]', 'int'),
            n.value('(event/action[@name="database_id"]/value)[1]', 'int')) as
[database_id],
        n.value('(event/data[@name="database_name"]/value)[1]', 'nvarchar(128)') as
[database_name],
        n.value('(event/data[@name="object_id"]/value)[1]', 'int') as [object_id],
        n.value('(event/data[@name="index_id"]/value)[1]', 'int') as [index_id],
        CAST(n.value('(event/data[@name="duration"]/value)[1]', 'bigint')/1000000.0 AS
decimal(6,2)) as [duration_seconds],
        n.value('(event/data[@name="lock_mode"]/text)[1]', 'nvarchar(10)') as [file_handle],
        n.value('(event/data[@name="transaction_id"]/value)[1]', 'bigint') as [transaction_id],
        n.value('(event/data[@name="resource_owner_type"]/text)[1]', 'nvarchar(10)') as
[resource_owner_type],
        CAST(n.value('(event/data[@name="blocked_process"]/value)[1]', 'nvarchar(max)') as
XML) as [blocked_process_report]
    FROM
    (   SELECT td.query('.') as n
        FROM
        (
            SELECT CAST(target_data AS XML) as target_data
            FROM sys.dm_xe_sessions AS s
            JOIN sys.dm_xe_session_targets AS t
                ON s.address = t.event_session_address
            WHERE s.name = 'MonitorBlocking'
              AND t.target_name = 'ring_buffer'
        ) AS sub
        CROSS APPLY target_data.nodes('RingBufferTarget/event') AS q(td)
    ) as tab
    GO
```

Your result, retrieving the data from the ring buffer, should look like this:

```
event_name     package_name    timestamp    database_id    database_name    object_id
index_id    duration_seconds    file_handle    transaction_id    resource_owner_type
blocked_process_report
blocked_process_report    sqlserver    2015-02-17 12:08:34.1500000    12
AdventureWorks2012    1765581328    0    11.90    IS    137307    LOCK
SELECT * FROM Person.Person;
BEGIN TRANSACTION
SELECT * FROM Person.Person WITH (TABLOCKX, HOLDLOCK);
WAITFOR DELAY '00:00:30' ---Wait a minute!
ROLLBACK TRANSACTION
--Release the lock
```

Monitoring Errors with Extended Events

You can use Extended Events to capture and track SQL Server errors without the need to have a server trace running, and you can instantly query the data as it becomes available. The system_health session collects information about errors, including the sql_text and session_id for any sessions that encounter an error with a severity greater than or equal to 20. In addition, sql_text and session_id for any sessions that encounter a memory-related error. The errors include 17803, 701, 802, 8645, 8651, 8657, and 8902. Extended Events will also get a record of any nonyielding scheduler problems, which appear in the SQL Server error log as error 17883.

Since the system_health session tracks errors with a severity greater than 20, you can test that functionality by simulating a severity 21 error using RAISERROR. First, run the following RAISERROR code to create a fatal error situation:

```
RAISERROR (N'This is a test of the Severity 21 Alert System, Thank goodness it is only a
test', -- Message text.
          21, -- Severity,
          1, -- State,
          N'number',
          5) WITH LOG;
```

You will see this error message displayed:

```
Msg 2745, Level 16, State 2, Line 1
Process ID 58 has raised user error 50000, severity 21. SQL Server is terminating this
process.
Msg 50000, Level 21, State 1, Line 1
This is a test of the Severity 21 Alert System, Thank goodness it is only a test
Msg 0, Level 20, State 0, Line 0
A severe error occurred on the current command. The results, if any, should be discarded.
```

You can query the system_health sessions with the following query to view the captured error data:

```
SELECT CAST(target_data as xml) AS targetdata
INTO #system_health_data
FROM sys.dm_xe_session_targets xet
JOIN sys.dm_xe_sessions xe
    ON xe.address = xet.event_session_address
```

```
WHERE name = 'system_health'
AND xet.target_name = 'ring_buffer';

SELECT
    DATEADD(mi, DATEDIFF(mi, GETUTCDATE(), CURRENT_TIMESTAMP), xevents.event_data.value
    ('(@timestamp)[1]', 'datetime2')) AS [err timestamp],
    xevents.event_data.value('(data[@name="severity"]/value)[1]', 'bigint')
    AS [err severity],
    xevents.event_data.value('(data[@name="error_number"]/value)[1]', 'bigint')
    AS [err number],
    xevents.event_data.value('(data[@name="message"]/value)[1]', 'nvarchar(512)')
    AS [err message],
xevents.event_data.value('(action/value)[2]', 'varchar(10)') as [session id],

    xevents.event_data.value('(action[@name="sql_text"]/value)[1]', 'nvarchar(max)')
    AS [query text],
    xevents.event_data.query('.') as [event details]
FROM #system_health_data
CROSS APPLY targetdata.nodes('//RingBufferTarget/event') AS xevents (event_data)
WHERE xevents.event_data.value('(@name)[1]', 'nvarchar(256)')='error_reported';

DROP TABLE #system_health_data;
GO
```

You will get similar results such as the following:

```
err timestamp      err severity    err number    err message    query text
2015-02-14 20:17:55.4740000    21    50000    This is a test of the Severity 21 Alert
System, Thank goodness it is only a test    RAISERROR (N'This is a test of the Severity 21
Alert System, Thank goodness it is only a test', -- Message text.
            21, -- Severity,
            1, -- State,
            N'number',
            5) WITH LOG;
```

■ **Caution**   There is a known bug in SQL Server. Microsoft claims to have fixed it in SQL Server 2008R2 SP1. The bug is that the Extended Event session `system_health` records incorrect timestamps. You can read more about the problem here: https://connect.microsoft.com/SQLServer/feedback/details/649362/extended-event-session-system-health-diferent-timestamp-datetime-and-datetime-on-server-getdate.

Monitoring Software

You are now aware of various ways to accomplish monitoring and alerting right out of the box. Maybe you thought about building your own, but other priorities and projects take precedence. Therefore, you may decide you want to acquire an enterprise-wide or SQL Server–specific monitoring and alerting system to keep track of and alert on multiple SQL Server instances under one interface. This, in fact, may be the right way to go for your organization because, quite simply, you don't have the time to develop your own solution.

That's why several vendors have dedicated development and marketing teams for creating a ready-made solution and selling it your organization. In this section, you will learn the various aspects of evaluating which type of monitoring software is right for you.

Build vs. Buy

Let's talk about a common scenario called "build vs. buy." Value does exist when considering the potentially billable hours vs. the cost of purchasing monitoring software; time is money after all. In fact, this decision may provide a great service and value in the long run, as well as a considerable return on investment (ROI). This section will not make any specific recommendations or reviews for third-party monitoring software but will simply inform you what you should look for in a monitoring system and the types of software and features that are out there. A couple of monitoring solutions will be mentioned as examples, in the context of the types of systems out there.

In addition, you should clearly implement a monitoring solution that has the lowest overhead and performance impact on the SQL Server instances that you seek to monitor. This may sound obvious, but the last thing you want is a performance monitoring system that causes performance issues. Yes, there has been such software that created overhead and even masked itself by not reporting its own resource utilization and impact on the system.

If you're just focusing on the SQL Server database platform, then you will want to consider SQL Server–specific monitoring software. This software usually excels in all your SQL Server monitoring needs because it focuses on the DBA and various metrics related to SQL Server only. This is a good option for DBAs and their respective teams that manage the SQL Server real estate exclusively.

Proactive monitoring allows the DBA to be able quickly pinpoint and resolve issues before they escalate into bigger issues and many times before anyone, such as management, even notices. This is a catch-22 in a sense: if the DBA is so efficient at resolving issues before anyone knows about them, how will you, the DBA, get the recognition you justly deserve? Well, this is why you should maintain a log, document all the issues that occur, and keep track of the resolution. Some monitoring software has this type of statistical runtime report so you can present these metrics to your manager.

This brings us to the different categories of monitoring systems. There are some broad and feature-rich enterprise-wide monitoring systems out there, including Microsoft's own System Center Operations Manager (SCOM). Many of these enterprise monitoring systems manage multiple devices and cross-platform components, such as network, Exchange (mail servers), operating systems, hypervisors (VMs), and of course SQL Server (as well as other database systems). They are often deployed as a core monitoring system, with management packs and agents specific to the product for an additional cost.

You should also be aware that you may want to avoid a software package that has too high of a learning curve. Besides the time it will take to fully understand how to install and use, some monitoring software solutions may require training, at additional cost, and vendors may bundle their value-added services (VAS) to be on-site to train on and deploy the product. This may be fine for large corporations and organizations but could be too expensive for small and medium businesses.

Pearl Knowledge Solution's SQLCentric monitoring and alert system has a built-in historical runtime trending report, which allows the user to select the measures and time period to report on and outputs table and chart display. For example, you can retrieve results showing the percentage of uptime for server, services and databases, successful job run executions, disk space, memory/CPU status, number of error log occurrences, and so on. You should be able to show your managers an overall holistic view of the state and health of your SQL Server instances, and this is where reporting comes in.

Features, Polling, Agents, Push vs. Pull

Some monitoring systems are considered polling software, and others are deploy agents. They are also distinguished as push vs. pull. What this means is polling software will connect to all of your SQL Server instances at some specified scheduled interval, run some processes and queries, "pull" or collect status information, and report or alert on the data based on various thresholds. In this regard, some polling software employs the "connect and collect" methodology, where the software logs onto SQL Server, for example, collects its information, and logs off, usually storing this data in a central repository, whether it's a database or file. This way it can minimize the impact of computing and processing on the monitored server itself. Alternatively, many software monitoring solutions deploy client agents, which need to be installed on each monitored server in the environment. These agents monitor in real time for conditions that would exceed the maximum configured thresholds and "push" the information out by uploading it to the central repository and sending an alert notification. Collected statistics could be stored either on the client system or on the central repository server for later reporting and historical trend analysis.

Some software monitoring solutions use triggers, stored procedures, and work databases on each server, all of which can introduce some additional overhead, including the agents themselves. Ideally, you want to look for monitoring software that is minimally invasive to the SQL Server instances it monitors and is a zero-impact solution.

Many third-party vendors do build and base their software solution by leveraging the internal and available features in SQL Server. For example, using and collecting metadata from DMVs and from Performance Monitor metrics and reading from the SQL Server error logs are all methods behind the scenes of monitoring software. The software uses this data to create reporting dashboards, tables, graphs, and charts to present the data in an eye-pleasing user-friendly front end.

The user interface or front-end is important in terms of usability. Ideally, it should be intuitive enough for the user to figure out what to do with little or no training. Some vendors still deploy their software as client-based Windows applications, but other more modern ones integrate their systems with the Web. Having the application as a front-end web application is significant in that it is portable and accessible via a website through an Internet browser from any computer within the company (that is, a corporate intranet) or available externally from anywhere in the world via the Internet. This enables manageability and makes support more efficient because you do not have to be on-site at the computer where installed.

The next logical step is to integrate monitoring systems with cloud technologies, such as Azure, which opens up possibilities of Monitoring as a Service (MAAS) and has performance metadata stored in the cloud (or at least monitored from the cloud). This may have some security implications, but vendors are working every day to overcome these challenges to make it a feasible option. Therefore, you may want to consider a third-party vendor hosting and monitoring your SQL Server instances remotely.

Another feature that is inherent in sophisticated monitoring and alert systems is the ability to control the number of alerts per event. For example, if the software reports on a failed job, how many times do you want to be alerted for the same job in a day? Another feature would be one where you can turn alerting on and off for an individual server. Going even further is an advanced solution that allows you to schedule maintenance or outage periods so that when you are working on a server that will require a reboot or restart of services, you can create a maintenance window where there will be no alerts generated. Basically, you are preventing false alarms by preventing a threshold to be tripped, otherwise known as a false positive. A false positive is where a test result incorrectly indicates that a particular condition or attribute is present. You are aware that a service is down, but it is not an issue while you work on the server to perform maintenance, upgrades, apply service packs, and so on.

Licensing and Pricing

There are many solutions out there at varied price entry points and different licensing schemes. Ultimately you need to decide based on all these factors, as well as pricing, what is the right solution for your environment. Different vendors have different licensing models. Typically, monitoring software may be based on the number of SQL Server instances you have in your environment. A simple licensing model is per-monitored server or per-monitored instance licensing. Per server could mean physical server, while per instance could mean x number of SQL Server instances on a physical server. Other licensing models could be per CPU, per core, or per socket as relative to each physical server. With virtualization in the mix, the pricing model could be based per VM. So, for example, if you have ten SQL Server instances across ten VMs but residing on the same host, you would still pay for ten separate licenses. Similar to a per-monitored instance, some vendors charge per number of SQL Server agents installed.

Evaluating Monitoring Software

You should be aware that not all monitoring systems are alike, and I would make a few suggestions when considering purchase. Don't listen to the sales/marketing hype. As I mentioned, their job is to sell, sell, sell. There are a lot of objective reviews out there from SQL experts and software users on their real-life experiences with the product. You should not settle on one product straightaway. It is highly recommended that you take advantage of as many of the vendor's free trial periods as possible. Create a product spreadsheet matrix of the various features, functionality, ease of use, licensing, and price for comparing the ideal solution based on your organization's needs. Evaluate whether the software offers such items as alerting, reporting, action recommendations, and so on. In addition, does it scale, is it web-based, does it do any performance tuning, are there any limitations, and does it support all versions of SQL Server?

You should evaluate each monitoring solution individually and take the features, functionality, ease of installation, deployment, and of course price all into consideration. Annual maintenance contracts are usually required with purchase, which cover technical support, bug fixes, and updates. Vendors typically charge 15 to 20 percent of the original purchase price for maintenance, and this maintenance cost can be raised with each renewal, according to your agreement. Feel free to make the vendors compete for your business and let them know the other products you are evaluating. You will be surprised how quickly the price comes down!

Reporting on Server Health

Your baselines have long been established, your servers are humming along, and continuous and automated monitoring and alerting are running and configured. Now, what's the best way to get a snapshot of the state of your SQL Server environment? Having user-friendly, intuitive, and interactive reports will allow you to quantify and visualize the vast array of collected data and analyze the results with graphical displays. If you want your bosses to know what you are doing as a DBA and want to prove that your SQL Server environment has a clean bill of health, you'll want to invest your time into learning how to create reports.

Management really likes organized data, numbers, charts, and graphs. As a DBA, you can provide this invaluable information to your managers so they can plan and budget for more hardware, software, and even potentially additional head count that will help ease your DBA workload. Anyway, as you progress in your DBA career, you'll want to move beyond the monotonous day-to-day support and operations and be freed up to participate and work on more complex projects. Microsoft offers some assistance on getting familiar with and using SQL Server Reporting Services by providing Reporting Service tutorials on

MSDN, including how to create a data-driven subscription, which allows you to generate dynamic reports automatically and send them to a distribution list on a regular schedule, create a basic table report, and even more. You can access these tutorials here:

https://msdn.microsoft.com/en-us/library/bb522859.aspx

In Chapter 7, I walked you through deploying the management data warehouse (MDW) and configuring the data collection as a means of a central repository of performance stats. In addition, you were shown how to create your own custom repository using the example of collecting wait statistics. In this chapter, you will finally get to report on this grand collection of metadata that's sitting in your central repository, waiting to be mined and reported on. Here I will show you the available reports from the MDW and then demonstrate how to create a custom SSRS report based on a custom collection.

MDW Reports

Fortunately, if you deployed the MDW in your environment, you have a set of canned reports ready to go at your fingertips. To access the MDW report collection, you will navigate to the MDW database being used as the repository, right-click, and from the pop-up menu select Reports ➤ Management Data Warehouse ➤ Management Data Warehouse Overview. Refer to Figure 8-14.

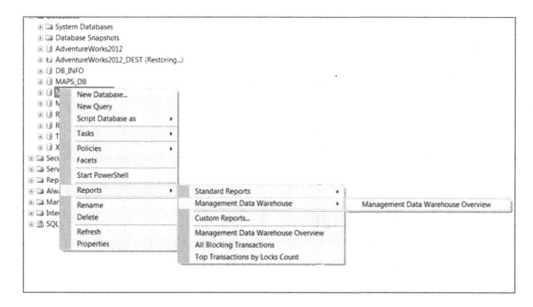

Figure 8-14. *Accessing the MDW reports*

The Overview report, which drills down to further snapshot reports, is displayed in Figure 8-15. The three main report groupings here are Server Activity, Query Statistics, and Disk Usage.

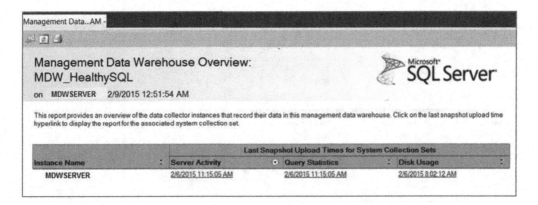

Figure 8-15. *MDW Overview report*

Figure 8-16 shows a sample of the MDW report for server activity. This report provides an overview of the resources that are consumed by SQL Server and the server activity for the selected instance and host OS. CPU, memory, disk I/O, and even network usage stats are displayed for the chosen time period. You can navigate through the historical snapshots of data using the timeline on the screen. Top wait types are shown as a bar graph, as well as various performance counter data representing SQL Server activity.

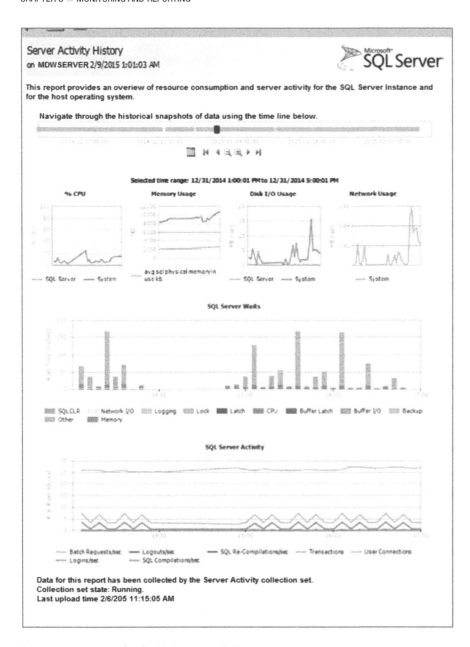

Figure 8-16. *Example of MDW server activity report*

Building the Custom SSRS Report

As you recall from Chapter 7, you set out to create a custom repository of waits statistics metadata that you can build reports from. Please refer to that chapter to learn how to create the repository in order to follow along with creating your reports. Using the `sys.dm_os_wait_stats` DMV, you were provided with scripts to create the initial baseline, create the historical wait stat table to persist the data for retrieval, create a flag table to allow the user to exclude certain wait types, and create a stored procedure around this code that you can schedule as a SQL Agent job to populate wait stats data on a scheduled interval. Once you have the job scheduled and sample data is collected, you can build your custom report.

This section is dedicated to creating the daily wait stats report from the wait statistics in the dbo.waitstats table you created in Chapter 7. SSRS is the report building tool and a component that is part of the native SQL Server Suite Business Intelligence product stack, which allows you to design, deploy, and manage reports.

Here is what you will do to create your custom SSRS report:

1. Use SQL Server Data Tools (SSDT) to create the initial report with the Report Wizard.

2. Create a data source connection to connect to the source database.

3. Create three data set queries to use for this report, one for the report data and the other two for use with user parameter selection.

   a. Base query to retrieve the data for the report

   b. Query for the capture date from the base table

   c. Query to get all the wait types

4. Create user input parameters.

   a. Begin Date

   b. End Date

   c. Wait Type

5. Create the Chart/Line Graph for display.

Create the Report Framework

First I'll discuss what SQL Server Data Tools (SSDT) are. Included with SQL Server 2012 and newer, you have SSDT, which is contained in the Visual Studio 2010 shell and a subset of the Visual Studio 2010 Microsoft development platform. It is one of the shared features you must select when installing SQL Server 2012 and newer, as shown in Figure 8-17, which will be accessible as part of the SQL Server 2012 program group. SSDT replaces the previous Business Intelligence Development Studio (BIDS). Visual Studio 2010 is a powerful development platform that goes way beyond the scope of this book, but you will learn how you can use it to create simple and more complex reports, which will be deployed via SSRS.

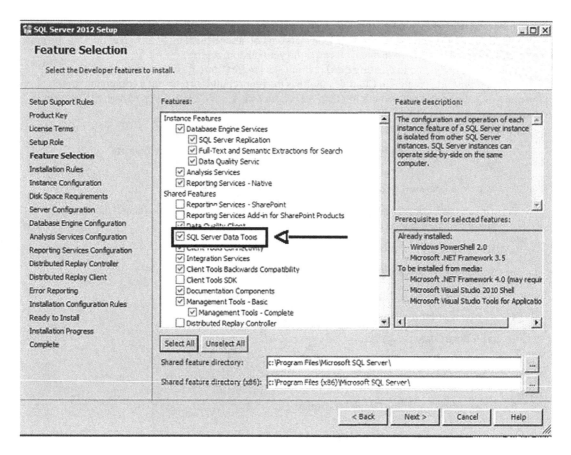

Figure 8-17. *Feature selection during SQL Server 2012 installation, highlighting SSDT*

To launch SSDT (Visual Studio 2010), go to Start ➤ All Programs ➤ Microsoft SQL Server 2012 ➤ SQL Server Data Tools. From the Start Page, click New Project, and then you will be presented with a list of Installed Templates under Business Intelligence. Select Report Server Project Wizard, as shown in Figure 8-18. You will use the wizard to create the basic report and then modify it to your custom needs.

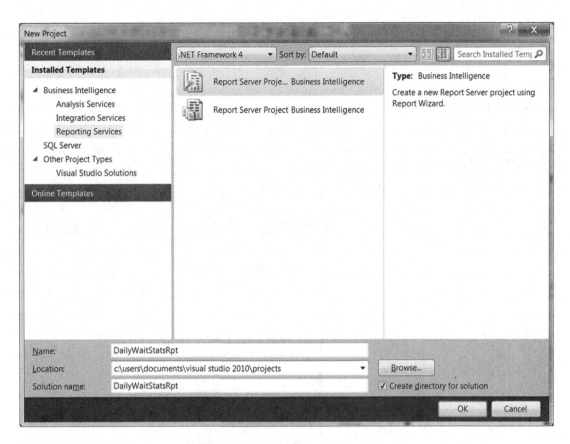

Figure 8-18. *Creating a new report project, Report Server Project*

The next thing you need to do is follow the wizard through the steps and create a new data source for your report data. In the Select the Data Source window, click Edit to set the connection properties by selecting the source server and database that is the repository for the wait statistics. Click Test Connection just to ensure that you are able to connect to the server and database. After you confirm that, click OK, and then you will see the connection string parameters appear. These steps to create the data source are represented in Figure 8-19. Now click Next to proceed with the wizard.

Select the Data Source

Select a data source from which to obtain data for this report or create a new data source.

○ Shared data source

[▼]

◉ New data source

Name:

DataSourceToWaitStatsRepository

Type:

[Microsoft SQL Server   ▼]

Connection string:

Data Source=MDWSERVER;Initial Catalog=DB_INFO

[Edit...   ]

[Credentials...   ]

Connection Properties   [?] [X]

Data source:

Microsoft SQL Server (SqlClient)   [Change...]

Server name:

[MDWSERVER   ▼] [Refresh]

Log on to the server

◉ Use Windows Authentication

○ Use SQL Server Authentication

User name: [   ]

Password: [   ]

☐ Save my password

☑ Make this a shared data source

Connect to a database

◉ Select or enter a database name:

DB_INFO   [▼]

○ Attach a database file:

[   ] [Browse...]

Logical name:

[   ]

[Help]   [< Back] [Next >]

[Advanced...]

[Test Connection]   [OK] [Cancel]

Figure 8-19. *Creating the data source for the report*

Create the Data Sets

You must now create the actual data sets for the report to pull the data from. Here you will specify a query to return specific data. You will create three data sets: the main query for the report, a subset of the data that will be used later for the datetime selection period (begin and end date), and the wait type. This is the Design the Query step shown in Figure 8-20.

Figure 8-20. *Designing the base query to retrieve report data*

In the Design the Query window, you will create the first data set with your main query by simply cutting and pasting the query into the window, as shown in Figure 8-17. You will retrieve the report data from the dbo.waitstats table you created in Chapter 7, using the dbo.waitstats query. Included are all the table columns, but you will need only wait_type, WaitSec, Percentage, and CaptureDate for this report. All other columns are commented out because they are optional. You can remove the /* and */ comment tags if you want to include those columns. In addition, the WHERE clause, which filters based on user input parameters, is commented out for the sake of creating the initial report via the wizard.

```
SELECT [wait_type]
      ,[WaitSec]
   /* ,[ResourceSec]
      ,[SignalSec]
      ,[WaitCount]
      ,[AvgWait_Sec]
      ,[AvgRes_Sec]
      ,[AvgSig_Sec] */ -- you only need WaitSec, Percentage & CaptureDate
      ,[Percentage]
      ,[CaptureDate]
  FROM [dbo].[waitstats]
/*Where CaptureDate  between @BeginDate AND @EndDate
 AND (@WaitType= 'ALL'
OR [Wait_type] in (@WaitType) )*/ --REMOVE COMMENTS AFTER PARAMS ARE CREATED.
```

■ **Note** You will create the dbo.waitstats query with the WHERE clause commented out, so later you will uncomment this section once your parameters are created in the next step.

You need to complete the Report Wizard first before you proceed. Once you finish with the design query step, click Next, leave Tabular selected as the Report Type, and click Next again.

The Design the Table step is where you will select the fields and indicate how you want to group your report data. For this report, you will group the data by wait_type. This means all the other column data details will be displayed by wait_type. In the details box, you will want to select WaitSec, Percentage, and CaptureDate. Figure 8-21 shows how your data fields should be organized.

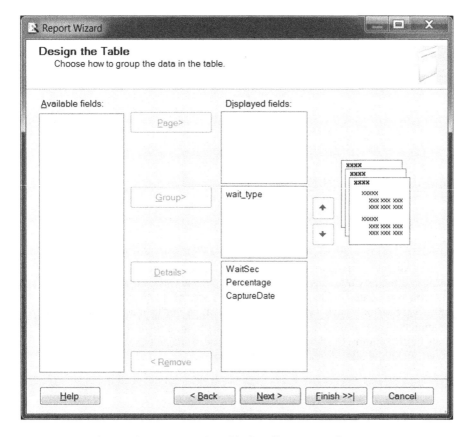

Figure 8-21. *Choosing how to group the table data (by wait_type)*

After you select your fields, click Next to choose the table layout. Here you can choose Stepped or Blocked, but I would say Stepped looks better. Also on this window, you can decide whether you want to enable drill down. Basically, if you choose this option, the wait types will be displayed in linear fashion, and their associated data can be viewed by expanding the view by clicking the drill-down (+) button. Decide and click Next.

The steps following allow you to choose the table style, the deployment location for the report to be accessed from your Reporting Services report server, and the desired deployment folder path. Select your table style, click Next, and then click Next after you choose the deployment locale. In the final step, name your report DailyWaitStatsReport and click Finish.

You should now be on the Design View tab of the report you just created.

Now you will create another data set from the same table data, dbo.waitstats, to retrieve all available dates in the table. This will allow you to select a date range for the report to serve as the begin and end dates. Set the name to CaptureDate, for simplicity sake; you'll see this when you create the parameters. Go to the Report Data tree on the left pane and navigate to Datasets. Right-click and select Add Dataset. Once the Dataset Properties window appears, click the "Use a dataset embedded in my report" option and select the data source (DataSource1) as created in the first step. Cut and paste the following query in the Query textbox, as demonstrated in Figure 8-22. Click OK to create the data set.

```
Select Distinct(CaptureDate) from [dbo].[waitstats]
```

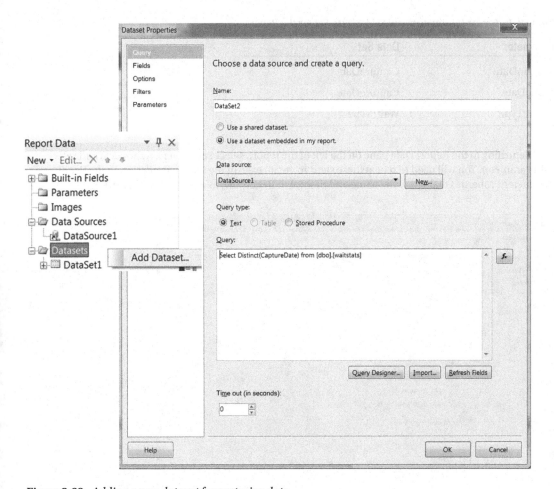

Figure 8-22. *Adding a new data set for capturing data*

The third and last data set you will create will allow you to choose to report on one particular wait type or simply return data on *all* of the actively monitored wait types in the table. To do this, basically repeat the previous steps (as in Dataset2) to add a new data set, Dataset3, naming it WaitType, and cut and paste the following query in the Query text box. Click OK.

```
Select [Wait_type] from [dbo].[waitstats]
UNION
Select 'ALL' from [dbo].[waitstats]
```

Create Parameters

Here you will create the parameters that will allow an interactive report where the user will be able to select the period/date range, as well as the wait type. Table 8-1 shows the parameters that will be created.

Table 8-1. *Create Parameters and Select Data Set for the Report*

Parameter	Data Set
@BeginDate	CaptureDate
@EndDate	CaptureDate
@WaitType	Wait_Type

Returning to the Report Data pane on the left of the report, select Parameters, right-click, and select Add Parameter. You will need to repeat these steps to create each of the three parameters. In the Report Parameter Properties dialog, set the name and prompt to BeginDate, as displayed in Figure 8-23.

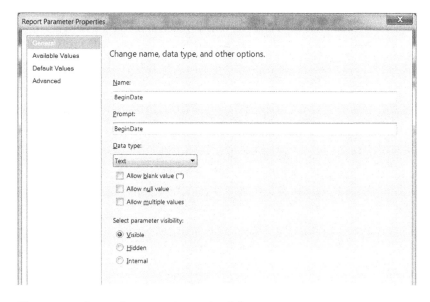

Figure 8-23. *Report Parameter Properties dialog*

Highlight and select the available values. On this screen, you will select the option Get Values from Query. The next steps should be intuitive now. You are setting the parameters to select from the previous data set queries you created, and you will select the CaptureDate data set from the data set drop-down, as well as for the Value and Label field drop-downs. Repeat the same step, only for the EndDate parameter, setting this to CaptureDate as well. Finally, create the WaitType parameter by adding parameter as shown previously, only this time set the data set, values, and label drop-downs to Wait_type, as demonstrated in Figure 8-24. Once you've selected these fields, you can click OK.

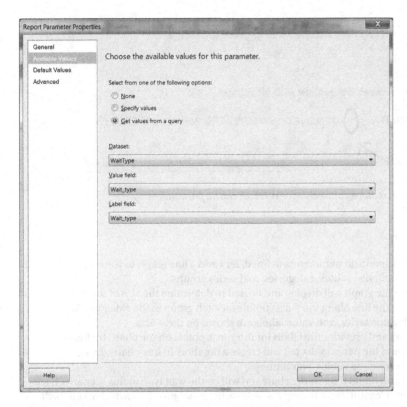

Figure 8-24. *Selecting the data set values for parameters*

Now that your report parameters have been created, let's go back to the main dataset1 for the report query and uncomment the WHERE clause, which filters on the user input. Do this by right-clicking dataset1 to display the properties and then remove the comment tags /* and */ from this code:

```
Where CaptureDate between @Begin AND @End AND (@WaitType= 'ALL' OR [Wait_type] in (@WaitType))
```

See Figure 8-25 for a graphical representation of what you need to uncomment.

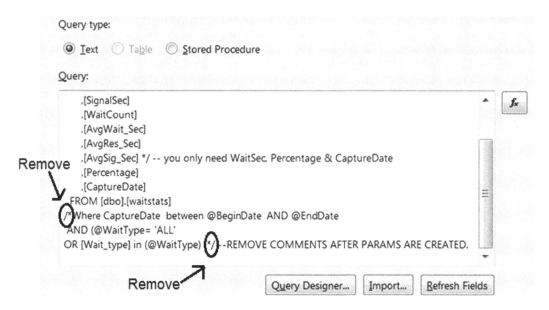

Figure 8-25. *Main query data set, remove comments for WHERE clause parameters*

Create Chart/Line Graph

Now that you have the report designed and parameters defined, let's add a line graph to your report. First I'll define and talk about the chart elements: values, categories, and series groups.

The value is the actual value the graph will display and is used to determine the size of the chart element, in this case the height of the line along the y-axis points for each group in the category. An individual line appears for each value series, and value labels are shown on the y-axis.

The category groups the data and provides the labels for the x-axis points on the chart. In this case, you will group the data by date, and the period selected will create a timeline. In line charts, categories are usually time-related and used to compare values over time.

The series are displayed as individual lines in the chart and will be the wait type in this scenario. Each series is also displayed in the chart legend. Here is what the fields will be assigned for each chart element:

1. Data Values = Percentage

2. Category Groups = CaptureDate

3. Series Groups = Wait_Type

On the Design View tab, you want to select the Chart item from Toolbox ➤ Report Items. The toolbox should be visible on the left of the report but can also be accessed by selecting View ➤ Toolbox or by pressing Ctrl+Alt+X. Click and drag the Chart item onto the report canvas area. Select the first Line Graph option from the chart type and click OK.

Double-click the chart area to make the Chart Data window appear. Once the fields are selected, it should look like Figure 8-26.

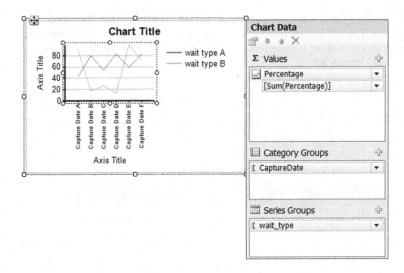

Figure 8-26. *Creating the chart and selecting the data*

Finally, size both the body and chart elements so they fill the screen. You'll need to click and drag them so they resemble Figure 8-27.

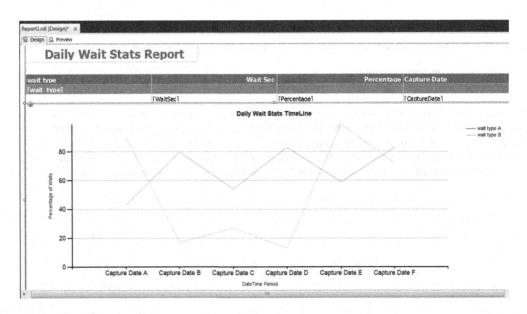

Figure 8-27. *The final report design in Design view with line graph*

Once you finish designing your report, you will want to test it by clicking the Preview tab; the report should render via Reporting Services. You will be prompted to select your user input parameters, BeginDate, EndDate, and WaitType. Once you've selected the parameters, you will click the View Report button, and your report preview will display as in Figure 8-28.

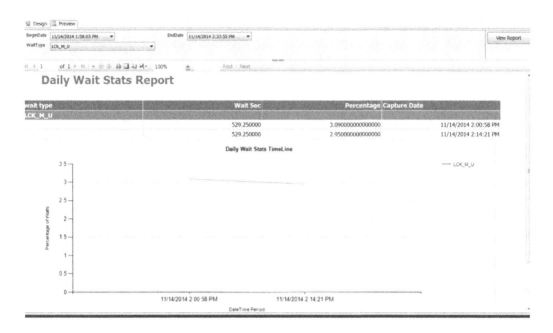

Figure 8-28. *Final report preview mode*

You will deploy the report to the Reporting Services web server and publish it to an SSRS site. When you go to your SSRS web site (for example, `http://localhost/reports/`), you can upload your report using Report Manager. A dialog box will appear, and you will browse to the folder that contains the report, which will be an `.rdl` file, which stands for "report definition language." In this example, you will select the `DailyWaitStatsReport.rdl` file, as shown in Figure 8-29. Click Open to add it as a custom report.

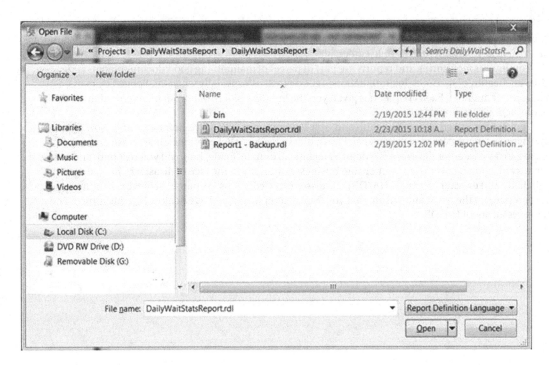

Figure 8-29. *Adding a custom report to SSMS*

Summary

This chapter dealt with two main tasks that a good DBA should endeavor to do: implement a SQL Server monitoring and alert solution and be able to create and generate performance status reports. Monitoring and alerting are essential so that the DBA can proactively monitor and be notified when a potential server or database issue arises in order to resolve it before escalation.

Once you have a comprehensive monitoring and alert system in place, it will not only allow you to manage and keep up with multiple SQL Server instances 24/7 but also give you peace of mind and even the ability to sleep better at night! Therefore, I would argue that automated monitoring/notification is essential not only for the reasons stated earlier but for a happier DBA by preventing burnout and for a greater satisfaction in your database professional career.

The second part of this chapter, dedicated to reporting, demonstrated how to leverage the native MDW reports based on your earlier setup and deployment of the MDW. It also walked you through how to build and deploy a custom report using SQL Server Reporting Services, SSDT, and Visual Studio. The custom SSRS report was one example, based on the baseline and benchmark wait statistics collected in Chapter 7. Reporting is most essential in presenting the fruits of your healthy SQL labor. Reporting is a tangible document, a visual representation, and an evidentiary record of the statistics, measures, and hard data that should be at the fingertips of all database professionals who are managing a SQL Server database infrastructure and can be easily generated on demand. The sky is the limit on designing fancy report dashboards with table data, drill-downs, colorful charts, pie graphs, line graphs, and so on; this also provides the visual eye candy that so many managers crave.

Business folks and executives love hard data, visual displays, numbers, and percentages that reflect what it is that you are telling them. For example, if you say that your SQL Server instances are performing fantastically and have had 95 percent uptime over the last six months, you must be able to back this up with documentation such as reports. In this chapter, you were given the framework you need to get started, from implementing a monitoring and notification process to creating a simple report using SSRS. I hope that this chapter has provided you with the strategies you need to accomplish these essential elements of healthy SQL and to excel in your DBA professional career.

Continuous monitoring and reports are part in parcel of maintaining good documentation and achieving healthy SQL. Good documentation is good practice, especially when challenged by peers, managers, or auditors. Each chapter has given you the building blocks of how to manage and maintain a healthy SQL server environment.

Thus far I've talked about the health and well-being of your SQL Server infrastructure. Now I'll cover what happens in the case of SQL Server sickness, that is, if your SQL Server instances crash and fail. If disaster strikes, whether the event is a natural, technical, or man-made, how will you respond, and how will your organization recover? Can your ensure business continuity in the face of disaster? The notion of high availability and disaster recovery (HA/DR) addresses these concerns. As part of achieving healthy SQL, you must prepare for the worst and ensure that your SQL Server instances have healthy SQL insurance. The next chapter is all about HA/DR.

■ ■ ■

CHAPTER 9

High Availability and Disaster Recovery

Up until now, I have been talking thus far about the health and well-being of your SQL Server infrastructure and how to maintain and monitor it. However, there's a time you hope never comes, but it is inevitable, and it's a reality you must prepare for. Let's cover what happens in the case of SQL Server sickness, that is, if your SQL Server instances crash and fail. If disaster strikes, whether the event is natural, technical, or man-made, how will you respond, and how will your organization recover? Can you ensure business continuity in the face of disaster? High availability and disaster recovery (HA/DR) address these concerns. Not only will I discuss strategy, I will talk about the features and technology around SQL Server to enable HA/DR. As part of achieving healthy SQL, you must prepare for the worst. A good disaster recovery plan is your insurance. This chapter is dedicated to this eventuality.

Evolution of Disaster Recovery and SQL Server

Let's take a look at the evolution of disaster recovery and SQL Server. In the beginning, there was SQL Server 6.5 (well, that's as far as I'm going back here), Microsoft's first major independent release of a database management platform. There wasn't much in the way of high availability, or at least anything mature, and certainly not much fanfare about the need for high availability and disaster recovery around SQL Server. When Microsoft realized there was a critical need to have built-in HA and DR, new and improved features were introduced with each new version of SQL Server.

In addition, with the ability to implement a standby or high availability disaster recovery solution, many companies wanted to leverage these standby resources for reporting or read-only usage. Many IT managers considered this for dual-use purposes. Not only could they use the standby server for reporting, but they could spread out and balance the read-write load between databases. The thinking was that if the majority of time you have another expensive piece of hardware hosting another SQL Server or database copy standing around with low activity waiting for a disaster to occur, perhaps you can make use of it in the interim. This itself presented technical and licensing challenges but has grown more sophisticated and now is a fully attainable goal.

Regarding licensing, Microsoft generally allows for one standby or passive server that doesn't require an additional license for SQL Server, but the minute you decide to use it for any other purpose, including reporting, license fees will apply. Always check on licensing requirements with your Microsoft technical account manager (TAM) to discuss your specific setup and scenario. Remember, license terms and conditions are subject to change.

■ **Note** Always check with your Microsoft TAM regarding software licensing because it is subject to change.

Exceptions and challenges came with each HA/DR feature, as discussed more in "SQL DR Drawbacks." Take note that these exceptions are separate from licensing and cost. For example, with log shipping, the secondary database was in standby mode or always restoring and not user accessible for any considerable use. With mirroring came snapshot reporting, which is the ability to create a snapshot of the mirror, but a new snapshot needed to be continuously generated if the user wanted up-to-date data. Finally, the ability to have both HA/DR and a fully up-to-date, synchronized reporting database was achieved with multiple read-only replicas using SQL Server 2012 and AlwaysOn features.

When SQL Server 6.5 Enterprise Edition was released, there weren't many native features for HA/DR from Microsoft out of the box. Features available included backup/restore, clustering, and transactional replication. With transactional replication in the mix, many folks creatively deployed replication as a data redundancy method. In other words, by replicating data to another SQL Server or subscriber database, you could have a copy of the data up-to-date and in sync across the network in disparate physical locations. Therefore, it was possible to use replication to have redundant databases at other sites or data centers. I think of replication more as a data availability and portability solution rather than disaster recovery, but nonetheless it's a viable method for this purpose. There are of course caveats, overhead, and potential latencies in maintaining replication.

Microsoft allowed SQL Server as early as version 6.5 to be clustered. This was a crude attempt at clustering SQL Server that was rarely implemented in the real world. If you were a system administrator back in the days of SQL Server 6.5 and Windows NT Server, you may recall Microsoft Cluster Server (MSCS). During its development, "wolfpack" was the code of Microsoft Cluster Server, with Windows NT 4.0 being the first version of Windows to include MSCS. Attempts to install and configure MSCS were labored, and sometimes many wished the wolf had stayed in the forest. Fast-forward to Windows Server 2008 and Windows Server 2008 R2; the MSCS service has been renamed to Windows Server Failover Clustering (WSFC). Keep in mind that server clustering is a Windows feature and *not* a SQL Server–specific solution. SQL Server is among the many Microsoft products that is cluster-aware and can be deployed on top of a cluster as a clustered resource.

Of course, backing up your servers, files, and databases was easily attainable and something frequently implemented across all organizations. Tape backups were the standard operating procedure of most networks and server infrastructures and part of the normal rotation. Restoring from backup was one of the few options available for disaster recovery. Naturally, business continuity was dependent on how fast you could recover from tape. Certainly, you could not achieve high availability with the tape backup and restore method. These conventional backups are known as *offline* or *cold* backups.

Any backup system will easily back up files that are quiesced and closed. However, database files are different in nature because they could always be open and in an active state. This prevented traditional backup systems from backing up these online databases. Some companies even excluded them from backup altogether, though this was not a very wise decision. Some third-party backup systems had a client agent component installed that would back up the online databases and not require downtime.

With respect to databases, an online backup, also referred to as a *hot* or *dynamic* backup, is a backup performed on data even though it is actively accessible to users and may currently be in a state of being updated. There are some typical methods that companies use to back up their database infrastructure. Using the SQL Server native backup engine, the databases are backed up to the file system. With this method, backups would be dumped either locally or to attached network storage. Now that you have backup copies of the database that are essentially offline, the network backup solution can back up all the file server files, in addition to the database backup files, ensuring that data is preserved in case of failure.

As of SQL Server version 7.0, the log shipping wizard was introduced out of the box and allowed the user to easily set up a warm standby server using an interactive GUI. Soon this became a viable solution, also referred to as the "poor-man's high availability." The context was used in comparison of log shipping vs. clustering. Clustering required purchasing and maintaining at least two server nodes of similar hardware, not to mention an expensive shared SAN. Log shipping could be achieved with any two existing SQL Server instances of the same version, regardless of hardware or edition. In addition, it was possible to log ship over long distances and to other data centers in disperse geographic locations. This was one that advantage log shipping (and mirroring, a later version feature, for that matter) had over clustering in terms of site redundancy. Building upon the concepts of log shipping, SQL Server 2005 introduced database mirroring between two SQL Server instances that provided a level of both HA and DR. With mirroring, you can achieve automatic failover. This is accomplished by using a witness sever, whose only role is to monitor whether to initiate an automatic failover. The witness is optional and comes into play in high-safety mode, discussed more later.

Peer-to-peer replication also came about with SQL Server 2005; it provides a high availability solution that can scale out by maintaining copies of data across multiple server instances, also called *nodes*. Peer-to-peer replication propagates transactionally consistent changes in near real time and is built around the same concepts of transactional replication. This enables applications that require a scale-out of read operations to distribute the reads from clients across multiple nodes. Because data is maintained across the nodes in near real time, peer-to-peer replication provides data redundancy, which increases the availability of data. However, because the nodes aren't in sync, data loss is possible.

Finally, culminating with the release of SQL Server 2012, originally code-named Denali, the Microsoft engineers thought, what if you can take the best of HA and DR, having a mix of Windows clustering and database mirroring, and create the concept of availability. That is essentially what AlwaysOn is. AlwaysOn is not a single, specific feature. Rather, it is a set of availability features such as failover cluster instances and availability groups. AlwaysOn was more marketing than a specific feature of SQL Server 2012. Availability groups allow for automatic failover, as well as multiple read-only replicas that can be used for querying and reporting.

Business Continuity

Even though the concepts of high availability, disaster recovery, and business continuity are used interchangeably, there are some distinct differences. So, I'll first define what business continuity (BC) is.

Business continuity is a simple concept that is often completely overlooked. BC includes the procedures and processes enacted to ensure the continuance of business. It is often used only to cover what happens in the event of a disaster, but a disaster isn't the only thing that affects the continuance of business. BC should cover any event that could impede or halt the business workflows of your systems. All aspects of business continuity should be documented and included in the run book (discussed more in the upcoming "DR Run Book" section).

To ensure business continuity, a certain amount of planning must take place that typically will account for how the business will recover its operations or move operations to another location after damage by events such as natural disasters, acts of terrorism, theft or criminal destruction, or technical glitches. This is referred to as *business continuity planning* (BCP). To devise a comprehensive plan for business continuity, the internal teams responsible for its business unit must evaluate and consider the elements of the BCP life cycle, consisting of five phases: analysis, design, implementation, testing, and maintenance. Figure 9-1 shows a graphical representation of the phases of the BCP life cycle.

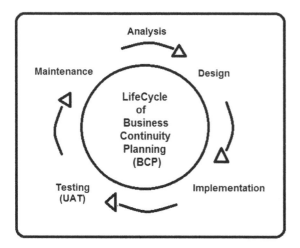

Figure 9-1. *Life cycle of business continuity planning phases*

The analysis phase covers the business impact analysis, the threat and risk analysis, and the impact scenarios that will help determine the recovery requirements. First the business impact analysis lays out the difference between the critical (urgent) and noncritical (nonurgent) organizational functions and applications. Critical functions and applications are those whose disruption is regarded as unacceptable. Here you will want to prioritize and define which servers, databases, and applications are your Day 1 recovery objectives. In other words, which of your critical servers, databases, and applications must be brought back online first in the event of a disaster?

Then you should continue to prioritize for Day 2 objectives, Day 3, and so on. This will allow you to focus on the Day 1 objectives that will make or break the company's ability to recover and minimize the amount of loss sustained as a result of being down. Of course, when considering which servers, applications, and databases are Day 1, all business units will chime in and attempt to get theirs at the top of the recovery priority list. This of course doesn't help your analysis, so ultimately the upper management and those at the executive level will make these decisions.

Data loss may equate to monetary loss, which is one determining factor. Perceptions of acceptability and criticality are also affected by the cost of recovery solutions. If a business unit determines that the technology budget needed to recover fully their apps, servers, and databases is too exorbitant, then they may find a less expensive solution that guarantees that, for example, Day 3 recovery is acceptable. Of course, the case should be made to upper management. If in fact a business's core functions constitute a Day 1 recovery objective, the case should be made to upper management. This is the time to make such a business case and not in the aftermath of a disaster. Management may determine the priority and criticality of recovery in terms of the effect it has on the company's bottom line.

The urgency and requirement for a Day 1 recovery objective may also be considered critical if dictated by law. Recent regulatory and compliance laws will often trump all other concerns and set the recovery priority.

To help businesses and IT understand the criticality of systems, two principles are applied that assist in determining priority. You will hear these terms used often, as well as throughout this book, and you should be familiar with them when planning DR and discussing database backup strategy. These terms are known as RPO and RTO.

- *Recovery point objective* (RPO) is the maximum acceptable level of data loss or of data that will not be recovered.

- *Recovery time objective* (RTO) is the acceptable amount of time to restore the system (such as the application or database).

Therefore, following an unplanned event, such as a disaster (natural or man-made), act of crime or terrorism, or any other business or technical disruption that could cause such data loss, the RPO will dictate the acceptable level of data loss that must not be exceeded. The RTO will dictate how long it will take to restore the database/server in accordance with acceptable time frames. For each critical function, the impact analysis yields the recovery requirements consisting of both the business and technical requirements, respectively.

As part of the impact analysis, the threat and risk analysis phase evaluates each potential disaster scenario and seeks to address all contingencies. The impact for common threat events are considered such as for earthquake, fire, flood, cyber attack, sabotage, hurricane/storm, power outage, terrorism, war, and civil disorder. In most Western first-world countries, you don't expect war and civil disorder, but global companies with assets all over the world must consider such scenarios. The solution/design phase identifies the most cost-effective DR solution and lays out the specific recovery steps that should be taken for the threats and risks defined in the impact analysis stage.

Here is a short but true story that relates to impact threat analysis. I was close to securing a client with my SQLCentric monitoring software in a small African country, and had to be put on hold pending the fallout of a coup that was happening in the kingdom. While this type of occurrence seems more common in a Tom Clancy novel, it does happen in the real world, no matter how far away it seems. A natural disaster closer to home struck the Northeast in 2012, Super Storm Sandy. Meteorologists (and insurance companies) argued whether it was a hurricane, a tropical super storm, or even a tsunami, but whatever they referred to it as, it was a true nightmare scenario that left a big part of the North East without power for several days. Sandy was the deadliest and most destructive hurricane of the 2012 Atlantic hurricane season, as well as the second-costliest hurricane in U.S. history. Many data centers in Sandy's path caused major web sites, services, and hosted apps to go offline.

Utility companies shut down portions of the power grid to prevent damage to electricity infrastructure substation equipment, which affected data centers and online services around the world. Because of storm surges, many buildings and data centers were flooded, especially those that were housed below ground level in basements. If you didn't know before why Water Street in downtown Manhattan was named as such, Superstorm Sandy presented an unfortunate circumstance to show us why. Listening to all the news on the storm as it occurred, one New York hospital thought it was well prepared with backup generators. Unfortunately, in the time of disaster, those generators did not come online and failed. They needed to be evacuated to another facility.

Therefore, based on all the information gathered from your analysis, impact, and threat assessment, you can come up with a proper solution to each potential disaster scenario, from a business and technical aspect. The solution design will depend upon your needs, RPO and RTO requirements, region and threat/risk analysis, budget, and current infrastructure. From a corporate perspective, a redundant colo (a commonly used acronym for co-location) site is the ideal situation that covers most probabilities.

Budget is a big consideration as well. Even though one financial firm I worked at had $78 billion assets under management, the CIO was forced at the time not to balloon the budget for a widescale company disaster recovery project. A colo site was identified and secured for the purpose of DR. As for actual technology and infrastructure, although a SAN-to-SAN replication implementation would have been the best solution, this was not within the budget at that time. So, I basically pieced our DR solution together with various software solutions.

Once this DR/BC solution was implemented, testing and user acceptance were key to ensuring that the DR/BC plan was foolproof. This testing and UAT phase of the CP life cycle was essential to validate the solutions implemented and that they work as intended in the event of a real disaster. Therefore, to demonstrate proof of concept, members from each business unit and IT department in the company were enlisted to varying degrees of DR testing to make sure all the servers, components, applications, and databases come online in mock DR exercises. They weren't the most fun days but absolutely necessary to ensuring the business continuity in the face of any disaster. As part of the maintenance phase, regular or quarterly testing soon became the norm and likely continues today. Therefore, your company should also have such a DR and BC strategy, using the BCP life cycle as your guide.

Concepts of High Availability and Disaster Recovery

High availability and disaster recovery are often tackled as distinct undertakings without understanding how they are related. HA and DR fall under the single umbrella of business continuity. The problem with considering the two concepts as individual plans is that you completely miss out on where they overlap. Log shipping is a prime example of an overlapping technology. Log shipping can be used as a warm failover for HA or as an alternate data source in the event of data loss on the primary database for DR.

Some of the most valuable options that SQL Server offers out of the box are features that allow for high availability and disaster recovery. This is the section where you need to ask yourself as a database professional the following set of questions when thinking about sufficient high availability and disaster recovery for your organization's database servers:

- Do you have "healthy SQL" insurance?

- Can you ensure there is business continuity?

- Do you have a proper backup and recovery plan for your databases?

- Are you comfortable knowing that your backups are securely backed up and that you can perform a point-in-time restore?

- Do you know where you would restore your database in the event of a disaster?

If the answer to any of these questions is no, then you need to read this chapter and learn what you can do to ensure that you can answer these in the affirmative.

High availability is a design that allows for systems to be available and accessible by clients and refers to a system or component that is continuously operational and can continue to perform the tasks with minimal downtime. Should one or more of the servers or devices fail, it is transparent to the end user. The levels of high availability and how much downtime is incurred over the cost of a year are measured in percentages and represented by tiers. The tier you are in is determined by the criticality of the application/database. Ideally, you want your high availability to come as close as possible to 99.999 percent, which is represented by Tier 1.

- *Tier 1*: >99.99 percent uptime (1 hour or less of downtime acceptable annually)

- *Tier 2*: 99.9 percent to 99.99 percent uptime (1 to 8.5 hours of downtime acceptable annually)

- *Tier 3*: <99.9 percent uptime (hours to days of downtime acceptable annually

The various tiers, 1, 2, and 3, show the percentage of time that SQL Server (or an application that depends on it) is available, along with the actual downtime in hours or days. For example, 99.999 percent uptime is often called the "five 9s of availability," which means about five minutes of downtime a year.

Using that definition, an uptime of 99.999 percent equates to a total downtime of 5.265 minutes a year (365*24*60 *.001). My company doesn't have a five 9s requirement. Most servers actually have only a three 9s requirement, but you generally meet four 9s of uptime, which equates to 52.56 minutes of downtime a year or less.

Disaster recovery, specifically, is the process or procedure related to preparing for the continuation of resources after a disaster or failure. With DR, you are prepared to incur a certain amount of downtime. How fast can you recover from failure and get systems back online? You need to ensure that your DR is reliable and that you can recover from failure in a reasonable amount of time. From a technology and DBA standpoint, you want to make sure the HA/DR features are in place, within your organization, and continuously monitor their state of health and perform regular testing.

From a healthy SQL perspective, having a comprehensive DR plan in place is definitely part of an overall healthy SQL Server strategy. While the primary objective of healthy SQL health checks is to help prevent unnecessary downtime by ensuring that your SQL Server instances are performing optimally and are well maintained. However, in the event of unforeseen circumstances, you need to prepare for every possible contingency.

Database Backups and Recovery Models

I'll reiterate some concepts discussed early on in Chapter 1. As I mentioned, the one word that is used in terms of DBA job security is *backup*. While frequently backing up your databases is good practice, verifying the integrity of the backup and restoring the backup when needed are just as important, if not more so. Therefore, don't just have a backup plan; have a restore plan as well. The restore plan must be incorporated into your overall backup strategy.

There are types of backups in SQL Server, such as the commonly known full, differential, and transaction log backups as well as the lesser-known file/file group, partial, and copy-only backups. Full backups are the most common and back up the entire contents of a database and are usually taken daily. However, as the databases grow, file system storage, file retention policy, and actual backup time become potential concerns. For example, if you are doing full daily database backups of 500GB and more in size, that's about 2500GB in five business days (not counting the weekend) each week. Now, you will need to explore options such as database backup compression, smaller retention intervals, and differential backups. Differential backups allow the DBA to do a full database backup, weekly, for example (say, Monday) and daily differentials Tuesday through Friday. Differentials back up only the changes, or *deltas*, from the last full database backup and save on backup time and storage. In the event of the need for recovery, you must restore the full backup and then apply the latest differential backups. Transaction log backups are taken much more frequently, depending on the business need for RPO and the acceptable amount of data loss, and allow for point-in-time database recovery, discussed more in the "Backup and Recovery" section.

The recovery model of a database (full, simple, or bulk-logged) comes into play when the requirements for backup and restore are considered. Many of the database-level DR features rely on the transaction log for recovery. The choice for the recovery model will depend on the need to recover all the data and allow you to recover to up to the point of failure. The recovery models can be explained as follows.

The full recovery model requires continuous transaction log backups to ensure that you can recover the database to a specific point in time. All of the HA/DR features that require transaction log backups will be discussed in this chapter with regard to how they factor in to your overall healthy SQL insurance policy, namely, your HA/DR strategy. Incidentally, most of the SQL Server HA/DR features require the database to be only in full recovery mode, including the following:

- Log shipping

- AlwaysOn availability groups

- Database mirroring

- Media recovery without data loss

- Point-in-time restores

Simple recovery mode has no transaction log backups and reclaims log space automatically, which prevents the log from growing out of control, and therefore there is no need to manage the transaction log size. In earlier versions, simple recovery was also known as Truncate Log on Checkpoint, which is in essence the operation that automatically manages transaction log growth. However, this option gives you no ability to recover point-in-time data, and therefore all those changes must be redone.

Please note that if the business finds it acceptable that, in the event of a disaster, the changes from the latest full database backup are sufficient and point-in-time restores aren't necessary, then then the simple recovery model should be selected.

Bulk-logged is the least common recovery model and is similar to the full recovery model in that it requires transaction logs. Moreover, bulk-logged is used for increased performance of bulk data load operations and reduces space the log takes up by using minimal logging for bulk operations. Because of its special purpose and minimal logging, point-in-time recovery is not supported here.

As databases grew exponentially and terabyte sizes became more common, backups became more cumbersome to manage and store. SQL Server 2008 introduced native database compression, although third-party compression software existed for earlier versions of SQL Server. You can review these features and concepts in the MSDN article at http://msdn.microsoft.com/en-us/library/ms175477.aspx.

In addition, you must set the file retention period of backups so you don't run out of space. Retention period is also determined by the business needs. You must also make sure the database backups are corruption free, and the DBA must be sure to check database integrity, which can be scheduled to occur as part of the backup maintenance plan. You need to schedule backups to occur accordingly, and you need to manage them and ensure they complete in a timely fashion.

To help ensure that backups are healthy and backup jobs are completed successfully, there must be extensive monitoring around your backup process. You can query SQL Server to find out the most recent status of your SQL Server native backups and related jobs. The following Backup_Stat script will return the most important information as related to your SQL Server database backups. You will get the name of the database backed up, the backup start date and time, the backup finish date and time, the running time (in other words, how long the backup took to complete), the path and file name of the backup, and the size of the backup in megabytes. The msdb database keeps a log and history of its backups, as well as jobs scheduled to run under the SQL Server Agent. The system tables msdb.dbo.backupset and msdb.dbo.backupmediafamily keep historical information about backups. The table msdb.dbo.backupset contains a row for each backup set, while msdb.dbo.backupmediafamily contains one row for each media family and will get you the physical path where the backup is stored. A backup set contains the backup from a single, successful backup operation, and a media family is how many backups are stored on a single file or device. Here is a T-SQL script that will return information about the status of your SQL Server backups:

```
SELECT          A.database_name  as 'DBName',
                    A.backup_finish_date as 'Backup Finished',A.backup_start_date,
RIGHT('00'+RTRIM(CONVERT(CHAR(2),DATEDIFF(second,a.backup_start_date,a.backup_finish_
date)%86400/3600)),2) + ':' +
RIGHT('00'+RTRIM(CONVERT(CHAR(2),DATEDIFF(second,a.backup_start_date,a.backup_finish_
date)%86400%3600/60)),2) + ':' +
RIGHT('00'+RTRIM(CONVERT(CHAR(2),DATEDIFF(second,a.backup_start_date,a.backup_finish_
date)%86400%3600%60)),2) AS 'Run Time',
                    B.physical_device_name as 'Backup Filename',
              (a.backup_size/1024/1024) as backup_size_mb
    FROM      msdb.dbo.backupset A, msdb.dbo.backupmediafamily B,
                    (SELECT database_name,
                        MAX(backup_finish_date) as 'maxfinishdate'
                FROM    msdb.dbo.backupset
                    WHERE Type = 'D'
                GROUP BY database_name) C
    WHERE         A.media_set_id = B.media_set_id AND
                    A.backup_finish_date = C.maxfinishdate AND
                    A.type = 'D'
    ORDER BY DBName
```

```
DBName     Backup Finished     backup_start_date     Run Time     Backup Filename     backup_size_mb
AdventureWorks2012     2012-06-25 15:53:31.000     2012-06-25 15:53:24.000     00:00:07
C:\Users\Q07642\Downloads\AdventureWorks2012-Full Database Backup\AdventureWorks2012-Full
Database Backup.bak     189.07421875000
MAPS_DB     2014-09-05 12:08:38.000     2014-09-05 12:08:12.000     00:00:26
C:\CANON_MAPS_DB_09052014.bak     467.53222656250
```

When all goes wrong and you need to recover, backups are your first line of DBA defense. Your job security as well as your database is always as good as your last backup. Good backups are part of your healthy SQL strategy. One important thing to remember as a DBA is it is simply not good enough to say you have backed up the databases. A DBA must be able to verify backups. Unfortunately, most folks *do not* validate their backups. The time-tested way to verify a backup is to periodically restore the database and ensure that it comes online. Often, it is recommended that a database consistency check (DBCC 'CheckDB') be run against the restored database to check integrity and ensure that it is free of any corruption. Another occasion to restore your databases is to test your disaster recovery plan. I'll discuss the recovery side of things in the "Backup and Recovery" section in this chapter.

■ **Caution**　A completed backup does not mean it is corruption free.

Challenges of High Availability

Now that you know what high availability is, you need to know about all the challenges to high availability and the features that address each of them so you can plan accordingly. Companies may experience serious outages that affect their business functions and continuity. Each type of outage has some unique characteristics but also overlaps, in that any of these, from a healthy SQL perspective, will incur database downtime. The following scenarios can cause downtime, in varying degrees:

- Server outage
- Network outage
- Database outage
- Hardware subsystem outage
- Authentication failures
- Data center site outage
- Data deletion
- Corruption

A server outage can occur in many ways, whether it's software or hardware related, such as a failed disk, an operating system error, or even the blue screen of death. Even stressed resources that hang the system, such as high CPU, I/O, or memory peak usage can incur downtime where applications and user connections cannot access the server. Even if the server is online but inaccessible, this is still considered an outage. Whether it's a software or hardware failure, the end result is server downtime.

A network outage is when servers become inaccessible and network resources are lost. Such an outage is beyond the database administrator's control but nonetheless affects system uptime and ultimately your SQL Server database server. You may even be the first in line for client support calls. A network outage is usually more widespread, affecting multiple systems and servers at one time. There could be many causes of a network outage, whether it's a bad NIC card, mismatched speed settings, network access path, dropped packets, down switches, routers, or even a denial-of-service attack. Any reason for disconnects or lack of connectivity can account for poor network performance, latency, and outages.

Database outage can occur when one or more databases are offline or unavailable. A database can be restoring or in recovery, or even stuck in single-user mode, and therefore considered inaccessible by the users and front-end applications. Another scenario is where the physical database files themselves (data or log) are missing or deleted. All this can occur even though the server itself is up and running and can turn a normal day into a database downtime disaster.

A hardware subsystem outage nowadays is a less frequent occurrence but is still a challenge for availability, especially when many high availability methods rely on a stable subsystem for redundancy. To protect against a subsystem failure, with the storage system, redundant disks (RAID), or SAN storage would be the order of the day to prevent against subsystem outages. Redundant Array of Inexpensive Disk (RAID) storage was a must for traditional servers with network attached storage and had built-in redundancy, depending on the RAID level, to ensure that if one or more disks failed, the server would still stay online and continue processing on other disks in the array. In some systems, there was also a slot reserved for what was called the *hot spare* so that the system administrator could dynamically swap disks without any downtime.

There are different types of RAID configurations, but the ideal recommended RAID configuration is RAID 1+0 or RAID 10, giving you the mirroring of RAID 1 with the striping of RAID 0. RAID 0 provides high performance for reads and writes, but there is no data redundancy and therefore is rarely implemented by itself. RAID 5, disk striping with parity, can provide good availability and performance for reads and allows the use of a hot spare to rebuild a failed disk. Normally a RAID 5 array would not be considered for a high read-write environment, especially writes, because every transaction has to also write to the parity disk, which potentially creates a performance bottleneck.

So, RAID 10 provides you with fault tolerance, mirroring, and striping. (RAID mirroring should not be confused with database mirroring, discussed later in this chapter.) In most modern server environments, RAID 10 is the most prevalent for high-end applications and very large databases. With disk mirroring (RAID 1), data is written to a mirrored pair of disk drives simultaneously. As you may have gathered, the type of RAID configuration implemented has a major impact on SQL Server performance and availability. This is why it is important for you, the DBA, to be involved up front when planning for SQL Server builds. The ideal disk configuration for some applications will be very different for a SQL Server build and even further will be different for a data warehouse/reporting database vs. an OLTP high transaction environment.

There are all sorts of new advances in technology for storage and disk subsystems that are out of scope for this book. Solid-state drives (SSDs) are becoming more and more implemented for high performance, but I'm discussing here disks in the context of high availability.

▪ **Note**   The ideal disk configuration will be different for an OLAP/DW database vs. an OLTP transactional database.

Authentication failures are mostly related to security policy issues and basically because of a node or device denying the connection. Authentication to network servers and databases has become more complex because of the Internet and exposure of weak systems to outside networks. Authentication failures occur in the simple form of expired passwords, incorrect or changed passwords, invalid certificates, firewalls, denial-of-service attacks, and even network outages as discussed earlier.

A data center site outage is a big one. What if the entire site goes down or becomes unavailable? This can happen because of a number of causes, such as fire, flood, power loss, network outage, terrorism, or natural disaster, such as a hurricane, tsunami, or earthquake, for example. As touched on earlier, the day the world changed, as I refer to 9/11, caught everyone off-guard and unprepared. The lessons of 9/11 on a technical DR and BC scale highlighted the need for site redundancy. A co-located data center site would need to be built out and able to come online rather quickly in the event of a site outage. Not only would redundant technology need to be in place at the colo, but also a redundant workspace would be needed for employees to assemble and ensure the DR plan was implemented and business functions continued.

My personal experience was recounted in Chapter 1, where I had two sites but no redundancy. Even though I had two data centers and office locations, in downtown and midtown Manhattan, the servers at each site hosted completely different applications and databases. I needed to "rack and stack" from scratch, build a new infrastructure, and restore backups from tape. As I can personally attest, this is a most arduous, drawn-out process.

Data deletion is what I like to describe as the big "oops"! In actuality, this can occur both accidentally or on purpose. Malicious intent by competitors, users, disgruntled employees, corporate spies, or hackers can delete data, and none would be the wiser, if proper security is not in place. What's worse is if there is no way to recover the data. Either way, if critical data goes missing because of records being deleted, this is a major faux pas that will ultimately be blamed on the DBA. Despite all the DBA "blame game" misattributions throughout the book, for this one you will rightfully be responsible if you are unable to recover deleted data.

Even if you are not the one who actually deleted the data, it will fall upon your shoulders to quickly recover the missing data. And oftentimes, an inexperienced DBA with system administrator access to SQL Server can accidentally delete data and mistake one server for another. SSMS is a great DBA tool but can wreak havoc if you're not careful. That is why errors and omissions insurance was invented! Your insurance policy will monetarily compensate your company's loss while you are on the unemployment line looking for a new gig!

In this case, good database backups are in order, and you need transaction log backups for point-in-time recovery, discussed in depth in the "Backup and Recovery" section, if you know approximately at what point the data was deleted. You can also restore the latest database copy with another name and import/export data records for individual tables using SQL Server Integration Services (SSIS), which is Microsoft's out-of-the-box ETL platform. It is possible to set up auditing features such as Change Data Capture (CDC) to track and store database DML changes, such as inserts, update, and deletes, and to recover the data, as well as track down the culprit.

Data corruption is definitely a bad thing to have happen, but it does happen, and you need to be prepared. If the database suddenly goes into an offline state or becomes suspect and is no longer accessible, one probable cause is that your database is corrupt. Database corruption can occur in many ways, including instances when the disk goes bad or when internal page structures get out of sequence or unlinked. One example of how corruption can happen is when SQL Server is writing data to disk, and this operation is interrupted by a power or disk failure. If this happens, it can result in what is known as a *torn page*.

Corruption can go undetected for a while, and by the time it becomes apparent, data loss is already great, and the DBA may not even be sure how far back they need to go to restore the last known good backup. In this case, preventative strategies are suggested. Some of these are discussed in the upcoming "Backup and Recovery" section.

I will discuss strategies, documentation, best practices, and the need for every company to have a run book with respect to bringing SQL Server instances back online and ensure they are up and running with minimal effort. To do this, I will point out how to leverage the existing features and technologies available out of the box.

SQL DR Drawbacks

As mentioned earlier, there were some challenges and things that you weren't able to do with various HA and DR solutions for SQL Server. With each of the available HA/DR choices and features, there are some pros and cons, and in this section I will discuss some of the drawbacks.

Log shipping and database mirroring allow for database failover and are database-level features offering protection for an individual database. Clustering allows for server failover and is an instance-level feature ensuring you against server failure. If one clustered server node fails or is unavailable, the SQL Server instance will fail over to another clustered node. Log shipping and mirroring can be used against site failure by log shipping or mirroring to another geographically disparate data center. However, clustering doesn't protect you against site failure. Until recently, third-party solutions aside, clusters were usually physically located in the same data center. If your site goes down or becomes unavailable, your cluster isn't going to be very useful in this situation because it presents a single point of failure (SPOF). This begins the broader conversation for the need to have site redundancy and co-locations. With clustering, you also have no protection against a disk array failure.

Database mirroring and log shipping have their own drawbacks; mirroring offers automatic failover but allows for only one target, and log shipping allows multiple targets but failover is a manual process. With mirroring you can mirror the primary database to only one destination database, and the mirror target is unreadable. Log shipping requires user intervention and a number of steps to get the secondary standby online. Logins must be manually synced, and connection strings must be changed. The secondary database in standby mode makes it briefly accessible and read-only but is not accessible when restoring.

With database mirroring, while the SQL Server engine itself was able to read the mirror's copy of the data to accomplish page repairs, the rest of us weren't given the ability to do anything helpful with the data. You couldn't directly access the database. The best you could do was take a snapshot of that database and query the snapshot, but that snapshot was frozen in time. Having your snapshot frozen in time is not terribly useful if you want to, say, run read-only queries against the mirror for reporting purposes while alos wanting the results from those queries to be fairly close to real time. Some companies implemented a series of snapshots for end-user access, even automating and scheduling them, but this sort of process is cumbersome to manage.

Unlike log shipping and replication, mirroring allowed for only two SQL Server instances to be involved. You could either use mirroring for high availability inside the same data center or use it for disaster recovery with two servers in different data centers, but not both. Because of this limitation, a common HA/DR scenario involved using a cluster for the production server (giving local high availability in the event of a server failure) combined with asynchronous mirroring to a remote site. You'll learn more about the database mirroring modes available in the "Mirroring" section.

The next problem is because database failovers are database-level events, DBAs can fail over one database from the principal to the secondary server but can't coordinate the failover of multiple databases simultaneously. Instance-level items such as jobs, linked servers, and logins could not be failed over. In applications that required more than one database, this made automatic failover a nonoption.

Even with availability groups (AG), which address some of the drawbacks of the other HA/DR features, AG is not without its own disadvantages. Even though AG is intended to replace the deprecated mirroring feature, there is no simple migration path from mirroring to AG, especially where mirrored SQL Server instances are in different domains. Because AG requires Windows failover clustering, the servers must be in the same domain. Even the ability to build a WFC can be a disadvantage to deploying AG in some shops. Moreover, AG is an Enterprise Edition feature, whereas mirroring is available in Standard Edition.

If you're looking to replace your current SQL Server cluster setup with AlwaysOn AG, automatic failover is possible only with synchronous-commit mode, which comes at a cost of increased transaction latency. Synchronous commit mode specifically emphasizes high availability over performance because transactions wait for transaction confirmation to the client, ensuring transactions are hardened to disk on the replica.

Every technology comes with a trade-off, such as performance vs. high availability, which must be balanced in accordance with your particular needs. Every aspect of the pros and cons must be weighed when deciding on what solution to implement. Remember, some form of high availability is better than none.

Backup and Recovery

In this section on backup and recovery, the importance of a good recovery strategy is highlighted. Moreover, point-in-time restores, which allow you to recover a database to a particular point in time, are covered. Database corruption and detection and repair are also discussed with information on how to avoid potential corruption, verify databases, and repair if necessary.

First Line of Defense

Backup and recovery are your first line of defense in the event of a disaster. You should have extensive monitoring and notification around your backup process and take regular transaction log backups if you need point-in-time recovery. You will learn some techniques and how to set up monitoring and notification for this and other important metrics later in the book. Backup and recovery are an essential part of the overall healthy SQL HA/DR strategy of your SQL Server instances.

In addition to simply ensuring that you in fact have regular database backups, for purposes of recovery you must also ensure that backups are secure, reliable, and corruption-free. They need to be accounted for, properly named, and safe from tampering, foul play, or deletion. You will also want to append the backup file with a datetime stamp to keep track of them. Who has the ability to access the backup folder and files or restore them? Are they encrypted, if they need to be? The physical backups should be secured and often are shipped offsite, in case of a disaster and so you know where to retrieve them in the event of a disaster. Finally, all of the previous information should be documented and part of your DR run book.

With all of the HA/DR features through SQL Server 2014, such as AlwaysOn HA/DR, one of the lesser known features is something DBAs should be aware of: the Database Recovery Advisor, which is covered in the next section, "Point in Time Restore." With the addition of this feature in SQL Server 2012, manageability has been enhanced for SSMS.

A good backup strategy is essential in every SQL Server environment, and a good recovery strategy is even more critical. To meet the needs and expectations of the business, you need to consider the recovery point objective and recovery time objective when devising a comprehensive backup strategy. Here you will need to do some interfacing with the business and involve them in this strategy since only they can tell you how critical the data is, how much downtime is acceptable, and how much data loss can be sustained.

Point-in-Time Restore

One persistent feature throughout the SQL Server product evolution has the ability to restore a SQL Server database to a point in time. This MSDN article on how to restore a database to a point in time, using both the SSMS GUI as well as T-SQL, is a good one:

http://msdn.microsoft.com/en-us/library/ms179451.aspx

Of course, to recover this way, you have to ensure that the recovery model of a database is set to full and you are taking regular transaction log backups throughout the day. How frequent these transaction log backups should occur depends on your company's business needs and what the minimal acceptable amount of data loss is.

Under one common scenario, end users would want to recover to a particular point-in-time because of user error, where perhaps several rows of data were accidentally deleted. For example, users may realize at 1 p.m. that at 12:15 p.m. a large number of records were accidentally deleted from a database. The ideal case for recovery is to restore to a point in time before 12:15 p.m. In this scenario, the transaction logs are being regularly backed up every 30 minutes on the hour.

The DBA then must restore the latest full backup from 10 p.m. and then apply every single transaction log backup in sequence up and until 12 p.m. There are about two dozen log backups in this case (see Figure 9-2). But even before you can recover a SQL Server database to its latest point in time, you must oftentimes back up the tail of its transaction log to ensure minimal data loss. This is known as the *tail log*. If the tail of the log is damaged, the changes since the most recent log backup must be redone.

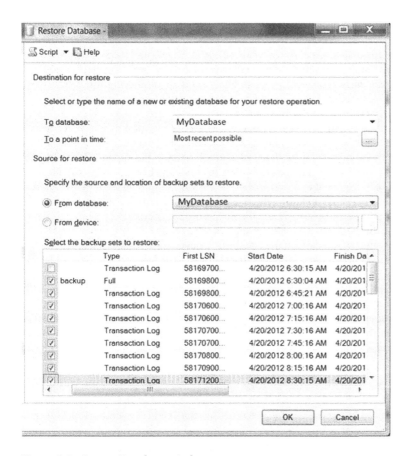

Figure 9-2. *Restore Database window*

A skilled DBA would need to know when the tail log backup is necessary, as well as the correct recovery sequence. Even with SSMS in previous versions, SQL Server wants to restore from the latest backup/log to the most recent possible by default. This process can get a bit confusing with all the different types of backups and multiple log backups.

To get to the database restore options, right-click a database and select Tasks ➤ Restore ➤ Database. On versions prior to SQL Server 2012 you can click the ellipsis, and a window will appear asking to input the desired date and time, as shown in Figures 9-3 and 9-4.

Destination for restore		
Select or type the name of a new or existing database for your restore operation.		
To database:	my_db|	
To a point in time:	Most recent possible	

Figure 9-3. *Selecting a point in time to restore*

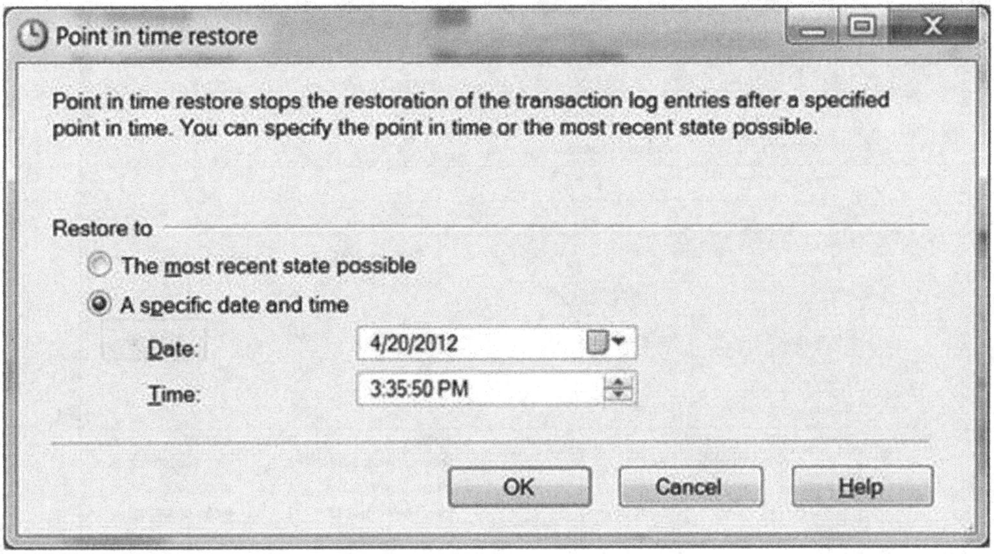

Figure 9-4. *Specifying a date and time for restore*

If you are using SQL Server 2012 or newer, it will look a little different from SSMS. The window that appears presents a Timeline button in the "Restore to" field in the Destination section, as shown in Figure 9-5, which will take you to the Backup Timeline window (in the Database Recovery Advisor), discussed next.

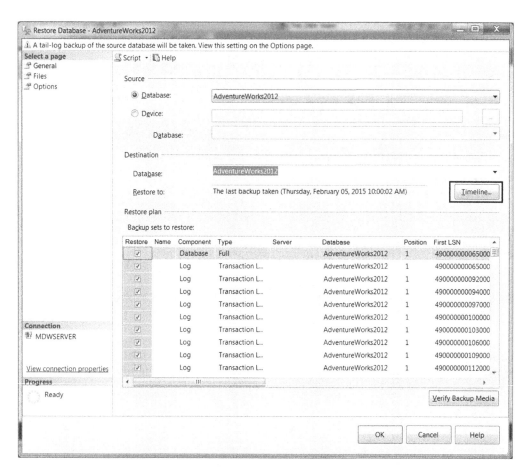

Figure 9-5. *The Restore Database window with the Timeline button*

With the introduction of the Database Recovery Advisor, otherwise known as Timeline Recovery, restoring databases to a point in time will be made much easier. The advisor provides a visual timeline that allows you to select a recovery time down to the second, for data you want to restore. The Database Recovery Advisor is available with SQL Server Studio Management versions 2012 and 2014, via the Restore Database dialog box. Figure 9-6 shows the timeline.

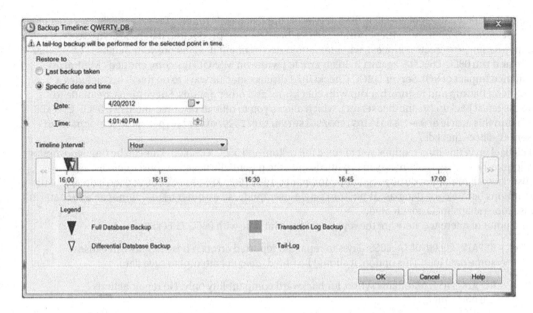

Figure 9-6. *Restore backup timeline*

Based on your selection, the advisor will create and perform the necessary commands and tasks to restore the database to the specified time. When you select a point in time, a restore plan that includes setting relevant restore operations is automatically generated. It will also let you know if you need the additional tail log backup or to set the database to single-user mode and do this for you!

Database Corruption: Detection, Recovery, and Repair

So, how do you ensure that your backups are corruption free? As of SQL Server version 2005, a new improved option was introduced over torn page detection, from early versions, called page checksum. When checksum is enabled on databases, SQL Server computes the checksum of the page whenever a page is read from disk to memory or written to disk from memory.

When SQL Server reads the page, it recomputes the checksum comparing it with the values stored in the page header. If the checksum value matches, then it is assumes the page did not get corrupted during the read-write process.

BACKUP CHECKSUM will compute a combined CHECKSUM of all pages and stored on the backup media. This value can be used to re-compute the CHECKSUM before restoring to make sure the backup itself is valid. Note that I am talking about corruption of the backup file, not database corruption. The backup file might still contain valid pages but is not readable by SQL Server because the data is corrupted. It's straightforward to tell whether the backup has any corruption during a restore or while doing a restore in verify-only mode. A backup checksum uses same algorithm as used by a page checksum. You can choose to generate a backup checksum during a backup that can then later be used during a restore to validate that the backup is not corrupt. Additionally, the page checksum, if available, can be verified during backup and recovery.

However, there is a caveat of using backup checksums that Books Online (BOL) talks about: "Due to the overhead verifying and generating backup checksums, using backup checksums poses a potential performance impact. Both the workload and the backup throughput may be affected. Therefore, using backup checksums is optional. When deciding to generate checksums during a backup, carefully monitor the CPU overhead incurred as well as the impact on any concurrent workload on the system."

Another traditional way of checking the integrity of your database is running DBCC CHECKDB. This operation can also be quite I/O intensive with performance overhead on your production databases. Therefore, the recommendation is to create a process, whether automated or manual, to restore your database to another instance and run DBCC CHECKDB against it. In an article I wrote on MSSQLTips.com, entitled "Minimize Performance Impact of SQL Server DBCC CheckDB," I discuss specific ways to do this. This includes a discussion on backup and restore, backup with checksum, and other options. Suggestions are made to restore the latest backup (to another server), which allows you to offload resource-intensive DBCC CHECKDB. You can find this article at www.mssqltips.com/sqlservertip/2399/minimize-performance-impact-of-sql-server-dbcc-checkdb/.

Full backup verification requires you to run a full restore and DBCC CHECKDB. This can be time-consuming and resource-heavy and is often easy to put off, despite the potentially negative consequences.

Also, keep in mind that during regular maintenance, DBCC CHECKDB should *not* be used with any of the repair options because the database is put into single-user mode, so no other transactions can alter data. In this case too, a snapshot is not created.

As a point of reference, here are the repair options available with DBCC CHECKDB:

- REPAIR_ALLOW_DATA_LOSS: Tries to repair all reported errors. These repairs can cause some data loss. This option, it should be noted, *does not* attempt to save data.

- REPAIR_FAST: Maintains syntax for backward compatibility only. No repair actions are performed.

- REPAIR_REBUILD: Performs repairs that have no possibility of data loss. This can include quick repairs, such as repairing missing rows in nonclustered indexes, and more time-consuming repairs, such as rebuilding an index.

For example, if you want to use DBCC repair, you must first put the database in single-user mode, as shown here:

```
ALTER DATABASE SQLCentric
SET single_user WITH ROLLBACK IMMEDIATE;
GO
DBCC CHECKDB (SQLCentric, REPAIR_REBUILD);
GO
```

With respect to corruption, one great feature in SQL Server 2008 R2 is the ability to automatically repair corrupt pages during database mirroring and also can be helpful with AlwaysOn AG. Automatic page repair is an asynchronous process that runs in the background. See the following MSDN article for information about automatic repair for mirroring and AG:

```
https://msdn.microsoft.com/en-us/library/bb677167.aspx
```

You can view stored history on suspect pages by querying the suspect_pages table, introduced in SQL Server 2005.

```
SELECT *
FROM msdb..suspect_pages;
GO
```

You can specifically look for bad pages such as a bad checksum and torn page errors by filtering by event type, as such:

```
-- Select nonspecific 824, bad checksum, and torn page errors.
SELECT *
FROM msdb..suspect_pages
WHERE (event_type = 1 OR event_type = 2 OR event_type = 3);
GO
```

SQL error 823 is page-level corruption, and the 824 error message usually indicates that there is a problem with the underlying storage system or the hardware or a driver that is in the path of the I/O request. You can encounter these errors when there are inconsistencies in the file system or the database file is damaged. Error 825 is also an indication of potential disk subsystem issues on the horizon. These errors will also appear in the SQL Server error logs. You'll learn more about errors 823, 824, and 825 in Chapter 8 and how to alert on them.

Log Shipping

Log shipping is one of those trusted HA/DR solutions that has been around from early SQL Server 7.0 through the latest version. Let's talk a little more in-depth about log shipping concepts and guide you through how to set it up through SSMS.

About Log Shipping

Log shipping provides a minimal of high availability using a second, warm standby server. The log shipping process involves taking a full backup of one or more databases and regular backups of the transaction logs, restoring them to the second "standby" server, otherwise known as the *secondary server*. The databases on the "standby" server are continuously in standby or in recovery mode, in a ready state to receive the transaction logs that are "shipped" or copied over the network. Then, the transaction logs are applied sequentially to the databases. The databases that are participating in log shipping are read-only when in standby mode, except when a log backup is being restored. It is not possible to use the server for anything much else but as a standby because every time the database transaction log is restored, an exclusive database lock prevents any user access. Restoring means the database is not accessible. Standby means it is read-only. When you set up the log shipping, you can indicate to leave it in restoring, or standby, mode. You can also specify whether the log shipping restore job will disconnect users or whether the restore is delayed until after the users are disconnected. As a reporting server, the standby is not very reliable because it is available only during the interval between restores. However, the shorter interval between restores is better for recovery.

To use the secondary server, you must apply the last transaction log backup to the closest point in time possible before the primary server failure and restore the databases using WITH RECOVERY. You must keep in mind and document, in your DR run book, the steps necessary to bring the log shipping standby server online for use as the primary database server.

In the event of a failure, you need to break the log shipping process by disabling the copy and restore jobs. Because you will want to reestablish log shipping again, you will need to restore the standby database from a full backup of the source database and start the process over. The easiest way to do this is to ensure that you script the log shipping configuration via SSMS and create the script from the source database. There is actually the option Script Configuration during setup, which will script the entire log shipping configuration for you. To bring the database online, you run the following statement: RESTORE DATABASE [DatabaseName] WITH RECOVERY. Once the database is online, you'll need to reconcile the SIDs for user logins/database users. Finally, test connectivity and access through SQL Server and your applications.

It was possible to automate and script a log shipping process as early as SQL Server version 6.5. As of SQL Server version 7.0, introduced the Log Shipping wizard and GUI out of the box.

Deploy Log Shipping

The Log Shipping interface and setup process are much more streamlined. Using SSMS, you can easily set up log shipping for an individual database. Right-click, go to Tasks, and then select Ship Transaction Logs, as shown in Figure 9-7.

Figure 9-7. *Setting up log shipping*

In the Database Properties window displayed in Figure 9-8, enable the database as the primary and schedule the transaction log backups for continuous log shipping.

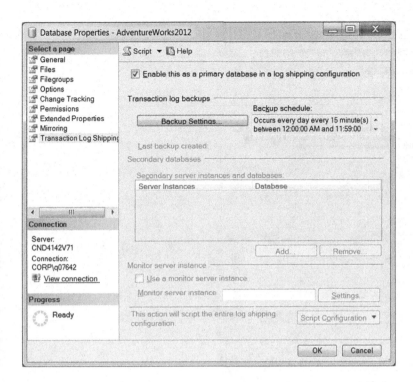

Figure 9-8. *Database Properties window transaction log shipping selected*

Set the network and local path to the transaction log backups and set the following in the Transaction Log Backup Settings dialog, as in Figure 9-9: file retention, alert if backups stop, job name, schedule, and compression level. When done, click OK.

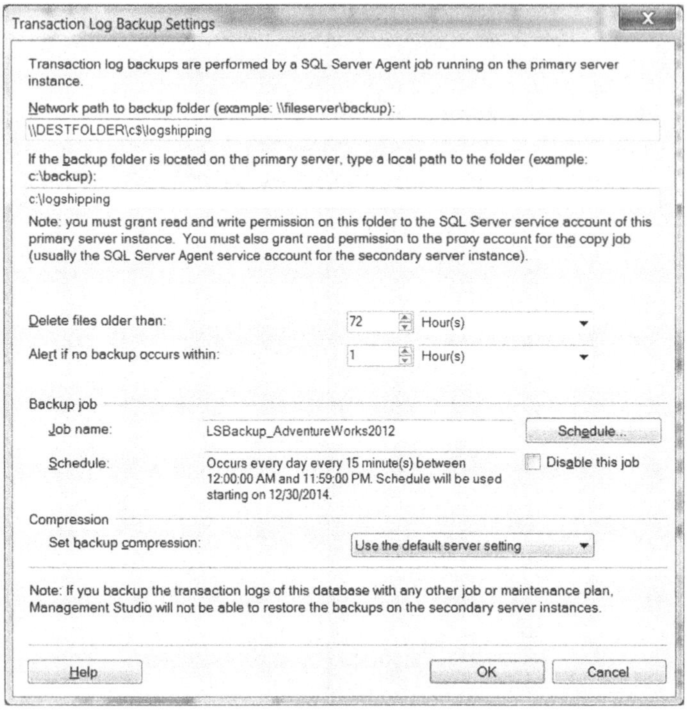

Figure 9-9. *Transaction Log Backup Settings dialog*

On the secondary database settings page, you have three configuration tabs, shown in Figure 9-10. On the Initialize Secondary Database tab, connect to the secondary instance and database. Choose the options to create the secondary database and restore it if necessary, manually or automatically. Then click the Copy Files tab to set the destination folder to receive the logs, file copy retention, job name, and schedule for the copy job. Finally, on the Restore Transaction Log tab, you can set the restore mode for no recovery or standby. Remember, if you want to allow the secondary database to be readable, you can choose "Standby mode." Set the restore job name and schedule, and click OK.

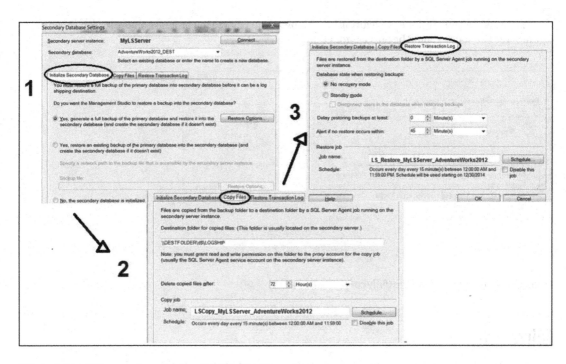

Figure 9-10. *The secondary database settings configuration*

Now on the Database Properties page, shown in Figure 9-11, log shipping has been populated, and you have the option of setting up a separate instance for monitoring. There the status and history of log shipping activity are recorded, and the alert job runs for the primary database.

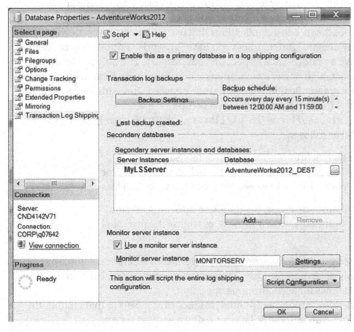

Figure 9-11. *Database properties for log shipping completed*

Finally, when you are done configuring log shipping, you will see the progress on the screen shown in Figure 9-12. The status should be Success for all steps.

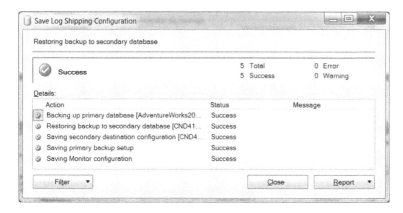

Figure 9-12. *Log shipping successfully configured!*

Mirroring

This section will talk about the various configuration modes and how to configure database mirroring.

About Database Mirroring

Mirroring is probably the best high availability option in versions SQL Server 2005 through 2008 R2. Mirroring is based on the similar process as log shipping, with new added capabilities to ensure automatic failover. With a witness server (a server that sits in between the two mirrors), you get automatic failover in the event of the failure of your primary database goes down. Most applications that use Microsoft connections to your database can support mirroring. The only negative is that unless you have Enterprise Edition, you are limited to synchronous mirroring, which can have a performance impact on your primary. The only mode allowed for in SQL Server Standard Edition is, in fact, high-safety synchronous mode. Enterprise Edition brings in asynchronous mirroring, which allows for greater flexibility and distance between sites with no performance impact. In mirroring, a failover will occur if the principal database is corrupt.

As defined by MSDN (`http://msdn.microsoft.com/en-us/library/dd207006.aspx`), the database mirroring operating modes are described as follows:

> In high-performance mode or asynchronous mode, the database mirroring session operates asynchronously and uses only the principal server and mirror server. The only form of role switching is forced service (with possible data loss).

> With high-safety mode or synchronous mode, the database mirroring session operates synchronously and, optionally, uses a witness, as well as the principal server and mirror server.

A mirroring-specific database property called *transaction safety* determines whether a database mirroring session operates synchronously or asynchronously. There are two safety levels: full and off. Full enables synchronous operation, and off allows for asynchronous operation.

As discussed, for use only with high-safety mode, an optional instance of SQL Server that enables the mirror server to recognize whether to initiate an automatic failover, using a witness server.

You should know a few other things about database mirroring and the optional use of a witness server. Mirroring in synchronous mode will ensure that your two databases, the principal and mirror, will remain in sync transactionally, all the time, without any data loss. However, this introduces potential latency because the transactions will not commit on the principal until all these transactions are committed to the mirrored database. Until the mirror sends back an acknowledgment of committed transactions, the principal can continue. Therefore, the partners must remain in continuous communication for the databases to remain synchronized.

SQL Server Enterprise Edition allowed for high-performance mode in that you have the option to set the "Transaction safety" property to full (on) or off. Allowing the mirroring feature to operate asynchronously would not require transaction committals to disk before the principal can proceed. With asynchronous mode, data loss is possible, but the mirror would be up-to-date in near real enough time. Asynchronous node allows for higher performance because it reduces any latency and the mirror can catch up as soon as possible. Therefore, you are trading off high availability for high performance. With the introduction of stream compression in SQL Server 2008, mirroring and log shipping are greatly improved, significantly reducing network traffic. Unfortunately, for many companies using SQL Server Standard Edition, database mirroring is deprecated as of SQL Server 2012, in favor of AG, discussed in later in the chapter.

Configuring Database Mirroring

The tasks of configuring and setting up database mirroring are fairly straightforward and can be deployed in a few clicks. The first thing you need to know are the instances you will be using for the principal, the mirror, and, optionally, the witness. Databases participating must be in full recovery mode. Before you start mirroring, the first step is to manually back up the principal database and restore it to the mirror server, specifying the restore option WITH NORECOVERY. You can do all this using T-SQL or via the SSMS GUI with backup and restore. Of course, the database name on the mirror must be the same as the principal.

Use SSMS to navigate to the database, you want as the principal database and right-click. Select Tasks and then Mirror to bring up the Database Properties window shown in Figure 9-13.

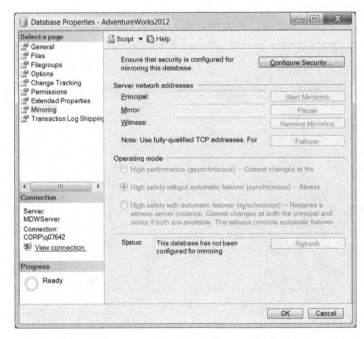

Figure 9-13. *Database Properties, configuring mirroring*

> ■ **Caution** The first step for mirroring is to back up and restore the database to the mirror server using WITH NORECOVERY.

To populate this window, click Configure Security to launch the Configure Database Mirroring Security Wizard. For communication purposes and to exclusively receive connections from other instances, an endpoint is used exclusively to receive connections from other server instances. Each SQL Server instance participating in mirroring must have an endpoint created manually for the database mirroring session because no endpoint is created by default. Here you will be configuring all the endpoints for security settings for the principal, mirror, and witness server instances. Click Next to advance.

> ■ **Note** To learn all about database mirroring endpoints, you can go to this MSDN article for reference: http://msdn.microsoft.com/en-us/library/ms179511.aspx.

The first question is, do you want to have a witness server for automatic failover and to operate in synchronous mode? If you choose Yes, then you will be prompted to select and connect to that server acting as the witness, as shown in Figure 9-14.

Figure 9-14. *Including a witness server*

Once you choose to include a witness server instance in your mirroring setup, you will then be asked to choose the witness server to configure and where to save the security configuration, as displayed in Figure 9-15.

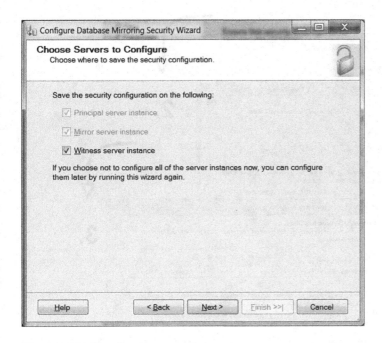

Figure 9-15. *Congfiguring a witness server*

With Figure 9-15, you have chosen to configure a witness server instance. In the following three screens you will be prompted to select and connect to the principal, witness, and mirror instances, respectively. I have combined these steps in one screenshot, shown in Figure 9-16.

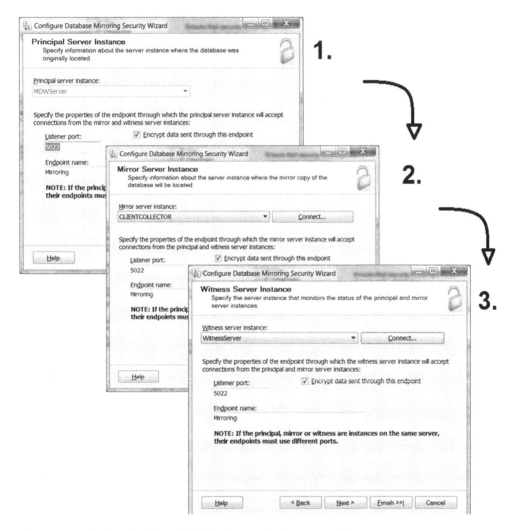

Figure 9-16. *Configuring the principal, mirror, and witness server instances*

After the previous configurations for all instances are completed, you then will need to specify the service accounts for the server instances. The one screen shown in Figure 9-17 allows you to do this for the principal, witness, and mirror.

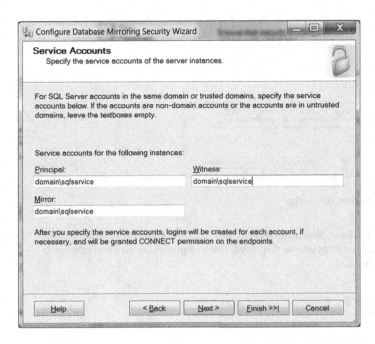

Figure 9-17. *Specifying the service accounts of principal, witness, and mirror*

To complete the mirroring setup and configuration, click Finish, and you will be presented with the progress screen for configuring the endpoints, as in Figure 9-18.

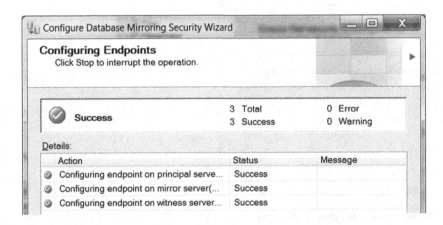

Figure 9-18. *Configuring the endpoints progress screen*

At the end of the wizard, you will get a pop-up window asking whether you want to start mirroring. You can click Start Mirroring here or from the database properties screen, which is now populated. To begin mirroring, select Start Mirroring, and the mirroring process will begin, as you can see in Figure 9-19.

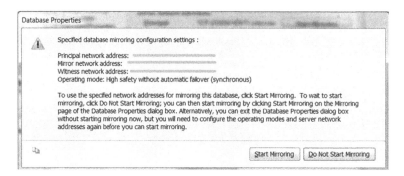

Figure 9-19. *Choosing to start or not to start mirroring*

After completing the Configure Database Mirroring Security Wizard, you will be brought back to the Database Properties screen, where your settings will be displayed, like in Figure 9-20, and you can opt to start mirroring from here. Click OK to exit.

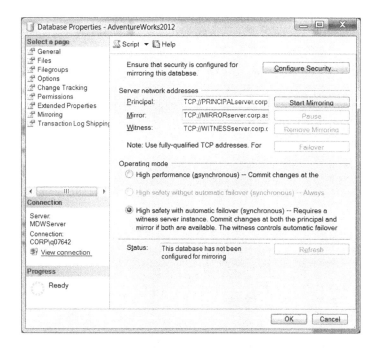

Figure 9-20. *Completed database mirroring properties screen*

Clustering

When you think about a server failure, having a second server to fail over to that will come back online within minutes can be comforting. This scenario is supported by a technology known as *failover clustering*. Failover clustering provides one form of high availability, as discussed in this section.

About Clustering

Clustering technology has been around for quite some time, starting with Microsoft Clustering Services (MCS) in Windows NT 4.0. The latest and proper name for Windows clustering is Windows Server Failover Clustering (WSFC). WSFC allows you to present shared storage to multiple servers and to fail over an entire instance. A server cluster is a group of independent servers working collectively and running the WSFC. The benefits of server clusters are that they provide high availability, via automatic failover, failback, scalability, and manageability for resources and applications. The following are the benefits:

- *High availability*: With server clusters, the ownership of resources such as disk drives and Internet Protocol (IP) addresses is automatically transferred from a failed server to a surviving server. When a system or application in the cluster fails, the cluster software restarts the failed application on a surviving server or disperses the work from the failed node to the remaining nodes. As a result, users experience only a momentary pause in service.

- *Failback*: The cluster service will automatically re-assign the workload in a cluster when a failed server comes back online to its predetermined preferred owner. This feature can be configured but is disabled by default.

- *Manageability*: You can use the Cluster Administrator tool (Cluadmin.exe) to manage a cluster as a single system and to manage applications as if they were running on a single server. You can move applications to different servers within the cluster. Cluster Administrator can be used to manually balance server workloads and to free servers for planned maintenance. You can also monitor the status of the cluster, all nodes, and all resources from anywhere on the network.

- *Scalability*: Cluster services can grow to meet increased demand. When the overall load for a cluster-aware application exceeds the cluster's capabilities, additional nodes can be added, up to 16 as of Windows Server 2008/R2.

Server clusters allow client access to applications and resources in the event of failures and planned outages. If one of the servers in the cluster is unavailable because of a failure or maintenance requirements, resources and applications move to other available cluster nodes.

WSFC protects you against individual server failure by creating a virtual Windows cluster name assigned its own virtual IP (VIP). This is what makes failover, and which physical node that is currently active, transparent to the end user. The typical setup for a WSFC with SQL Server is a two-node active/passive configuration. Another common setup that attempts to leverage the existing cluster server resources is an active/active cluster. Many cluster experts will say this is a misnomer and should not be confused with load balancing. All what this does is allow each node to host a separate individual SQL Server instance and fail over to each other's node. So in reality, for example, SQL Server instance 1 will fail over to the server node hosting SQL Server instance 2, and vice versa. This makes the respective node a passive node to the other SQL instance. As for licensing, since you are actively utilizing each SQL Server instance, then it must be properly licensed because you are allowed a passive node without additional licensing.

You can scale out the number of nodes and thus can have, for example, a three-node active-active-passive cluster. This means in this three-node scenario that each active node participating in the cluster will host a separate SQL Server instance that in the event of a failover will fail over to the passive node. This simply means that a server node currently hosting and owning the cluster resources is active, while the failover server node is passive. Figure 9-21 shows a more common cluster configuration, a typical two-node active/passive WSFC with SQL Server.

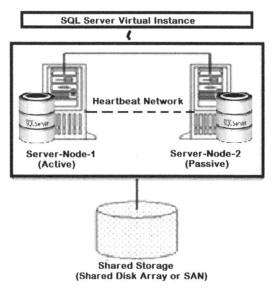

Figure 9-21. Common two-node Windows failover cluster with SQL Server

The technology for WSFC is part of the backbone of AlwaysOn. A WSFC cluster is a group of independent servers that work together to increase the availability of applications and services. It does this by monitoring the health of the active node and failing over to a backup node, with automatic transfer of resource ownership when problems are detected.

To set up and install SQL Server as a cluster, there are several steps and preplanning that must be done. Cluster installation roles and responsibilities depend on your internal team because often the SAN administrator will allocate shared storage and the Windows administrator will configure and install WSFC. The point at which the DBA comes in varies in each environment. If you have SAN and Windows administrators who are savvy about SQL Server clustering, they may set up the entire cluster. Or, they might just take it to the point where you're ready to launch the SQL Server installer. Oftentimes, you'll need to direct the other team members on the installation and environmental prerequisites. For example, you must ensure that the latest .NET Framework is installed, that the disks and LUN have been presented to the cluster, and that the correct numbers of IP addresses have been reserved. The best way to ensure a smooth SQL Server cluster install is to use a checklist for the perquisites before double-clicking the SQL Server EXE.

Fortunately for you, I have assembled such a precluster installation checklist, which is part of my white paper on clustering. The document is a comprehensive step-by-step SQL Server 2012 cluster installation guide. The purpose of the white paper is to provide a step-by-step guide on the prerequisites, planning, installation, and deployment of a SQL Server 2012 cluster, including a checklist and post-verification. Complete with screenshots, it will take you through the SQL Server setup and installation. The white paper will be included with the e-copy of this book as a bonus. You can download the white paper directly at this URL:

```
http://bit.ly/SQLServerClustering
```

Multisubnet Clusters

Although the WSFC is able to span multiple subnets, a SQL Server that is cluster-aware has not, until now, been able to support a clustered instance of SQL Server across multiple subnets. Prior to SQL Server 2012, implementing a geocluster required a stretch VLAN so that all nodes are in the same subnet. It also was quite expensive to set up clustering across multiple data centers because of the WSFC requiring shared storage in both data centers as well as the block-level SAN replication. SAN-to-SAN replication is one of the most expensive HA/DR solutions. There was additional complexity of managing and configuring SAN replication technology, which required a lot of work with your storage vendors to get your setup correct.

Now, multisite clustering with no SAN replication and with no shared storage is possible. Essentially, SAN-less HA/DR allows for flexible failover and can offer an alternative to traditional SAN-based clusters, as well as potential cost savings of thousands of dollars. This was a big thing with the release of SQL Server 2012, where multisubnet clustering is supported. A SQL Server multisubnet failover cluster is a configuration where each failover cluster node is connected to a different subnet or different set of subnets. It enables you to set up a failover cluster using nodes in different subnets, eliminating the need for a stretch VLAN. These subnets can be in the same location (local cluster) or in geographically dispersed sites (geocluster). Clustering across geographically dispersed sites is sometimes referred to as *stretch clusters* or *geoclustering*.

Figure 9-22 is an example of a SAN-less two-node cluster in each data center, for a total of four nodes, where each node has its own storage. The implementation of Windows Server Failover Clustering for SQL Server is set up, configured, and supported in the usual way, but this gives you the flexibility to implement clustering with servers that are not attached to shared storage and the ability to replicate your data to geographically dispersed data centers. With SQL Server 2012 AlwaysOn HA/DR, your solution does not have to utilize shared storage but can use SAN, DAS, NAS, or local disk depending on your budget and requirements. I suggest working with your storage providers to come up with the solution you need.

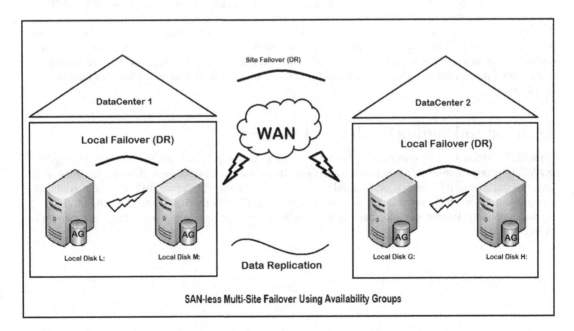

Figure 9-22. A sample of multisite failover using AG and no SAN

Availability Groups (2012)

In this section, you will be introduced to SQL Server 2012 AlwaysOn availability groups. You will explore some of the architecture, concepts, and steps for configuring high availability in SQL Server 2012. You'll learn a bit on how to configure and implement SQL Server AlwaysOn availability groups.

Introduced in Microsoft SQL Server 2012, the AlwaysOn availability groups feature is a high availability and disaster recovery solution that provides an enterprise-level alternative to database mirroring. AG allows you the ability to group databases into failover groups so that multiple databases can be failed over together. However, do be aware that the databases are not in sync until the transactions are committed or hardened on the secondaries. If a failover occurs where one database's transactions are committed but another database's transactions are not, the data from this database will not show on the secondary. AlwaysOn availability groups maximize the availability of a set of user databases for an enterprise. Deploying AlwaysOn availability groups involves creating and configuring one or more availability groups. Each availability group is a container for a discrete set of user databases, known as *availability databases*, which fail over together. An availability group can have multiple possible failover targets (secondary replicas). AG uses database mirroring features to allow multiple readable secondary replicas and groupings of databases for failover, backup, and reporting.

Because AG's components are based on database mirroring technologies, Microsoft has announced that database mirroring has been deprecated as of SQL Server 2012 and will be removed in later versions of SQL Server, with AG as its replacement. This leaves many Standard Edition customers out in the cold as far as database mirroring is concerned because AG is currently an Enterprise Edition feature. Whether this will change in future versions is unknown as of this book's printing. Currently, Standard Edition users are suggested to consider other types of HA/DR, discussed in this chapter, such as log shipping, Windows failover clustering, and even replication.

To implement availability groups, you will need to have Windows Enterprise Edition and SQL Server Enterprise Edition (or Developer Edition for testing) and WSFC. As a prerequisite, the host computer must be a WSFC node. No shared storage is required, and a quorum disk is preferred. AG uses the WSFC APIs for failover, works similarly to how a failover clustered instance fails over, and has a similar quorum model to Windows Failover Clustering as well. The instance is connected every 30 seconds to perform a health check, monitors the health of the active node, and fails over to a backup node, with automatic transfer of resource ownership, when problems are detected. To assist in these tasks, SQL Server now has a "listener" called the Availability Group Listener, which is used for redirection of connections in case of a failover or for read-only functionality.

Enabling and Setting Up the AG Feature

Once the Windows Server failover cluster has been created, you can proceed with enabling the AlwaysOn availability groups feature in SQL Server 2012. This needs to be done on all of the SQL Server instances that you will configure as replicas in your availability group. To enable the SQL Server 2012 AlwaysOn availability groups feature, open SQL Server Configuration Manager. Double-click the SQLServer (MSSQLSERVER) service to open the Properties dialog box. Right-click the SQL Server Service and select Properties, as shown in Figure 9-23.

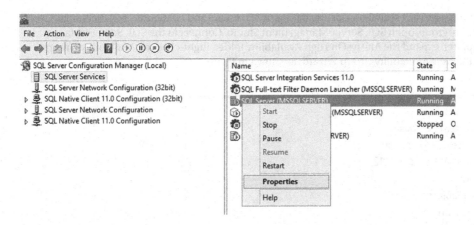

Figure 9-23. *SQL Server Services properties*

In the Properties dialog box, select the AlwaysOn High Availability tab. Check the Enable AlwaysOn Availability Groups box, as shown in Figure 9-24. This will prompt you to restart the SQL Server service. Click OK. Restart the SQL Server service. You will be stepped through a simple AG setup here. However, you can review the MSDN collection of articles under the title. Create and configure SQL Server 2012 AlwaysOn availability groups at this URL:

https://msdn.microsoft.com/en-us/library/ff878265.aspx

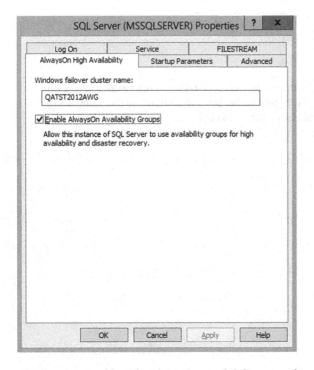

Figure 9-24. *Enabling the AlwaysOn availability group feature*

Availability groups can be created on existing databases. To create and configure a SQL Server 2012 AlwaysOn availability group, open SQL Server Management Studio. Connect to the SQL Server instance.

In Object Explorer, expand the AlwaysOn High Availability folder. Right-click the Availability Groups folder and select the New Availability Group Wizard, as shown in Figure 9-25.

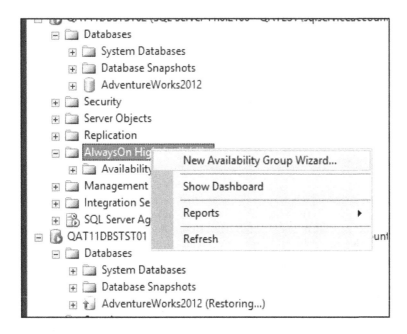

Figure 9-25. *Launching the New Availability Group Wizard*

From the Introduction page, click Next.

Click Next. In the Specify Availability Group Name page, enter the name of your availability group. This can be the name of the cluster, or it could be a different name, but it should not be the name of any active server on your network, and the name should be less than 16 characters. See Figure 9-26.

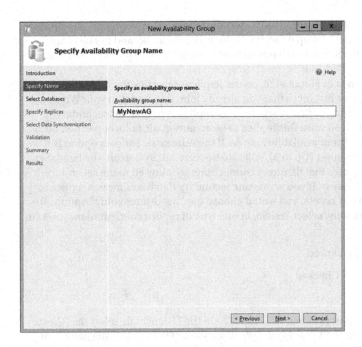

Figure 9-26. Specifying the availability group name

In the Select Databases page, shown in Figure 9-27, select the check box beside the database that you want to include in your availability group. Click Next.

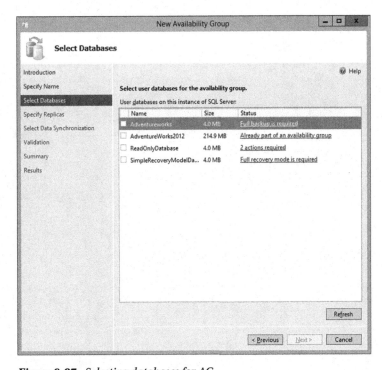

Figure 9-27. Selecting databases for AG

For a database to be added to an availability group, it must meet the following requirements. The database must be in full recovery model, have a recent backup done, not be in read-only mode, and not be in any other availability groups. The wizard, at the Select Databases step, will check for these prerequisites and display them in the Status column.

On the Specify Replicas page, as shown in Figure 9-28, on the Replicas tab, click the Add Replicas button and connect to the other SQL Server instances that you already joined as nodes in your Windows Server failover cluster. The Initial Role setting indicates whether the replica is primary or secondary. Automatic Failover (Up to 2) is checked if you want this replica to be an automatic failover partner. Both replicas here will use the synchronous-commit availability mode. If the Automatic Failover option is selected, the next option, Synchronous Commit (Up to 3), will also be selected. By default, the Readable Secondary setting will be No, which indicates that no direct connections are allowed to the secondary databases and are not available for read access. If you want your secondary databases for this replica to allow direct read-only connections for read access, you would choose the "Read-intent only" option. To allow all connections but for read access only, select Yes. So, in one type of replica configuration, you can configure the following options:

- *Automatic Failover (Up to 2)*: Checked

- *Synchronous Commit (Up to 3)*: Checked

- *Readable Secondary*: No

On the Endpoints tab, verify that the port number value is 5022. On the Listener tab, select the "Create an availability group listener" option. Enter the following details. The listener DNS name is the name that you will use in your application connection string Port: 1433. Click the Add Replica button to provide an IP address. In the Add IP Address dialog box, enter your preferred virtual IP address in the IPv4 Address field. Click OK and then click Next. You should see similar to Figure 9-28.

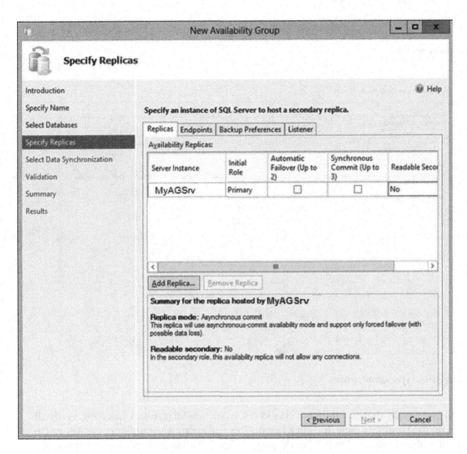

Figure 9-28. *Specifying replicas configuration information*

On the Select Initial Data Synchronization page, select the Full option. Provide a shared folder that is accessible to all the replicas and that the SQL Server service account used by both replicas has write permissions to. This is just a temporary file share to store the database backups that will be used to initialize the databases in an availability group, as shown in Figure 9-29. If you are dealing with large databases, it is recommended that you manually initialize the databases prior to configuring them because your network bandwidth may not be able to accommodate the size of the database backups. Click Next.

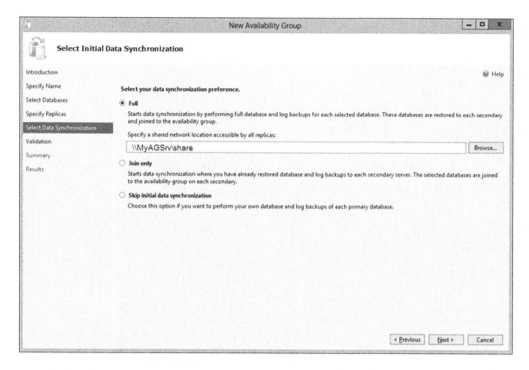

Figure 9-29. *Selecting initial synchronization*

On the Validation page, verify that all validation checks return successful results. Click Next. Verify all configuration settings on the Summary page and click Finish. This will create and configure the AlwaysOn availability group and join the databases. On the Results page, verify that all tasks have been completed successfully.

Congratulations! You have just created a basic implementation of SQL Server 2012 AlwaysOn availability group. You can now use the availability groups listener name in your application connection string. Please note that you need to manually add new databases in the availability group even though your application has already been using the listener name. Also, make sure to monitor the replicas in your availability groups to be alerted when new databases are created.

Read-Only Replicas

Read-only replicas, or active secondaries, are a new feature of 2012 AlwaysOn HA/DR that allow for up-to-the-minute readable database replicas, available for querying and reporting. When first introduced in SQL Server 2012, you were able to create up to four readable secondary replicas, but with SQL Server 2014 this increased from four to eight. Other useful things you can do with replicas are that you can take backups from read-only copies and perform DBCC statements against a secondary replica, which offloads the overhead from production, that DBCC often causes. Indexing must be same on replicas as the primary. Poorly performing queries can also affect the status of a replica in that if they are poorly coded, they will perform just as bad on the replica. There would be no difference in query performance on the primary compared to the secondary. The only potential difference is if there is resource contention issues on the primary or snapshot isolation is turned on for the secondary.

Virtualization

Virtualization is a viable option to throw into the HA/DR mix and can offer many options for database availability and disaster recovery, utilizing the best features from both virtual technologies and Microsoft.

For example, VMware's vSphere high availability can help to recover SQL Server instances in the case of host failure. At the application level, all SQL Server features and techniques are supported on vSphere, including AlwaysOn availability groups, AlwaysOn failover cluster instances database mirroring, and log shipping. In fact, SQL Server 2012 high availability features can be combined with vSphere features to create flexible availability and recovery scenarios, applying the most efficient and appropriate tools for each use case.

With SQL Server, you can incorporate a level of DR into a virtual environment using a mix of HA/DR features and technologies. Using AlwaysOn features, you can create availability groups across multiple VMs.

In the event of a disaster, businesses think that operating at a slower rate of performance is better than not operating at all. Therefore, I implemented a physical-to-virtual (P2V) scenario where all servers were replicated from physical rack servers in New York to virtual machines backed by blade servers in New Jersey, thus minimizing the cost of space, cooling, and power consumption. For the SQL Server instances, at the time I actually used database mirroring between data centers; in this case, the primary database was on a physical box, and the mirror was on a VM.

Virtualization and the technology behind it are a huge topic not covered in this book. From a DR perspective, there are endless possibilities as virtualization becomes more and more implemented. While I'm not endorsing VMware as the only virtual platform for SQL Server, here is one of its white papers detailing its platform for availability and recovery options, as related to SQL Server:

https://www.vmware.com/files/pdf/solutions/SQL_Server_on_VMware-Availability_and_Recovery_Options.pdf

Peer-to- Peer Replication

Peer-to-peer replication (P2P) can provide some measure of HA, but there are caveats to this, and some data loss is possible. This feature is primarily a scalability solution and provides data availability. As inserts, updates, and deletes are propagated to all server nodes participating in P2P, the databases are synchronized in near real time.

With peer-to-peer replication, you have the capability to keep multiple copies of the data on multiple instances, which could span multiple sites, providing a scale-out HA (if bandwidth permits) and DR solution. Because data is maintained across the nodes, peer-to-peer replication provides data redundancy, which increases the availability of data. Replication is mainly intended for reporting offloading. Because of the nature of the distribution database architecture, higher latencies are more prevalent than would be expected with the availability groups.

A benefit of peer-to-peer replication topology is you can have multiple nodes participate, with multiple publishers and subscribers. You can choose to replicate only a subset of tables within the database (table level or filtered rows). You can create different indexes optimized for the reporting environment because all databases are writeable. This is an optimal solution if you are running expensive reporting queries that need custom indexes.

Unlike most other DR solutions discussed in this chapter, with peer-to-peer replication the database can be in simple recovery mode. The database on secondary is both readable and writeable. However, in the case of DR, there is no automatic redirection, and some manual intervention is necessary. You will have to change the connection string to an available node if the node it is connected to becomes unavailable. Because all of the "nodes" participating in this replication model are always "active," there is really no concept of a failover.

Conflicts are not handled well and require the user to ensure that data modified at different sites does not conflict. For example, if a row is modified at more than one node, it can cause a conflict or even a lost update when the row is propagated to other nodes. P2P replication will simply overwrite data unless configured to fail when a conflict occurs, which requires manual intervention. Other things to note about peer-to-peer are that initialization and re-initialization via snapshots are not supported, and replicated tables must all have a primary key. Figure 9-30 shows a simple topology of peer-to-peer replication, where each node serves as a publisher and a subscriber.

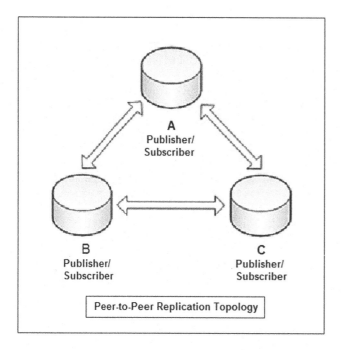

Figure 9-30. *Simple representation of peer-to-peer replication*

Because peer-to-peer replication is not typically deployed as a high availability solution, it is out of the scope of this book to delve into its setup and use. It is an interesting feature that deserves mentioning because it provides data availability and redundancy at multiple sites. A more common use for peer-to-peer replication is where multiple sites should be updated and in sync, such as ATMs or movie rental kiosks like Redbox. The importance of near-real time data varies, of course, but these are two examples where you would want the data up-to-date almost instantly. You can find more information on P2P replication here:

https://msdn.microsoft.com/en-us/library/ms151196.aspx

To learn how to configure P2P replication, with guidance, you can access this TechNet article here:

https://technet.microsoft.com/en-us/library/ms152536%28v=sql.105%29.aspx

DR Run Book

Earlier in the book you were introduced to the concept of the run book. A *run book* is an operational book or set of documents that contain instructions on what to do in case of a disaster recovery scenario. The run book is among your most important pieces of documentation in the company. It is your guide, your contingency plans, and your emergency handbook for when all things can and will go wrong. This is something that is so essential to the contingency planning of any company or organization that it should be considered negligent not to have one. In fact, the run book may even be required by certain compliance laws.

Imagine the day-of-disaster scenario. You probably don't even want to think about it, but it does happen, as I can personally attest to. So, let's just say there's a power outage and UPS supplies fail (I know what you were going to say what about UPS, but just stick with me for sake of argument). All of the servers have gone offline, and the building that houses your servers is offline and has been evacuated. Now what? What do you do? Everyone is in panic mode. Have no fear, your run book is here (don't forget to take it with you on the way out of the building). It contains names, places, addresses, phone numbers, contacts, instructions, colo, VPN, logins, passwords, and all the vital information to get your company back up and running. It is the nuclear football of sorts because it contains such high-value information and details critical to the company's survival and business continuity.

Having a comprehensive disaster recovery run book takes a lot of collaborative effort requiring teamwork and is based on documenting your DR plan and covering what actions and steps are required for as many contingencies as possible. This effort involves three main categories to ensure business continuity and rapid recovery in an orderly fashion: people, process, and technology. There are a lot of moving parts, but you should be mindful of being able to provide the key information specific for SQL Server. The run book is a continuously updated document and must be flexible and adaptive to changes in the environment. In fact, the run book should always have a version number, a created/last-modified date, and last-modified-by information appended to it.

In Chapter 2, you were provided with details on conducting an inventory to find out where all the SQL Server instances are in your current environment. This inventory is definitely something you want to include in your run book. If you have a complete inventory, you should have a good tally of the number of servers you will need to consider, along with network names, SQL Server instance names, IP addresses, and ports. Also, as part of your master inventory list, you will want to have included applications and other SQL Server components with connection information. Most important is to have the department and complete contact information of the business owner of this SQL Server's data. An even more detailed inventory will include the databases residing on each instance, including their names, sizes, physical locations, latest backup paths, and dates.

In an actual disaster, communication will be absolutely essential. You will want to refer to the run book for a contact list of folks, with their roles listed, including their contact information and order of escalation. These people will be the ones most familiar with the servers/applications/databases or be able to follow procedures to get you to the right resource; they make up the team conducting the DR operations. Table 9-1 shows a matrix you can include in your run book.

Table 9-1. *Sample Matrix for DR Contact List*

Name	Title	Department	Tel #1	Tel #2	Email	Escalation Order	Service Vendor
	Call Center Operator	Operations Center				1	
	DBA1	IT Database				2	
	DBA2	IT Database				3	
	DB Lead/Mgr	IT Database				4	
	SysAdmin1	Network Ops				5	
	SysAdmn2	Network Ops				6	
	NetOps Mgr	Network Ops				7	
	Vendor Acme	3rdPartyHost				8	Yes
	AppOwner	LineOfBusiness				9	
	CTO	C-Executive				10	

Of course, a disaster needs to be officially declared to initiate and activate DR contingency plans. Monitoring, as discussed in Chapter 8, is essential to determining this, and the run book should include monitoring procedures, thresholds, alerts, operators, and steps to resolve. If after some effort and time exceeding service level agreements (SLAs) a server or database cannot be brought online or is not accessible, it may be time to activate your DR plan.

From a SQL Server database perspective, by understanding your company's backup and recovery requirements, you can build a solid backup/restore strategy. The recovery point objective and recovery time objective were discussed early in the "Business Continuity" and "Backup and Recovery" sections. All this information will determine the priority of database applications and dictate the order of restoration. You should document your restore procedures, the backup locations, and the steps to reestablish production systems.

Finally, protect the run book! In addition to having printed copies, you should keep multiple electronic copies offsite and uploaded to a shared document drive, somewhere in the cloud, outside the company's network but secured. The point is if the company's network is completely inaccessible, you will need to access your run book.

Summary

SQL Server instances and their databases are critical components in DR planning and ensuring business continuity, but the databases are just one component in a bigger, interrelated, and interdependent scheme of applications, servers, storage, and networks, all of which must come online once disaster strikes. BCP/DR planning is a tremendous undertaking and collaborative team effort of the entire IT and business units, and therefore, you should not think this is a lone effort on the part of the DBA. In fact, many companies will hire a DR planning professional to help assemble and put the plan into action. Yes, you are responsible for the DR component of the SQL Server databases. One of the objectives of this chapter, assuming the typical DBA working in a corporate environment, is to make you aware of these concepts and terms, as well as the technologies and features available for high availability and disaster recovery. Given all the available options, you could decide to use one or any combination of them to come up with an HA/DR plan suited to your company's needs and budget. With the knowledge in this chapter, you should be able to evangelize, if necessary, and greatly contribute to the overall corporate IT BCP and HA/DR strategy.

CHAPTER 10

■ ■ ■

Surviving the Audit

In this chapter, I will discuss the various methods to retrieve audit-related information, such as the default trace, SQL Audit, DDL triggers, and more. I will explore the internals of the transaction log and give you a glimpse into how read it in its native hexadecimal format, which is how the popular third-party vendors do it in their compliance and data recovery software. Luckily, with the advent of SQL Server 2008's Change Data Capture, you will see an easier way to capture DML.

What happens now if you hear the dreaded five-letter word *audit*? Your organization's legal department has just been put on notice that your systems will be audited. Even if you work for a small or midsize firm that doesn't necessarily fall under the legal compliance requirements, you most certainly should be concerned about the security, health, and stability of your SQL Server instances and their databases. In many cases, you will want your SQL Server infrastructure and department to be organized in a way that shows management you are in full control of the environment and things are automated, efficient, and running like a well-oiled machine. The tenets of auditing, even self-auditing, will prove to your managers and higher-ups that their business systems and databases are secure, that performance is great, and that you have a DR plan that will ensure the business is protected on several levels.

The process of auditing your servers was discussed in Chapter 1. To reiterate, a health check is a performance assessment and review (also referred to as a *performance audit* or *analysis*). Basically, it is a comprehensive check to see whether your systems are up to snuff and adhere to industry standards and best practices. When you first started out on your healthy SQL journey in Chapter 1, I asked the following questions: How healthy are your SQL Server instances? How do you know? Are they performing optimally? Are you providing high availability? Do you have a disaster recovery plan?

In this sense, you've been learning in-depth the ins and outs of auditing your SQL Server environment. You already have the knowledge and foundation to successfully prepare for and pass an audit. There is one more question that was asked at the beginning of this book that should be answered in this chapter: can you prove all this in an IT audit? This chapter will give you the knowledge and the tools available to pass an audit.

Overview

Throughout my own database career, I have had to address audit and compliance issues on several levels at various clients. Whether it was to secure and lock down the database, clean up database access, set up auditing processes, evaluate and deploy auditing software, generate security reports, track down unauthorized database changes, parse XML logs, create policy documentation, or implement change controls, they all had some things in common: compliance, regulations, and legal implications. My career has spanned many industries—financial, legal, government, and healthcare—all of which must follow some specific set of compliance laws.

I have even written software reviews for third-party auditing solutions and done a presentation on a topic I'll discuss in the next section: database forensics. My presentation about database forensics focused specifically on how to employ native SQL Server views, functions, and features to find out who did what to your database and when. This presentation was meant to provide ideas on how to get your SQL Server in compliance without using third-party solutions.

Although database forensics, auditing, and security are definitely specialties among database professionals, often with dedicated roles/job titles (database security and compliance officer), as a DBA you will certainly come across audit and compliance issues in some form or another. This chapter will prepare you.

Database Forensics

Even to this day, there aren't many resources published on the subject of database forensics. This is a critical and invaluable function to ensure database compliance, secure your database, and track down and report on the source of all database user activity. It doesn't matter the size of your company or complexity of your databases, your databases hold vital information and play a critical role in storing electronic evidence. Since this data is deemed so crucial, compliance laws regulate how databases are accessed, stored, backed up, managed, and maintained. IT audits and electronic forensics in general make up a broad subject. Here you are dealing with the narrow scope of your SQL Server databases and what you can do to secure and ensure databases and servers are in compliance.

The integrity of the databases and its contents may one day serve as the "smoking gun" evidence needed in legal matters, such as intellectual property cases and other civil and criminal matters. So, how does that translate to your life? For example, a database may store and archive e-mail chains and communications that show evidence of discrimination or sexual harassment in the workplace. Or a database may store information useful in financial litigation cases involving tampering and manipulation of numbers and other data that is illegal, which can result in your financial investments, pensions, and retirement accounts being raided. Database forensics can also be used to identify the source of credit card and banking fraud and the breach of your personal data, such as medical, Social Security, place of residence, and activity that often leads to identity theft. In financial firms, accounting is critical, and money laundering is an example of an illegal act that can be traced to suspicious database activity. Malicious intent to tamper with the integrity of a database and its contents can have profound effects on the company's business, industry reputation, and your job, and it can put you out of business. Even simple omissions and accidental deletions can hurt a business.

Database forensics allows you to apply investigative techniques to database contents and metadata. Using database forensics, you will be able to answer the questions of who, what, and when and gather evidence of potential illicit or harmful database activity. For example, who deleted what records on such and such date and time? Database forensics, if applied correctly, can derive this information and, in the best circumstances, allow you to recover from this data loss.

Third-party software and native SQL Server features allow you to easily recover the data and reverse transactions such as deleted and modified records. Update, insert, and delete statements executed on SQL Server are all logged operations and can be tracked and reversed. Many software solutions can read the raw transaction log and give you the ability to get the database back to a certain point in time before this activity occurred. I already discussed point-in-time recovery using regular transaction log backups to get you back to a particular point in time. There are other recovery methods as well, and some are discussed in this chapter.

To apply database forensics, you will need to use software tools and features that can track, capture, and analyze this data. SQL Server has several out-of-the-box solutions to help you in this regard and provide you with logging and audit capabilities, which can provide you with documentary evidence of database and user activity. This is what you will learn in this chapter.

Much of the stuff you will learn in this chapter will in fact be an exercise in database forensics. You will be exposed to database investigation and analysis techniques, such as how to set up auditing and evidence collection and how to leverage the native SQL Server features out of the box.

A forensic examination of a database may relate to the timestamps that apply to the update time of a row in a relational table being inspected and tested for validity in order to verify the actions of a database user. Alternatively, a forensic examination may focus on identifying transactions within a database system or application that indicate evidence of wrongdoing, such as fraud. If you are interested in expanding your knowledge on database forensics, I recommend an excellent book on the topic (although covering SQL Server 2005) called *SQL Server Forensic Analysis* by Kevvie Fowler.

Benefits of Database Forensics

I'll discuss the benefits of database forensics and the types of information that can be discovered. Sources of extremely valuable information can be, and routinely are, overlooked. In intellectual property cases, for example, financial databases may be important for damages, but knowledge management systems, source code repositories, and document management systems can yield amazing insight into an alleged infringement, while helping defendants protect against troublesome fishing expeditions or invalidate claims against them. These specialized databases can be used to review document life cycle and versioning. Even extended metadata, such as keywords, descriptions, annotations, and comments, can give insight to the purpose of a document, reveal who authored or accessed information, and expose where it was routed.

If you consider the use of database forensics as an investigation, you can draw an analogy to the National Security Agency (NSA) leak story in recent news. It was reported by senior intelligence officials that the NSA is collecting and perusing hundreds of millions of contact lists from personal e-mail and instant messaging accounts around the world, many of them belonging to Americans, as well as other foreign nationals.

Let's leave all political commentary aside to focus on the alleged act of what was happening. Rather than targeting individuals, the operation was looking at contact lists and address books online, which of course includes e-mail address, telephone numbers, street addresses, business information, and family information. This information is metadata, and they were analyzing this metadata to search for hidden connections and to map relationships, in the hopes of finding critical patterns leading to actionable intelligence data to prevent or break up, for example, a terrorist plot. The content itself wasn't as important as the metadata that would lead to a big catch. So, they wouldn't be looking for specific e-mail content of "Let's take out the bridge" but patterns of e-mails fitting into a bigger picture, for example, who's hanging out with who, doing what, when, and why are there so many e-mails to Jake's AK-47 and Explosives Shop. The NSA in essence is looking for a haystack so they can find the needle. Database forensics can derive the following:

- Retrace user DML and DDL operations

- Identify data pre- and post-transaction

- Recover previously deleted data rows

- Help prove/disprove a data security breach

- Help determine the scope of a database intrusion

- Do this with no dependency on third-party auditing tools

Regulatory Compliance

One of the biggest challenges for organizations today is how to observe, obey, and maintain legal standards of regulatory compliance, which is governed by a myriad of laws, rules, regulations, and guidelines. Failure to comply with such regulations could result in severe penalties, which can tarnish a company's reputation and hinder its ability to conduct its business. However, although such laws were passed, many argue in a reactive manner (such as the public accounting scandals in the news) that the rules are vague and subject to broad interpretation. What exactly are the steps to ensure that they are in compliance? This question left several companies scrambling to figure out what it is they needed to do. Sure, in general, organizations are required to take proactive measures to establish documented security processes and procedures for detecting anomalies, attacks, and other vulnerabilities that can cause harm, as well as maintain logs and audit trails to comply. Moreover, they need to be able to prove and demonstrate their compliance to outside auditors. Sound familiar? Let's briefly mention the main bodies of regulatory compliance, which you may have heard about in your career travels, or those in which your company must comply with.

Industry Rules and Regulation

Each industry may be regulated under a specific set of regulatory compliance laws. One or more of these standards (such as the more commonly known SOX, HIPPA, PCI DSS and others like FISMA, GLBA, and ISO 27001) may apply to your organization. Just so you know what these dizzying acronyms are and what they are, I'll briefly discuss them.

The Sarbanes-Oxley (SOX-404) legislation requires all public companies and public accounting firms to show the auditors the accuracy of their financial reporting. The act requires companies to implement processes and controls to protect financial data. All companies need to produce the SOX report that tells the auditors in detail how the data security is handled internally.

The Health Insurance Portability and Accountability Act (HIPAA) regulation impacts organizations in healthcare that exchange patient information electronically. HIPAA regulations were established to protect the integrity and security of health information, including protecting against unauthorized use or disclosure of the information, and a breach of the information will result in penalties.

You need to observe the Payment Card Industry Data Security Standards (PCI DSS) guidelines if your organization stores, transmits, or processes customer credit card data. The PCI DSS was created to meet the rising threat to credit cardholder personal information.

■ **Tip**   The key to DB compliance is this: "Say what you do and do what you say."

Database Access Control and Compliance

The criteria in this section are meant to serve as a general guideline to follow in a drafting database compliance policy. You must aim to adhere to the general principles of compliance (as broadly defined) but more importantly follow the precedence of other public entities. Specifically, you define your policies, document them, adhere to them, and enforce them. This entire process is in effect self-contained. Say what you do and do what you say. Auditors look for this consistency in ensuring your compliance and applying these rules.

For example, document what the access rights are and who needs them and then have a trail of it by having a record of someone being granted access, whether via e-mail, a log (electronic or print), or some auditing system/database that notes when you granted access. I have written such requirements at various clients financial and other industries. The following sections explain the things you should do.

Control Access to the Database Environment

Give people only the bare minimum rights necessary. Have access authorized (you may need an approved list of authorizers, called an *access control list* [ACL]) and keep copies of the authorization. There should be no developer access to production without proper approval, documentation, and expiry. Review access regularly and have it re-authorized.

Treat generic or service accounts like people and don't give them too much access. Service accounts should be secured to reduce the surface area of attack. Keep track of and try to control who knows the service account credentials and keep a catalog of these accounts and functions. You should create a spreadsheet of the various service accounts and the servers and services they are used for. Service accounts should be assigned their necessary rights but restricted from logging on interactively. This restriction will help prevent humans from utilizing the account.

Segregation of Duties

This is a tough one, but make sure that no one has too much access such that they can modify the production system without having to ask anyone for permission. Try to keep the control over the production and test environments separate. This forces people who prepare a change or new release to seek approval and show their homework is done before they can release their change. There will always be someone with full control over a system, so make sure their actions are monitored. Review segregation of duties regularly. Consider it for every process or rights assignment you have.

The segregation of duties ensures that everyone's role is clearly defined and documented with their purpose and function so as not to allow undue access and make changes not accounted for. For example, the people who develop the application and database code must also not be allowed to modify the live or production versions of the application and database. In the ideal and compliant SQL Server world, the DBA would be designated with production access and responsible for code rollouts and production changes. The DBA would also need some oversight, and the actions of the DBA would need to be monitored and documented. The developers would not have access to production. The relationship of the DBA and developers are discussed in "The Tale of the DBA and the Developer" section.

Moreover, segregation of duties makes sure that at least two individuals are responsible for the separate parts of any task. Organizations can apply this knowledge to help manage against segregation of duties violations by enforcing the principle of least privileges, meaning grant users only the privileges that they need to do their job.

Monitoring

You may be able to trade off some segregation of duties concerns if you are able to provide strong monitoring of actions. Using the audit methods and features described in this chapter will allow you do so. DBA activity should also be included in any monitoring process and documented. Follow up all issues discovered in the monitoring process. You should be able to generate ad hoc reports regularly and create alerts on any activity.

Monitoring should be implemented for a variety of reasons, discussed in Chapter 8, and should ensure that all server and database user activity is recorded. Activity to be monitored includes the need to audit schema and DDL changes to database objects, structures, and login/user creation. As part of monitoring such activity, you should audit all access activity by privileged users, any change to database user privileges, and any failed login attempts. Later in the chapter, you will learn methods to capture and track this activity using SQL Server's native feature set.

Backup/Recovery

We discussed this topic extensively in Chapter 8. To reiterate, with respect to auditing, have processes written for both backup and recovery. This written documentation needs to also be stored somewhere safe and secure, outside the network, because it may be offline in the event of an actual disaster. Test and verify your backups regularly, particularly by restoring them. Document the testing. Review backup logs and document the reviews to show that you're looking at them. Review backup jobs and schedules and make sure they represent current agreements with your business units and align with the client's service level agreement (SLA). If the auditor finds an unreported error, their trust in what you say will take a hit. You don't want to be caught saying that you check the backups every day and they're fine, without documented proof.

SQL Code

SQL code should be managed, maintained, and versioned in source repository. There should be a companion change control ticket (see the next section). Define development and deployment best practices and policies. Code should be accompanied with deployment documentation.

For production deployment, scripts should be verified against the source repository for the latest version/schema/data. There should be no direct ad hoc updates to the database. All changes should be compiled into a deployable SQL script and must include the "Use <database>" syntax at the header of every script. Data migration and process logic deployments should be wrapped in a DTS/SSIS package file (and of course versioned as well). All deployment scripts must have matching rollback scripts so that in the event of failure, you can roll back the environment to the exact state it was in prior to the attempted code release. All these scripts should of course be tested and certified against a user acceptance testing (UAT) environment.

Change Control

The objective of change management in this context is to ensure that standardized methods and procedures are used for efficient and prompt handling of all changes to control IT infrastructure in order to minimize the number and impact of any related incidents upon service. Changes in the IT infrastructure may arise reactively in response to problems or externally imposed requirements, such as legislative changes, or may arise proactively from seeking improved efficiency and effectiveness or enabling or reflecting business initiatives, or from programs, projects, or service improvement initiatives. Change management can ensure standardized methods, processes, and procedures that are used for all changes, facilitate efficient and prompt handling of all changes, and maintain the proper balance between the need for change and the potential detrimental impact of changes.

In the DBA world, you will require change tickets, generated from a change control ticketing system, for any changes to production, including a new SQL Server build. You may be part of a queue, where the server administrator will stand up the hardware, put it on the network, install and configure Windows, and then reassign the ticket to the DBA for the final phase of installing and implementing SQL Server. For existing SQL Server installations, common tasks that should require a change control ticket are applying a new service pack, applying a cumulative update or hotfix, troubleshooting, or deploying new code, such as stored procedures, triggers, or new object creation (tables, views, indexes, and so on). All this will fall under your responsibility as the de facto DBA, and in order to keep track of all these requests and changes, that's where change control becomes your friend. Not only as part of compliance and documentation, but also best practice, in the event that something goes awry, you can back up with evidence that you fulfilled your duties in compliance with any IT corporate or governmental policy. Moreover, this documentation will help when sometimes mistakes are made or instructions aren't clear. Documenting the steps taken allows root-cause analysis to proceed when things go wrong. Always create a paper trail and always have complete documentation of your actions. Having a change management system in place to keep track of changes can streamline the documentation process.

Login and Password Policy Enforcement

One of the things you want to ensure in an audit is that you have documented login and password policies and are able to enforce them. An audit might expect you to demonstrate how you enforce login and password policy. With Windows-authenticated logins, it was easier to enforce and set password policies and complexity requirements because by default member computers inherit the password policy configuration from the domain. Since SQL Server 2005, password policies and enforcement were made possible for SQL Server logins by leveraging the Windows API responsible for enforcing password policies and the password expiration policies feature. Now you can document and prove SQL Server login policy as well. This section will give you technical know-how to implement and enforce SQL login and password policies, which in turn you can present in a potential audit.

Although it is often recommended to have Windows Authentication only, this is not, for many reasons, always possible. Microsoft SQL Server allows Mixed Mode where a SQL Server–authenticated account and password are enforced by the same API and protocol that enforces Windows login policies.

Strong password policies require and check for minimum password length, proper character combinations, and passwords that are regularly changed every so often. This practice leads to more secure passwords and makes security breaches of database servers much more preventable.

SQL Server supports password complexity and password expiration, which allows for more secure password policies. Therefore, database security is now enhanced by the same Windows password policies that can also be applied to SQL Server password policies. The password enforcement options available in the Login dialog, under SQL Server authentication, are shown in Figure 10-1.

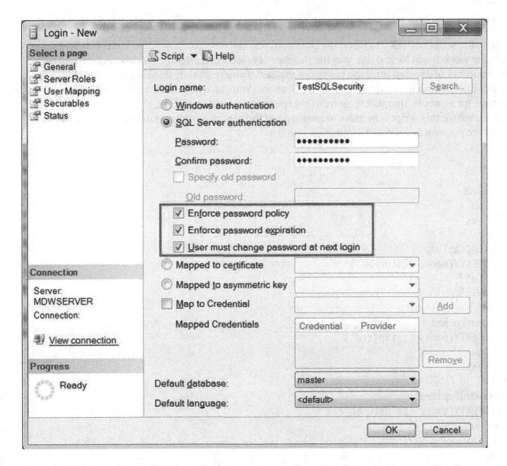

Figure 10-1. *Creating a SQL login with password policies enforced*

As you can see, there are three options outlined:

- Enforce password policy

- Enforce password expiration

- User must change password at next login

So, once you create your SQL authenticated login and of course map the login to a database user and grant access and roles, how can you keep track of this login and its policies? As of SQL Server 2008, you can use LOGINPROPERTY and the sys.sql_logins system view to keep track of and get information about the login policy settings.

With the following SQLLoginSecurity script, you can quickly answer various inquiries about the status of the login and see whether the login is set to any of the following:

- Disabled

- Locked

- Expired

- Must User Change Password at Next Login

In addition, the script will tell you when the password was last reset, the last failed login date and time, the date and time when it was locked out, and the number of failed login attempts. Moreover, you will be able to get the number of days left until the password expires! If you're already thinking what I'm thinking, you can use this information to set up alerts and notifications. You can even create a user notification warning the user, for example, that their password is expiring in *x* number of days.

The only caveat for this script is in order to return *all* of the previous information, you must in fact enable the enforce password and policy expiration options.

```
SELECT
Name,
CASE Is_disabled
WHEN 0 THEN 'No'
WHEN 1 THEN 'Yes'
ELSE 'Unknown'
END as IsLoginDisabled,
CASE LOGINPROPERTY(name, 'IsLocked')
WHEN 0 THEN 'No'
WHEN 1 THEN 'Yes'
ELSE 'Unknown'
END as IsAccountLocked,
CASE LOGINPROPERTY(name, 'IsExpired')
WHEN 0 THEN 'No'
WHEN 1 THEN 'Yes'
ELSE 'Unknown'
END as IsPasswordExpired,
CASE LOGINPROPERTY(name, 'IsMustChange')
WHEN 0 THEN 'No'
WHEN 1 THEN 'Yes'
ELSE 'Unknown'
END as MustChangePasswordOnNextLogin,
LOGINPROPERTY(name, 'PasswordLastSetTime') as PasswordLastSetDate,
LOGINPROPERTY(name, 'BadPasswordCount') as CountOfFailedLoginAttempts,
LOGINPROPERTY(name, 'BadPasswordTime') as LastFailedLoginTime,
LOGINPROPERTY(name, 'LockoutTime') as LoginLockedOutDateTime,
LOGINPROPERTY(name, 'DaysUntilExpiration') as 'NoDaysUntilthePasswordExpires'
From sys.sql_logins
order by name
```

Name	IsLoginDisabled	IsAccountLocked	IsPasswordExpired
sa	No	No	No
TestSQLSecurity	No	No	No
UPLMDW	No	No	No

MustChangePasswordOnNextLogin	PasswordLastSetDate	CountOfFailedLoginAttempts
No	2014-05-05 12:05:09.803	0
No	2015-02-10 11:36:59.540	0
No	2014-09-17 09:32:03.897	0

LastFailedLoginTime	LoginLockedOutDateTime	NoDaysUntilthePasswordExpires
1900-01-01 00:00:00.000	1900-01-01 00:00:00.000	NULL
2015-02-10 11:36:05.513	1900-01-01 00:00:00.000	76
1900-01-01 00:00:00.000	1900-01-01 00:00:00.000	NULL

The Tale of the DBA and the Developer

One the many challenges the DBA must face, especially in an environment that does not have an already established hierarchy, is dealing with developers who, for a variety of reasons, have unfettered access to production systems. This could be the case where you have joined a startup, it could be a company that did not previously have a dedicated DBA, or perhaps your company just acquired a company that must be integrated. So, the developers by default act as the de facto DBAs or in startups simply feel they need to rapidly deploy code and schema changes, unhindered by control processes, to get the product to market for customers' immediate gratification. This may be fine initially but will certainly require, as the company grows and the business matures, a segregation of duties (as discussed in the "Database Access Control and Compliance" section) and a change control process.

The nature of this challenge may be more urban legend of the "rivalry" between DBAs and developers. However, if this is the case, it is important to remember that neither the DBA nor the developer is working for themselves but for the company as a whole. When faced with this challenge myself, throughout my career, I have approached it in a way to promote the message that this is the company's directive and that all parties must collaborate as a team to meet the company's overall objectives.

Basically, as long as you have upper management behind you, and certainly you should, I have followed this tenet: if a DBA is overly strict, the developers will become untrustworthy; if the DBA over-trusts, the developers will become unruly.

Therefore, do not take a hammer approach to kicking developers out of production in one fell swoop. Instead, educate them to the need to follow protocol and try to make the developers your friend; make their lives easier, *not* harder. Explain that by creating a barrier to each developer's access to production, you are actually protecting them and insulating them from blame if the server comes crashing down or doesn't work as intended. Set up a developer's sandbox and a QA/UAT environment that will mirror production that they will have full access to. Work with them and set up regular meetings for code reviews, best-practice discussions, SQL Server scripting (deployment and rollback), ticketing, and change control processes.

All changes to the database environment must follow the standard change management process and policies. This process should follow the ITIL change management process where a change control ticket must be created for all production changes. Each change control ticket should include the following:

- Description of the change

- Reason for the change

- Documentation and scripts attached (deployment and rollback)

- Evidence/support of testing in nonproduction environment

- Risk statement/backout plan

- Ticket assignment

- Approvals (technical, PM, and, if necessary, customer)

All the previous information could also be in an e-mail chain, as long as it is saved and archived for auditing purposes.

Transaction Log

The transaction log is the primary source that is often used for auditing and database forensics. All throughout various sections of the book, I have talked a lot about the transaction log and its importance for point-in-time recovery, as well as the database recovery models. In addition, I discussed the properties and atomicity in a transaction. In this section, I will discuss the internals of the transaction log, just so you understand its ultimate importance in recovery. The transaction log architecture is a bit complex, so I will stick with the basics. The details of the transaction log can take up an entire book itself. Table 10-1 shows you all the column data stored in the transaction log.

Table 10-1. *Inside the Transaction Log*

1. CurrentLSN	27. Oldest Replicated Begin LSN	53. Rowbits Bit Value	79. File ID
2. **Operation**	28. Next Replicated End LSN	54. Number of Locks	80. Physical Name
3. Context	29. Last Distributed End LSN	55. Lock Information	81. Logical Name
4. **Transaction ID**	30. Server UID	56. LSN Before Wrties	82. Format LSN
5. Tag Bits	31. UID	57. Pages Written	83. RowsetID
6. Log Record Fixed Length	32. **SPID**	58. Data Pages Delta	84. TextPtr
7. Log Record Length	33. BeginLogStatus	59. Reserved Pages Delta	85. Column Offset
8. PreviousLSN	34. Begin Time	60. Used Pages Delta	86. Flags
9. Flag Bits	35. Transaction Name	61. Data Rows Delta	87. Text Size
10. AllocUnitID	36. Transaction SID	62. Command Type	88. Offset
11. AllocUnitName	37. End Time	63. Publication ID	89. Old Size
12. **Page ID**	38. Transaction Begin	64. Article ID	90. New Size
13. **Slot ID**	39. Replicated Records	65. Partial Status	91. Description
14. Previous Page LSN	40. Oldest Active LSN	66. Command	92. Bulk allocated extent count
15. PartionID	41. Server Name	67. Byte Offset	93. Bulk rowinsertID
16. RowFlags	42. Database Name	68. New Value	94. Bulk allocationunitID
17. Num Elements	43. Mark Name	69. Old Value	95. Bulk allocation first IAM Page ID
18. **Offset in Row**	44. Master XDESID	70. New Split Page	96. Bulk allocated extent ids
19. Checkpoint Begin	45. Master DBID	71. Rows Deleted	97. **RowLog Contents 0**
20. CHKPT Begin DB Version	46. PrepLogBegin LSN	72. Bytes Freed	98. **RowLog Contents 1**
21. MaxXDESID	47. PrepareTime	73. CI Table ID	99. RowLog Contents 2
22. Num Transactions	48. Virtual Clock	74. CI Index ID	100. RowLog Contents 3
23. Checkpoint End	49. Previous Savepoint	75. NewAllocationUnitID	101. RowLog Contents 4
24. CHKPT End DB Version	50. Savepoint Name	76. FilegroupID	
25. Minimum LSN	51. Rowbits First Bit	77. Meta Status	
26. Dirty Pages	52. Rowbits Bit Count	78. File Status	

You know already that each SQL Server database has at least one transaction log and can have multiple files making up the log. Internally transaction logs are divided into virtual log files (VLFs), which are graphically represented in Figure 10-2. VLFs are created with a new log or when there is growth of the log. A VLF is the unit of truncation for the transaction log. Physical log files consist of multiple VLFs. All transactions that occur in a database are within the VLFs and marked with log sequence numbers. The information used to recover is guided by the LSNs, which organize the transactions sequentially and allow you to restore them in order. A continuous sequence of log backups is called a *log chain*, which starts with a full backup of the database. Note that if one of the transaction logs in the chain is missing, you will not be able to restore past the previous log; you must take a new full backup immediately and start the transaction log backup process over. Each backup creates header details containing the LSN.

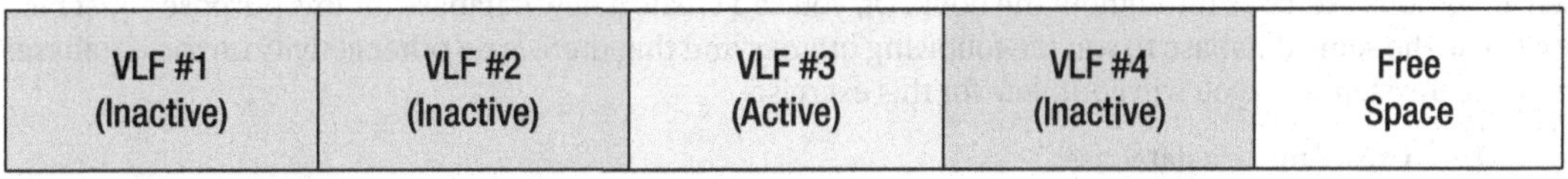

VLF #1 (Inactive)	VLF #2 (Inactive)	VLF #3 (Active)	VLF #4 (Inactive)	Free Space

Figure 10-2. Transaction log divided into VLFs

By reading the transaction log, it is possible to reverse the effects of a transaction, roll back, and recover from malicious or accidental changes. Yes, you can determine who changed what and when the change occurred by reading the transaction log; however, it is not a task I recommend for the DBA, without the use of specific third-party software tools that read and translate the transaction log. In this case, it's much more economical to employ the use of software or SQL Server features such as CDC and SQL Audit to track, capture, and recover from modifications or deletes. Reading the transaction log is an undertaking that is not really something you'd want to do in your DBA daily life. Doing so is more of an academic exercise in curiosity than a real-life scenario.

This is because the data is stored natively in the transaction log in hexadecimal format, with bytes that are intentionally swapped and endian ordered. Hexadecimal is a base-16 number system, as in [0-9] [A-F], with two hex digits representing a byte. Endian order specifies how the bytes are stored. Data is either stored in big or little endian order. In big endian, you store the *most* significant byte first, while in little endian, you store the *least* significant byte first. The standard is big endian order, but Microsoft SQL Server stores double-byte ntext data type values in little-endian byte order.

Therefore, to translate and decode the transaction log into plain English, there are several steps to be taken. You really need a Rosetta Stone type of decoding chart. Among the things you need to know to reconstruct a data row are the schema and column order of the table, whether or not the column is fixed or variable, the number and name of columns in the row, the position of the column data, and the offsets. On the internal pages of the log, you will have the page header, the data rows, and the row offset array. Data rows can be fixed or variable length. Then, you swap the bytes and translate the data types.

If you wanted to actually capture and track transaction log activity to a particular user or session, you would need to also know the server process ID (SPID), which is a unique value used by SQL Server to track a given session within the database server. In an active transaction log, you can map the transaction to a current SPID where transaction log activity is logged against the executing SPID. However, while using the transitional sys.sysprocesses system view will get you the currently active data sessions, the information here is highly volatile and has no historical trail. The transaction log will allow you to identify DML and DDL statements. Moreover, you can find out who executed the transaction because the actual login username is stored in the Transaction SID column. You can use the SUSER_SNAME function to retrieve the login username, as will be shown in the upcoming section.

Reading the Transaction Log

You can examine the contents of the transaction log using a function provided by Microsoft called fn_dblog. A simple T-SQL construct will let you output the raw contents of the SQL Server transaction log. The fn_dblog function allows you to examine the contents of the transaction log and even filter it for specific data. For example, you can filter transactions by target database object, specific columns, and SPID, as well as datetime range, which is useful in narrowing down a certain transaction that occurred. For a quick look of the information stored in the log, you can run the following:

```
Select * from fn_dblog(null,null)
```

Let's complete a short exercise in database forensics and actually translate and read the transaction log using fn_dblog. You can use the AdventureWorks2012 database that you already downloaded and have used for various exercises throughout the book. Or, you can create a new database for this purpose—just be sure to use the same database to run the following queries and that there is no other activity on the database. These are the steps that you will complete for this exercise:

1. Create the test database.

2. Create a table.

3. Insert a record.

4. Update/modify a record.

5. Get the transaction log record for the transaction ID.

6. Read/translate the transaction log for the modified row.

■ **Note** This exercise is a specific to a set of conditions, such as how data is translated for a data string, as opposed to an integer, datetime, and so on.

First, select the database and create a table called DECODE_TLOG with one column as a VARCHAR(100) using the following code. After the table is created, you will run an insert statement to insert the first record into the table, which will be "Hello World". You will then run a simple update statement to modify the record to "Find Me". Open a query window in SSMS and run the following statements, from the DECODE_TLOG script, to create the table, insert a record, and then update it:

```
Create Database DECODE_TLOG_DB
Go

Use DECODE_TLOG_DB
GO

CREATE TABLE DECODE_TLOG(COL1 VARCHAR(100));
GO
INSERT INTO DECODE_TLOG VALUES ('Hello World');
GO
UPDATE DECODE_TLOG SET COL1 = 'Find Me';
GO
```

Now you will want to look for and examine the transaction just completed. You have to start at the beginning of a transaction. In this case, you will examine the transaction of the update statement you just ran. Inside the transaction log, you will locate where the transaction began. The entry in the log you are looking for is where the log marked the start of the transaction and will appear as an LOP_BEGIN_XACT operation. The begin transaction is the only record that contains the date and time when the transaction started and the SID (LoginUserName) of the user who had issued the statement. So, let's find this transaction by querying for the begin transaction operation for where [Operation] = 'LOP_BEGIN_XACT'. It should be the last record inserted in your database transaction log, so you will run the following T-SQL code:

```
Use DECODE_TLOG_DB
Go
select [Current LSN], [Operation], [Transaction ID], [Parent Transaction ID],
    [Begin Time], [Transaction Name], [Transaction SID]
from fn_dblog(null, null)
where [Operation] = 'LOP_BEGIN_XACT'
order by [Begin Time] Desc
Go
```

You will want to find the timestamp that matches the time you ran the update statement. You will see results similar to the following:

```
Current LSN Operation Transaction ID Parent Transaction ID Begin Time Transaction Name
Transaction SID
0000003f:0000012f:0001 LOP_BEGIN_XACT 0000:000022eb NULL 2015/04/06 13:30:22:680 UPDATE
0x0105000000000000515000000112445B13A17C1C62513D89645C50000
0000003f:0000012d:0007 LOP_BEGIN_XACT 0000:000022ea NULL 2015/04/06 13:30:22:677 INSERT
0x0105000000000000515000000112445B13A17C1C62513D89645C50000
0000003f:0000012d:0001 LOP_BEGIN_XACT 0000:000022e9 NULL 2015/04/06 13:30:22:667 CREATE
TABLE 0x0105000000000000515000000112445B13A17C1C62513D89645C50000
```

Because I am using my results in this example, you will need to run the following code with the transaction ID that is generated on your system. Based on the previous results, the first transaction ID returned in the result set is 0000:000022eb; you can use this to examine a single transaction more closely. Run the following query with [Transaction ID] ='0000:000022eb'. Reviewing the results, you can see the entire transaction from beginning to end, LOP_BEGIN_XACT, then LOP_MODIFY_ROW, and finally the LOP_COMMIT_XACT to mark the end of the transaction. Everything occurs between the LOP_BEGIN_XACT and LOP_COMMIT_XACT. The LOP_BEGIN_XACT indicates this is the beginning of the transaction. LOP_COMMIT_XACT indicates the end of the transaction, and that it is committed to the database. Here LOP_MODIFY_ROW means there was an update.

```
select [Current LSN], [Operation],
    [AllocUnitName], [Page ID], [Slot ID],
    [Lock Information],
    [Num Elements], [RowLog Contents 0], [RowLog Contents 1], [RowLog Contents 2],
SUSER_SNAME([Transaction SID]) as [LoginUserName]
from fn_dblog(null, null)
where [Transaction ID]='0000:000022eb'
```

```
Current LSN Operation AllocUnitName Page ID Slot ID Lock Information Num Elements RowLog
Contents 0 RowLog Contents 1 RowLog Contents 2 LoginUserName
0000003f:0000012f:0001 LOP_BEGIN_XACT NULL NULL NULL NULL NULL NULL NULL NULL Domain\LoginName
0000003f:0000012f:0002 LOP_MODIFY_ROW dbo.DECODE_TLOG 0001:00000343 1 HoBt
720575940058571776:ACQUIRE_LOCK_IX OBJECT: 12:1028198713:0 ;ACQUIRE_LOCK_IX PAGE: 12:1:835 ;
ACQUIRE_LOCK_X RID: 12:1:835:1 6 0x160048656C6C6F20576F726C64 0x120046696E64204D65 0x NULL
0000003f:0000012f:0003 LOP_COMMIT_XACT NULL NULL NULL NULL NULL NULL NULL NULL NULL
```

Finally, with all of the information derived previously, you can construct a T-SQL statement that will give you the complete forensic footprint of the who, what, when, and where of the transaction. To wit, you will get who updated the row, with what data, when (datetime), and what database, table, and object. Using the following script, DECODE_TLOG1.sql, you will complete your first lesson in database forensics. Remember, this example is specific to a one-column table with varchar data.

```
SELECT [MainLogRec].[Transaction ID],
cast(substring([RowLog Contents 0],3,Len([RowLog Contents 0])) as varchar(max))BEFORE_UPDATE,
cast(substring([RowLog Contents 1],3,Len([RowLog Contents 1])) as varchar(max))AFTER_UPDATE,
[Operation],
    GetLoginName.[Transaction Name],
    [AllocUnitName],
    GetLoginName.LoginUserName, GetLoginName.[Begin Time],
    [Lock Information],[Page ID], [Slot ID],
    [Num Elements], [RowLog Contents 0], [RowLog Contents 1]
from
(
Select  [transaction id],cast(substring([RowLog Contents 0],3,Len([RowLog Contents 0])) as
varchar(max))BEFORE_UPDATE,
cast(substring([RowLog Contents 1],3,Len([RowLog Contents 1])) as varchar(max))AFTER_UPDATE,
[Operation],
    [AllocUnitName], [Lock Information],[Page ID], [Slot ID],
    [Num Elements], [RowLog Contents 0], [RowLog Contents 1] FROM ::fn_dblog(NULL, NULL) AS l
WHERE CHARINDEX('Hello World', l.[RowLog Contents 0]) > 0 -- Find "Hello World"
AND Operation='LOP_MODIFY_ROW'
--AND [transaction id]='0000:000022e8' --uncomment to set tran_id
) As MainLogRec
inner join
(
    Select SUSER_SNAME([Transaction SID]) as [LoginUserName], [Transaction ID], [Transaction
Name], [Begin Time]
    FROM ::fn_dblog(NULL, NULL)
    WHERE /*[transaction id]='0000:000022e8'*/ ----uncomment to set tran_id
    Operation='LOP_BEGIN_XACT'
) As GetLoginName
  On [MainLogRec].[transaction id]=GetLoginName.[transaction id]
```

You will return the translated data as shown next. The record set is broken up here so you can better see the values.

Transaction ID	BEFORE_UPDATE	AFTER_UPDATE	Operation	Transaction Name
0000:000022e8	Hello World Find Me	LOP_MODIFY_ROW	UPDATE	dbo.DECODE_TLOG

AllocUnitName	LoginUserName	Begin Time
CORP\Q07642	2015/04/06	11:14:57:003

```
Lock Information Page ID Slot ID Num Elements RowLog Contents 0 RowLog Contents 1
HoBt 72057594058571776:ACQUIRE_LOCK_IX OBJECT: 12:1028198713:0 ;ACQUIRE_LOCK_IX
PAGE: 12:1:835 ;ACQUIRE_LOCK_X RID: 12:1:835:0 0001:00000343 0 6
0x160048656C6C6F20576F726C64 0x120046696E64204D65
```

So, even though it *is* possible to read the transaction log, it's just too much information to attempt to reconstruct every row or all inserted, updated, or deleted data. Reading the log using fn_dblog may come in handy some time, but don't rely on fn_dblog. The system function fn_dblog is an "undocumented" function, which means it is not officially supported by Microsoft and could change in any version. There are third-party recovery solutions out there that read and recover deleted and modified data from the transaction log. Let's move on now to more practical ways to audit and capture data and other changes using native features out of the box.

C2 Auditing and Common Criteria Compliance

C2 Auditing and Common Criteria options are intended for specific compliance requirements and are not generally used. If you have no specific legal reason to use them, you should not and should consider other auditing options for your SQL Server instances. You should be aware of these configurable audit options, but I will not elaborate on them because they are rarely used. To learn more about them, you can visit the following URLs:

- Common Criteria Compliance: https://technet.microsoft.com/en-us/library/bb153837%28v=sql.105%29.aspx

- C2 Auditing: https://msdn.microsoft.com/en-us/library/ms187634.aspx

In addition, keep in mind that from a resource use point of view, these auditing options are extremely intensive and can take up huge amounts of disk space fairly quickly. In addition, these options are an all-or-none proposition, meaning that they are configured to stop the instance if audit data can no longer be written, usually because of running out of disk space. The last thing you desire is for some audit process to bring down your production servers.

C2 Auditing has been depreciated and will be removed in a future version of SQL Server. You can enable these options from the Server Properties screen, as in Figure 10-3, or you can enable them via sp_configure. The ability to enable Common Criteria compliance via sp_configure was added in SQL Server 2012. Here are the statements to enable them. Do not enable both!

```
sp_configure 'c2 audit mode', 1 --enable c2 audit
go
sp_configure 'common criteria compliance enabled',1 --enable
go
```

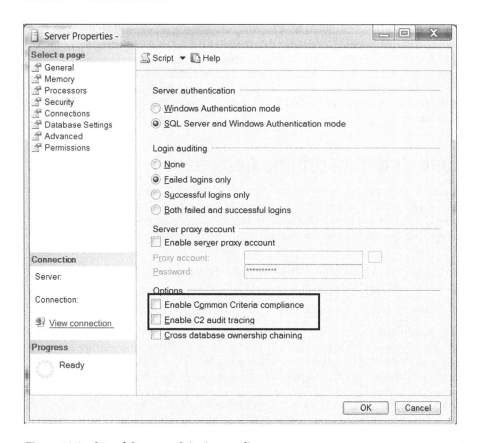

Figure 10-3. *C2 and Common Criteria compliance*

SQL Audit

SQL Audit was introduced in SQL Server versions 2008. The SQL Server Audit feature in SQL Server 2008 is intended to replace SQL Trace as the preferred auditing solution. SQL Audit uses and is built upon Extended Events to audit SQL Server events. Since it is leveraging Extended Events, it is intended to be fast and lightweight to capture audit data without major performance overhead, unlike its bulkier predecessor SQL Trace. It is relatively easy to set up and enable, although the myriad of events it can capture do not make it the most intuitive tool. You can use T-SQL as well to set it up, but clearly there is a visual advantage to using and managing it with SSMS. Once all your audit specifications are set up, you can easily script it so you can deploy your custom audit processes to multiple SQL Server instances. SQL Server Audit was designed with the following objectives:

- *Security*: The audit feature, and its objects, must be truly secure.

- *Performance*: The performance impact must be minimized.

- *Management*: The audit feature must be easy to manage.

- *Discoverability*: Questions concerning the audit must be easy to answer.

At the top level, SQL Audit allows you to audit both instance-level and database-level events. SQL Audit is a comprehensive auditing platform that offers a high level of granularity. You can define audits to capture SELECT, INSERT, UPDATE, DELETE, REFERENCES, and EXECUTE statements for individual users at the object level. Not only can you audit for changes that are made via insert, update, and delete, but the mere act of reading the database through SELECT statements can also be captured. This means, for example, you can track users and potential intruders to databases that shouldn't even be reading sensitive and personal information.

The Server Audit object describes the target for audit data, plus some top-level configuration settings. Think of a Server Audit object as the destination for audit data. This destination can be a file, the Windows Application log, or the Windows Security log. The allowable delay for writing events to the destination can also be configured on this object. Note that the Server Audit object contains no information about what is being audited, just where the audit data is going. Multiple Server Audit objects can be defined, with each object being specified and operational independent from one another. A server audit can be enabled or disabled only outside of the scope of an active transaction.

The Server Audit Specification object describes what to audit at the server level. As its name suggests, this object is focused on server instance-wide actions. A Server Audit Specification object is associated with a Server Audit object in order to define where the audit data is written. There is a one-to-one relationship between the Server Audit Specification object and the Server Audit object. However, a single audit can have one server specification and one database-level specification.

The Database Audit Specification object also describes what to audit. But, as its name suggests, this object is focused on actions that occur in a specific database. Where the audit data is written is defined by the association of a database audit specification with a Server Audit object. Each database audit specification can be associated with only one server audit. A server audit, for its part, can be associated with only one database audit specification per database.

In SQL Server Management Studio, server audits are created and managed in the Audits folder, which is under the server-level Security folder. They are quite simple to enable.

Creating an Audit in SQL Server Management Studio

To enable and configure SQL Audit, the easiest way is to use SSMS and navigate down the tree and expand the Security folder. Select and right-click the folder Audits and then New Audit. The Audit Properties dialog will appear, as in Figure 10-4. Here you are presented with several audit configuration options. As of SQL Server 2012, some notable options were added, specifically, what to do on audit log failure. Previously, the only option was to shut down SQL Server, or not, but now you have three options available. You can choose Continue, regardless of whether audit information is recorded. The next option is Shutdown Server, which gives me goose bumps thinking about it. The third option is Fail Operation, which will prevent audit data from being written for a particular operation, but at least it will not affect the whole server.

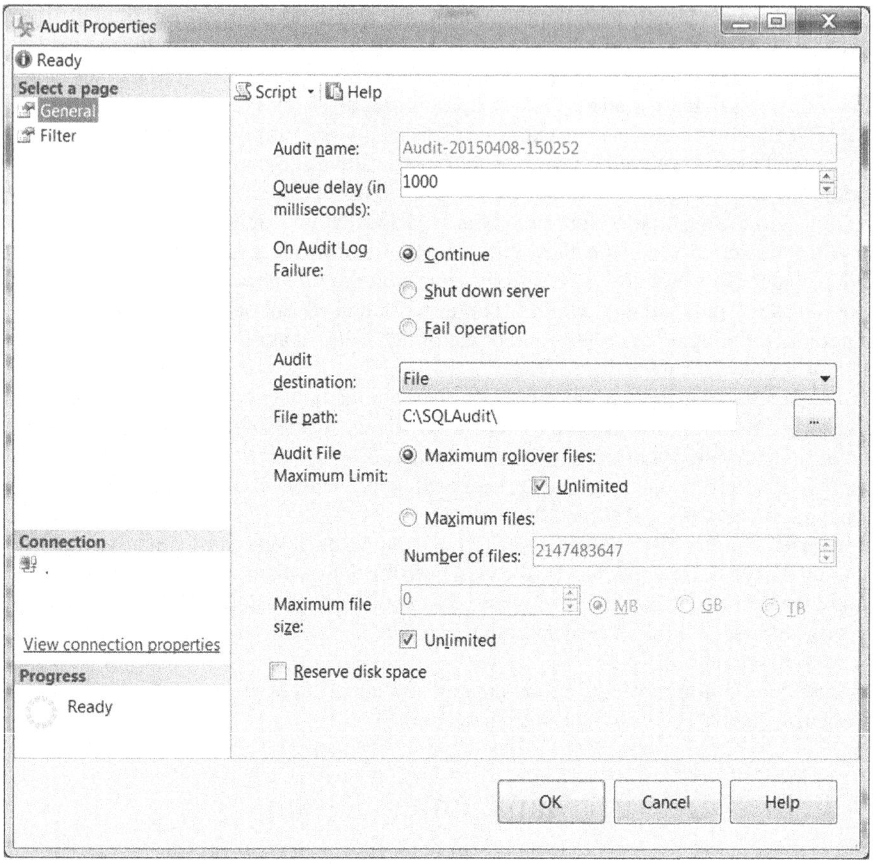

Figure 10-4. *Creating an audit in SQL Server Management Studio*

You will give the audit a name and a destination and set where the audit data will be logged. These options include a file, the Windows Application log, or the Windows Security log (which requires further configuration). Queue Delay specifies how long to wait on a transaction before processing audit actions. By default, Queue Delay, which is set in milliseconds, is set at 1000ms (1 second). The Queue Delay default setting is usually sufficient, even under heavy load, but do not set this property to zero. You don't want audit actions processed synchronously because this may cause some performance overhead.

Next are the settings for maximum files and maximum rollover files. When the maximum number of rollover files, specified by the user, is reached, the oldest file will be overwritten. Once the maximum of the "Maximum files" option is reached, it will cause all further auditing writes to fail. I suggest you skip the "Maximum files" option and instead opt for rollover files. However, I would implement a file-copy process to copy the audit files off the server on a regular basis. Copying these files will allow you to preserve audit logs and create a historical archive. You will also be able to set the maximum file size for each audit file in megabytes, gigabytes, and even terabytes, or you can just check unlimited size.

One great addition for SQL Audit in SQL Server 2012 is the option to filter out any unwanted activity or objects from the audit output. To do this, select the Filter page, enter something like `database_name='AdventureWorks2012'`, and click OK.

After you have created the initial audit, right-click the new entry and select Enable Audit. You should get
a success message, as shown in Figure 10-5.

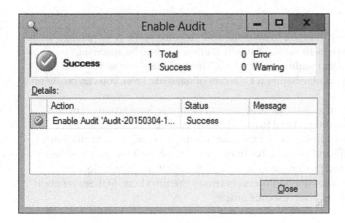

Figure 10-5. *Audit successfully enabled*

You can then check on the current status of the audit by executing this T-SQL:

```
SELECT name,status_desc, audit_file_path FROM sys.dm_server_audit_status
```

The results will show you the name of the audit, the status (stopped or started), and the name
status_desc audit_file_path.

```
Audit-20150408-150252 STARTED C:\SQLAudit\Audit-20150408-150252_3550C2CC-9E61-417A-B045-
53D226155792_0_130733200041640000.sqlaudit
```

You can also go back any time to the SQL Audit object you created, in SSMS, and script it for future use.
This is best practice once you define your audits and specifications for rapid deployment and recovery of
your audit definitions. Right-click the Audit object in SSMS and select Script Audit as ➤ CREATE to ➤ New
Query Editor Window. The T-SQL to create and define your SQL Audit options is shown next, in the disabled
state. You would need to change it to STATE=ON to enable it via script.

```
USE [master]
GO
CREATE SERVER AUDIT [Audit-20150408-150252]
TO FILE
(    FILEPATH = N'C:\SQLAudit\'
    ,MAXSIZE = 0 MB
    ,MAX_ROLLOVER_FILES = 2147483647
    ,RESERVE_DISK_SPACE = OFF
)
```

```
WITH
(    QUEUE_DELAY = 1000
    ,ON_FAILURE = CONTINUE
    ,AUDIT_GUID = '3550c2cc-9e61-417a-b045-53d226155792'
)
WHERE ([database_name]='AdventureWorks2012')
ALTER SERVER AUDIT [Audit-20150408-150252] WITH (STATE = OFF)/*change to STATE=ON" to
enable*/"
GO
```

The Audit object you just created deals with where to write the audit records and how to manage them but doesn't actually tell SQL Server which events to audit. That information needs to be specified. Once you define your Audit object, you have to create your audit specifications. This includes both server-level and database-level audit specifications. Keep in mind, whether it's a server or database level, you can create only one audit specification per audit.

The SQL Server Audit feature enables you to audit server-level and database-level groups of events and individual events. A server audit specification is used to audit events that occur at the server level such as logins, creating or dropping databases, linked server creation, permission and ownership changes, and more. A database audit specification will audit events that occur at the database level such as schema changes (create, alter, drop) executing a stored procedure, creating a user, and dropping a table.

Because there are too many server and database audit-level events to mention here, SQL Server audit action groups are described in the following TechNet resource article:

```
http://technet.microsoft.com/en-us/library/cc280663.aspx
```

If you are so inclined, you can query the sys.dm_audit_actions system view for every audit action and audit action group that can be recorded and configured in the audit log for SQL Server Audit. As of version SQL 2014, there are more than 500 such actions.

```
select action_id,name,class_desc,covering_parent_action_name from sys.dm_audit_actions
```

Server Audit Specification

In addition to using SSMS, server audit specifications can be created with the CREATE SERVER AUDIT SPECIFICATION statement. The server audit specification collects many server-level action groups raised by Extended Events. You can create a simple server audit specification with the following example using SSMS.

Under the Security ➤ Audit folder, find the Server Audit Specification folder and right-click. Select New Server Audit Specification from the pop-up menu. Doing so opens a dialog box. Give the specification a name and select the previously created audit.

You can give the specification any name relevant to the specified audit events you will select. You will select one example here. Choose Database_Change_Group for Audit Action Type as shown in Figure 10-6, and click OK. This action relates to the event that is raised when a database is created, altered, or dropped.

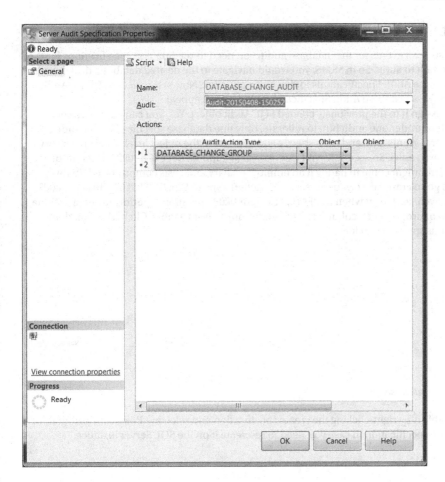

Figure 10-6. *Creating the server audit specification*

Now, just as you did before, you can script the server audit specification and build a deployment script. Navigate using Object Explorer in SSMS to the Server Audit Specifications folder, right-click, and select "Script Server Audit Specification as." Then select CREATE to, and finally select New Query Editor Window. You will see the specification defined as shown here, again in disabled state:

```
USE [master]
GO
CREATE SERVER AUDIT SPECIFICATION [DATABASE_CHANGE_AUDIT]
FOR SERVER AUDIT [Audit-20150408-150252]
ADD (DATABASE_CHANGE_GROUP)
WITH (STATE = OFF) /*change to STATE= ON to enable*/
GO
```

343

Database Audit Specification

To configure the database-level events for the database audit, you need to set database specifications for the particular database you want to audit. So in SSMS, you would navigate to the desired database, drill down to the Security folder's Database Audit Specifications folder, and right-click. Now select New Database Audit Specification. The Create New Database Audit Specification window will appear.

Give it a name and assign it to the previously created SQL Audit object. Yes, you can have both server and database specifications under one audit but, to reiterate, only one database specification per audit.

You can choose several events here and even specify audits down to the object level. You can get very detailed with your database audits. So, example, you can choose to audit for DELETE or UPDATE events of a specific table or tables. This might come in handy if an employee salary table was compromised. In this simple example, I won't go so granular, so you can set Audit Action Type to SCHEMA_OBJECT_CHANGE_GROUP. This action will raise an event and log it when a CREATE, ALTER, or DROP operation is performed on a schema, such as a table is created or dropped or a column is added or removed from a table. Click OK when done. Figure 10-7 shows how this specification looks.

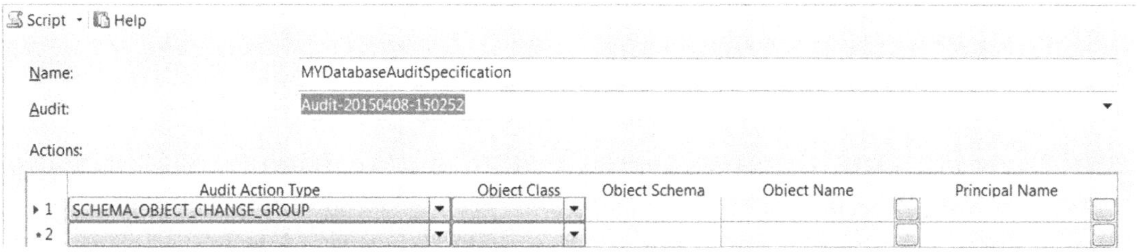

Figure 10-7. *Creating the database specification*

You should also enable it by right-clicking the create specification and selecting Enable. In addition, be sure to script the database specification in case you need to re-create it on the SQL Server instance.

```
USE [YourDatabase_2B_Audited]
GO
CREATE DATABASE AUDIT SPECIFICATION [MYDatabaseAuditSpecification]
FOR SERVER AUDIT [Audit-20150408-150252]
ADD (SCHEMA_OBJECT_CHANGE_GROUP)
WITH (STATE = OFF)/*change to STATE=ON to enable*/
GO
```

Generating Audit Activity

With your audit and specifications created in the previous sections, let's simulate some activity that will trigger the selected audit events and then view them in the log. Let's first perform some server-level activity and create and drop a sample database. You can run the following in your query editor in SSMS, with separators (GO) and a built-in delay of ten seconds between each operation. Don't worry about not seeing the database, which is the point of auditing. You can increase the delay or run the CREATE and DROP operations separately.

```
Create Database "DetectThisDB"
Go
WAITFOR DELAY '00:00:10'
Go
Drop Database "DetectThisDB"
GO
```

Now, generate some simple database activity. Create a table in the audited database (in my case AdventureWorks2012) to first create a table with one column and then add another column after.

```
USE [AdventureWorks2012]
CREATE Table "AuditMe"
        (col1 nvarchar(50)
        )
Go
WAITFOR DELAY '00:00:10'
Go
ALTER Table "AuditMe"
    ADD col2 int
GO
```

After the previous statements are executed, you should have triggered server-level and database-level events for CREATE DATABASE, DROP DATABASE, CREATE TABLE, and ALTER TABLE...ADD.

Viewing the Audit Log

Now that you have set up your SQL Audit server and database specifications and generated some server/database event activity, you can see the actual audit data captured by viewing the audit log in SSMS. To view the audit log in SSMS, simply navigate to the Audit folder where you created and have your existing SQL Audit object. Right-click the Audit object and select View Audit Logs from the pop-up menu. You will see some of the audit data reflecting all the actions you've taken via the scripts provided earlier. I have rearranged some of the columns to highlight the most relevant data captured for this audit, as displayed in Figure 10-8. You can also examine the other column data by expanding the window.

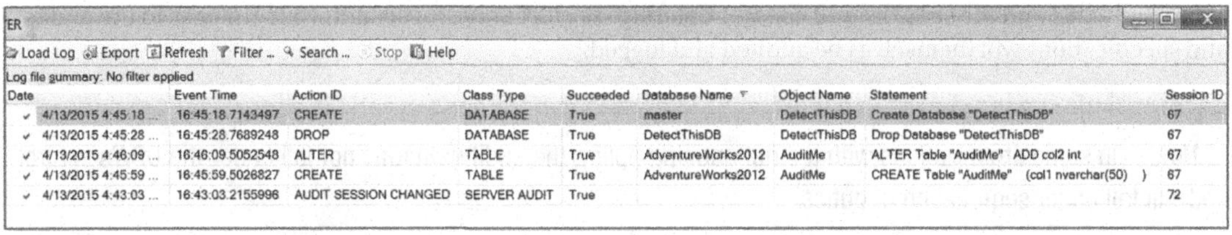

Date	Event Time	Action ID	Class Type	Succeeded	Database Name ▼	Object Name	Statement	Session ID
4/13/2015 4:45:18 ...	16:45:18.7143497	CREATE	DATABASE	True	master	DetectThisDB	Create Database "DetectThisDB"	67
4/13/2015 4:45:28 ...	16:45:28.7689248	DROP	DATABASE	True	DetectThisDB	DetectThisDB	Drop Database "DetectThisDB"	67
4/13/2015 4:46:09 ...	16:46:09.5052548	ALTER	TABLE	True	AdventureWorks2012	AuditMe	ALTER Table "AuditMe" ADD col2 int	67
4/13/2015 4:45:59 ...	16:45:59.5026827	CREATE	TABLE	True	AdventureWorks2012	AuditMe	CREATE Table "AuditMe" (col1 nvarchar(50))	67
4/13/2015 4:43:03 ...	16:43:03.2155996	AUDIT SESSION CHANGED	SERVER AUDIT	True				72

Log file summary: No filter applied

Load Log ⊗ *Export* ⊞ *Refresh* ▼ *Filter ...* ⚲ *Search ...* Stop ⓘ *Help*

Figure 10-8. Viewing audit log activity in SSMS

In addition, you can use the system function sys.fn_get_audit_file to read into and return information from an audit file created by a server audit in SQL Server. You can specify the exact file location and path to read a specific audit log file or use * to read all existing ones and select only the most relevant column data, as follows:

```
SELECT
event_time,
succeeded,
object_id,
server_principal_name,
server_instance_name,
database_name,
```

```
schema_name,
object_name,
statement FROM
sys.fn_get_audit_file (('<Audit File Path and Name>',default,default);
GO
```

The results will appear similar to the following output:

```
event_time succeeded object_id server_principal_name server_instance_name database_name
schema_name object_name statement
2015-04-13 16:43:03.2155996 1 0 domain\loginname MYSQLServer
2015-04-13 16:45:18.7143497 1 10 domain\loginname MYSQLServer master  DetectThisDB Create
Database "DetectThisDB"
2015-04-13 16:45:28.7689248 1 10 domain\loginname MYSQLServer DetectThisDB  DetectThisDB
Drop Database "DetectThisDB"
2015-04-13 16:45:59.5026827 1 1380199967 domain\loginname MYSQLServer AdventureWorks2012
dbo AuditMe CREATE Table "AuditMe"
        (col1 nvarchar(50)
        )
2015-04-13 16:46:09.5052548 1 1380199967 domain\loginname MYSQLServer AdventureWorks2012
dbo AuditMe ALTER Table "AuditMe"
    ADD col2 int
```

This section ought to get you started on setting up and configuring your own SQL Audit settings, as well as creating server and database specifications. Here are some final notes about SQL Audit. To examine and persist audit data, consider loading the previous query results to a history table. A central server repository to house all the audit data of multiple SQL Server instances may be desirable, in terms of centralized data as well as security. Keep in mind if you need to alter the audit or any of the specifications, the audit must be in a disabled state, and the same as well goes for deleting specifications. By default, your changes to the audits and specifications will themselves be audited and logged.

■ **Note**   In some organizations with a strict auditing policy, the audit data may not fall under the DBA's control and will fall under segregation of duties.

Finally, you need to be aware that the file location and folders need to be secured and locked down because it is easy to delete these log files if the user has access to them. For a comprehensive overview of SQL Server Audit feature, you can read the SQL Server 2008 white paper, located here:

```
https://technet.microsoft.com/en-us/library/dd392015(v=sql.100).aspx
```

DDL Triggers

DDL triggers were first introduced in SQL Server 2005, as a special kind of trigger that fire in response to Data Definition Language (DDL) statements. They can be used to perform administrative tasks in the database such as auditing (DDL) events and control database operations and preventing changes happening to a database. You can use DDL statements to regulate commands such as CREATE, DROP, and ALTER that are used against objects. For example, you can create a trigger to flag, identify, and roll back a DROP TABLE command to prevent tables from being dropped.

DDL triggers, like regular triggers, fire in response to an event. However, unlike DML triggers, they do not fire in response to UPDATE, INSERT, and DELETE statements on a table or view. Instead, they fire in response to a variety of DDL events. These events primarily correspond to Transact-SQL statements that start with the keywords CREATE, ALTER, and DROP. Certain system stored procedures that perform DDL-like operations can also fire DDL triggers. You can create, for example, a DDL trigger for ALL login events on SQL Server by running the following CREATE trigger statement:

```
CREATE Trigger on ALL Server for DDL_LOGIN_Events
```

And now if you wanted to raise a message in response to triggering a server-level login event, you can construct the T-SQL as follows:

```
Create trigger ddl_trigger_logins on ALL Server for DDL_LOGIN_Events
 as Print 'You cannot create Logins in this server. This action is not permitted'
Rollback;
```

To test this, open a new query window and execute the following:

```
CREATE LOGIN PleaseCreateMyLogin WITH PASSWORD = 'AintGonnaHappen';
GO
```

You will receive the following error message:

```
You cannot create Logins in this server. This action is not permitted.
Msg 3609, Level 16, State 2, Line 1
The transaction ended in the trigger. The batch has been aborted.
```

You can also create a DDL trigger to respond to database events, such a CREATE, ALTER, and DROP objects. The syntax for this for tables is as follows:

```
CREATE Trigger test_ddl_dbtrigger on Database for CREATE_TABLE, DROP_TABLE, ALTER_TABLE
```

To raise an error and prevent any attempts of creating new tables, create this trigger:

```
Create TRIGGER ddl_database_prevent_tables ON DATABASE
 FOR CREATE_TABLE AS PRINT 'CREATE TABLE Issued.'
select eventdata() RAISERROR
('New tables cannot be created in this database.', 16, 1) ROLLBACK ;
```

```
Test the database DDL trigger just created by issuing the following tsql statement:
Create Table NoChance (
col1 nchar(50)
)
```

An error will be returned, and the CREATE TABLE will be rolled back. You get results with EVENTDATA(), which returns data when referenced directly inside a DDL or logon trigger.

```
CREATE TABLE Issued.
Msg 50000, Level 16, State 1, Procedure ddl_database_prevent_tables, Line 1
New tables cannot be created in this database.
Msg 3609, Level 16, State 2, Line 1
The transaction ended in the trigger. The batch has been aborted.
```

To disable the DDL triggers, you can run this:

```
USE Database;
GO
DISABLE Trigger ALL ON ALL SERVER;
GO
```

■ **Caution**   Be aware when running the previous script with ALL because it will in fact disable all DDL server triggers. You can replace ALL with the actual name of the individual trigger.

In sum, you can use DDL triggers for the following:

- To prevent certain changes to your database schema

- To have something occur in the database in response to a change in your database schema

- To record changes or events in the database schema

To get more information about DDL triggers, you can refer the MSDN library at http://msdn.microsoft.com/en-us/library/ms184304.aspx.

Default Trace

The first thing most people want to know when learning about the default trace is, what information does it capture? You were introduced to the default trace, the events it captures, and how to check and ensure that it's running in Chapter 5. There are a number of events that are captured for you by the default trace, and many of these can assist you with your system audit, keeping track of and reporting on certain changes, such as dropping or altering a table, as well as a myriad of database, audit, and security events. The default trace contains useful information for audit purposes, including but not limited to the complete authentication history, SQL Server configuration changes, DDL operations (schema changes), and the IP addresses of SQL Server client connections.

In this chapter, however, you will apply the default trace to real auditing scenarios and use it to track certain events, specifically, laying out a beginning-to-end process to capture changes to SQL Server configurations. This is the information you get when you run sp_configure, and the information stored in sys.configurations. If you want to capture and be alerted when, for example, xp_cmdshell is turned on or there are changes to the max/min memory settings, maximum degrees of parallelism, and more, this process will allow you to do this.

Reviewing the Default Trace Output

The default trace records these useful events to a trace file, which can be loaded and reviewed in SQL Profiler or queried using the fn_trace_gettable(@trcpath) system function. The options available to allow you to read and query the output are as follows:

- Query window, fn_trace_gettable()

- SQL Server Profiler

- Schema Changes History report (via SSMS, as shown in Figure 10-9)

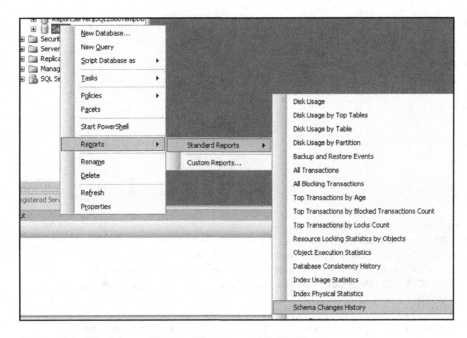

Figure 10-9. The Schema Changes History report in SSMS

Since you already brushed up on SQL Profiler in Chapter 5, I will demonstrate the power and usefulness of the default trace using T-SQL and other components out of the box.

Let's first start with a simple example to capture the DELETION of a database table in the AdventureWorks2012 database. You'll create a quick sample table to use to keep the database intact. Execute the following T-SQL against the AdventureWorks2012 database:

```
CREATE TABLE [dbo].[DropThisTableNow](
    [Col1] [nchar](10) NULL,
    [Col2] [nchar](10) NULL
) ON [PRIMARY]

GO
```

Verify that the table has been successfully created; check out in SSMS if it exists. Once confirmed, go ahead and subsequently drop the table:

```
USE [AdventureWorks2012]
GO
DROP TABLE [dbo].[DropThisTableNow]
GO
```

Observe that the [DropThisTableNow] table has been dropped; you can now interrogate your default trace file for this event using the GetDeletedTableTrc script, which searches on EventClass=47, which is the Object:Delete event.

```
DECLARE @path NVARCHAR(260);

SELECT
   @path = REVERSE(SUBSTRING(REVERSE([path]),
   CHARINDEX(CHAR(92), REVERSE([path])), 260)) + N'log.trc'
FROM    sys.traces
WHERE   is_default = 1;

SELECT
  LoginName,
  HostName,
  StartTime,
  ObjectName,
  TextData
FROM sys.fn_trace_gettable(@path, DEFAULT)
WHERE EventClass = 47      -- Object:Deleted
AND EventSubClass = 1 -- represents a single pass over the data
--AND DatabaseName = N'ENTER-DB_NAME' -- you can filter for a specific database
--AND ObjectName = N'ENTER-OBJ-TABLENAME' -- you can filter on a specicific object
ORDER BY StartTime DESC;
```

The results will tell you who dropped what, where, and when, which can be extremely valuable in tracking down the culprit and can be used for auditing. You could potentially receive much more information with this script, such as previous trigger event data.

LoginName	HostName	StartTime	ObjectName	TextData
AD\HisLogin	CND4142V71	2015-03-03 12:09:36.110	Table_DropThisShitNow	NULL

Using the Default Trace to Capture SQL Server Configuration Changes

With the default trace, you know you can capture when a change is made, who made the change, and which option was changed. It will trace data for event class 22, which is the ErrorLog event.

Here are the overall requirements:

- Default trace enabled

- Database Mail turned on and configured with at least some profile

- Creation of a history/tracking table

- Creation of a stored procedure

- Capture and alert on SQL Server configuration changes

By using the default trace, combined with fn_trace_gettable, sp_send_dbmail, a custom tracking table, and a stored procedure, you can capture all of the configuration changes. Let's check out how this works.

Once a SQL Server is initially configured, you probably would love nothing but to "set it and forget it." However, in the real world, especially with multiple SQL Server environments to manage, you need to keep track of any changes to the configuration that could impact the environment. As a DBA, you need to be aware of any ad hoc changes and ideally be alerted to address the issue.

In SQL Server 2008, Microsoft introduced the Policy Management Framework (or policy-based management). This powerful new framework allows DBAs to define a set of policies that can control several aspects of SQL Server. For example, the DBA can define a policy that specifies how a particular configuration option should be set on all the servers in the enterprise. Based on a particular facet, a policy can evaluate a condition as true or false and then log or prevent an unauthorized action. In this section, I'll offer a solution where you can use the SQL Server default trace, which is a lightweight server-side trace running continuously in the background. Let's check out how this works.

Creating the History Tracking Table

The purpose of this table is twofold. First, it will store and archive all configuration changes that can be reported on. Second, when dynamically retrieving and querying the trace for any configuration changes, it will capture only the latest changes. It does this by comparing the EventSequence column, which is a unique row identifier and is the order in which the trace event occurred. Because the trace is an ongoing continuous process, it will always contain older changes as well. By comparing the result sets where EventSequence does not exist in this table, you can ensure there are no duplicate occurrences.

You'll either want to use an existing administrator database or create a database where this table will reside. You can first simple create the database, if needed, using this code:

```
Create Database AdminDB
Go
```

Now, let's create the tracking table in the database just created or an existing one.

```
/****** Object: Table [dbo].[SQLConfig_Changes] ******/
SET ANSI_NULLS ON
GO
SET QUOTED_IDENTIFIER ON
GO
SET ANSI_PADDING ON
GO

CREATE TABLE [dbo].[SQLConfig_Changes](
[TextData] [varchar](500) NULL,
[HostName] [varchar](155) NULL,
[ApplicationName] [varchar](255) NULL,
[DatabaseName] [varchar](155) NULL,
[LoginName] [varchar](155) NULL,
[SPID] [int] NULL,
[StartTime] [datetime] NULL,
[EventSequence] [int] NULL
) ON [PRIMARY]
GO

SET ANSI_PADDING OFF
GO
```

Methodology

Now that you have your table created, I'll discuss each portion of the code to capture the SQL configuration changes.

1. Create a temp table, matching the definition of the dbo.SQLConfig_Change table to capture the needed data from the trace.

```
CREATE TABLE #temp_cfg (
TEXTData VARCHAR(500),
HostName VARCHAR(155),
ApplicationName VARCHAR(255),
DatabaseName VARCHAR(155),
LoginName VARCHAR(155),
SPID INT,
StartTime DATETIME,
EventSequence INT
)
```

2. Query for the physical path of the current active trace file on your SQL Server.

```
DECLARE @trc_path VARCHAR(500)
SELECT @trc_path=CONVERT(VARCHAR(500),value) FROM fn_trace_getinfo(DEFAULT)
WHERE property=2
SELECT @trc_path
```

3. Next, you will query the trace to capture the needed data for the fn_trace_gettable function, and filter the data with the predicate TextData like '%configure%'. The event will be inserted to your SQLConfig_Changes table only if it has not already been captured. You also order by the StartTime descending, so you can force the latest data to the top of the query results.

```
INSERT INTO #temp_cfg
SELECT TEXTData,HostName,ApplicationName,DatabaseName,LoginName,SPID,StartTime,EventSequence
FROM fn_trace_gettable(@trc_path,1) fn
WHERE TEXTData LIKE '%configure%'
AND SPID<>@@spid
AND fn.EventSequence NOT IN (SELECT EventSequence FROM SQLConfig_Changes)
AND TEXTData NOT LIKE '%Insert into #temp_cfg%'
ORDER BY StartTime DESC
```

4. At this point, you insert the new rows from the temp table #temp_cfg into the dbo.SQLConfig_Changes table.

```
INSERT INTO dbo.SQLConfig_Changes
SELECT * FROM #temp_cfg
```

Finally, you will invoke the Database Mail feature to alert you to any new configuration changes on the server. (This use of Database Mail must be set up in advance). Because #temp_cfg contains the new data, you check to see whether in fact the table is populated by issuing the command in this script: If @@ROWCOUNT > 0. So, only if there are any rows, meaning configuration changes have been made since the last time it ran, it will send an e-mail alert. You use a cursor to interrogate the temp table's data row-by-row and send out one e-mail alert for each configuration change detected. You can also truncate the message to show only the text message of the configuration change and eliminate the "Run the RECONFIGURE statement to install" message.

```
IF @@ROWCOUNT > 0
--select @@ROWCOUNT
BEGIN
DECLARE c CURSOR FOR
SELECT LTRIM(REPLACE(SUBSTRING(TEXTdata,31,250), '. Run the RECONFIGURE statement to
install.', ''))
FROM #temp_cfg

OPEN c
FETCH NEXT FROM c INTO @textdata
WHILE (@@FETCH_STATUS <> -1)
BEGIN
--FETCH c INTO @textdata

SELECT @message = @textdata + 'on server ' + @@servername + CHAR(13)

EXEC msdb.dbo.sp_send_dbmail --@profile_name='ProfileName - otherwise will use default
profile',
@recipients='SQLAdmin@SomeSQLCompany.com',
@subject='SQL Server Configuration Change Alert',
@body=@message

FETCH NEXT FROM c INTO @textdata
END
CLOSE c
DEALLOCATE c
END
DROP TABLE #temp_cfg
```

Creating the Stored Procedure

Now that you understand each part of the code, you can put all of it together and compile it into a stored procedure, called usp_Capture_SQL_Config_Changes. This stored procedure requires only one parameter, @SendMailTo, which consists of the e-mail recipients for the alerts.

```
SET NOCOUNT ON
GO

CREATE PROCEDURE dbo.usp_Capture_SQL_Config_Changes @SendEmailTo VARCHAR(255) AS

CREATE TABLE #temp_cfg (
TEXTData VARCHAR(500),
HostName VARCHAR(155),
ApplicationName VARCHAR(255),
DatabaseName VARCHAR(155),
LoginName VARCHAR(155),
```

```
SPID INT,
StartTime DATETIME,
EventSequence INT
)

DECLARE @trc_path VARCHAR(500),
@message VARCHAR(MAX),
@message1 VARCHAR(MAX),
@textdata VARCHAR(1000)

SELECT @trc_path=CONVERT(VARCHAR(500),value) FROM fn_trace_getinfo(DEFAULT)
WHERE property=2

INSERT INTO #temp_cfg
SELECT TEXTData,HostName,ApplicationName,DatabaseName,LoginName,SPID,StartTime,EventSequence
FROM fn_trace_gettable(@trc_path,1) fn
WHERE TEXTData LIKE '%configure%'
AND fn.EventSequence NOT IN (SELECT EventSequence FROM SQLConfig_Changes)
AND TEXTData NOT LIKE '%Insert into #temp_cfg%'
ORDER BY StartTime DESC

INSERT INTO dbo.SQLConfig_Changes
SELECT * FROM #temp_cfg

/*select TextData,HostName,ApplicationName,DatabaseName,LoginName,SPID,StartTime,EventSequence
from fn_trace_gettable(@trc_path,1) fn
where TextData like '%configure%'
and SPID<>@@spid
and fn.EventSequence not in (select EventSequence from SQLConfig_Changes)
order by StartTime desc*/

--select * from SQLConfig_Changes

IF @@ROWCOUNT > 0
--select @@ROWCOUNT

BEGIN
DECLARE c CURSOR FOR

SELECT LTRIM(REPLACE(SUBSTRING(TEXTdata,31,250), '. Run the RECONFIGURE statement to
install.', ''))
FROM #temp_cfg

OPEN c

FETCH NEXT FROM c INTO @textdata
```

```
WHILE (@@FETCH_STATUS <> -1)
BEGIN
--FETCH c INTO @textdata

SELECT @message = @textdata + 'on server ' + @@servername + CHAR(13)

EXEC msdb.dbo.sp_send_dbmail --@profile_name='ProfileName - otherwise will use default
profile',
@recipients=@SendEmailTo,
@subject='SQL Server Configuration Change Alert',
@body=@message

FETCH NEXT FROM c INTO @textdata

END
CLOSE c
DEALLOCATE c

END

DROP TABLE #temp_cfg
```

Testing the Process

Once you have created the table and stored procedure as well as ensured that the default trace and Database Mail are enabled, you are ready to test your process in a test environment. The easiest way to test this logic is to start changing some of the configuration options with the sp_configure system stored procedure. Let's turn on Ad Hoc Distributed Queries, for example.

```
sp_configure 'show advanced options',1
GO
RECONFIGURE WITH override
GO

sp_configure 'Ad Hoc Distributed Queries',1
GO
RECONFIGURE WITH override
GO
```

You should see the query output as follows:

```
"Configuration option 'Ad Hoc Distributed Queries' changed from 1 to 1. Run the RECONFIGURE
statement to install."
```

Now, go to any query window on the server and run your stored procedure.

```
exec dbo.usp_Capture_SQL_Config_Changes 'SQLDBA@SomeSQLCompany.com'
```

With everything set up properly, within seconds you should see a message in your inbox, as in Figure 10-10.

```
Cc:
Subject:        SQL Server Configuration Change Alert

Configuration option 'Ad Hoc Distributed Queries' changed from 1 to 0 on server NCSQL2K8DEV01
```

Figure 10-10. *Configuration change alert*

In addition, you can query the SQLConfig_Changes table to return configuration change history.

```
SELECT *
FROM dbo.SQLConfig_Changes
ORDER BY StartTime DESC

 HostName Application DatabaseName LoginName SPID StartTime
Configuration option 'Ad Hoc Distributed Queries changed from 0 to 1 MYSQLCLIENT Microsoft
SQL Server SQLCentric MYWINDOWS\LOGIN 105 2015-03-10 10:46.09.06
```

The previous process is meant to offer one solution of capturing configuration changes, using the default trace. Clearly there are many things that can be captured and alerted on using this method. It is likely that this is one method the major third-party monitoring vendors use in their software.

To take this a step further, you can schedule the stored procedure to run as a job. Since the data is cumulative within the trace capture, you can determine the interval to run the job as desired. The only caveat is that the trace files will roll over at some point, and this interrogates only the active trace file. You most likely do not need to run it every few minutes and probably can start with hourly or maybe even twice a day depending on your environment. Ideally, with the previous process, you will have some peace of mind that you will be alerted on any changes made to the SQL Server configuration. Once SQL Server is initially configured, you probably would love nothing but to "set it and forget it." However, in the real world, especially with multiple SQL Server environments to manage, you need to keep track of any changes to the configuration that could impact the environment. As a DBA, you need to be aware of any ad hoc changes and ideally be alerted to address any issues.

In this section, you were provided with a solution that used the SQL Server default trace, which is a lightweight server-side trace running continuously in the background.

Change Data Capture

Change Data Capture (CDC) was introduced in SQL Server 2008 and is just available in the Enterprise, Developer, and Evaluation Editions of SQL Server 2008 and newer. This solution is database specific and intended to capture database activity and changes to actual data in the database. CDC focuses on DML (insert, update, and delete) activity and can be applied only to user databases. To use CDC, you must follow the requirements, and the person using CDC must be in the sysadmin fixed server role as well as in a db_owner fixed database role.

The details of the changes are available in an easily consumed relational format. Column information and the metadata required to apply the changes to a target environment are captured for the modified rows and stored in change tables that mirror the column structure of the tracked source tables. Table-valued functions are provided to allow systematic access to the change data by users.

Since CDC will create tracking and cleanup jobs, SQL Server Agent must be running as well. You will see the jobs created in a few minutes. The steps involved are to enable CDC on your database and then to enable CDC on each table you want to capture activity on. Of course, you can select from a handful of specific tables or all tables in the database.

You can use the AdminDB account you created for your sample process in the previous section on the default trace or the same database used for creating your default trace process for running some example code to see how CDC works and captures data changes.

To enable and configure CDC on the database, you would run the following system stored procedure, selecting the database to apply it to:

```
Use AdminDB
GO
exec sys.sp_cdc_enable_db
Go
```

Confirm which databases have CDC enabled by running the following:

```
select name, is_cdc_enabled from sys.databases
```

You can see now that AdminDB has been enabled for CDC, with the following results, where 1=enabled is in the is_cdc_enabled column:

```
name is_cdc_enabled
AdminDB 1
MAPS_DB 0
DECODE_TLOG_DB 0
XEvents_ImportSystemHealth 0
AdventureWorks2012 0
```

To enable CDC on each table, use this:

```
exec sys.sp_cdc_enable_table [TABLENAME]
```

For this demo, you will enable CDC on the SQLConfig_Changes table by executing the following statement:

```
EXEC sys.sp_cdc_enable_table
@source_schema = N'dbo',
@source_name   = N'SQLConfig_Changes',
@role_name     = NULL
GO
```

Once you run the previous code, you will get an output message indicating that CDC jobs have been created and started successfully.

```
Job 'cdc.AdminDB_capture' started successfully.
Job 'cdc.AdminDB_cleanup' started successfully.
```

To confirm which tables have CDC enabled and see that the SQLConfig_Changes table is now CDC enabled, run the following:

```
select name, is_tracked_by_cdc from sys.tables
```

You will see under the is_tracked_by_cdc column the status, where 1 equals enabled, as with the following results:

```
name is_tracked_by_cdc
SQLConfig_Changes 1
MSSQL_InventoryOLD 0
systranschemas 0
change_tables 0
ddl_history 0
```

Once you enable CDC on your selected tables, CDC system tables are created and listed here:

- cdc.captured_columns: This table returns a list of captured columns.

- cdc.change_tables: This table returns a list of all the tables that are enabled for capture.

- cdc.ddl_history: This table contains the history of all the DDL changes since CDC was enabled.

- cdc.index_columns: This table contains indexes associated with the change table.

- cdc.lsn_time_mapping: This table maps the LSN number (you will learn about this later) and time.

- cdc.SourceSchema_SourceTable_CT: This will be the name of the schema and tables you enabled CDC on.

Once CDC is enabled on the database and tables, you can also view the CDC tables as system tables in the database via SSMS, under the Tables ➤ System Tables folder, as shown in Figure 10-11.

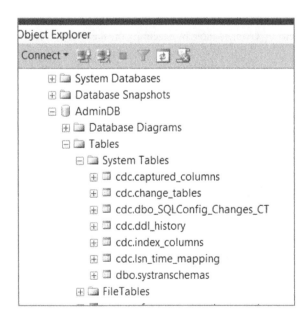

Figure 10-11. CDC tables created as shown in SSMS

You can also take a look at the Jobs Activity Monitor under the Jobs folder in SQL Server Agent for the CDC jobs created, as displayed in Figure 10-12.

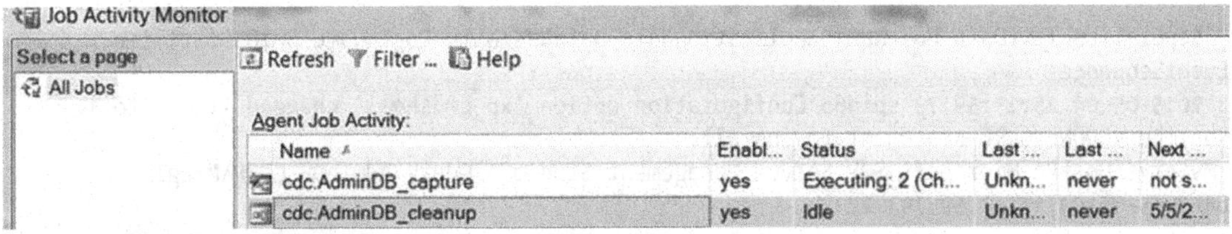
Job Activity Monitor
Select a page
All Jobs
Refresh
Filter ...
Help
Agent Job Activity:
Name
Enabl...
Status
Last ...
Last ...
Next ...
cdc.AdminDB_capture
yes
Executing: 2 (Ch...
Unkn...
never
not s...
cdc.AdminDB_cleanup
yes
Idle
Unkn...
never
5/5/2...

Figure 10-12. *CDC jobs shown in SQL Agent Job Activity Monitor*

Now, let's make a change to `SQLConfig_Changes` table by inserting a configuration change. Drawing on the capture default trace process created earlier, you can run any configuration change. Here's an example:

```
sp_configure xp_cmdshell, 1
go
reconfigure with override
go
```

As you recall, to insert a record into the history tracking table `SQLConfig_Changes`, you must run the stored procedure `usp_Capture_SQL_Config_Changes`. Therefore, run the following:

```
exec [dbo].[usp_Capture_SQL_Config_Changes] 'SomeEmail@MyCompany.com'
```

Once you insert a row, you can ensure that the data change was in fact captured, by querying the associated CDC table, in this example, `[cdc].[dbo_SQLConfig_Changes_CT]`. Let's query the most relevant columns that are mostly self-explanatory, except `__$operation`, which will be discussed in a minute.

```
select __$operation,TextData,HostName,
ApplicationName,DatabaseName, LoginName,
SPID, StartTime, EventSequence
from [cdc].[dbo_SQLConfig_Changes_CT]
```

■ **Note** The `usp_Capture_SQL_Config_Changes` stored procedure is not part of CDC.

The `__$operation` column is used to indicate and store the type of change to the table: insert, update, or delete. The values of the `__$operation column` are defined as follows:

1=Delete

2=Insert

3=Update with the row filter option set to `all update old` for before update

4=Update with a more typical update operation for the value after update

You will see the results capturing the type of operation, the actual data inserted, the host, the application, and the database and login names, as well as the SPID, start time of the transaction, and the event sequence. The output resembles the following:

```
__$operation TextData HostName ApplicationName DatabaseName LoginName SPID StartTime
EventSequence
2 2015-05-04 15:13:59.79 spid64 Configuration option 'xp_cmdshell' changed from 1 to 1.
Run the RECONFIGURE statement to install.
 MyServerHostPC Microsoft SQL Server Management Studio - Query AdminDB CORP\MYLgID
64 2015-05-04 15:13:59.793 272
```

You can observe that the column value of __$operation is 2, which indicates that a record was inserted.

If you want to disable CDC, there are system functions for that as well. Do not simply drop the database, tables, or jobs related to CDC. For example, to disable CDC on the tables and database, simply select that database and execute sys.sp_cdc_disable_table and sys.sp_cdc_disable_db to turn off CDC, before dropping the objects.

To turn off Change Data Capture, use this:

```
exec sys.sp_cdc_disable_table
@source_schema = N'dbo',
@source_name   = N'SQLConfig_Changes',
@role_name     = NULL
GO
```

Then you can drop the tables, as shown here:

```
DROP Table [TABLENAME]
GO
```

Finally, disable CDC on the database.

```
exec sys.sp_cdc_disable_db
go
```

For further reference all CDC stored procedures can be found on MSDN at http://msdn.microsoft.com/en-us/library/bb500244.aspx

There are additional CDC functions that you will want to explore if you choose to dig deeper into CDC, such as cdc_get_all_changes and cdc_get_net changes, which can be used to retrieve the history of changes, such as current values or both current and previous. You can find a reference for all the CDC functions here:

http://msdn.microsoft.com/en-us/library/bb510744.aspx

In addition to auditing and tracking changes in source tables, a common usage scenario for CDC is where incremental data loads from source tables to data warehouses using extraction, transformation, and loading (ETL). To learn more about CDC, refer to the MSDN article here:

https://msdn.microsoft.com/en-us/library/cc645937.aspx

Policy-Based Management

In SQL Server 2008, Microsoft introduced the Policy Management Framework, also called *policy-based management* (PBM). This powerful new framework allows DBAs to define a set of policies that can control several aspects of SQL Server. For example, a DBA can define a policy that specifies how a particular configuration option should be set on all the servers in the enterprise. Based on a particular facet, a policy can evaluate a condition as true or false and then log or prevent an unauthorized operation. PBM can prove instrumental in complying with SOX/HIPPA and other regulatory laws, as well as assist in proving to auditors that your servers are actively enforcing compliance with standards defined by the company and enforced by the DBA. PBM allows database administrators to define rules for one or more SQL Server instances and enforce them so one administrator can manage any and all of them by preventing servers from being out of compliance with defined policies. PBM was the first step toward using the SQL Server out-of-the-box feature to set standardization for multiple SQL Server instances throughout an organization.

PBM gives the DBA the ability to define standard policies, enforce these policies selectively, and automate checking and enforcement of policies, as well as correct conditions that are not compliant with policies. PBM can be used in a variety of ways, most of which augments a documented policy manual. Documented policy guidelines were the only way to ensure compliance. PBM can now streamline this manual task via automation and allow policy violations to be discovered, along with who is responsible, via SQL Server Management Studio (SSMS).

Policy-based management can be extremely helpful in standardizing and enforcing SQL Server configuration and other policies across the enterprise. The database professional can configure different conditions that allow you to discover when one of those servers goes out of compliance with internal database policies. You can also use PBM to enforce desired policies that prevent servers from being out of compliance. Furthermore in this chapter, I will introduce the basic PBM concepts and demonstrate an example of how it works. Because I cannot cover every aspect of PBM in the scope of this book, I suggest you take a look at and download the original PBM white paper, authored by longtime SQL Server consultant Sharon Dooley from Microsoft, located at this URL:

```
http://bit.ly/19BdOJJ
```

Ultimately, because policies are custom and vary for each environment, no policies are initially created for you; however, Microsoft has included a number of sample policies, stored as XML files in your SQL Server installation, that you can review and learn from. You can choose to import one or more of these policies if they apply to your environment or use the policies as examples to create your own policies. You should definitely take a look at them and can find them in the default folder path of your SQL Server installation.

```
Drive_letter:\Program Files(x86)\Microsoft SQL Server\ {vbuild}\Tools\Policies\
DatabaseEngine\1033
```

By using the following information, you can derive the version build number to use for the default folder path where the policies are. Therefore, {vbuild} equals the build number you should specify in place of vbuild.

- 90 = SQL Server 2005

- 100 = SQL Server 2008 and SQL Server 2008 R2

- 110 = SQL Server 2012

- 120 = SQL Server 2014

To see what policies are currently loaded into your SQL Server instance or after you import them into SQL Server from the installation path, you can run this against the msdb system database:

```
SELECT name
, description, date_created
FROM msdb.dbo.syspolicy_policies
order by date_created desc
```

The output will look like this:

```
name description date_created
SQL Server Login Mode Checks for Windows Authentication. When possible, Microsoft
recommends using Windows Authentication. 2015-03-29 14:39:06.610
SQLLoginPWPolicy  2015-03-27 23:09:26.563
SQLPWExpiration  2015-03-27 23:06:37.827
DISALLOW_XP_CMDSHELL  2014-07-13 22:22:59.497
AlwaysOnArJoinStateHealthPolicy Alwayson Policy Description ID:41428 2014-05-05 13:05:31.583
```

At a minimum, you should know the key concepts of PBM to configure and set up some initial policies you can use in your SQL Server environment.

- Facets

- Conditions

- Policies

- Categories

- Targets

- Execution mode

The simplest recommended way to define policies is to use SQL Server Management Studio. Under the Management folder, you can navigate to the Policy Management subfolder, and you will see three main folders that need to be configured for policy management: Policies, Conditions, and Facets.

Before you can set up your policy, you must configure the policy's properties by choosing a predefined facet, which is used to test various conditions. There are dozens of available facets to choose from, each having one or more properties. Therefore, facets are collection of properties for an object such as a table, a stored procedure, or an audit. For example, the Login facet has properties including name, create date, login type, password expiration enabled, password policy enforced, must change password, and so on.

A policy must have a condition. After choosing the facet for the policy, you must then define the condition of the facet's property or properties. Expanding on use of the Login facet, you want to set the condition of the state of this facet's property to enforce. For example, you want all the logins' passwords to have an expiration. In this scenario, the facet's login property is PasswordExpirationEnabled, and the condition would be set to true. You will actually set the condition @PasswordExpirationEnabled=True so later you will evaluate whether your SQL Server's settings are in compliance with this condition, defined within the policy. Such true/false Boolean expressions can be combined with AND, OR, and NOT, which could become overly complex.

A target, also called an *object set*, can be at several levels. A target can be at the SQL Server instance level, database level, table level, or index level. In that the targets form a hierarchy, if a policy is created at the server level, it cascades the policy to all the lower levels in the hierarchy.

A policy is a rule based on a single condition and applied to one or more targets. A policy has an automation mode that describes what SQL Server should do when a policy is violated.

Categories are really only a logical grouping and used simply to group related policies. If you specify that a particular category is mandated for all databases, policies in the category will be applied to all databases. Otherwise, a database owner can subscribe to one or more policy categories. For example, using your Login policy again, the category Microsoft Best Practices: Security might be an appropriate choice. Policies that do not have a specific category assigned will be placed in the default category, where policies are applied to all databases.

With the available evaluation modes, there are four choices for policy evaluation.

- On Change: Prevent

- On Change: Log only

- On Schedule

- On Demand

The On Change: Prevent mode uses DDL triggers to roll back any unwanted changes. The DDL triggers' On Change: Prevent mode allows you to reverse the effects of undesirable changes from being made permanent. On Change: Log only allows the change to be made but records it in the event log. The On Change evaluation modes are available only for those changes that can be trapped with a DDL trigger. On Schedule evaluates policy compliance on a given schedule. Compliance or noncompliance is reported in the policy history. Finally, On Demand requires that the administrator manually perform policy evaluation. The On Change: Prevent, On Schedule, and On Demand modes will all record errors in the event log. Some facets do not support all the evaluation modes.

An administrator can create alerts that respond to the error and send notifications about the policy violations.

An important aspect of security, as discussed, is password policy enforcement. SQL Server allows you during installation to select the preferred authentication mode. Available choices are Windows Authentication mode and mixed mode. Windows Authentication mode only enables Windows Authentication and therefore disables SQL Server Authentication. Mixed mode enables both Windows Authentication and SQL Server Authentication. Windows Authentication is always available and cannot be disabled.

I'll now take the login example and walk you through creating a policy for enforcing that the SQL Server password policy is enabled, ensuring that all SQL-authenticated passwords are set to @PasswordPolicyEnforced=True. You will create the facet, condition, and policy; select evaluation mode; and finally set up an alert to notify that your server is out of compliance.

Creating a Implementing a SQL Password Enforcement Policy

In this section, you will set up a policy for Enforcing SQL Login Password Policy. Using SSMS, navigate to and expand the Management and Policy Management folders. Right-click Conditions and select New Condition from the pop-up menu. Now, enter an appropriate name in the Create New Condition dialog such as **EnforceSQLPWPolicy**. Next, from the Facets drop-down list, select the Login Options facet. In the Expression section, you can use the drop-downs for Fields and Values, or you can simply specify the condition shown in Figure 10-13 and then click OK. Here I will set @PasswordPolicyEnforced = True.

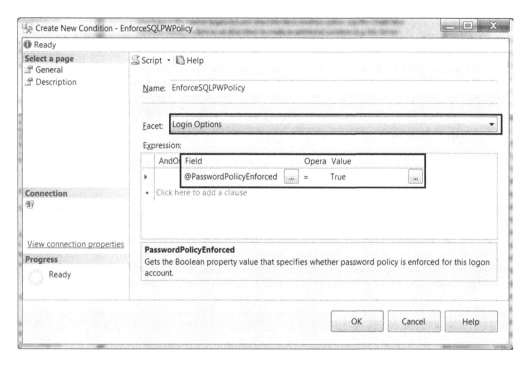

Figure 10-13. *Creating a new condition for enforcing a SQL password policy*

Now you will create the policy based on the condition you set up in the previous step. From the Policy Management folder, right-click the Policies folder, and select New Policy from the pop-up menu. Enter an appropriate name for the new policy, similarly named here as the associated condition, EnforceSQLPWPolicy, in the Create New Policy name field. From the Check Condition drop-down list, select the *condition* created in the previous step, EnforceSQLPWPolicy, which is located under the Login Options facet.

You need to now specify the *target* for enforcing the password policy, which you will modify to exclude Windows-authenticated logins and focus only on SQL-authenticated logins. Once you do this, all policy evaluation results will only include logins created for SQL Server Authentication and whether they satisfy compliance with your set condition. In the "Against targets" box, click the drop-down, and from here you will create another condition called SQLServerLoginsOnly by selecting the New Condition menu item. Using the Create New Condition screen that appears, set the Expression field from the drop-down to @LoginType and set Value to SqlLogin. Click OK. This new condition is shown in Figure 10-14. The expression reads as @LoginType = SqlLogin. Once you click OK in the Condition dialog, you will see that SQLServerLoginsOnly is the target for this policy condition, as in Figure 10-14.

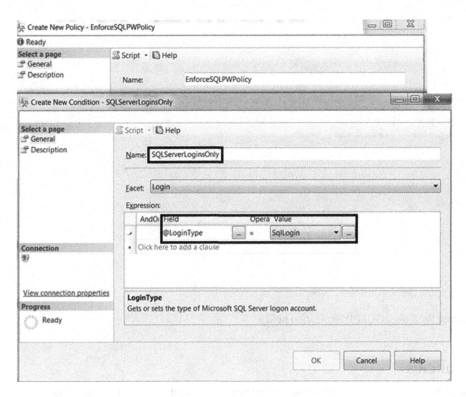

Figure 10-14. *Creating a new condition to specify SQL logins only*

Using the described steps, create an additional policy (such as SQL Login Password Policy). Use the Password Policy Enforced condition for the Check condition value and the same SQL Server Authenticated Logins condition you created to narrow down the policy targets. Here are the summarized steps for creating the second policy:

1. Right-click Policies, select New Policy, and enter **EnforceSQLPWExpiration** for the name.

2. Check Condition, select New Condition, and enter **EnforceSQLPWExpiration** for the name.

3. For the Facet, access the drop-down menu and select Login.

4. For the Expression field, select @PasswordExpirationEnabled and set Value to True.

5. In the "Against targets" section, click the drop-down, and you should see the condition you created previously. Select SQLServerLoginsOnly, and click OK. The selection should appear as in Figure 10-15.

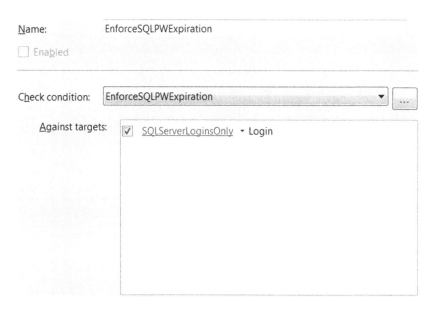

Figure 10-15. *Creating the EnforceSQLPWExpiration policy*

Testing the Policies

To test the previous policies, you can create a new login using SQL Server Authentication. Using SSMS, do not check the "Enforce password policy" and "Enforce password expiration" options. You can also create the login by default this way if you add a login via T-SQL.

```
CREATE LOGIN SAM123
  WITH PASSWORD= 'ABC123',
CHECK_POLICY=OFF
```

To evaluate the declared policies against their targets, select the Evaluate option from the SQL Login Password Expiration context menu. The Evaluate Policies dialog will provide the result of the evaluation, as in Figure 10-16.

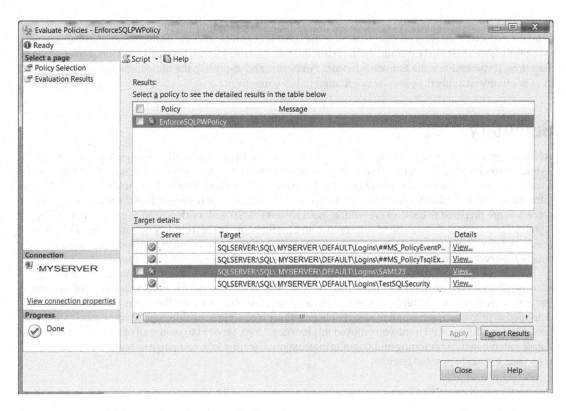

Figure 10-16. Policy evaluation results

Applying Policies

As per the results in Figure 10-16, the policy evaluation results come back with a noncompliant message for login SAM123. You can manually change the target object properties, in this scenario, by going to the login properties for the noncompliant login, or you can apply the policy automatically. You have the option of selecting the noncompliant target object and clicking Apply to place it in compliance with the policy. You may see the Policy Evaluation Warning dialog, as in Figure 10-17, so click Yes to confirm.

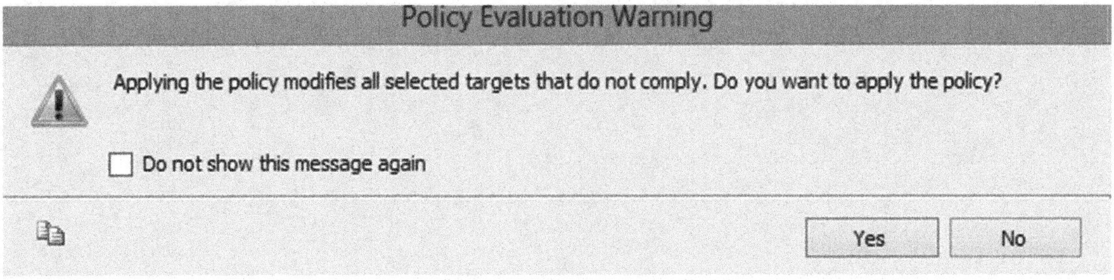

Figure 10-17. Policy evaluation warning, when applying policies

Just remember, with respect to enforcing password policy, this property must be set first, before the enforce password expiration property, because the latter is dependent on the former being enabled. Trying to apply Enforce Password Expiration policy with Enforce Password Policy first will result in an error. Therefore, if you evaluate the Enforce Password Policy first and apply it to the noncompliant login, you can then evaluate and apply the password expiration policy correctly.

Summary

Your journey to a SQL Server healthy environment is almost complete, but really the adventure never ends. As long as you have SQL Server instances, ongoing maintenance, tuning, and performance optimization will always be necessary. The information in this book will empower you to take a holistic view of your SQL Server infrastructure and insulate you against SQL Server audits. Now that you have your healthy SQL strategy in place, you are prepared to back up everything you have done so far with evidence, and you can survive any IT audit. I hope you find this to be an informative and useful book, full of technical tips and know-how, best practices, DBA strategies, hands-on exercises, T-SQL code and scripts, references, and tools for managing your SQL Server environment, as well as safely navigating through the minefield of corporate IT.

This book is intended to instill confidence in you, the de facto DBA, to carry out your DBA duties successfully and execute them faithfully. You are now familiar with the native and powerful out-of-the-box feature set, as well as some third-party assets, to carry out your objectives. Furthermore, you should now be equipped with as much information as possible to achieve a certifiably healthy SQL Server environment and excel in your DBA career! I hope you enjoyed this journey. I look forward to seeing all of you someday soon. Please join me in the continuing and ongoing international healthy SQL campaign to build awareness to keep your servers happy and healthy!

Index

■ I, J, K

Get the eBook for only $5!

Why limit yourself?

Now you can take the weightless companion with you wherever you go and access your content on your PC, phone, tablet, or reader.

Since you've purchased this print book, we're happy to offer you the eBook in all 3 formats for just $5.

Convenient and fully searchable, the PDF version enables you to easily find and copy code—or perform examples by quickly toggling between instructions and applications. The MOBI format is ideal for your Kindle, while the ePUB can be utilized on a variety of mobile devices.

To learn more, go to www.apress.com/companion or contact support@apress.com.

Printed in the United States
By Bookmasters